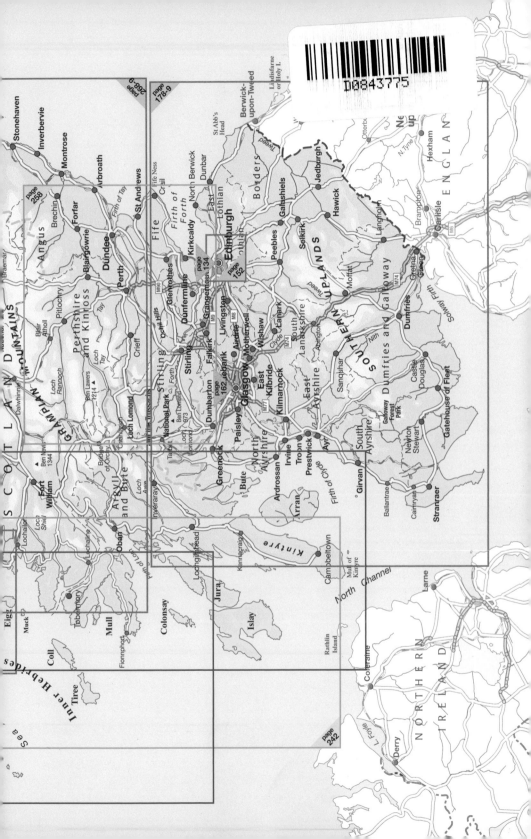

INSIGHT GUIDES
SCOTLAND

APA PUBLICATIONS

L

Part of the Langenscheidt Publishing Group

※ INSIGHT GUIDE

SCOTLAND

Editorial
Project Editor
Alexia Georgiou
Art Director
Steven Lawrence
Picture Researcher
Tom Smyth
Publishing Manager
Rachel Fox
Series Manager
Rachel Lawrence

Distribution

UK & Ireland
GeoCenter International Ltd
Meridian House, Churchill Way West
Basingstoke, Hampshire RG21 6YR
sales@geocenter.co.uk

United States
Ingram Publisher Services
One Ingram Blvd
PO Box 3006
La Vergne, TN 37086-1986
customer.service@ingrampublisherservices.com

Australia
Universal Publishers
PO Box 307
St Leonards, NSW 1590
sales@universalpublishers.com.au

New Zealand
Hema Maps New Zealand Ltd (HNZ)
Unit 2, 10 Cryers Road
East Tamaki, Auckland 2013
sales.hema@clear.net.nz

Worldwide
**Apa Publications GmbH & Co.
Verlag KG (Singapore branch)**
7030 Ang Mo Kio Ave 5,
08-65 Northstar@AMK, Singapore
569880
apasin@signet.com.sg

Printing

CTPS-China

©2011 Apa Publications GmbH & Co.
Verlag KG (Singapore branch)
All Rights Reserved

First Edition 1984
Fifth Edition 2011

CONTACTING THE EDITORS

We would appreciate it if readers would alert us to errors or outdated information by writing to:
Insight Guides, PO Box 7910, London SE1 1WE, England.
insight@apaguide.co.uk

www.insightguides.com

ABOUT THIS BOOK

The first Insight Guide pioneered the use of creative full-colour photography in travel guides in 1970. Since then, we have expanded our range to cater for our readers' need not only for reliable information about their chosen destination but also for a real understanding of the culture and workings of that destination. Now, when the internet can supply inexhaustible (but not always reliable) facts, our books marry text and pictures to provide those elusive qualities: knowledge and discernment. To achieve this, they rely heavily on the authority of locally based writers and photographers.

How to use this book

The book is carefully structured to convey an understanding of Scotland and its culture and to guide readers through its sights and attractions:

◆ The **Features** section, with a pink colour bar, covers the country's history and culture in lively authoritative essays written by specialists.

◆ The **Places** section, with a blue bar, provides full details of all the sights and areas worth seeing. The chief places of interest are coordinated by number with specially drawn maps.

◆ The **Travel Tips** section, with a yellow bar at the back of the book, offers a convenient point of reference for information on travel, accommodation, restaurants and other practical aspects of the country. Information may be located quickly by using the index printed on the back cover flap, which also serves as a bookmark.

The contributors

This new edition of *Insight Guide: Scotland* was managed by Insight

the inside for newspapers and TV.

Other Scottish journalists who have contributed to this guide include **Julie Davidson**, who wrote five of the Places chapters (Glasgow, the Southwest, Forth and Clyde, the West Coast and the East Coast).

An important contributor was Glasgow-born **Marcus Brooke**, a globe-trotting writer and photographer. A contributor to many Insight Guides, he wrote the chapters on Skye, the Outer Hebrides and Orkney, and those on festivals, Highland games, golf, Edinburgh architecture, and the feature on castles and abbeys. Also from Glasgow is the novelist and artist **Naomi May**, who wrote the chapters on art and religion.

Two contributors to *The Scotsman* – **Alastair Clark** and **Conrad Wilson** – added their insight to the music and food of Scotland, whilst **Stuart Ridsdale**, **Roland Collins**, and **Dymphna Byrne** shared their enthusiasm for the Borders, Central Scotland and the Hebrides. **Andrew Eames**, who wrote the features on crofting and Highland flora and fauna, is a journalist and author of *Four Scottish Journeys;* while **Christopher Smout** offers a refreshing alternative to the myth of Highlanders and Lowlanders, drawing on his expertise as the author of the *History of the Scottish People*. Remaining chapters – on the Scottish character, early history, whisky, and Shetland – are written by Brian Bell.

Many of the stunning photographs are the output of **David Cruickshanks**, with contributions by other photographers. Thanks also go to **Pam Barrett**, who proofread the guide, and to **Helen Peters**, who indexed it.

Guides editor **Alexia Georgiou**, edited by **Caroline Radula-Scott** and updated by **Jackie Staddon** and **Hilary Weston**. **Colin Hutchison**, a Glasgow-born, Edinburgh-based journalist and travel writer provided the new introduction on Scotland the Brave.

The current edition builds on the original one produced by **Brian Bell**, a journalist with wide experience in newspapers and magazines and former editorial director of Insight Guides.

A leading contributor – he wrote the chapters on Edinburgh, the age of rebellion, modern Scotland, Scots geniuses, tartan and hunting – is **George Rosie**, who began his career in Dundee with publisher D.C. Thomson. Rosie moved to London and joined the *Sunday Times* in 1974, but has since returned to Scotland and writes about it from

Map Legend

▬ ▬ ▪ ▬	International Boundary
▬ ▬ ▬ ▬	County Boundary
▬ ▪ ▬ ▪ ▬	National Park/Reserve
▬ ▬ ▬ ▬	Ferry Route
Ⓜ	Metro
✈ ✈	Airport: International/Regional
🚌	Bus Station
❶	Tourist Information
† † ⛪	Church/Ruins
†	Monastery
☾	Mosque
✡	Synagogue
▓ ▓	Castle/Ruins
∴	Archaeological Site
∩	Cave
⚑	Statue/Monument
★	Place of Interest
⚑	Beach

The main places of interest in the Places section are coordinated by number with a full-colour map (eg ❶), and a symbol at the top of every right-hand page tells you where to find the map.

Contents

LEFT: view towards Isle of Harris from Taransay, Outer Hebrides.

THE BEST OF SCOTLAND: TOP ATTRACTIONS

There is so much to discover about Scotland, from historic cities and majestic castles to misty mountains and dramatic lochs and glens

△ **Burns National Heritage Park**. The birthplace of Scotland's most famous poet Rabbie Burns provides an insight into how much he has contributed to Scotland's life and culture. *See page 204*

△ **Glen Coe** is full of drama for its bloody massacre of the MacDonalds in 1692, its powerful scenery and its challenging and notoriously dangerous mountain climbs. *See page 224*

▽ **Edinburgh** is Scotland's capital city and home to the Scottish Parliament. The city is steeped in history, dominated by Scotland's oldest castle, and a centre of culture and world-renowned festivals. *See page 133*

△ **Glasgow** has shaken off its grimy past and is now more noted for a trendy nightlife, first-class arts venues, great shopping and some lovely parks. *See page 161*

△ **Loch Lomond and the Trossachs**. The bonnie banks of Loch Lomond enclose the largest body of water in Britain which, along with the Trossach hills, form part of the magnificent national park. *See page 262*

△ **Stirling** has been a settlement since prehistoric times due to its strategic position. Raised to city status in 2002, it offers fine shopping and excellent cultural venues, plus a national park on its doorstep. *See page 211*

△ **St Andrews** is a breezy seaside town acknowledged as the home of golf, and possesses Scotland's oldest university. *See page 261*

△ **Isle of Skye**, romantically associated with Bonnie Prince Charlie and Flora MacDonald, is the most scenically spectacular spot of the western seaboard, with superb mountain landscapes and dramatic sea lochs. *See page 231*

◁ **The Cairngorms**, lying between Speyside and Braemar, are home to rare wildlife, such as the golden eagle, and to beautiful alpine plants – a magnet for walkers, climbers and skiers. *See page 276*

▷ **Iona** has been known since the 6th century as the cradle of Christianity in Scotland. Beyond the abbey are beautiful beaches and an unspoilt landscape rich in birdlife. *See page 243*

THE BEST OF SCOTLAND: EDITOR'S CHOICE

With so much to see and experience in this bonnie land, you may wish to set some priorities for your trip. Here, at a glance, are the editor's recommendations plus some handy money-saving tips

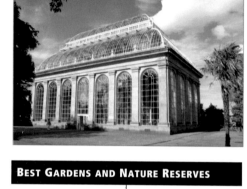

BEST CASTLES

● **Edinburgh Castle** High above the city stands Scotland's most popular tourist attraction. Listen out for the ritual firing of the One o'Clock Gun. See *page 140*

● **Stirling Castle** Perched atop a craggy outcrop, a wealth of Scottish history is crammed into every corner of this ancient fortress. See *page 212*

● **Dunvegan Castle** Northwest of Portree, Dunvegan Castle has been the stronghold of the chiefs of MacLeod for more than seven centuries. See *page 234*

● **Glamis Castle** This beautiful, turreted castle in Angus has a rich and

royal history, not least as former home of Queen Elizabeth, the Queen Mother. See *page 272*

● **Dunnottar Castle** A ruined fortress in a striking setting that has been witness to Scotland's stormy and bloodstained past. *See page 273*

● **Eilean Donan** Built against a backdrop of brooding mountains and a picturesque sea loch, every inch of Eilean Donan portrays the image of a romantic Scottish castle. See *page 226*

BEST GARDENS AND NATURE RESERVES

● **Inverewe Garden (Wester Ross)** Created by Osgood Mackenzie in 1862, this subtropical oasis is one of Scotland's most popular, set on the shores of Loch Ewe. The diverse plant collection includes specimens from the far ends of the earth. *See page 227*

● **Royal Botanic Garden (Edinburgh)** The garden was founded as early as 1670 as a resource for medical research. The Temperate Palmhouse, a huge Victorian glasshouse, is impressive and packed with ferns and palms. See *page 149*

● **Arduaine Garden (Argyll)** A 20-acre (8-hectare) woodland garden, with superb coastal views, specialising in magnolias, rhododendrons, ferns and

azaleas. See *page 222*

● **Sands of Forvie (Aberdeenshire)** Part of the Forvie National Nature Reserve. The reserve has a large sand dune sytem, and the biggest breeding colony of eider duck in Britain. *See page 280*

● **Beinn Eighe National Nature Reserve (Wester Ross)** Overlooking Loch Maree, parts of the reserve are home to the elusive pine marten, buzzards and golden eagles. Caledonian pine wood partly covers the forest. See *page 290*

● **Hermaness National Nature Reserve** (Shetland) Overlooking Britain's most northerly tip, Hermaness is a haven for more than 100,000 nesting sea birds, including gannets, great skuas and puffins. *See page 311*

ABOVE: the majestic towers and turrets of Glamis Castle.
ABOVE RIGHT: Edinburgh's Temperate Palmhouse.

ISLANDS OFF THE BEATEN TRACK

● **Rum** (Inner Hebrides) Not only does Rum have some of the best scenery in this group of islands but the best hill walking, too. *See page 246*

● **Barra** (Outer Hebrides) A wild, stunning place, with empty white beaches and open roads. Don't miss a trip to Kisimul Castle. *See page 253*

● **Taransay** (Outer Hebrides) This idyllic island has many sandy beaches – access relies on the kindness of the Atlantic Ocean. *See page 250*

● **Rousay** (Orkney) An archaeological delight, along with nearby Egilsay, and dubbed the "Egypt of the North". *See page 304*

● **Foula** (Shetland) Probably Britain's remotest inhabited island and a stronghold of true Shetland culture. *See page 311*

ABOVE: the view to Taransay.
BELOW: a slice of traditional Selkirk bannock.

TOP MUSEUMS AND ART GALLERIES

● **Kelvingrove Art Gallery and Museum (Glasgow)** Housed in an imposing red sandstone building, Scotland's most popular gallery is a treasure trove of cultural antiquities. *See page 169*

● **Shetland Museum and Archives (Lerwick)** Housed in a striking timber-clad building, the museum charts Shetland's history and heritage with an amazing collection of artefacts and archives of written, photographic and musical records. *See page 310*

● **National Museum of Scotland (Edinburgh)** This remarkable museum charts the history of Scotland through its artefacts, from Neolithic standing stones to Viking treasures. *See page 143*

● **Aberdeen Art Gallery** The neoclassical building has a permanent collection of 18th–20th-century art by the likes of Raeburn and Toulouse Lautrec. *See page 282*

ENTICING LOCAL DELICACIES

● **Loch Fyne kippers** These herrings are caught in Loch Fyne, a sea loch north of Arran. They are soaked in brine and slowly cured over smouldering oak fires.

● **Forfar Bridie** A delicious minced meat pie that is said to have been made by Maggie Bridie of Glamis, when the county of Angus was called Forfarshire.

● **Arbroath smokie** Arbroath's speciality of lightly smoked haddock.

● **Highland malts** Among the famous Highland malts are Glenmorangie, Glenfiddich, Macallan and Laphroaig.

● **Selkirk bannock** This rich fruit bun was originally made by a baker in Selkirk, and eaten at Christmas.

● **Moffat toffees** A toffee-based sweet with a sherbert centre, traditionally made in Moffat in the southwest.

● **Scottish cheeses** Lanark blue, Seater's Orkney and Isle of Mull – just a few of the best.

Caledonian MacBrayne

MONEY-SAVING TIPS

● **Travel** Look out for FirstScotrail's Freedom of Scotland Travelpasses and Citylink Explorer bus passes (*see Getting Around, page 315*). If sailing to several islands, invest in a Caledonian MacBrayne Rover ticket (*see page 316*). Avoid taking your car on a ferry and save money by walking, cycling or using public transport on the island.

● **Eating** Many restaurants offer substantially reduced rates between 5.30–7pm on a pre-theatre menu.

● **Drinking** "Happy hour" is a convenient way for pubs and clubs to entice people in for a drink at cheaper prices – usually 5–6pm or 6–7pm on weekdays.

● **Attractions** From Edinburgh Castle to wildlife cruises, ask about special family, children and senior citizen prices.

● **Paying for the view** The views from Edinburgh and Stirling castles may be impressive, but they are free from the Pentland and Ochil hills, respectively. With so many walking trails across the country, it can be rewarding in every sense to take a picnic and head for the hills.

SCOTLAND THE BRAVE

A country of such diverse and challenging
landscapes and ever-changing fortunes, Scotland
has never been afraid to stand up for herself

F àilte gu Alba. Tongue-tied visitors may struggle to pronounce the name of many a Scottish mountain, decipher a Hebridean road sign or toast friends with the words *"Slàinte mhath"* over a fine malt. But whether spoken in Gaelic or English, few can mistake the sincerity of the Scots' welcome to their homeland.

Officialdom states only 2 percent of Scots "speak the Gaelic". Though the very fact it survives and flourishes is a sign that from Shetland to the Borders, the Scotsman (and woman) is proud of his or her regional differences, and fiercely protective of their national identity.

Alas, for a nation that gave the world penicillin and the telephone, it's the same "inventiveness" in the Scots' genes – or overzealous promotion of a national stereotype – that can confound the visitor in search of the "authentic" contemporary Scotland.

It is true that Scots possess a healthy dollop of self-deprecating humour and are not averse to poking fun at their southern neighbour. But the image of being a kilt-wearing, bagpipe-playing people who bemoan their weather while tucking into a diet of tartan-tinned shortbread, oatcakes, haggis and malt whisky is, well, only half true.

To the consternation of Scotland's health minister, there are some who still enjoy a drink and cholesterol-enhancing fare. Yet the increasing availability of traditional, regional foodstuffs like Uist hot-smoked salmon, Perthshire venison and Arbroath smokies underlines that Scots still possess the entrepreneurial and adventurous spirit that has served them so well in centuries past.

Arguably, too, Scotland's natural environment, a land renowned for its misty glens, dramatic peaks and habitat-rich wildscape has played its part in carving out the resilient, complex Scottish character. Indeed, it's not Nessie but Scotland's most annoying wee monster, the midge, that continues to sorely test the Scots resilience. In fact, this unloved airborne terror has even inspired the phrase: "A midge in your hand is better than two up your kilt!" Welcome to Scotland! ❏

PRECEDING PAGES: working sheepdogs take control in Aviemore; the Massed Highland Dancers perform at the Royal Edinburgh Military Tattoo. **LEFT:** three cheers for Culzean Castle. **ABOVE LEFT:** the prickly, purple thistle, the national emblem of Scotland. **ABOVE RIGHT:** the ancient mountain landscape of Assynt Coigach.

THE SCOTTISH CHARACTER

A confusing mix of dourness and humour, the Scots are unanimous only when identifying the common cause of their problems: England – of course

Natives of Scotland, it has been said, consider themselves as Scots before they think of themselves as human beings, thus establishing a clear order of excellence. This attitude does not make them popular with the rest of the human race, especially their nearest neighbour, England. Indeed, English literature is so peppered with anti-Scots aphorisms that the cumulative impression amounts to national defamation.

"I have been trying all my life to like Scotchmen," wrote the essayist Charles Lamb, "and am obliged to desist from the experiment in despair." P.G. Wodehouse was no kinder: "It is never difficult," he wrote, "to distinguish between a Scotsman with a grievance and a ray of sunshine." And Dr Samuel Johnson, whose tour of the Hebrides in 1773 was immortalised by his Scottish biographer James Boswell, has said: "The noblest prospect that a Scotchman ever sees is the high road that leads him to England."

The playwright J.M. Barrie – creator of Peter Pan and a Scot himself – once had one of his characters say, "You Scots are such a mixture of the practical and the emotional that you escape out of an Englishman's hand like a trout."

Shotgun marriage

It is a road that many have taken: an estimated 20 million people of Scots descent, one of the most inventive peoples on earth, are scattered throughout every continent – four times as many as live in Scotland itself. Yet an unease towards the English, a suspicion that they are their social superiors, has for centuries blighted the Scots psyche. The union of the two countries in 1707, after centuries of sporadic hostility, was regarded by most Scots as a shotgun marriage, and over 300 years have scarcely diluted the differences in outlook and attitude between the ill-matched partners.

It is an old tune, often played. When the future Pope Pius II visited the country in the 15th century, he concluded: "Nothing pleases the Scots more than abuse of the English." In that respect, the Scots resemble England's other close neighbours, the French, with whom they have intimate historical connections.

LEFT: taking a break at the Scottish Game Fair.
RIGHT: fishing for prawns.

Both share an outspokenness, which the English mistake for rudeness. Both are proud peoples, a characteristic which, in the case of the Scots, the English translate as ingratitude.

Calvinist traditions

It is noticeable that the butt of most of these waspish epigrams is the Scots *man*. Until recently, women, though no less strong in character, played a subsidiary role in the country's public affairs. It was very much a man's world: it has taken many centuries to allow a woman to become a Clan Chief. And although Scottish law introduced desertion as grounds for divorce in 1573 (364 years before England), it retained a robust, Calvinistic view about what wives ought to put up with.

Certainly, the Calvinist tradition is central to the Scots character. While England absorbed the Reformation with a series of cunning compromises, Scotland underwent a revolution, replacing the panoply of Roman Catholicism with an austere Presbyterianism designed to put the ordinary people directly in touch with their God. No person was deemed inherently better than the next – and that included the clergy, who were made directly answerable to their congregations. This democratic tradition, allied with a taste for

SCOTTISH HOME RULE

The long-standing resentment of Scotland towards England finally found a political focus in 1997, when the second referendum on autonomy within the UK in two decades resulted in a "yes" vote to the setting up of the first Scottish parliament since 1707. The lack of majority in 1999 forced Labour into a coalition with the Liberal Democrats, and the SNP formed the main opposition.

Furthermore, the results of the 2007 Scottish elections, which have brought the SNP, led by Alex Salmond, to power (albeit narrowly) for the first time in its history, suggest the "hot potato" of Scottish independence is far from resolved.

argument born of theological wrangling, runs deep and once led more than one English politician to label firebrand Glasgow shipyard workers, for example, as Communists. Some might have been; but most were simply exercising their right to be individualists. It was an attitude that would allow a riveter to regard himself as being every bit as good as the shipyard boss and, whenever necessary, to remind the boss of that fact.

The Scots character is a confusing one. It combines dourness and humour, meanness and generosity, arrogance and tolerance, cantankerousness and chivalry, sentimentality and hardheadedness. One aspect of these contradictions is caught by a *Punch* cartoon showing a hitchhiker with a sign reading "Glasgow – or else!"

On the positive side, a bad climate and a poor soil forged an immensely practical people. But there was a price to be paid: these disadvantages encouraged frugality and a deep-seated pessimism. "It could be worse," comes easily to the lips of the most underprivileged.

The situation is redeemed by laughter. Scottish humour is subtle and sardonic and, in the hands of someone as verbally inventive as the comedian Billy Connolly, can leave reality far behind.

It has also been used, over the years, to cement many a Scottish stereotype. "My father was an Aberdonian," the veteran comedian Chic Murray would say, "and a more generous man

ings takes his glass into the lavatory." Matters have greatly improved, and some say that the introduction of Scotland's smoking ban in public places in 2006 has encouraged more women into pubs for a drink and meal with friends.

The cult of the kilt

Like the Irish, the Scots have realised that there's money to be made from conforming to a stereotyped image, however bogus it may be. If haggis isn't universally popular (once described as looking like a castrated bagpipe), it is offered to tourists as the national dish. Heads of ancient Scottish clans, living in houses large enough to generate

you couldn't wish to meet. I have a gold watch that belonged to my father, he sold it to me on his deathbed... so I wrote him a cheque, postdated of course."

Alcohol features prominently in Scottish jokes, as it does in many other aspects of the country's life. Until recently the single aim of Scottish pubs was to enable their clientele to get drunk as fast as possible, a purpose reflected in their decor. "Some of them," wrote the journalist Hugh McIlvanney, "are so bare that anyone who wants to drink in sophisticated surround-

cash flow problems, have opened their homes to tour groups of affluent overseas visitors. Others have opened "clan shops" retailing an astonishing variety of tartan artefacts, such as tartan teddies, with clan heraldry stamped on everything from tea towels to key fobs. And the cult of the kilt – based, someone mused, on the self-deception that male knees are an erogenous zone – is a huge commercial success.

But the image obscures the real Scotland. It's worth lingering long enough to draw back the tartan curtain and get to know one of Europe's most complex peoples. There's no guarantee that the more innocent visitors won't have the wool pulled over their eyes; but, if it's any consolation, it's sure to be best-quality Scottish wool. ❏

LEFT: students sit it out at St Salvator's Quad, St Andrews University. **ABOVE:** sporrans to the rear as drummers beat a tattoo at the Perth Highland Games.

DECISIVE DATES

PREHISTORIC TIMES

c.6000 BC
First sign of human settlement on west coast and islands.

c.1000 BC
First invasion of Celtic tribes.

THE ROMANS

AD 82
Agricola's forces enter Scotland and reach Aberdeenshire.

142
Second Roman invasion reaches Firth of Forth.

185
Withdrawal of Roman forces behind Hadrian's Wall.

EARLY CHRISTIANS

397
First Christian church founded at Whithorn by St Ninian.

563
St Columba lands on Iona and founds monastery.

THE BIRTH OF SCOTLAND

843
Kenneth MacAlpin becomes first king of Scots.

973
Kenneth II defeats the Danish Luncarty, near Perth.

1018
Malcolm II defeats the Northumbrians at Battle of Carham.

THE EARLY YEARS

1040
Macbeth becomes king by murdering Duncan I.

1124–53
Reign of David I. Royal burghs founded, and Border abbeys established.

1249
Alexander III becomes king. Start of "Golden Age".

WARS OF SUCCESSION

1286
Death of Alexander III. Succeeded by infant granddaughter Margaret. Rival claimants to throne include John Balliol and Robert Bruce.

1290
Margaret dies en route to Scotland. Edward I of England declares himself feudal overlord of Scotland.

1291–6
Edward I (the Hammer of the Scots) invades Scotland; wins Battle of Dunbar.

1297
Rebellion led by William Wallace defeats English forces at Stirling Bridge.

1305
English put Wallace to death as a traitor.

1306
Robert the Bruce becomes King Robert I and is crowned at Scone. After a defeat he spends a year in exile.

1314
Scots forces under Robert the Bruce defeat English at Battle of Bannockburn.

1333
English defeat Scots at Halidon Hill.

THE EARLY STUARTS

1371
Robert II, first of Stuarts, becomes king.

1406–1542
Reigns of James I–V.

1513
James IV killed in Battle of Flodden.

1542
James V dies after Battle of Solway Moss. Baby daughter, Mary Queen of Scots, succeeds.

1547
Hertford wins Battle of Pinkie. Mary taken to France.

1561
Mary returns to Scotland to reclaim throne.

1566
Birth of James VI.

1587
Mary Queen of Scots executed.

THE UNION OF CROWNS AND PARLIAMENTS

1603
Elizabeth I dies. James VI becomes James I of England.

1650
Cromwell seizes power in England. Scots proclaim Charles II as king in defiance. Lose to Cromwell at Dunbar.

1660
Charles II restored as king.

1689
James VII/II deposed by William and Mary. Scots supporters of James (Jacobites) win Battle of Killiecrankie.

1692
Massacre of Glencoe.

1707
Treaty of Union, abolition of separate Scottish parliament.

PRECEDING PAGES: *Mary of Scotland mourning over the dying Douglas at the Battle of Langside*, by F. Hartwich. **FAR LEFT:** Robert the Bruce. **ABOVE:** the Battle of Culloden. **RIGHT:** Alex Salmond, the First Minister of Scotland.

JACOBITE REBELLIONS AND THE CLEARANCES

1715
Rebellion led by Earl of Mar fails after battle at Sheriffmuir.

1745
Prince Charles Edward Stuart, Bonnie Prince Charlie's success at Prestonpans puts much of Scotland in Jacobite hands.

1746
Campaign ends in débâcle at Culloden on 16 April.

1780s
Highland Clearances, people evicted to make room for sheep; "Age of Enlightenment" in literature and the arts.

THE INDUSTRIAL AGE

1823
Caledonian Canal opened.

1836
Highland potato crop fails.

1850 onwards
Fast industrial expansion.

1852
Queen Victoria and Prince Albert buy Balmoral.

1882
The "Crofters War", including Battle of the Braes on Skye.

THE MODERN AGE

1924
Ramsay Macdonald becomes first Labour prime minister.

1934
Scottish National Party (SNP) formed.

1964
Forth Road Bridge opened.

1975
Start of North Sea gas and oil exploitation.

1997
Referendum votes in favour of a 129-member Scottish Parliament with tax-varying powers.

1999
Scottish Parliament is elected.

2004
The Scottish Parliament's new building, budgeted at £40 million, opens in Edinburgh at a cost of more than £431 million. Unesco names capital as the world's first City of Literature.

2007
Alex Salmond (SNP) is elected first minister of Scotland.

2010
The Referendum Bill to be implemented giving people of Scotland the chance for more independence from UK.

BEGINNINGS

An endless battle for power, early Scottish history was dominated by the continual conflicts of ruthlessly ambitious families, who not only needed strength but cunning and determination too, to keep a king on the throne

On a bleak, windswept moor three witches crouch round a bubbling cauldron, muttering oaths and prophesying doom. A king is brutally stabbed to death and his killer, consumed by vaulting ambition, takes the throne, only to be killed himself soon afterwards. "Fair is foul, and foul is fair."

To many people, these images from William Shakespeare's *Macbeth* are their first introduction to early Scottish history. But of course, the Scots will tell you, Shakespeare was English, and, as usual, the English got it wrong. There is perhaps some truth to the tale, they admit – Macbeth, who reckoned he had a better hereditary claim to the throne than its occupant, did kill Duncan in 1040 – but thereafter he ruled well for 17 years and kept the country relatively prosperous.

Power games

Where Shakespeare undeniably showed his genius, however, was in managing to heighten the narrative of a history that was already (and remained) melodramatic beyond belief. Scotland's story was for centuries little more than the biographies of ruthlessly ambitious families jostling for power, gaining it and losing it through accidents of royal marriages, unexpected deaths and lack of fertility.

A successful Scottish king needed cunning as well as determination, an ability to judge just how far he could push powerful barons without being toppled from his throne in the process. In a continuous effort to safeguard the future, marriage contracts were routinely made between royal infants and, when pre-

mature death brought a succession of kings to the throne as children, the land's leading families fought for advancement by trying to gain control over the young rulers, occasionally by kidnapping them.

Summarise some of the stories and they seem more histrionic than historical. An attractive young widow returns from 13 years at the French court to occupy the throne of Scotland, lays claim to the throne of England, conducts a series of passionate affairs, marries her lover a few weeks after he has allegedly murdered her second husband, loses the throne, is incarcerated for 19 years by her cousin, the queen of England, and is then, on a pretext, beheaded.

LEFT: Romans building Hadrian's Wall.
RIGHT: a Pictish sculpted stone at St Vigeans.

No scriptwriter today would dare to invent as outrageous a plot as the true life story of Mary Queen of Scots.

Nameless people

Our earliest knowledge of Scotland dates back more than 6,000 years, when the cold, wet climate and the barren landscape would seem familiar enough to a time-traveller from the present day. Then the region was inhabited by nameless hunters and fishermen. Later, the mysterious Beaker People from Holland and the Rhineland settled here, as they did in Ireland, leaving as a memorial only a few tantalising

tany, and mastered the use of iron implements. The blueprint for a tribal society was in place.

It was the Romans who gave it coherence. The desire of Emperor Vespasian in AD 80 to forge northwards from an already subjugated southern Britain towards the Grampian Mountains and the dense forests of central Scotland united the tribes in opposition. To their surprise, the Romans, who called the natives Picti, "painted men", encountered fearsome opposition. An early Scots leader, called Calgacus by the Romans, rallied 30,000 men – a remarkable force but no match for the Roman war machine.

Soon, however, the "barbarians" began to per-

Feuds between clans were frequent and bloody, provoking one visiting scholar to state: "The Scots are not industrious and the people are poor. They spend all their time in wars and, when there is no war, they fight one another."

pots. Were the eerie Standing Stones of Callanish, on the island of Lewis, built by them as a primitive observatory? Nobody can be certain.

A tribal society

Celtic tribes, driven by their enemies to the outer fringes of Europe, settled in Scotland, as they did in Ireland, Cornwall, Wales and Brit-

fect guerrilla tactics. In the year 118, for instance, the Ninth Legion marched north to quell yet another rebellion and was never seen again. Was it really worth all this trouble, the Romans wondered, to subdue such barbarians?

Hadrian's answer, as emperor, was no. He built a fortified wall that stretched for 73 miles (117km) across the north of England, isolating the savages. A successor, Antoninus Pius, tried to push back the boundaries in 142 by erecting a fortified wall between the Rivers Forth and Clyde. But it was never an effective exercise. The Roman Empire fell without ever conquering these troublesome natives, and Scottish life carried on without the more lasting benefits of Roman civilisation, such as good roads. A complex clan system evolved, consisting of large families bound by blood ties.

Birth of the true Scots

Europe's Dark Ages enveloped the region. What records remain portray raiders riding south to plunder and pillage. True Scots were born in the 6th century when Gaels migrated from the north of Ireland, inaugurating an epoch in which beautifully drawn manuscripts and brilliant metalwork illuminated the cultural darkness.

Like much of Western Europe, Scotland's history at this time was a catalogue of invasions. The most relentless aggressors were the Vikings,

for power was continuous. It was in this period that Macbeth murdered his rival, Duncan, and was eventually killed in turn by Duncan's son.

The Norman conquest

The collapse of England to William the Conqueror in 1066 drove many of the English lords northwards, turning the Lowlands of Scotland into an aristocratic refugee camp. Scotland's king, Malcolm, married one of the refugees, Margaret, a Hungarian-born Christian reformer and strong supporter of English standards. Partly to please her, Malcolm invaded England twice. During the second incursion, he lost his

who arrived in the 8th century in their Scandinavian longships to loot the monasteries that had been founded by early Christian missionaries such as St Ninian and St Columba.

Eventually, in 843, the warring Picts – a fierce Celtic race who dominated the southwest – united with the Scots under Kenneth MacAlpin, the astute ruler of the west coast kingdom of Dalriada. But Edinburgh was not brought under the king's influence until 962, and the Angles, a Teutonic people who controlled the south of the country, were not subjugated until 1018. Feuding

life. This gave William Rufus, the Conqueror's son and successor, an opportunity to involve himself in Scottish affairs by securing the northern throne for Malcolm's eldest son, Edgar, the first of a series of weak kings. A successor, David I, having been brought up in England, gave many estates to his Norman friends. Also, he did nothing to stop English replacing Gaelic and introduced feudalism into the Lowlands.

But true feudalism never really took root. French knights, accustomed to deference, were surprised to find that, when they rode through a field of crops, the impertinent Scottish peasants would demand compensation. Although the Normans greatly influenced architecture and language, they in no sense conquered the

LEFT: Clava Cairns, the Bronze Age burial site.
ABOVE: William Wallace rallies his Scottish forces against the English.

country. Instead, they helped create a social division that was to dominate Scotland's history: the Lowlands were controlled by noblemen who spoke the same Norman French and subscribed to the same values as England's ruling class, while the Highlands remained untamed, under the influence of independent-minded Gaelic speakers, and the islands were loyal, more or less, to

> Some believe Queen Margaret gave the Scots their inferiority complex by forcing them to measure themselves against the English.

Norway. The Highland clans, indeed, were virtually independent kingdoms, whose chiefs, under the old patriarchal system, had the power of life and death over their people.

Over the next three centuries the border with England was to be constantly redefined. The seaport of Berwick-upon-Tweed, now the most northerly town in England, was to change hands 13 times. In the 1160s the Scots turned to French sympathisers for help, concluding what eventually came to be known as the Auld Alliance. In later years the pact would have a profound influence on Scottish life, but on this occasion it was no match for England's might. After a comparatively peaceful interlude, England's insidious interference provoked a serious

backlash in 1297. William Wallace, a violent youth from Elderslie, became an outlaw after a scuffle with English soldiers in which a girl (some think she was his wife), who helped him escape, was killed herself by the sheriff of Lanark. Wallace returned to kill the sheriff, and raised enough of an army to drive back the English forces, making him for some months master of southern Scotland.

But Wallace, immortalised in the film *Braveheart*, wasn't supported by the nobles, who considered him low born, and, after being defeated at Falkirk by England's Edward I (the "Hammer of the Scots"), he was executed.

Bruce's victory

The next challenger, Robert the Bruce, who was descended from the Norman de Brus family, got further as a freedom fighter – as far as the throne itself, in fact, in 1306, though getting off to a bad start, he spent a year's exile on Rathlin Island, off the coast of Ireland. This is where he is said to have been inspired by the persistence of a spider building its web in a cave, and he returned to Scotland full of determination and proceeded to win a series of victories. Soon the French recognised him as king of Scotland and the Roman Catholic Church gave it its backing.

England's new king, Edward II, although he had little stomach for Scottish affairs, could not ignore the challenge and, in 1314, the two forces collided at Bannockburn, south of Stirling. Bruce's chances looked slim: he was pitching only 6,000 men against a force of 20,000 English. But he was shrewd enough to hold the high ground, forcing the English into the wet marshes, and he won.

Because the Pope did not recognise the new monarch, Bruce's subjects successfully petitioned Rome, and the Declaration of Arbroath in 1320 confirmed him as king.

However, England's Edward III decided that Scotland was more trouble than it was worth and in 1328 granted it independence. He recognised Bruce as king and married his sister to Bruce's baby son. Peace had been achieved between two of the most rancorous of neighbours. It seemed too good to be true – and it was. ❑

LEFT: Robert the Bruce.
RIGHT: Robert the Bruce kills Sir Henry de Bohun in single combat at Bannockburn.

Robert Bruce sends a defiance to Edward III.

BATTLE FOR THE THRONE

For centuries the throne of Scotland was a source of conflict, inextricably part of the turbulent relationship with England which was always there, breathing down the monarch's neck. But help was at hand from France...

The outbreak in 1339 of the intermittent Hundred Years War between England and France kept Edward III's mind off Scotland. He failed, therefore, to appreciate the significance of a pact concluded in 1326 between France and Scotland by Robert the Bruce. Yet the Auld Alliance, as the pact came to be known, was to keep English ambitions at bay for centuries and at one point almost resulted in Scotland becoming a province of France.

Principal beneficiaries of the deal were the kings of the Stuart (or Stewart) family. Taking their name from their function as High Stewarts to the king, they were descended from the Fitzalans, Normans who came to England with William the Conqueror in 1066.

When the Bruce family failed to produce a male heir, the crown passed in 1371 to the Stuarts because Marjorie, Robert the Bruce's daughter, had married Walter Fitzalan. The first of the Stuarts, Robert II, faced a problem that was to plague his successors: he had constantly to look over his shoulder at England, yet he could never ignore another threat to his power – his own dissident barons and warring chieftains.

Youthful monarchs

His son, Robert III, trusted these ambitious men so little that he sent his eldest son, James, to France for safety. But the ship carrying him was waylaid and young James fell into the hands of England's Henry IV. He grew up in the English court and didn't return to Scotland (as James I) until 1422, at the age of 29. His friendliness with the English was soon strained to breaking

ous auez men ouy recordes de tregues entre les anglois z les

point, however, and he renewed the Auld Alliance, siding with France's Charles VII and Joan of Arc against the English. But soon James was murdered, stabbed to death in front of his wife by his uncle, a cousin and another noble.

His son, James II, succeeded at the age of six, setting another Stuart pattern: monarchs who came to the throne as minors, creating what has been called an infantile paralysis of the power structure. In 1460 James, fighting to recapture Roxburgh from the English, died when one of his own siege guns exploded. James III, another boy king, succeeded. He had time to marry a Danish princess (bringing the Norse islands of Orkney and Shetland into the realm) before he

---

LEFT: Robert the Bruce meets with Edward III.
RIGHT: Edward III takes Berwick in 1333.

was locked in Edinburgh Castle by the scheming barons and replaced by his more malleable younger brother. The arrangement didn't last, and soon James's son, James IV, was crowned king, aged 15. He cemented relations with England in 1503 by marrying Margaret Tudor, the 12-year-old daughter of Henry VII, the Welsh warrior who had usurped the English throne 18 years before. The harmony was short-lived: the French talked James into attacking England, and he was killed at the battle of Flodden Hill. James's heir, predictably, was also called James and was just over a year old. The power-brokers could continue plotting.

should Scotland ally itself with Catholic France or Protestant England? In the ensuing tug-of-war between the English and the French, the infant Mary was taken to France for safety and, at the age of 15, married the French dauphin. The Auld Alliance seemed to have taken on a new life, and Mary made a will bequeathing

> The Battle of Flodden Hill was Scotland's worst defeat to the English, wiping out the cream of a generation, and some argue that the country never recovered from the blow.

Mary Queen of Scots

Torn between the French connection and the ambitions of England's Henry VIII, who tried to enrol him in his anti-Catholic campaign, the young James V declared his loyalties by marrying two Frenchwomen in succession. Life expectation was short, however, for kings as well as for peasants, and James V died in 1542 just as his second queen, Marie de Guise, gave birth to a daughter. At less than a week old, the infant was proclaimed Mary Queen of Scots.

Ever an opportunist, Henry VIII despatched an invasion force which reduced Edinburgh, apart from its castle, to rubble. It was known as the "Rough Wooing" and left hatred that would last for centuries. The immediate question was:

Scotland to France if she were to die childless.

When the king of France died in 1558, Mary, still aged only 16, ascended the throne with her husband. Her ambitions, though, didn't end there: she later declared herself queen of England as well, basing her claim on the Catholic assumption that England's new queen, Elizabeth I, was illegitimate because her father, the much-married Henry VIII, had been a heretic.

When Mary's husband died in 1560, she returned to Scotland, a vivacious, wilful and attractive woman. She married a Catholic, Henry Darnley, who was by contemporary accounts an arrogant, pompous and effeminate idler, and soon she began spending more and more time with her secretary, David Rizzio, an Italian.

When Rizzio was stabbed to death in front of her, Darnley was presumed to be responsible, but who could prove it? Mary appeared to turn back to Darnley and, a few months later, gave birth to a son. Immediately afterwards, however, Darnley himself was murdered. Mary and her current favourite, James Hepburn, earl of Bothwell, were presumed responsible.

A Protestant, Bothwell divorced his wife and became Mary's third husband, three months after Darnley's death. Even Mary had gone too far this time. Protestant Scotland forced its Catholic queen, still only 24, to abdicate, locking her in an island castle on Loch Leven. Bothwell fled to

flimsy evidence, of plotting Elizabeth's death and was beheaded at Fotheringay Castle.

James I of England

Mary's son, by this time secure on the Scottish throne, made little more than a token protest. Because Elizabeth, the Virgin Queen, had no heir, James had his sights set on a far greater prize than Scotland could offer: the throne of England. On 27 March 1603 he learned that the prize was his. On hearing of Elizabeth's death, he departed for London, and was to set foot in Scotland only once more in his life.

Scots have speculated ever since about how

Norway, where he died in exile. And so, in 1567, another infant king came to the throne: Mary's son, James VI.

Still fact rivalled fiction. Mary escaped from Loch Leven, tried unsuccessfully to reach France, then threw herself on the mercy of her cousin, Elizabeth I. Her previous claim to the English throne, however, had not been forgotten. Elizabeth offered her the bleak hospitality of various mansions, in which she remained a prisoner for the next 19 years.

In 1587 she was convicted, on somewhat

LEFT: Robert Herdman's depiction of the execution of Mary Queen of Scots. **ABOVE:** Scottish border raiders. **ABOVE RIGHT:** James I of England.

PREACHERS OF FIRE

The bid for power by a Catholic – Mary – in the mid-16th century, set alarm bells ringing among Protestants. Their faith had been forged in fire, with early preachers such as George Wishart burned at the stake, and it contained little room for compromise. The Protestants' visionary was John Knox, a magnetic speaker and former priest whose aim, inspired by Calvinism, was to drive Catholicism out of Scotland. His followers had pledged themselves by signing the First Covenant to "forsake and renounce the congregation of Satan", and carrying Calvin's doctrines to extremes by outlawing the Latin Mass throughout all of Scotland.

differently history would have turned out had James VI of Scotland made Edinburgh rather than London his base when he became James I of England. But he was more in sympathy with the divine right of kings than with the notions of the ultra-democratic Presbyterians, who were demanding a strong say in civil affairs. And, as he wrote, ruling from a distance of 400 miles (644km) was so much easier.

His son Charles succeeded to the throne in 1625, not knowing Scotland at all. Without, therefore, realising the consequences, the absentee king tried to harmonise the forms of church service between the two countries.

because of their support for the National Covenant of 1638) backed parliament and the Roundhead forces of Oliver Cromwell; their hope was that a victorious parliament would introduce compulsory Presbyterianism in English and Irish churches as well as in Scotland. Soon the Roundheads began to outpace the Cavalier supporters of the king. Charles tried to gain the Scots' support by promising a three-year trial for Presbyterianism in England. But his time had run out: he was beheaded on 30 January 1649.

Charles's execution came as a terrible shock north of the border. How dare England kill the king of Scotland without consulting the Scots!

Conflict and civil war

The Scots would have none of it: religious riots broke out, and one bishop is said to have conducted his service with two loaded pistols placed in front of him. A National Covenant was organised, pledging faith to "the true religion" and affirming the unassailable authority in spiritual matters of the powerful General Assembly of the Church of Scotland. Armed conflict soon followed: in 1639 the Scots invaded northern England, forcing Charles to negotiate.

Charles I's luck ran out in England too. Needing money, he unwisely called together his parliament for the first time in 10 years. A power struggle ensued, leading swiftly to civil war. At first the Scottish Covenanters (so named

Many turned to Charles's 18-year-old son, who had undertaken not to oppose Presbyterianism, and he was proclaimed Charles II in Edinburgh. But Cromwell won a decisive victory at the Battle of Dunbar and turned Scotland into an occupied country, abolishing its separate parliament.

By the time the monarchy was restored in 1660, Charles II had lost interest in Scotland's religious aspirations and removed much of the Presbyterian Church's power. Violent intolerance stalked the land and the 1680s became known as the Killing Time. The risk to Covenanters increased when, after Charles died of apoplexy in 1685, his brother James, a Catholic, became king. With the rotten judgement that dogged the Stewart line, James II imposed the death penalty for worshipping as a Covenanter. His power base in London soon crumbled, however, and in 1689 he was deposed in favour of his Protestant nephew and son-in-law, William of Orange.

Highland Jacobites

Some Scots, mostly Highlanders, remained true to James. The Jacobites, as they were called, almost annihilated William's army in a fierce battle at Killiecrankie in 1689. But their leader Claverhouse was killed, and most of them lost heart and returned to the Highlands.

Determined to exert his authority over the

ald younger than 70 to the sword. The Campbells were thrilled to carry out their commission, and the Massacre of Glencoe in 1692 remains one of the bloodiest dates in Scotland's history. The barbarity of the massacre produced a public outcry, not so much because of the number killed but because of the abuse of hospitality.

Queen Anne, the second daughter of James II, succeeded William in 1702. None of her 17 children had survived, and the English were determined to keep both thrones out of Stuart hands. They turned to Sophie of Hanover, a granddaughter of James VI/James I. If the Scots would agree to accept a Hanoverian line of succession, much-

Scots, William demanded that every clan leader swear an oath of loyalty to him. Partly due to a misunderstanding of where the swearing would take place, one chieftain, the head of the Clan MacDonald, took his oath after the deadline.

Bloody massacre

Here was a chance to make an example of a prominent leader. Members of the Campbell clan, old enemies of the MacDonalds, were ordered to lodge with the MacDonalds at their home in Glencoe, get to know them and then, having won their confidence, put every MacDon-

> "We are bought and sold for English gold," the Scots sang following the Treaty of Union of 1707. Like so many Scottish songs, it was a lament.

needed trade concessions would be granted. There was one other condition: England and Scotland should unite under one parliament.

As so often before, riots broke out in Edinburgh and elsewhere. But the opposition was fragmented and, in 1707, a Treaty of Union incorporated the Scottish parliament into the Westminster parliament to create the United Kingdom. Unknown to the signatories, the foundation of the British Empire was being laid. ❏

LEFT: Scottish Covenanters meet in Edinburgh.
ABOVE: grief after the Massacre of Glencoe.

THE AGE OF REBELLION

The 18th and 19th centuries witnessed rebellions in Scotland not only against the Union, but also in ideas, industry, agriculture and the Church

The ink was hardly dry on the Treaty of Union of 1707 when the Scots began to smart under the new constitutional arrangements. The idea of a union with England had never been popular with the working classes, most of whom saw it (rightly) as a sell-out by the aristocracy to the "Auld Enemy". Scotland's businessmen were outraged by the imposition of hefty, English-style excise duties on many goods and the high-handed government bureaucracy that went with them. The aristocracy who had supported the Union resented Westminster's peremptory abolition of Scotland's privy council. Even the hardline Cameronians – the fiercest of Protestants – roundly disliked the Union in the early years of the 18th century.

Jacobite insurgency

All of which was compounded by the Jacobitism (support for the Stuarts) which haunted many parts of Scotland, particularly among the Episcopalians of Aberdeenshire, Angus and Perthshire, and among the Catholic clans (such as the Mac-Donalds) of the Western Highlands.

And, given that one of the main planks of Jacobitism was the repeal of the Union, it was hardly surprising that the Stuart kings cast a long shadow over Scotland in the first half of the 18th century. In fact, within a year of the Treaty of Union being signed, the first Jacobite insurgency was under way, helped by a French regime ever anxious to discomfit the power of the English.

In January 1708 a flotilla of French privateers

commanded by Comte Claude de Forbin battered its way through the North Sea gales, carrying the 19-year-old James Stuart, the self-styled James VIII and III. After a brief sojourn in the Firth of Forth near the coast of Fife, the French privateers were chased round the top of Scotland and out into the Atlantic by English warships. Many of the French vessels foundered on their way back to France, although James survived to go on plotting.

On dry land, the uprising of 1708 was confined to a few East Stirlingshire lairds who marched around with a handful of men. They were quickly rounded up, and that November five of the ring-leaders were tried in Edinburgh for treason. The

---

PRECEDING PAGES: David Morier's portrayal of Culloden, painted in 1746. **LEFT:** Prince Charles Edward Stuart leaving Scotland, from a painting by J.B. MacDonald, and **ABOVE:** in his finery as the Young Chevalier.

verdict on all five was "not proven" and they were freed. Shocked by this display of Scottish leniency, the British parliament passed the Treason Act of 1708, which brought Scotland into line with England, ensuring traitors a gruesome death.

Bobbing John v Red John

The next Jacobite uprising, in 1715, was a serious affair. By then disaffection in Scotland with the Union was widespread, the Hanoverians had not secured their grip on Britain, there were loud pro-Stuart mutterings in England, and much of Britain had been stripped of its military.

But the insurrection was led by the Earl of Mar,

a few others), leaving his followers to the wrath of the Whigs. The duke of Argyll was sacked as commander of the government forces for fear he would be too lenient. Dozens of rebels – especially the English – were hanged, drawn and quartered, and hundreds were deported.

> *Bealach-n-Spainnteach (the Pass of the Spaniards), a niche in the Kintail Mountains, recalls the rout suffered by the Spanish at the hands of the British when they joined forces with the Jacobites in 1719.*

a military incompetent known as "Bobbing John", whose support came mainly from the clans of the Central and Eastern Highlands. When the two sides clashed at Sheriffmuir near Stirling on 13 November, Mar's Jacobite army had a four-to-one advantage over the tiny Hanoverian force commanded by "Red John of the Battles" (as the duke of Argyll was known). But, instead of pressing his huge advantage, Mar withdrew his Highland army after an inconclusive clash.

The insurrection of 1715 quickly ran out of steam. The Pretender himself did not arrive in Scotland until the end of December, and the forces he brought with him were too little and too late. He did his cause no good by stealing away at night (along with "Bobbing John" and

Not that the débâcle of 1715 stopped the Stuarts trying again. In 1719 it was the Spaniards who decided to try to queer the Hanoverian pitch by backing the Jacobites. Again it was a fiasco. In March 1719 a little force of 307 Spanish soldiers sailed into Loch Alsh where they joined up with a few hundred Murrays, Mackenzies and Mackintoshes. This Spanish-Jacobite army was easily routed in the steep pass of Glenshiel by a British unit, which swooped down from Inverness to pound the Jacobite positions with their mortars. The Highlanders simply vanished into the mist and snow of Kintail, leaving the wretched Spaniards in their gold-on-white uniforms to wander about the subarctic landscape before surrendering.

The Young Pretender

But it was the insurrection of 1745, "so glorious an enterprise", led by Charles Edward Stuart (Bonnie Prince Charlie), which shook Britain, despite the fact that the government's grip on the turbulent parts of Scotland had never seemed firmer. There were military depots at Fort William, Fort Augustus and Fort George, and an effective Highland militia (later known as the Black Watch) had been raised. General Wade had thrown a network of military roads and bridges across the Highlands. Logically Charles, the Young Pretender, should never have been allowed to set foot out of the Highlands.

But having set up a military "infrastructure" in the Highlands, the British Government had neglected it. The Independent Companies (the Black Watch) had been shunted out to the West Indies, there were fewer than 4,000 troops in the whole of Scotland, hardly any cavalry or artillery, and Clan Campbell was no longer an effective fighting force. The result was that Bonnie Prince Charlie and his ragtag army of MacDonalds, Camerons, Mackintoshes, Robertsons, McGregors, Macphersons and Gordons, plus some Lowland cavalry and a stiffening of Franco-Irish

LEFT: Culloden's victor, the duke of Cumberland. **ABOVE LEFT:** Prince Charlie's much romanticised farewell in 1746 to Flora MacDonald. **ABOVE RIGHT:** Culloden Cairn.

mercenaries, was able to walk into Edinburgh and set up a "royal court" in Holyrood Palace.

In that September the Young Pretender sallied out of Edinburgh and wrecked General John Cope's panicky Hanoverian army near Prestonpans, and then marched across the border into England. But Stuart's success was an illusion. There was precious little support for his cause in the Lowlands of Scotland. Few Jacobite troops had been raised in Edinburgh, and Glasgow and the southwest were openly hostile. Some men had been drummed up in Manchester, but there was no serious support from the Roman Catholic families of northern England. Charles got as far as Derby and then fled back to Scotland with two powerful Hanoverian armies hot on his heels.

Battle of Culloden

After winning a rearguard action at Clifton, near Penrith, and what has been described as a "lucky victory" at Falkirk in January 1746, the Jacobite army was cut to pieces by the duke of Cumberland's artillery on Drummossie Moor, Culloden, near Inverness on 16 April 1746. It was the last great pitched battle on the soil of mainland Britain.

It was also the end of the Gaelic clan system, which had survived in the mountains of Scotland long after it had disappeared from Ireland.

The days when an upland chieftain could drum up a "tail" of trained swordsmen for cattle raids into the Lowlands were over.

Following his post-Culloden "flight across the heather", Charles, disguised as a woman servant, was given shelter on the Isle of Skye by Flora Mac-Donald, thus giving birth to one of Scotland's abiding romantic tales. He was then plucked off the Scottish coast by a French privateer and taken into exile, drunkenness and despair in France and Italy. A few dozen of the more prominent Jacobites were hauled off to Carlisle and Newcastle where they were tried, and some hanged. And for some time the Highlands were harried mercilessly by the duke of Cumberland's troopers.

In an effort to subdue the Highlands, the government in London passed the Disarming Act of 1746, which not only banned the carrying of claymores, targes, dirks and muskets, but also the wearing of tartans and the playing of bagpipes. It was a nasty piece of legislation, that impacted greatly on Gaelic culture. The British Government also took the opportunity to abolish Scotland's inefficient and often corrupt system of "Courts of Regality" by which the aristocracy (and not just the Highland variety) dispensed justice, collected fines and wielded powers of life and wealth.

The Age of Enlightenment

It is one of the minor paradoxes of 18th-century European history that, while Scotland was being racked by dynastic convulsions which were 17th-century in origin, the country was transforming itself into one of the most forward-looking societies in the world. Scotland began to wake up in the first half of the 18th century. By about 1740 the intellectual, scientific and mercantile phenomenon which became known as the Scottish Enlightenment was well under way, although it didn't reach its peak until the end of the century.

Whatever created it, the Scottish Enlightenment was an extraordinary explosion of creativity and energy. And while, in retrospect at least, the period was dominated by David Hume, the philosopher, and Adam Smith, the economist, there were many others, such as William Robertson, Adam Ferguson, William Cullen and the Adam brothers. Through the multifaceted talents of its literati, Scotland in general and Edinburgh in particular became one of the intellectual powerhouses of Western Europe.

The Clearances

But the Enlightenment and all that went with it had some woeful side effects. The Highland "Clearances" of the late 18th and early 19th centuries owed much to the "improving" attitudes triggered by the Enlightenment, as well as the greed of the lairds. The enterprising Sir John Sinclair, for example, pointed out that, while the Highlands were capable of producing from £200,000 to £300,000 worth of black cattle every year, "The same ground will produce twice as much mutton and there is wool into the bargain."

The argument proved irresistible. Sheep – particularly Cheviots – and their Lowland shepherds

began to flood into the glens and straths of the Highlands, displacing the Highland "tacksmen" and their families. Tens of thousands were forced to move to the Lowlands, coastal areas, or the colonies overseas, taking with them their culture of songs and traditions.

The worst of the Clearances – or at least the most notorious – took place on the huge estates of the countess of Sutherland and her rich, English-born husband, the marquis of Stafford. Although Stafford spent huge sums of money building roads, harbours and fish-curing sheds (for very little profit), his estate managers

Above: a Skye crofter prepares some winter comfort.
Right: Glasgow in the 18th century.

evicted tenants with real ruthlessness. It was a pattern that was repeated all over the Highlands at the beginning of the 19th century, and again later when people were displaced by the red deer of the "sporting" estates. The overgrown remains of villages are a painful reminder of this sad chapter in Scottish history.

Radicals and reactionaries

As the industrial economy of Lowland Scotland burgeoned at the end of the 18th century, it sucked in thousands of immigrant workers from all over Scotland and Ireland. The clamour for democracy grew. Some of it was fuelled by the ideas of the American and French revolutions, but much of the unrest was a reaction to Scotland's hopelessly inadequate electoral system. At the end of the 18th century, there were only 4,500 voters in the whole of Scotland and only 2,600 voters in the 33 rural counties.

And for almost 40 years Scotland was dominated by the powerful machine politician Henry Dundas, the first viscount Melville, universally known as "King Harry the Ninth".

As solicitor general for Scotland, lord advocate, home secretary, secretary for war and then first lord of the Admiralty, Dundas wielded awesome power.

INDUSTRIAL GLORY

The Enlightenment was not just confined to the salons of Edinburgh. Commerce and industry also thrived. "The same age, which produces great philosophers and politicians, renowned generals and poets, usually abounds with skilled weavers and ship-carpenters," the Scottish philosopher David Hume wrote in 1752.

By 1760 the famous Carron Ironworks in Falkirk was churning out high-grade ordnance for the British military and by 1780 hundreds of tons of goods on barges were being shuttled between Edinburgh and Glasgow along the Forth–Clyde Canal.

The Turnpike Act of 1751 improved the road system dramatically and created a brisk demand for carriages and stagecoaches. In 1738 Scotland's share of the tobacco trade (based in Glasgow) was 10 percent; by 1769 it was more than 52 percent.

There was also a huge upsurge of activity in many trades such as carpet-weaving, upholstery, glassmaking, china and pottery manufacture, linen, soap, distilling and brewing.

The 18th century changed Scotland from one of the poorest countries in Europe to a state of middling affluence. It has been calculated that between 1700 and 1800, the money generated within Scotland increased by a factor of more than 50, while the population stayed more or less static (at around 1.5 million).

But nothing could stop the spread of libertarian ideas in an increasingly industrialised workforce. The ideas contained in Tom Paine's *Rights of Man* spread like wildfire in the Scotland of the 1790s. The cobblers, weavers and spinners proved the most vociferous democrats, but there was also

> Lord Cockburn summed up the relentless grip of the powerful Henry Dundas, also known as King Harry the Ninth, on Scotland: "Who steered upon him was safe; who disregarded his light was wrecked."

riots were put down by musket-fire and the Scottish universities were racked by witchhunts.

Although Dundas himself was discredited in 1806, after being impeached for embezzlement, and died in 1811, the anti-radical paranoia of the Scottish ruling class lingered on. Establishment panic reached a peak in 1820 when the so-called Scottish Insurrection was brought to an end in the legally corrupt trial of the weavers James Wilson, John Baird, Andrew Hardie and 21 other workmen. A special (English) Court of Oyer and Terminer was set up in Glasgow to hear the case, and Wilson, Baird and Hardie were sentenced to a gruesome execution, after

unrest among farmworkers, and among seamen and soldiers in the Highland regiments.

Throughout the 1790s a number of radical "one man, one vote" organisations sprang up, such as the Scottish Friends of the People and the United Scotsmen (a quasi-nationalist group that modelled itself on the United Irishmen led by Wolfe Tone).

But the brooding figure of Dundas was more than a match for the radicals. Every organisation that raised its head was swiftly infiltrated by police spies and agents provocateurs. Ringleaders (such as the advocate Thomas Muir) were framed, arrested, tried and deported. Some, such as Robert Watt, who led the "Pike Plot" of 1794, were hanged. Meetings were broken up by dragoons,

making resounding speeches. The other radicals were sentenced to penal transportation.

Reform and disruption

By the 1820s most of Scotland (and indeed Britain) was weary of the political and constitutional corruption under which the country laboured. In 1823 Lord Archibald Hamilton pointed out the electoral absurdity of rural Scotland: "I have the right to vote in five counties in Scotland, in not one of which do I possess an acre of land," he said, "and I have no doubt that if I took the trouble I might have a vote for every county in that kingdom." Hamilton's motion calling for parliamentary reform was defeated by only 35 votes.

But nine years later, in 1832, the Reform Bill

finally passed into law, giving Scotland 30 rural constituencies, 23 burgh constituencies and a voting population of 65,000 (compared to a previous 4,500). Even this limited extension of the franchise – to male householders whose property had a rentable value of £10 or more – generated much wailing and gnashing of teeth among Scottish Tories.

No sooner had the controversy over electoral reform subsided than it was replaced by the row between the "moderates" and the "evangelicals" within the Church of Scotland. "Scotland," Lord Palmerston noted at the time, "is aflame about the Church question." But this was no genteel falling-out among theologians. It was a brutal and bruising affair which dominated political life in Scotland for 10 years and raised all kinds of constitutional questions.

At the heart of the argument was the Patronage Act of 1712, which gave Scots lairds the same right English squires had to appoint, or "intrude" clergy on local congregations. Ever since it was passed, the Church of Scotland had argued (rightly) that the Patronage Act was a flagrant and illegal violation of the Revolution Settlement of 1690 and the Treaty of Union of 1707, both of which guaranteed the independence of the Church of Scotland.

A Free Church

But the pleas fell on deaf ears. The English-dominated parliament could see no fault in a system that enabled Anglicised landowners to appoint like-minded clergymen. Patronage was seen by the Anglo-Scottish establishment as a useful instrument of political control and social progress. The issue came to a head in May 1843 when the evangelicals, led by Dr Thomas Chalmers, marched out of the annual General Assembly of the Church of Scotland in Edinburgh to form the Free Church of Scotland.

Chalmers, theologian, astronomer and brilliant organiser, defended the Free Church against bitter enemies. His final triumph, in 1847, was to persuade the London parliament that it was folly to allow the aristocracy to refuse the Free Church land on which to build churches and schools. A few days after he had given evidence, Chalmers died in Edinburgh.

The rebellion of the evangelicals was brilliantly planned, well funded and took the British establishment completely by surprise: 400 teachers left the kirk and, within 10 years of the Disruption, the Free Church had built more than 800 churches, 700 manses, three large theological colleges and 600 schools, and brought about a huge extension of education.

After 1847, state aid had to be given to the Free as well as to the established Church schools, and in 1861 the established Church lost its legal powers over Scotland's parish school system. This prepared the ground for the

Education Act of 1872, which set up a national system under the Scottish Educational Department. And, although it ran into some vicious opposition from landowners, especially in the Highlands, the Free Church prevailed.

In fact, it can be argued that the Disruption was the only rebellion in 18th- or 19th-century British history that succeeded. Chalmers and his supporters had challenged both the pervasive influence of the Anglo-Scottish aristocracy and the power of the British Parliament, and they had won. The Patronage Act of 1712 was finally repealed in 1874, and the Free Church merged back with the Church of Scotland in 1929, uniting the majority of Scottish Presbyterians in one Church. ❏

LEFT: a view of Trongate, Glasgow, possibly dating from the 19th century.
RIGHT: Scottish Presbyterians in the 17th century defying the law to worship.

THE MAKING OF MODERN SCOTLAND

Despite the economic and social problems of the 20th century, Scotland remains fiercely confident, particularly in moves towards political independence

During the Victorian and Edwardian eras, Scotland, like most of Europe, became urbanised and industrialised. Steelworks, ironworks, shipyards, coal mines, shale-oil refineries, textile factories, engineering shops, canals and, of course, railways proliferated all over 19th-century Scotland. The process was concentrated in Scotland's "central belt" (the stretch of low-lying land between Edinburgh and Glasgow), but there were important "outliers" like Aberdeen, Dundee, Ayrshire and the mill towns of the Scottish borders. A few smaller industrial ventures found their way deep into the Highlands or onto a few small islands.

It was a process that dragged in its wake profound social, cultural and demographic change. The booming industries brought thousands of work-seeking immigrants flocking into Lowland Scotland. Most came from the Highlands and Ireland, and many nursed an ancient distaste for the British establishment that translated itself into left-wing radicalism – one reason why Scottish politics are still dominated by the Labour Party today. The immigrants were also largely Roman Catholic, which did something to loosen the grip of the Presbyterian churches on Scottish life.

Glasgow – a huge metropolis

The small Georgian city of Glasgow became a huge industrial metropolis built on the kind of rectangular grid common in the United States, with industrial princes living in splendour while Highland, Irish, Italian and Jewish

immigrants swarmed in the noisome slums.

In many ways 19th-century Glasgow had more in common with Chicago or New York than with any other city in Britain. Working-class conditions were appalling. Rickets, cholera, smallpox, tuberculosis, diphtheria and alcoholism were rampant. The streets were unclean and distinctly unsafe. Violence was endemic as Highlanders and Irishmen clashed in the stews and whisky dens, while Orangemen from Ulster were used as violent and murderous strike-breakers. The city hangman was never short of work.

But there was no denying Glasgow's enormous industrial vitality. By the middle of the century the city was peppered with more than

---

PRECEDING PAGES: the distinctive Scottish Parliament Building. **LEFT:** *First Steamboat on the Clyde*, by John Knox. **RIGHT:** slum-dwellers in Glasgow's Gorbals.

100 textile mills (an industry which by that time employed more than 400,000 Scots). There were ironworks at Tollcross, Coatbridge and Monklands, productive coal mines all over Lanarkshire, and the River Clyde was lined with boiler makers, marine-engineering shops, and world-class

> Industry transformed the city of Glasgow and the River Clyde. Between 1740 and 1840 Glasgow's population leapt from 17,000 to 200,000 and then doubled again to 400,000 by 1870.

were more than 40 breweries within the city boundaries. And, in the latter part of the 19th century, the Scotch whisky industry boomed, thanks to the devastation of the French vineyards in the 1880s by phylloxera, which almost wrecked the thriving cognac industry.

As a result, Scotland, with an educated workforce and proximity to European markets, was attracting inward investment. The American-funded North British Rubber Company moved into Edinburgh in 1857. In 1884 the Singer Company built one of the biggest factories in the world at Clydebank to manufacture mass-produced sewing machines. It was the start of a

shipyards. For generations the label "Clyde built" was synonymous with industrial quality.

Nor was industry confined to Glasgow and its environs. The Tayside city of Dundee forged close links with India and became the biggest jute-manufacturing centre in Britain. The Carron Ironworks at Falkirk was Europe's largest producer of artillery by the year 1800, while in West Lothian a thriving industry was built up to extract oil from shale. Scotland's east coast fisheries also flourished, and by the end of the century the town of Wick in Caithness had become Europe's biggest herring port.

As well as producing large quantities of books, biscuits and bureaucrats, Edinburgh was a centre of the British brewing industry; at one stage there

100-year trend which did much to undermine the Scottish economy's independence.

Highland poverty

Despite the enthusiasm of Queen Victoria and the British gentry for the Highlands, dire poverty stalked upland Scotland. Land reform was desperately needed. Following riots in Skye in 1882 and the formation of the Highland Land League in 1884, Gladstone's Liberal government passed the Crofters (Scotland) Holdings Act of 1886, which gave crofters fair rents, security of tenure and the right to pass their crofts on to their families. But it was Lord Salisbury's Conservative government which put the Scottish Secretary in the

British cabinet, and established the Scottish Office in Edinburgh and London in 1886.

By the end of the 19th century the huge majority of the Scottish population was urban, industrialised and concentrated in the towns and cities of the Lowlands. And urban Scotland proved a fertile breeding ground for the British Left. The Scottish Labour Party (SLP) was founded in 1888, although it soon merged with the Independent Labour Party (ILP), which in turn played a big part in the formation of the (British) Labour Party. Britain's first Labour MP, Keir Hardie, was a Scot, as was Ramsay MacDonald, Britain's first Labour prime minister.

added up after the war it was found that more than 20 percent of all Britons killed were Scots.

In addition to which, the shipyards of the Clyde and the engineering shops of west central Scotland were producing more tanks, shells, warships, explosives and fieldguns than any comparable part of Britain. That explains why the British Government took such a dim view of the strikes and industrial disputes that hit the Clyde between 1915 and 1919 and led to the area being dubbed "Red Clydeside".

When Glasgow workers struck for a 40-hour week in January 1919, the Secretary of State for Scotland panicked and called in the military;

The Great War

When World War I broke out in 1914, the Scots flocked to the British colours with an extraordinary enthusiasm. Like Ireland, Scotland provided the British Army with a disproportionate number of soldiers. Like the Irish, the Scots suspended their radicalism and trooped into the forces to fight for king and empire, to the despair of left-wing leaders like Keir Hardie and John Maclean. With less than 10 percent of the British population, the Scots made up almost 15 percent of the British army. And when the butcher's bill was

LEFT: herring drifters near the port of Peterhead.
ABOVE: Labour Party leader Ramsay MacDonald with his son and daughter in 1929.

CASH INCENTIVES

The growth of industry in Scotland generated huge amounts of cash. Edinburgh and Dundee became centres for investment trusts which sank cash into ventures all over the world, particularly in America. In 1873 the Dundee jute man Robert Fleming set up the Scottish American Investment Trust to channel money into American cattle ranches, fruit farms, mining companies and railways.

The biggest cattle ranch in the US – Matador Land & Cattle Company – was operated from Dundee until 1951. The outlaw Butch Cassidy once worked for a cattle company that was being run from the fastidious New Town of Edinburgh.

Laying down the Law

Different in origin from that of England, Scottish law, along with the Kirk, plays a vital part in cementing a sense of national identity

One curiosity of the Scottish legal system is Not Proven – "that bastard verdict", as Sir Walter Scott called it. At the end of a criminal trial the verdict can be "guilty" or "not guilty", as in England, or the jury may find the charge "not proven". It's an

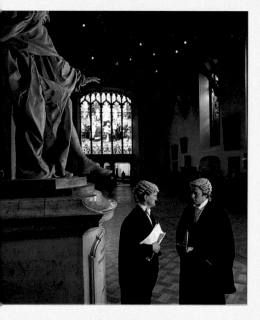

option that reflects Scots logic and refusal to compromise by assuming a person innocent until proved guilty, but it does confer a stigma on the accused.

The jargon of Scots lawyers is distinctive, too. If you embark on litigation you are a "pursuer". You sue a "defender". If you disagree too outspokenly with a judge's decision, you may be accused of "murmuring the judge".

From the abolition of the Scottish Parliament with the 1707 Act of Union until its re-establishment in 1999, the UK Parliament in London made laws for the country. However, though few outsiders realise it, the Scots still managed to maintain their own distinctive legal system.

Scottish law is quite different in origin from that of England and those countries (such as the US and

many Commonwealth nations) to which the English system has been exported, and is closer to those of South Africa, Sri Lanka, Louisiana and Quebec. It was developed from Roman law and owes much more to Continental legal systems than England does – thanks partly to the fact that Scottish lawyers, during the 17th and 18th centuries, studied in Europe.

Solicitors, the general practitioners of the law, regard themselves as men of affairs, with a wider role than lawyers in some countries have adopted. Advocates, the equivalent of the English barrister, to whom a solicitor will turn for expert advice, are based in Parliament House in Edinburgh and also refuse to become too narrowly specialised. This is important if they wish to become sheriffs, as the judges of the local courts are called.

Some practitioners have demonstrated outstanding talents beyond the confines of the law. Sir Walter Scott was, for most of his life, a practising lawyer. In Selkirk, you can still see the courtroom where he presided as sheriff. Robert Louis Stevenson qualified as an advocate, but he soon gave it up for literature.

Mutual influences

Inevitably, English law has had its influence. Much modern legislation, especially commercial law, has tended to be copied from England. But it hasn't been all one way. In Scottish criminal trials, the jury of 15 is allowed to reach a majority verdict, a procedure recently adopted by England. The English have also introduced a prosecution service, independent of the police, similar to Scotland's. Some in England would also like to import the "110-day rule": this requires a prisoner on remand to be released if his trial doesn't take place within 110 days of his imprisonment. More controversially, Scottish judges have power in criminal cases to create new crimes – a power they use sparingly.

Many in England envy the Scottish system of house purchase. Most of the legal and estate agency work is done by solicitors and seems to be completed far faster than in England. Scottish laws on Sunday trading are more liberal, and divorce was available in Scotland 500 years before it was in the south.

Along with the Kirk, the separateness of the Scottish legal system plays a vital part in establishing a sense of national identity. Many Scots lawyers resent the failure of Westminster to have proper regard to the fact that the law is different in Scotland. Whether it's better is another question; the best verdict in this case may be "not proven". ❑

LEFT: time for legal exchange between sessions.

Glaswegians watched open-mouthed as armed troops backed by tanks poured onto the Glasgow streets to nip the Red Revolution in the bud. At a huge rally in George Square on 31 January 1919, the police baton-charged the crowd.

The hungry years

The 1920s and 1930s were sour years for Scotland. The "traditional" industries of shipbuilding, steel-making, coal-mining and heavy engineering went into a decline from which they have never recovered: and the whisky industry reeled from the body blow of American Prohibition. The new light engineering industries – cars, electrics and

England went Conservative even if Scotland voted Labour.

The 1920s and 1930s also saw the revival of a kind of left-wing cultural nationalism which owed a lot to the poetry of Hugh MacDiarmid, the writing of Lewis Grassic Gibbon and the

> In 1937 Walter Elliot, Secretary of State for Scotland, described how in Scotland "23 percent of its population live in conditions of gross overcrowding, compared with 4 percent in England".

machine tools – stayed stubbornly south of the border. Unemployment soared to almost three in 10 of the workforce, and Scots boarded the emigrant ships in droves. An estimated 400,000 Scots (10 percent of the population) emigrated between 1921 and 1931.

Most of urban Scotland saw its salvation in the newly formed Labour Party, which not only promised a better life but also a measure of Home Rule. Support for the Labour Party began early. At the general election of 1922 an electoral pattern was set which has remained (with few exceptions) ever since:

enthusiasms of upper-crust nationalists like Ruaridh Erskine of Marr and R.B. Cunninghame-Graham. From the Scottish literary renaissance of the interwar years the nationalist movement grew increasingly more political. In 1934 the small (but right-wing) Scottish Party merged with the National Party of Scotland to form the Scottish National Party (SNP).

The world at war

It wasn't until World War II loomed that the Scottish economy began to climb out of the doldrums. And when war broke out in September 1939 the Clydeside shipyards moved into high gear to build warships like the *Duke of York*, *Howe*, *Indefatigable* and *Vanguard*, while the engineering

ABOVE: the Hungry Thirties: Glasgow kids keep smiling through the hard times.

firms began pumping out small arms, bayonets, explosives and ammunition. The Rolls-Royce factory at Hillington near Glasgow produced Merlin engines for the RAF's Spitfires.

The Germans were well aware of this and on 13 and 14 March 1941, hundreds of German bombers, operating at the limit of their range, devastated Clydeside. More than 1,000 people were killed (528 in the town of Clydebank) and another 1,500 injured.

War killed more than 58,000 Scots (compared to the 148,000 who had lost their lives in World War I) but had the effect of galvanising the Scottish economy for a couple of decades.

euphoria was that the Labour Government's policy of nationalising the coal mines and the railways was stripping Scotland of many of its decision-making powers, and therefore management jobs. The process continued into the 1970s with the steel, shipbuilding and aerospace industries also being "taken into public ownership".

This haemorrhage of economic power and influence was compounded by Scottish companies being sold to English and foreign predators. In 1988 British Caledonian, originally a Scotland-based airline, was swallowed up by British Airways. To an alarming extent, Scotland's economy now assumed a "branch factory" status.

And there's no doubt that the Labour Government that came to power in 1945 made major improvements to Scottish life.

The post-war period

The National Health Service proved an effective instrument against such plagues as infant mortality, tuberculosis, rickets and scarlet fever. Housing conditions improved in leaps and bounds as the worst of the city slums were pulled down and replaced by roomy (although often badly built) council houses. Semi-rural new towns like East Kilbride, Glenrothes, Cumbernauld, Irvine and Livingston were established throughout central Scotland.

What went largely unnoticed in the post-war

A bid for Home Rule

English enthusiasm for Labour's experiment flagged and in 1951 Sir Winston Churchill was returned to power. Scotland, of course, continued to vote Labour (although in the general election of 1955 the Conservatives won 36 of Scotland's 71 seats, the only time they have had a majority north of the border). And, while Home Rule for Scotland was off the political agenda, Scottish nationalism refused to go away.

In the late 1940s two-thirds of the Scottish electorate signed a "national covenant" demanding Home Rule. In 1951 a squad of young nationalists outraged the British establishment by whisking the Stone of Destiny out of Westminster Abbey and hiding it in Scotland. And in 1953 the British establishment outraged Scottish sentiment by insisting on the title of Queen Elizabeth II for the new queen, despite the fact that the Scots had never had a Queen Elizabeth I.

Industrial decline

But while Scotland did reasonably well out of the Conservative-led "New Elizabethan Age" of the 1950s and early 1960s, the old structural faults soon began to reappear. By the late 1950s the well-equipped Japanese and German shipyards were snatching orders from under the nose of the Clyde, the Scottish coalfields were proving woefully inefficient and Scotland's steelworks and heavy engineering firms were losing their grip on international markets.

And, although the Conservative Government did fund a new steel mill at Ravenscraig, near Motherwell, and enticed Rootes to set up a car plant at Linwood and the British Motor Corporation to start making trucks at Bathgate, it was all done under duress and they were abandoned. Scotland's distance from the marketplace continued to be a crippling disadvantage. The Midlands and south of England remained the engine-room of the British economy. The drift of Scots to the south continued.

Although the Scots voted heavily for the Labour Party in the general elections of 1964 and 1966, Labour's complacency was jolted in November 1967 when Mrs Winnie Ewing of the SNP snatched the Hamilton by-election. Despite losing the seat in 1970, her success marked the start of an upsurge in Scottish nationalism that preoccupied Scottish – and, to some extent, British – politics for the next decade.

Striking oil

When Harold Wilson's Labour Government ran out of steam in 1970, it was replaced by the Conservative regime of Edward Heath – although, once again, the Scots voted overwhelmingly Labour. But in the early 1970s, Scotland got lucky. The oil companies struck big quantities of oil. All round Scotland engineering firms and land speculators began snapping up sites on which to build platform yards, rig repair bases, airports, oil refineries and petrochemical works.

The SNP was quick to take advantage of the new mood of optimism. Running on a cam-

paign slogan of "It's Scotland's Oil", the SNP won seven seats in the general election of February 1974 and took more than 20 percent of the Scottish vote. In October 1974 they did even better, cutting a swathe through both parties to take 11 seats and more than 30 percent of the Scottish vote. It looked as if one more

> In the 1970s the Royal High School in Edinburgh was purchased ready for the new Scottish Assembly to be installed. After years of indecision it was sold again in 1994.

push by the SNP would see the United Kingdom dissolved, and the hard-pressed British economy cut off from the oil revenues it so badly needed.

The Labour Government responded to the nationalists' political threat with a constitutional defence. It offered Scotland a directly elected assembly with substantial (although strictly limited) powers if the Scottish people voted "yes" in a national referendum. At which point Westminster changed the rules. At the instigation of Labour MP George Cunningham, parliament decided that a simple majority was not good enough, and that devolution would go ahead only if more than 40 percent of the Scottish electorate voted in favour. It

---

LEFT: harvesting in Fife.
RIGHT: oil rig moored off Cromarty Firth.

was an impossible condition. Predictably the Scots failed to vote yes by a big majority in the referendum of March 1979 (although they *did* vote "yes") and the Scotland Bill lapsed. Shortly afterwards, the 11 SNP members joined a vote of censure against the Labour Government – which fell by one vote.

Margaret Thatcher came into power and promptly made it plain that any form of Home Rule for Scotland was out of the question.

The Thatcher years

The devolution débâcle produced a genuine crisis of confidence among Scotland's political classes. Support for the SNP slumped, the Alliance could do nothing. And the Labour Party, armed with the majority of the Scottish vote, could only watch helplessly as the aluminium smelter at Invergordon, the steel mill at Gartcosh, the car works at Linwood, the pulp mill at Fort William, the truck plant at Bathgate and much of the Scottish coalfields perished in the economic blizzard of the 1980s. Even the energetic Scottish Development Agency could do little to protect the Scottish economy and unemployment climbed to more than 300,000.

So the political triumph of Thatcherism in England found no echoes in Scotland. At the general election of June 1987 the pattern that first emerged in 1922 repeated itself; England voted Tory and Scotland voted Labour. Out of 72 Scottish MPs 50 were Labour and only 10 were Conservative. This raised the argument that the then Scottish Secretary, Malcolm Rifkind, was an English governor-general with "no mandate" to govern Scotland. Rifkind's response was that the 85 percent of the Scottish electorate who voted for "British" parties were voting for the sovereignty of Westminster and therefore had to accept Westminster's rules.

At the end of 1987, the Labour Party tabled yet another Devolution Bill, which was promptly thrown out by English MPs to the jeers of the SNP, who claimed that Labour's "Feeble Fifty" could do nothing without Westminster's say so.

A new parliament

The commitment to devolution remained, however, and following Labour's landslide victory in the general election of May 1997, which left Scotland with no Conservative MPs at all, the Scottish people were asked in a referendum whether they wanted their own parliament.

The proposal received a ringing endorsement, a majority of two-to-one voting "yes". Proposals for the new parliament to have the power to vary taxes from UK standard rates were also approved.

In the first elections to the Edinburgh-based Scottish Parliament in 1999, only three out of five Scots bothered to vote. Labour won 53 of the 129 seats. This was not an overall majority, so Labour was forced to negotiate with the Liberal Democrats (17 seats) who became their coalition partners in a joint bid to keep at bay the pro-independence SNP (35 seats). The new parliament building finally opened at

Holyrood in 2004, its construction costs having soared from an estimated £40 million to £431 million. Yet many voters regarded the assembly as a toothless beast, its energies sapped by the tendency of the more able politicians to direct their ambitions towards the London parliament rather than the Edinburgh one.

Ground-breaking legislation

Land reform was one area where the Scottish Parliament did assert itself, notably by introducing the Land Reform (Scotland) Act to tackle the iniquity of most of the land of Scotland being owned by a few lairds, many absentee and many foreign. The new law brought much of that land into public ownership by establishing two national parks – the Loch Lomond and

Trossachs, and the Cairngorms. Other ground-breaking legislation abolished upfront tuition fees at universities, provided better care for the old and disabled, and gave mothers the legal right to breastfeed in public.

The Falkirk Wheel

In 2002 Scotland reasserted itself in the world of engineering by unveiling an iconic landmark, the Falkirk Wheel. This, the world's only rotating boat lift, replaced derelict locks and transfers boats by means of gondolas between two canals – the Union and the Forth & Clyde – that stand at different levels and link Edinburgh and Glasgow. While Edinburgh is Scotland's powerful "financial hub", Glasgow's once-proud heavy industry has now been replaced by a thriving service sector. However, Glasgow and Edinburgh still both continue to have neighbourhoods plagued by poverty.

Scotland's economy is closely linked to the rest of Britain and the wider European community, and has also been badly affected by the recession of the early 21st century. Since the decline of industry and manufacturing, Scotland has been depending on the service and tourism industries, as well as the food and drink market and oil and gas. Figures reveal that the recession proved shorter in Scotland than in the rest of the UK but the future is still shaky and unsure and the pace of recovery slow.

The state of education

Scotland has a long history of universal provision of public education. In comparison with the rest of the UK, at secondary level Scottish children learn a wider range of subjects: the English system is confined to a smaller number of subjects, each studied in more depth. The Scottish educators, believing their students are better equipped to face the modern world, have considered this a narrow approach. Universities in Scotland normally offer four-year courses, one year longer than the rest of the UK, and with tuition fees abolished for Scottish students the percentage of Scots studying close to home is high. Parents in Scotland tend to play a bigger role in their children's education.

LEFT: the sun sets on a wind farm in the Highlands.
RIGHT: the Falkirk Wheel is an extraordinary feat of modern engineering.

The independence debate

Scots have now been members of the United Kingdom for over 300 years, and Scottish history is deeply enmeshed with that of Great Britain. With the SNP having seized power at the 2007 elections, and its leader, Alex Salmond now firmly installed as first

> With its new legislative powers, Scotland led the way in banning smoking in all public places in 2006, encouraging England and Wales to follow suit.

minister of the country, Scotland has once again taken a decisive step to challenge the status quo and the 1707 Treaty of the Union.

The intensified interest in stronger powers of devolution was highlighted with the launch of Independence 2010 Scotland, aiming to give the people the chance to vote for the future of Scotland's devolved government in a new referendum. A raft of new proposals are planned in the Referendum Bill, which would encourage total independence for Scotland, with its own say on the world stage, including the impacts of climate change and terrorism, as well as the general wellbeing of the people of Scotland. Only time will tell whether Scotland will benefit from becoming independent once more. ❑

HIGHLANDERS AND LOWLANDERS

Although the distinctions between Highlanders and Lowlanders are disappearing, many of the original Gaelic traditions live on and are being preserved

The division between the Highlander and the Lowlander was one of the most ancient and fundamental in Scotland's history. "The people of the coast", said John of Fordun, the Lowland Aberdeenshire chronicler, writing in 1380, "are of domestic and civilised habits, trusty, patient and urbane, decent in their attire, affable and peaceful… The Highlanders and people of the islands, on the other hand, are a savage and untamed nation, rude and independent, given to rapine, easy-living, of a docile and warm disposition, comely in person but unsightly in dress, hostile to the English people and language and, owing to diversity of speech, even to their own nation, and exceedingly cruel."

Different languages

The division was based on what Fordun called "the diversity of their speech": the Lowlanders spoke Scots, a version of Middle English, the Highlanders spoke Gaelic. The line between the two languages broadly coincided with the line of the hills. North of the Highland fault running from just above Dumbarton to just above Stonehaven, and west of the plains of Aberdeenshire and the Moray Firth, Gaelic was spoken. Outside that area, Scots was spoken, except in the northern isles of Orkney and Shetland, where a kind of Norse was spoken, and perhaps in a few pockets of the southwest where a form of Gaelic lingered until late in the Middle Ages.

Four hundred years later, things hadn't changed that much. When Patrick Sellar, the

PRECEDING PAGES: tug o'war at the Scottish Game Fair; opponents clash in a game of shinty.
LEFT: Lonach Highlanders stop for refreshments.
RIGHT: a walk through the Highland Wildlife Park.

Lowland sheep farmer, wrote to his employer, the countess of Sutherland, about the nature of the people over whom he was appointed as estate manager; John of Fordun would have recognised the tone. Sellar spoke of "the absence of every principle of truth and candour from a population of several hundred thousand souls". He compared these "aborigines of Britain" with the "aborigines of America", the Native American Indians: "Both live in turf cabins in common with the brutes: both are singular for patience, courage, cunning and address. Both are most virtuous where least in contact with men in civilised State, and both are fast sinking under the baneful effects of ardent spirits."

Then, in the 19th century, a startling turn-about occurred. Many Scots began to adopt as their national symbols the very trappings of the despised Highland minority: the kilt and the tartan, the bagpipe and the bonnet, the eagle's feather and the dried sprig of heather – it blended into a kitsch everyone across the world can recognise. In the late 1980s, when the American broadcasting networks wished to devote a minute of their national news bulletins to the question of why Scotland felt unsympathetic to the policies of Britain's then prime minister, Margaret Thatcher, they set the scene with hairy-kneed men throwing pine trees at a Highland gathering.

sought wives with better dowries than the mountains could provide.

By 1800, Highland landowners wanted their estates to produce more cash more quickly, just as landowners did elsewhere in Scotland. Over the next 50 years they cleared most of the land of peasant farms, which paid little rent, in order to accommodate the Lowlander and his sheep, which paid a good deal more.

Simultaneously, Gaelic began a catastrophic decline, from being the language of the Highland area to being the language, as it is today, only of the Outer Hebrides and a few other communities, mainly on islands, in the extreme west. In the

The fact that many Scots only wear a kilt on formal occasions and have never attended a Highland Games is not very relevant. The adoption of these public symbols has something to do with the campaigns of Sir Walter Scott to romanticise the Highlanders; with the charismatic powers of the police pipe bands, which in Victorian days were largely recruited from Highlanders; and with a music hall that loved a stereotype.

At the same time, ironically, true Highland society was in a state of collapse. Ever since the 17th century its distinctive character and Gaelic culture had been eroded by the steady spread of hostile government power, the march of commercial forces tying Scotland together as one market, and the Lowlandisation of the clan chiefs as they

current Scottish Parliament, however, members from those communities have tried to reverse the trend by introducing the Gaelic Language Bill. This aims to make more use of Gaelic in government matters and strengthens its use within the education system. There are now Gaelic language centres on Islay and Skye, while the BBC airs news and cultural programmes in Gaelic.

Blurred distinctions

So the Highland–Lowland division today has a different meaning from what it had in the past. It is certainly not any longer the most obvious or important division, ethnically and culturally, among the Scottish people as a whole. The Lowlanders themselves were never uniform: the folk of Aberdeenshire spoke "Doric", a dialect of their own, very different in vocabulary and intonation from, say, those of Lothian or Galloway. In the 19th century, this sort of regionalism was greatly compounded and complicated by the immigration of the Irish, about two-thirds of them Catholic and one-third Protestant.

A Catholic element

The Catholic Irish crowded into distinct areas – Glasgow and Dundee among the cities, and the small mining or iron-working towns of Lanarkshire, Lothian and Fife. Today, especially in the west, it is the Catholic–Protestant division that

What is a Highlander?

Being a "Highlander" has an uncertain and ambiguous meaning over most of the area covered today by the Highland and Grampian region. The citizens of Pitlochry or Inverness don't, for the most part, speak Gaelic, are mostly ordinary lukewarm Protestants, and enjoy a lifestyle and a culture not obviously very different

> Sports allegiances in Scotland are a blend of the regional and the religious. Celtic is Glasgow Catholic, Rangers is Glasgow Protestant.

continues to have most meaning in people's lives. The Catholics are, overall, still a minority in Scotland, but their Church now has more attenders on Sundays than any Protestant denomination – even the Church of Scotland itself. Intermarriage has dissolved animosities, but even today politicians deal cautiously with anything that touches, for example, on the right of Scottish Catholics to have their own state-aided schools.

Being a "Lowlander" has less meaning than having a religious affiliation, or coming from Edinburgh rather than Glasgow, or even than backing a particular football team.

LEFT: sheep drovers in the 19th century.
ABOVE: piping at the Perth Highland Games.

from that of the citizens of Perth or Aberdeen. They may have a name with the prefix "Mac" or theoretically belong to some clan like Grant or Munro; but, apart perhaps from a greater fondness for dressing in tartan and doing Highland reels at party time, there is little that is distinctive about being a Highlander in most communities that lie beyond the geological Highland line.

In the west, however, in the Inner and Outer Hebrides and along the extremities of the mainland coast from Argyll to Sutherland, the ancient significance and meaning of being a Highlander is very much alive. Not all these communities necessarily speak Gaelic, but in the Western Isles the power of the language is still strong.

All of them are, however, historically "crofting

communities": that is, they are the relics of a traditional peasantry who, thanks to a campaign of direct action in the 1880s, won from the British Parliament the right to live under the same kind of privileged land law as their brethren in Ireland. The Crofters Holding Act in 1886 conferred on them security of tenure, the right to hand on their holdings to heirs, and a rent fixed by the arbitration of a Land Court sitting in Edinburgh.

Today's crofters

Crofting is still largely the economic foundation of these communities. It can best be described as small-scale farming that involves

individual use of arable land and some communal use of grazing on hills and moors. It rarely provides a viable way of making a living. Very often, crofting is (or was) combined with some other activity, such as fishing or weaving, especially on the islands of Harris and Lewis. Today crofters often run a bed and breakfast or an outdoor activity to supplement their income.

Inevitably, crofting involves regulation and subsidy, and the crofter can become quite an expert in tapping the various grants available. This can cause old animosities to rise in the Lowlander but in return the Highlander resents the indifference of Edinburgh and London towards the real problems of remote living.

But the Highland way of life in these areas goes beyond the details of economic existence, and can best be understood in Scotland by a journey to the Outer Hebrides. In Lewis the visitor encounters the Protestant version of a Gaelic culture dominated, especially on Sundays, by grim Calvinist churches known to outsiders as the "Wee Frees". Jesus may have walked on water, but if he had dared walk on the glorious beaches of Harris or Lewis on a Sunday he would have been ostracised. In Barra and South Uist is the Catholic version, implanted by the 17th-century Counter-Reformation and not involving such denial of life's pleasures.

Some people argue that the Highland way of life exists in a still purer form in the Canadian Maritimes, especially the Catholic Gaelic-speaking communities of Cape Breton Island, who trace their origins directly to the 1745 Rebellion and the Clearances of the early 19th century.

Into the future

Wherever it survives, irrespective of religious background, the Gaelic tradition often defies the dominant world outside. In some ways, the Gaelic Highlander is indeed aboriginal, as the despised Patrick Sellar said, though he only meant it as an insult. The Highlander is often unmodern in priorities, is materialistic yet with little sense of individual ambition and attaches little importance to clock-watching. Gaelic society is supportive of its members, has an abiding sense of kinship and an unembarrassed love of a song and story, and a penchant for a dram.

With every passing year it appears superficially less likely that the Highlands' distinctiveness can survive another generation, but its efforts to do so become more determined as the 21st century deepens. The creation of a unified local government authority, the Western Isles Council, which conducts its business in Gaelic, has given a remarkable new confidence and ability to deal with modern political society. The Highland way of life is far from finished on these islands.

On the other hand, elsewhere in Scotland, John of Fordun and Patrick Sellar have really had the last word. It is their Anglicised Lowland Scotland that now runs from the Mull of Galloway to John o' Groats. The tartan and the bagpipe ought not to fool the visitor: the Scots are not fooled, though they enjoy the pretence of it all.   ❑

LEFT: seeing red at Ibrox Park, Glasgow.

Scots Idioms

From insult to endearment, the Scots will be sure to have a word for it that drives straight to the point...

There are moments in the lives of all Scots – however educated, however discouraged by school or station from expressing themselves in the vernacular – when they will reach into some race memory of language and produce the only word for the occasion.

The Scots idiom tends to operate at two ends of a spectrum: from abusive to affectionate. So the word for the occasion might well be "nyaff". There are few Scots alive who don't know the meaning of the insult nyaff – invariably "wee nyaff" – and there are few Scots alive who don't have difficulty telling you. Like all the best words in the Scots tongue, there is no single English word which serves as a translation. The most that can be done for nyaff is to say it describes a person who is irritating rather than infuriating, whose capacity to inspire contempt is just about in scale with his diminutive size, and the cockiness that goes with it.

Excuse my French

The long historical partnership between Scotland and France has certainly left its mark on the Scots tongue. Scottish cooks use "ashets" as ovenware – a word which derives from *assiette*, meaning plate – while the adjective "douce", meaning gentle and sweet-natured, is a direct import of the French *douce*, meaning the same. But the most satisfying Scots words – resounding epithets like "bauchle" (a small, usually old and often misshapen person) and evocative adjectives like "shilpit" (sickly looking) and "wabbit" (weak and fatigued) – belong to the tongue that was threatened in 1603 when King James VI moved south to become James I of England.

Until then, the Lowland Scots (as opposed to Gaelic-speaking Highlanders), whose racial inheritance was part-Celtic and part-Teutonic, spoke their own version of a northern dialect of English, and "Scots" was the language of the nobility, the bourgeoisie and the peasants. But when king and court departed south, educated and aristocratic Scots

RIGHT: a street entertainer gives a colourful performance.

adopted the English of the "elite", and the Scots tongue has never recovered. Yet what could be more expressive than a mother saying of her child, "The bairn's a wee bit wabbit today"? Or more colourful than describing the newspaper vendor as "a shilpit wee bauchle"? The words themselves almost speak their meaning and they are creeping back into the vocabulary of the middle classes.

The dialects of Glasgow and Scotland's urban west have been much influenced by the mass infusions of Gaelic and Irish from immigrants from the Highlands and Ireland, but Glasgow's legendary "patter" has an idiom all its own, still evolving and still conscious of every subtle shift

in the city's preoccupations. Glasgow slang specialises in abuse, which can be affectionate or aggressive. A "bampot" is a harmless idiot; a "heidbanger" is a dangerous idiot. Predictably, there is a rich seam of Glasgow vernacular connected with drink. If you are drunk you might be steamin', stotious, wellied, miraculous or paralytic. If you are drinking you might be consuming a wee goldie (whisky) or a nippy sweetie (any form of spirits).

If a Glaswegian calls you "gallus", it is a compliment. The best translation today is probably streetwise, although it covers a range of values from cocky and flashy to bold and nonchalant. The word derives from gallows, indicating that you were the kind of person destined to end up on them. In Glasgow that wasn't always a reason for disapproval. ❏

HOW THE KIRK MOULDS MINDS

The Church of Scotland has had a profound impact on the Scottish character, encouraging hard work, obedience and a rigorous independence of mind

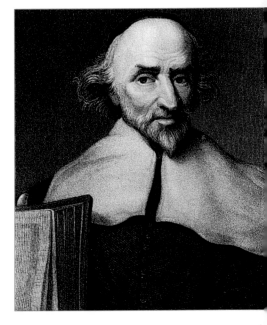

When Sunday was still solemnly observed as the Lord's Day, a young minister was asked to preach to George V at his Highland palace, Balmoral. Nervous at such an honour, the minister enquired: "What would the King like the sermon to be about?" His Majesty replied: "About five minutes." What he was dreading, of course, was an interminable exhortation to high moral endeavour.

The Church of Scotland (the Kirk) was formed as a result of the Reformation and the break with Rome in the 16th century, creating a radical Presbyterian Protestantism in its place. It was officially established as the national Kirk in 1690. Its Presbyterian ethic has been strict and challenging – well suited to promote survival in a poor country with a harsh climate. Until recent times the Sabbath was a day when profane activity ceased in some households. The intervals between services in the kirk were spent in prayer or with improving books. Whether the Kirk has shaped the Scots or the Scots their Kirk, it is impossible to understand Scottish character and attitude without taking into account the austere religious background.

No trimmings

Scots Protestants worship God, their Maker, in a plain dwelling dominated by a pulpit. There are no trimmings such as elaborate holy pictures, or altar hangings. The clergy are attired in sober black and a sparingly used Communion table replaces the altar. The appeal is to the conscience and to the intellect, with the minister's address based on a text from the Bible, the

LEFT: Lorimer's *Ordination of the Elders.*
RIGHT: the reformer John Knox.

only source of truth. The one concession to the senses is the singing of hymns and a psalm.

The reason for this lack of "outer show" is that ritual is thought irrelevant; what matters is the relation of the individual soul to his or her Maker. Hence the emphasis on self-reliance and personal integrity. With honesty a prime virtue, Presbyterians bow their heads in prayer, but feel no need to grovel on their knees; they talk to God directly. This directness characterises all other dealings, and strangers may be disconcerted by the forthright expression of opinion, prejudice, liking or disapproval.

The belief that all are equal in the eyes of the Lord has produced a people more obedient to the dictates of conscience than to rank or worldly status. A minister may have no qualms about berating sinners from the pulpit, but they in turn will take issue with him over errors in his sermon.

Strict education

Unlike the English, who avoid confrontation, the average Scot has an aggressive zest for argument, preferably "philosophical". At its worst this fosters a contentious pedantry, at its best moral courage and the independence of mind which, from a tiny population, has engendered an astonishing number of innovative thinkers in many diverse fields.

The academic excellence of which the Scots are so proud owes its merit to John Knox, who insisted that every child, however poor, must attend a school supervised by the Kirk. By the early 1700s Scotland was almost unique in having universal education. Knox's concern, however, was more spiritual than scholastic: the newborn babe is not innocent but "ignorant of all godliness" and has to undergo an arduous pilgrimage towards knowledge of the Lord. With the help of the *tawse* (a strap), children were brought up as slaves to the "work ethic": sober, frugal, compulsively industrious.

Values are positive: duty, discipline, the seri-

AN INDEPENDENT CHURCH

Rigorously democratic, the Church of Scotland is without bishops or hierarchy. In most other churches, the attenders have no say in the appointment of clergy, who are imposed from above. The Scots minister, however, is chosen by the congregation, whose elders, having searched far and wide for a suitable incumbent, will invite the favourite candidate to test their worth by a trial sermon. Where other churches' cardinals and archbishops hold office for life, the Kirk's leader, the Moderator, is elected for one year only.

The Kirk is also a symbol of national independence. At its General Assembly the Sassenach (English) queen or her representative, the Lord High Commissioner, is invited as a courtesy but is not allowed to take part in any of the debates. These are much publicised by the media, since, as there has been no Scottish parliament until now, politics and economics have been discussed along with matters clerical, and a report submitted to the government of the day.

The General Assembly meets once a year in May for a week in Edinburgh (usually in the Assembly Hall on the Mound) and is chaired by the Moderator. It is attended by ministers and elders from almost every kirk in the country and its deliberations are keenly observed (sometimes critically) by the general public, who can attend in the public gallery.

ous pursuit of worthwhile achievement and a role of benefit to the social good. Hard-headed and purposeful, Scots have no time to waste on frivolous poetics. Scotland has produced philosophers like David Hume, the economist Adam Smith, Watt, Telford and Macadam, whose roads revolutionised public transport; lawyers, doctors, scientists, engineers and radical politicians in search of Utopia – Knox's Godly Commonwealth in secular translation. Yet Scotland would give the world, especially Africa, more Protestant missionaries – such as David Livingstone, John Phillip, Robert Moffat, Mary Slessor – than any other European country.

Balance sheet

With the pressure to achieve so relentless, there's short shrift for the idle. Religious imagery is businesslike: at the Last Day people go to their *reckoning* to settle *accounts* with their Maker; it's not sins or trespasses for which pardon is implored but, "Forgive us our *debts* as we forgive our *debtors*". In a land where it's a struggle to survive, the weakest, who go to the wall, have *earned* their just deserts.

But with one slip from the "strait and narrow" leading to instant perdition, it's said the Scots have a split personality: Jekyll and Hyde. God's Elect are teetotal, but alcoholism is "the curse of Scotland"; while it's almost unheard of for a Kirk member to go to prison, Glaswegians proudly boast of having one of the busiest criminal courts in the UK. It would seem, therefore, that the unofficial influence of the Kirk is defiance of all it stands for.

Its ministers have, at all times, lashed "the filthy sins of adultery and fornication", and the taboo on the flesh is so intense that some critics have accused mothers, fearing to "spare the rod and spoil the child", of showing too little physical affection towards their babies. Yet the poet Robert Burns, a flamboyant boozer and wencher, is a national hero, the toasting of whose "immortal memory" provides an annual excuse for unseemly revels. Visitors to puritan Scotland may be puzzled by the enthusiasm for his blasphemous exaltation of sensual delights. But perhaps, if paradoxically, Burns's anarchic *joie de vivre* also stems from the teaching of the

Kirk, to whose first demand, "What is the chief end of man?" the correct response is: "To glorify God and *enjoy* Him for ever."

Though the Kirk's faithful have declined – today fewer than one in five is a regular communicant – its traditions die hard. Fire and brimstone sermons may be a thing of the past,

> It should not be forgotten that around 16 percent of Scotland's population is still Roman Catholic and there are a fair number of other Reformed churches that all contribute to the Scottish mix.

and it's only in some of the outer isles that the Sabbath is kept holy.

The Kirk, however, remains important both in politics, through the General Assembly, and socially as a principal dispenser of charitable aid to the poor and afflicted in this Vale of Tears.

More significant, though, than its public function is an enduring impact on the moulding of character. Scots are still brought up to be thrifty, upright and hard-working, while those who rebel put an energy into their pleasures that can often seem self-destructive. There's success or failure, no limbo in between. However secularised the goal, the spur remains: a punitive drive to scale impossible heights. The jaws of hell still gape for those found "wanting". ❏

LEFT: attending Mass at St Patrick's Church in Glasgow. **RIGHT:** the Papal visit to Scotland was an historic event for many.

SCOTS GENIUSES

For its size, Scotland has produced a disproportionate number of intellectual geniuses: great thinkers who have changed the face of the modern world

When the English social scientist Havelock Ellis produced his *Study of British Genius* (based on an analysis of the *Dictionary of National Biography*) he came up with the fact that there were far more Scots on his list than there should have been. With only 10 percent of the British population, the Scots had produced 15.4 percent of Britain's geniuses. And when he delved deeper into the "men of Science" category he discovered that the Scots made up almost 20 percent of Britain's eminent scientists and engineers.

Not only that, but the Scots-born geniuses tended to be peculiarly influential. Many of them were great original scientists like Black, Hutton, Kelvin, Ramsay and Clerk Maxwell, whose work ramified in every direction. Others were important philosophers like the sceptic David Hume or the economist Adam Smith, whose words, according to one biographer, have been "proclaimed by the agitator, conned by the statesmen and printed in a thousand statutes".

Great Scots

Scotland, like Ireland, produced a long string of great military men such as Patrick Gordon (Tsar Peter the Great's right-hand man), James Keith, David Leslie and John Paul Jones. There are also great explorers such as David Livingstone, Mungo Park, David Bruce and John Muir, and accomplished financiers like John Law, who founded the National Bank of France, and William Paterson, who set up the Bank of England. Andrew Carnegie, also a Scot, ruthlessly put together one of the biggest industrial empires America has ever seen, sold it when it was at its peak, then gave much of his money away on the fine Presbyterian basis that "the man who dies rich dies disgraced".

Just why a small, obscure country on the edge of Europe should produce such a galaxy of talent is one of the conundrums of European history. As nothing in Scotland's brutal medieval history hints at the riches to come, most historians have concluded that Scotland was galvanised in the 16th and 17th centuries by the intellectual dynamics of the Protestant Reformation. This is a plausible theory. Not only did the Reformation produce powerful and challenging figures such as John Knox and his successor Andrew Melville,

LEFT: Eureka! A popular version of how James Watt discovered steam power.

RIGHT: the possibly apocryphal meeting between Robert Burns and the young Walter Scott.

but it created a Church that reformed Scotland's existing universities (Glasgow and St Andrews), set up two new ones (Edinburgh and Aberdeen) and tried to make sure that every parish in Scotland had its own school.

Radical thinkers

When Thomas Carlyle tried to explain the proliferation of genius in 18th- and 19th-century Scotland, he found "Knox and the Reformation acting in the heart's core of every one of these persona and phenomena". This is a large claim, and overlooks the well-run network of primary schools inherited from the Roman Catholics.

But, whatever the reason, 18th-century Scotland produced an astonishing number of talents. As well as David Hume and his friend Adam Smith, Scottish society was studded with able men like Adam Ferguson, who fathered sociology, William Robertson, one of the finest historians of his age, and the teacher Dugald Stewart. There were also gifted eccentrics like the High Court judge Lord James Monboddo, who ran into a barrage of ridicule by daring to suggest (100 years before Darwin) that men and apes might, somehow, be related. It was a sceptical, questioning, intellectually charged atmosphere in which talent thrived.

Intellectual freedom

Interestingly, that talent didn't fall foul of established religion: few Scots had a problem squaring their faith with their intellectual curiosity. An extraordinary number of Scotland's most radical thinkers were "sons of the manse", born into clergy homes. This meant that, in 1816, when Anglo-Catholics were squabbling over the precise date of the Creation, the Presbyterian intellectual Thomas Chalmers could ask: "Why suppose that this little spot (the planet earth) should be the exclusive abode of life and intelligence?"

And nothing thrived more than the science of medicine. In the late 18th and early 19th centuries Edinburgh and Glasgow became two of the most important medical centres in Europe and produced physicians such as William Cullen, John and William Hunter (who revolutionised surgery and gynaecology in London), three generations of Munros, Andrew Duncan (who set up the first "humane" lunatic asylums), Robert Liston and James Young Simpson (who discovered the blessings of chloroform). It was a Scot, Alexander Fleming, who, in 1929, discovered the bacteria-killing properties of penicillin, the most effective antibiotic ever devised.

While Scotland has never produced a classical composer of any note, or a painter to compare with Rembrandt or Michelangelo, the reputation of 19th-century portraitists like Raeburn,

pneumatic tyre; John Macadam, the engineer who gave his name to the metalled road; Charles MacIntosh, who did the same to waterproofed fabric; James Nasmyth, who dreamed up the steam hammer; James "Paraffin" Young, who first extracted oil from shale; Alexander Graham Bell, who invented the telephone; and John Logie Baird, the father of television.

Makers of the modern world

More important in world terms were Scotland's "pure" scientists, such as John Napier, who invented logarithms; Joseph Black, who described the formation of carbon dioxide; James Hutton,

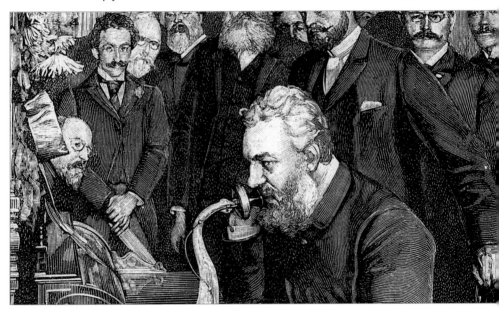

Wilkie and Ramsay are now being upgraded. And in the Adam family (father William and sons Robert, John and James), Scotland threw up a dynasty of architectural genius which was highly influential. (One of the scandals of modern Scotland is the number of Adam-designed buildings that are collapsing into ruin.)

However, the number of technologists born in Scotland is truly remarkable: they include James Watt, who greatly improved the steam engine; the civil engineer Thomas Telford; R.W. Thomson, inventor of the fountain pen and the

LEFT: an 1827 view of the engineer John Macadam.
ABOVE: Alexander Graham Bell, the inventor of the telephone.

Roderick Murchison and Charles Lyell, who developed modern geology; and Lord Kelvin, who devised the second law of thermodynamics and whose name is remembered (like Fahrenheit and Celsius) as a unit of temperature.

Then there's the Scotsman who is said to have virtually invented the modern world: James Clerk Maxwell, the 19th-century physicist who uncovered the laws of electrodynamics. Albert Einstein described his work as a "change in the conception of reality" which was the "most fruitful that physics has experienced since the time of Newton". And Max Planck, the German physicist, said he was among the small band who are "divinely blest, and radiate an influence far beyond the border of their land". ❑

THE GREAT TARTAN MONSTER

Tartanry is a big, colourful business in Scotland, displaying its gaudy wares to willing tourists at every opportunity. But the versatile pattern goes back a long way and links up with all things considered Scottish

When it comes to selling drink, the Mackinnons of Edinburgh (and formerly of Skye) are no slouches. In fact, their family company, the Drambuie Liqueur Co. Ltd, and their sweet-tasting liqueur continues to be successful as Scotch whisky enjoys a boom in worldwide sales.

And it has all been done on the coat-tails of that great loser, Bonnie Prince Charlie. Not only does Drambuie claim to be based on a "secret" recipe given to the Mackinnon family by the prince himself, but the Stuart's kilted portrait adorns every bottle. (On Skye, the drink became known locally as "dram buidhe", the yellow drink.) And the conference room in Drambuie's Edinburgh HQ is an exact replica of the 18th-century French frigate which sailed the Prince into exile (not to mention drunkenness and despair) in Europe.

But, thanks to Bonnie Prince Charlie, the Mackinnons are now turning over many millions of pounds. "The drink itself may be nothing famous," says one Edinburgh expert, "but the marketing has been superb." The Jacobite rising of 1745–6 was a major disaster for the Stuarts, but it was good news for the Mackinnon family.

The power of tartan

The success of Drambuie – "the Prince's Dram" – is tartanry in action. The Mackinnon millions are yet another tribute to that *mélange* of chequered cloth, strident music, mawkish song and bad history that has stalked Scotland for generations and refuses to go away. Tartan tea-towels and tartan tea-cosies, tartan pencils and tartan postcards, tartan golf club covers and a

wide assortment of comestibles packaged in tartan – all are eagerly purchased.

Tartanry is a vigorous subculture which, somehow, manages to lump together Bonnie Prince Charlie, John Knox, pipe bands, Queen Victoria, Rob Roy, Harry Lauder, Mary Queen of Scots, Edinburgh Castle and the White Heather Club dancers. It is a cultural phenomenon that has defied every attempt by the Caledonian intelligentsia to understand it or explain it away.

Many resent the fact that this debased and often silly version of Gaeldom has come to represent the culture of Adam Smith, David Hume, Robert Burns and James Clerk Maxwell. Others regard tartanry as a harmless effervescence which

LEFT: tartan comes in all shapes and sizes.
RIGHT: novelty tartan merchandise for sale.

has kept alive a sense of difference in the Scottish people that may yet prove politically decisive.

Serious tartan

But it certainly demands elaborate and expensive tribute. A full set of Highland "evening wear" consisting of worsted kilt, Prince Charlie Coatee, silver-mounted sporran, lace jabots and cuffs, ghillie shoes, chequered hose and *sgian dubh* can cost up to £1,000. Even day wear – a kilt in "hunting" tartan, Argyle Jacket, leather sporran and civilian brogues – will set the wearer back £600.

Of course, none of this applies to the Highlanders who actually live in the Highlands. As anyone who knows the area will confirm, the day dress of the Highland crofter or shepherd consists of boiler suit, wellington boots and cloth cap. For important evening occasions he takes off his cap.

Tartanry could be regarded as Gaeldom's unwitting revenge on the country that once despised and oppressed it. Right into the 19th century there was nothing fashionable (or even respectable) about Highlanders. Their kilts, tartans and bagpipes were hopelessly associated in the public mind with the Jacobite assaults on the Hanoverian ascendancy in 1715, 1719 and 1745. In fact, in 1746 (following the 1745 Rising) the

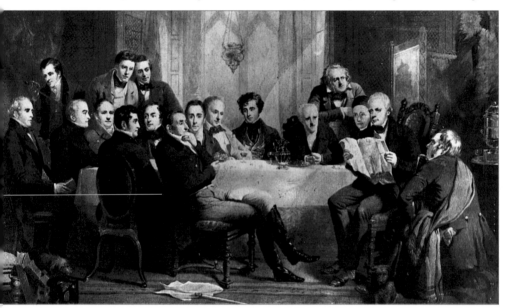

REGIMENTAL COLOURS AND CHANGING OF THE GUARD

The popularity of tartan was helped along by the stirring performances of the Highland regiments in the Crimean War and the Indian Mutiny. In their "government" tartans, red coats and feathered bonnets, the Highland battalions were an awesome sight. By 1881, the British military were so besotted with tartanry that the War Office ordered all Scotland's Lowland regiments to don tartan trousers and short Highland-style doublets.

Venerable Lowland regiments were outraged and protested that their military tradition was both older and a lot more distinguished than that of the Highlanders. But their pleas fell on deaf ears. Only the Scots Guards, as members of the elite Brigade of Guards, were granted the right not to wear tartan on their uniforms. However, in 2006 an efficiency-inspired decision by the British Government was taken to merge six Scottish infantry regiments, including the Royal Scots, the world's oldest active army regiment, into one "super-regiment", and it was met with a storm of protest.

Alas, the proud Black Watch, King's Scottish Borderers et al are now part of the new Royal Regiment of Scotland (www.royalregimentofscotland.org.uk). The new regimental cap badge incorporates the Saltire of St Andrew and the Lion Rampant, which are two recognisable symbols of Scotland. As a royal regiment, the cap badge is surmounted by a crown.

whole caboodle – bagpipes and all – was banned by the British Government until 1782.

Tartan order

But, with the Jacobite menace safely out of the way, the elites of Hanoverian Britain began to wax romantic over the Highland clans. The bogus "Ossian" sagas of James Macpherson became the toast of Europe (Napoleon loved them), while Sir Walter Scott's romantic novels became bestsellers. It was Scott who orchestrated the first ever outburst of tartan fervour: King George IV's state visit to Edinburgh in 1822.

Determined to make the occasion high strutting around Edinburgh in their Highland finery were the very people who were ousting their own clansfolk to make way for sheep, "It almost seems as if there was a cruel mockery in giving such prominence to their pretentions."

But there was no stopping the tartan bandwagon. "We are like to be torn to pieces for tartan," wrote an Edinburgh merchant to the weaving firm of William Wilson and Son of Bannockburn in the wake of George IV's visit. "The demand is so great that we cannot supply our customers." Taking the hint, Wilson installed 40 extra looms.

The tartan business got another boost when a

romance, Scott wheeled into Edinburgh dozens of petty Highland chieftains and their tartan-clad "tails" and gave them pride of place in the processions. The huge 20-stone (127kg) frame of George IV himself was draped in swathes of Royal Stewart tartan over flesh-coloured tights.

"Sir Walter Scott has ridiculously made us appear to be a nation of Highlanders," grumbled one Edinburgh citizen at this display of tartan power, "and the bagpipe and the tartan are the order of the day." Scott's own son-in-law, John Lockhart, pointed out that the same gentry

LEFT: Sir Walter Scott and friends, who helped create the romantic Highland image. **ABOVE:** a tartan-covered taxi in Edinburgh.

couple of amiable English eccentrics known as the "Sobieski Stuarts" (born Charles and John Allen) popped up, claiming to be the direct descendants of Bonnie Prince Charlie and his wife Louisa of Stolberg. They also claimed to have an "ancient" (in other words fake) manuscript which described hundreds of hitherto unknown tartans.

Royal favour

But the real clincher came in 1858 when Queen Victoria and Prince Albert bought Balmoral as a summer residence and furnished it almost entirely with specially designed (by Albert) "Balmoral" tartan. After that, the English mania for Highland Scotland knew no bounds. Every Lancashire industrialist and City of London financier had to have a shooting lodge in the mountains, while every family name in Scotland was converted into a "clan" complete with its own tartan.

Pipe bands a-piping

According to the Royal Scottish Pipe Band Association (RSPBA), there are now more than 400 pipe bands in the UK alone, with hundreds more all over the world. Every year the bands flock to one or the other of the RSPBA's five championships. The biggest prize is the World Pipe Band Championship, which invariably

count, had more than 20,000 members and 170 branches prancing and leaping around ballrooms all over the world.

This may be understandable in Scot-infested corners of the globe like the United States, Canada and New Zealand, but it isn't so explicable in France, Holland, Sweden, Kenya or Japan. Just why the sensible citizens of Paris, The Hague, Gothenburg, Nairobi and Tokyo should want to trick themselves out in tartan to skip around in strict tempo to tunes like *The Wee Cooper O'Fife*, *The Dukes of Perth*, *Cadgers in the Canongate* or *Deuks Dang Ower My Daddie* is a deep and abiding mystery.

used to be won by a Scottish band, but which in 1987 went to the 75th Fraser Highlanders from Canada and, in 1992 and 1993, to the Field Marshal Montgomery Band from Northern Ireland. More than 80 of the RSPBA's member bands are in Northern Ireland, where the hardline Protestants are happy to swathe themselves in the tartans of the Jacobite clans, most of whom were Catholic or Episcopalian. On the other side of the Irish fence, the saffron-kilted pipers of Ireland have abandoned their melodic "Brian Boru" pipes for the Great Highland Bagpipe.

Another (somewhat quieter) arm of tartan imperialism is the Royal Scottish Country Dance Society (RSCDS; www.rscds.org) which is run from Edinburgh and which, at the last

Famous patrons

It may have something to do with Scottish country dancing's royal and aristocratic connections. The Queen herself is patron of the RSCDS, and the royal prefix was granted by her father King George VI just before he died in 1952. Other exalted members include the Earl of Mansfield (who is president of the RSCDS) and the Right Honourable Peregrine Moncrieffe of Moncrieffe.

But it seems unlikely that the royal laying-on of hands will ever extend to the crowd of kilted warblers, accordion players, comics and fiddlers who make their living entertaining Scotland (and the Scottish diaspora). Usually showbiz tartanry finds its own niche, but occasionally, as in the case of the 1970s' band The Bay City Rollers or Rod Stewart's wearing of Royal Stewart tartan, it escapes into the mainstream of pop culture.

Yet another manifestation of tartanry is the Highland Games circuit. Every year between May and September villages and towns the

> In contrast to the loud dress sense of some of the Scottish pop world, the newer breed of Gaelic-speaking folk-rock bands has never been seen near a scrap of tartan.

attend), can easily pull in more than 20,000. But even Braemar cannot compete with the 40,000- or 50,000-strong crowds who flock to watch the big Highland Games in the US. The event at Grandfather Mountain in North Carolina celebrated its 55th anniversary in 2010 and is now one of the biggest of its kind in the world. American tartanry buffs are very keen on "clan gatherings" in which they get togged up in a kind of "Sword of Zorro" version of Highland dress, and march past their "chief" brandishing their broadswords.

But perhaps the daftest manifestation of competitive tartanry is "haggis-hurling". This is

length of Scotland (plus a few in England) stage a kind of Caledonian Olympics in which brawny, kilted figures toss the caber, putt the shot and throw the hammer while squads of little girls in velvets and tartans dance their hearts out to the sound of bagpipes.

Highland Games

The Scottish Games Association represents more than 60 annually held Highland Games. Most attract crowds of up to 5,000, although the Braemar Gathering (which the royal family

---

LEFT: tartan helps keep the royal family warm at the Braemar Gathering. **ABOVE RIGHT:** tartan gift shops line Edinburgh's Royal Mile.

a sport that allegedly has its origins in the Highlands, when clansmen would catch a haggis thrown across the river by their wives at lunchtime. It was revived in 1977 by an Edinburgh public relations man, Robin Dunseath, as "a bit of an up-market joke". To his astonishment the "ancient" sport of haggis-hurling (usually from standing on top of a whisky barrel) took off and went from strength to strength, with competitions taking place all over the globe.

So popular has the "sport" become that a world championship now takes place. The current world record was set in 1984 by Alan Pettigrew, who hurled a haggis a remarkable 180 ft 10 ins (55.11 metres) on the island of Inchmurrin, Loch Lomond. ❑

SCOTLAND'S PAINTERS

From the Edinburgh Enlightenment to the Glasgow rebels, Scottish painting retains an exuberance that defies its Calvinistic background through its flamboyant, sensuous works

In spite of its puritanism and thunderings from the Kirk against "vain outer show", Scotland is unique among the British provinces in having a distinctive painterly tradition. The art of Protestant Northern Europe tends to be tormented and morbid and, given a Calvinist shadow of guilt and sin, one would expect Scottish painting to be gloomily angst-ridden. Instead, as if in defiance of all that the Kirk represents, it is extroverted, joyful, flamboyant, robust – much more sensuous (even if less complex) than English art with its inhibiting deference to the rules of good taste.

It is significant that young Scottish artists have mostly bypassed the Sassenach (English) capital to study abroad; those from Edinburgh in Rome, the Glaswegians a century later in pleasure-loving Paris. Growth of the arts in Scotland is linked to the relative importance of its two major cities, and the rivalry between them (culture versus commerce) has resulted in aesthetic dualism: where Edinburgh's painters are rational and decorous, raw but dynamic Glasgow has produced exuberant rebels.

The Enlightenment

Before the 18th century, Scottish art scarcely existed. There was no patronage from the Kirk, which forbade idolatrous images, or from the embattled aristocracy. In a country physically laid waste by the Covenanter Wars and mentally stifled by religious fanaticism, painters were despised as menial craftsmen.

PRECEDING PAGES: Wilkie's *Pitlessie Fair.*
LEFT: Raeburn's perennially popular *Rev. Robert Walker Skating on Dunningston Loch.*
RIGHT: Ramsay's portrait of David Hume.

The return of peace and prosperity, however, gave rise to a remarkable intellectual flowering, the Edinburgh Enlightenment, which lasted, roughly, from 1720 until 1830 and caused the city to be dubbed the "Athens of the North". The rejection of theology for secular thought was accompanied by a new enthusiasm for the world and its appearance, the brothers Adam evolving a style in architecture and design that was adopted all over Europe and remains to this day the classic model of elegance and grace.

A need arose, meanwhile, for portraits to commemorate the capital's celebrated sons. Though the earliest portrait painters, Smibert and Aikman, achieved modest recognition as artists not craftsmen, Allan Ramsay, son of a poet and friend of the philosopher David Hume, expected to be treated as an equal by the intellectual establishment, many of whose members he immortalised with his brush.

Considering he grew up with a background

> *Raeburn's style is broader and more painterly than Ramsay's, the poses more dramatic: Judge Eldin looking fierce in his study, the Clerks of Penicuik romantically strolling, the Rev. Robert Walker taking a turn on the ice.*

Scottish arts established

Ramsay's achievement was rivalled in the next generation by Sir Henry Raeburn, knighted in 1822 by George IV and made King's Limner (painter) for Scotland. Raeburn also studied in Italy, and his oeuvre, like Ramsay's, was confined to portraiture with an emphasis on individual character – the fiddler Neil Gow or a homely matron receiving the same attention as a scholar or fashionable beauty.

Raeburn was the first Scottish painter of national renown to have remained in his native Edinburgh and, in doing so, he established the arts in Scotland and their acceptance by the

of visual austerity – Edinburgh had no galleries, no art school and only a few enlightened collectors – Ramsay's rise to fame is astonishing. Leaving home to study in Italy, he returned to London in 1739 and was an instant success, finally ending up as court painter (in preference to Reynolds) to George III. Despite his classical training, Ramsay cast aside impersonal idealism for "natural portraiture", concentrating on light, space and atmosphere and the meticulous rendering of tactile detail: ribbons, cuffs, the curl of a wig, the bloom on a young girl's cheek. The refined distinction of his best work, such as the portraits of his two wives, has earned him an honourable position in the history not just of Scottish but of British art.

public. Interest and prestige led to ventures in other genres, especially landscape. Though Alexander Nasmyth painted an Italianate Scotland, gilded and serene, the choice of local vistas – rather than a classical idyll in the manner of Claude – was startling in its novelty.

Equally novel was David Allan's transfer of the pastoral tradition of nymphs and shepherds into scenes from Scottish rural life. He was followed by David Wilkie, whose *Pitlessie Fair* (painted at 19) was the start of a career that earned him a knighthood and outstanding popularity; his "low-life" comedies like *The Penny Wedding* created a taste for such subjects that persisted throughout the Victorian era.

Although no one equalled Raeburn or Wilkie,

there was a new public interest in the arts, which flourished in Edinburgh during the 19th century. Notable in landscape are David Roberts with his views of the Holy Land and, later, William McTaggart, "the Scottish Impressionist".

The Glasgow Boys

The academic mainstream, however, was confined to historical melodrama, sentimental cottagers and grandiose visions of the Highlands as inspired by Sir Walter Scott. The 1880s saw a new departure when a group of students, nick-named the Glasgow Boys, united in protest against Edinburgh's stranglehold on the arts. Due to rapid

offence to the genteel. The public, devoted to gain, godliness and grand pianos (whose legs were prudishly veiled) was both affronted and bemused by Crawhall's lyrical cows, the voluptuous cabbages tended by James Guthrie's farm hands, the indecent brilliance of the rhubarb on Macgregor's *Vegetable Stall*.

Influenced by Whistler and the European Realists, most of the Glasgow Boys left Scotland in disgust to study in Paris – where they were subsequently acclaimed. This success abroad tickled civic pride (what Edinburgh artist could compete?) and the canny burghers, who had once been so hostile, began to pay high prices for their

industrial expansion, Glasgow had grown from a provincial town into "the second city of the Empire" and, in contrast to 18th-century Edinburgh, there were galleries, an art school and lavish collectors among the new rich (one of whom was William Burrell), who were anxious to buy status through cultural patronage.

Initially, though, the Glasgow Boys scandalised their fellow citizens. Rejecting the turgid subjects and treacly varnish of the academic "glue-pots", they abandoned their studios to paint in the open air, choosing earthy, peasant themes that lacked "message" or moral and gave

pictures. Sadly, the Glasgow Boys then lost their freshness and became respectable: Lavery a fashionable portrait painter, Guthrie a conservative president of the Royal Scottish Academy, while Hornel retreated into orientalism. Today, there is a revival of interest – and investment.

Experimental Colourists

The Glasgow Boys gave younger artists the courage to experiment through their flamboyant handling of paint and colour. Oppressed by the drab Calvinism of Scottish life, rebels of the next generation, led by Peploe, Cadell, Hunter and Fergusson, again fled to Paris, where they were intoxicated by the decorative art of Matisse and the Fauves. Discarding

LEFT: *Porlock Weir* by Charles Rennie Mackintosh.
ABOVE: Macgregor's *Vegetable Stall*.

conventional realism, they flattened form and perspective into dancing, linear rhythm, with colour an expression of a pagan *joie de vivre*. As with the Glasgow Boys, fame abroad brought the Scottish Colourists belated success at home. Peploe and Hunter returned to paint a Scotland brightened by Gallic sunshine and the witty Cadell to transform Glasgow house-wives into flappers of the Jazz Age.

A gloomier fate, though, awaited the architect and designer Charles Rennie Mackintosh. An originator of Art Nouveau, his distinctive style is typified by a simple geometrical manipulation of space based on combinations of straight

Confidence in Scottish painting has been boosted by superb municipal collections, notably the Burrell in Glasgow, which has always been a major tourist draw.

line and gentle curves. Glasgow School of Art, his architectural masterpiece, is one of the city's most remarkable buildings, and the Glasgow Style he initiated in furniture and the decorative arts is now admired the world over. Yet in his day "Toshie" was dismissed as a drunken eccentric and was such a failure professionally that he abandoned architecture to paint water-colours in France.

Modern times

From the 1930s, landscape has tended to pre-dominate in Scottish painting, but in the 1950s, Colquhoun and MacBryde adopted Cubism, not for formal reasons but as a means of conveying romantic melancholia.

Since World War II, while modern trends have been pursued with characteristic vigour, there's been a loss of optimism and sparkle. More poignant than the Modernists is Joan Eardley, who turned her back on artistic fashion to paint urchins in the Glasgow backstreets, then, after settling in a remote fishing village in the northeast, sombrely elemental landscapes.

John Bellany is unusual in that he has the tormented vision one might expect, but rarely finds, among artists brought up under Calvinism. Overwhelmed, after a visit to Buchenwald, by human wickedness, he gave up modish abstracts to return to figurative art of a tragic, often night-marish monumentality. Later, towards the end of his life, he unleashed a prolific output of superb, lyrical autobiographical canvases.

Glasgow graduates

German Expressionism, with its energy and gloom, replaced the hedonistic influence of the French, when Glasgow School of Art produced a new group of rebels. Known (unofficially) as the Glasgow Wild Boys, they have also rejected Modernism for gigantic narrative pictures with literary, political or symbolist undertones. The most successful, Adrian Wiszniewski and Stephen Campbell, have gone down well in New York.

Wiszniewski, a Pole born in Scotland, has adapted Slavic folk art to express nostalgia for the past, disenchantment with the present. Campbell, combining macho brutalism with whimsy, draws his inspiration from the contrasting writings of P.G. Wodehouse and Bram Stoker (author of *Dracula*).

Other brilliant Glasgow graduates include Stephen Conroy, Peter Howson, Mario Rossi, Craig Mulholland and Steven Campbell, who, except for Howson, are all local to Glasgow. And Allison Watt, Lesley Banks and Jenny Saville redress the balance for women, though their images of other women are far from conventional: Watt earned notoriety for her painting of the Queen Mother with a teacup on her head.

LEFT: James Guthrie's *Hind's Daughter*.
RIGHT: Joan Eardley's *Street Kids*.

SONG AND DANCE

The folk music revival has had a profound effect in Scotland, filling the clubs and pubs once more with traditional Celtic sounds, and the dancing continues unabated

The sound of Scottish music has changed dramatically in the past 25 years – and that's before you take into account the insidious influence exerted in recent years by phenomenally successful Scottish pop groups such as Simple Minds, Belle and Sebastian, Franz Ferdinand and Travis.

Nothing has been more dramatic than the forging of an alliance between two previously alien schools. On the one hand, the inheritor of the bagpipe tradition, regarded until then as a musical law unto themselves. On the other hand, the young adventurers of the folk music revival, ready to play and sing anything that had its roots embedded somewhere in Celtic culture.

Piped music

Whether the piping establishment has benefited is debatable. They are a gritty, stubborn lot, much given to internecine warfare over the etiquette and mystique of piping disciplines that have been handed down like family heirlooms through the generations. Discipline still rules at the sponsored competitions, where pipers from all over the world challenge each other at what in Gaelic is called *pìobaireachd* (pibroch).

Just to confuse the uninitiated, *pìobaireachd* has another title, *ceòl mór* (Great Music). This is a truly classical music, built to complex, grandiloquent proportions and actually playable only after years of study and practice. Those who *can* play it do so by memory, in the manner of the great Indian raga players. The pipe music that most of us are familiar with – stretching from *Mull of Kintyre* to

reels, marches, jigs and strathspeys – is referred to by the classicists as *ceòl beag* (Small Music).

Great or Small, much of it has survived thanks to patronage rather than household popularity. The earliest royal families in Scotland are credited with having a piper, or several, on their books, and no upwardly mobile landlord could afford to be without one. But it was in the warring Highland clan system that the pipes flourished. The blood-tingling quality of the Great Highland Bagpipe, with its three resonant drones, was quickly recognised by the early Scottish regiments, and the military connection remains to this day. Even now, the Scots use the pipes to soften up the English at football and rugby internationals.

PRECEDING PAGES: time for a fling at the local ceilidh.
LEFT AND RIGHT: busking is a popular money maker for some performers.

Despite being bearers of the country's national music, the pipes can offer nothing to compare with the phenomenal resurgence of Scots fiddle music, which had thrived only in certain areas until the folk music revival got its full head of steam in the 1960s. Today, there are probably more fiddlers in Scotland than ever before. The best-known folk musicians are the Shetland fiddler Aly Bain and accordionist/songwriter Phil Cunningham, who perform widely at home and abroad. A few groups such as Blazing Fiddles are also making their mark.

Another traditional instrument that has been revived is the *clarsach*, or Scots harp, which first appeared in 8th-century Pictish stone carvings. Some of the great *clarsach* music came from Ruaridh Dall Morrison (the Blind Harper) in the 17th century. Much smaller than the modern concert harp, the *clarsach* had become virtually extinct until its revival in the early 1970s.

But the fiddle and the *clarsach* were a long way behind folk song in returning to the mainstream of Scottish culture. The classic narrative ballads and *pawky bothy* (a Gaelic term meaning "hut") ballads had survived largely in the hands of farm workers and the travelling folk (the tinkers) of Perthshire and the northeast. Until the tape recorder enabled collectors like the late Ham-

FIDDLERS ON THE HOOF

The fiddle has been part of Scottish music for more than 500 years – King James IV had "fithelaris" on his payroll in the 15th century. The fiddle reached its Golden Age in the 18th century, when Scots musicians sailed across to Italy to study the art of playing the instrument and brought back not only the tricks of the classical trade, but also a steady supply of exquisite violins, which were soon copied by enterprising local craftsmen. At the same time, the dancing craze had begun.

Country fiddlers found their robust jigs and reels much in demand at balls, parties and other social gatherings, and the first major collections of Scots fiddle tunes were published, making the music widely accessible.

By the early 19th century, though, high society had turned its fancy to the new polkas and waltzes that were flooding in from Europe. But the rural fiddlers played on regardless, and it was the Aberdeenshire village of Banchory that produced the most famous Scots fiddler of all – James Scott Skinner, who was born in 1843.

Classically trained, and technically virtuosic, Skinner, who was also known as the "King of the Strathspey", was internationally acclaimed, and with the arrival of recording in the later part of his career, the message of his music was spread even further – even as far as fiddle-packed Shetland, which had until then resolutely stuck to its own Norse-tinged style.

ish Henderson to bring their songs to the young urban folk revivalists. Today's best-known singers are Fife-based Sheena Wellington (traditional) and Ishbel MacAskill from Lewis (Gaelic).

The folk clubs served, too, as spawning grounds for new songwriting, especially of the polemical brand, producing some of the best songs since Robert Burns. The 18th-century poet is credited with more than 300 songs, many of them set to traditional fiddle tunes, and you can still hear them in all sorts of venues. You'll also hear Scotland's unofficial national anthem, the sentimental *Flower of Scotland*, written by the late Roy Williamson of folk duo The Corries. Recalling the Scots victory over the English at Bannockburn in 1314, it is sung at major sporting events in the hope of firing the national teams on to equal success.

Clubs and festivals

Many of the early folk clubs are still in existence – notably those in Edinburgh, Aberdeen, Kirkcaldy, Stirling and St Andrews. Sadly, the type of *ceilidh* laid on for tourists tends to be caught in a time warp of kilt, haggis and musical mediocrity. In Gaelic, *ceilidh* means a gathering *(see page 346)*. The Gaelic-speaking community, now mostly confined to the West Highlands and islands, holds its great gathering, the Royal National Mod, of beautiful competitive singing every October.

From Easter until autumn, there is hardly a weekend when there isn't a folk festival somewhere in Scotland. Glasgow's Celtic Connections is among the biggest festivals of its kind in the world and runs for two weeks in January, featuring around 1,500 artists performing in more than 300 events. But there is nothing to beat the smaller traditional folk festivals in rural areas, where the talent tends to be local rather than imported. Among the best events, the Hebridean Celtic Festival (July) attracts a large crowd from as far away as the US. Kirriemuir (September), Shetland (April) and Orkney (May) are also famous for their annual celebrations of traditional music.

Most folk festivals have their unofficial "fringe", and many pub sessions can match the finest organised *ceilidh*. Today, it's also fashionable to have a *ceilidh* at a wedding reception or a private party.

LEFT: fiddlers hit the right notes.
RIGHT: the Belladrum Festival, Beauly.

The Highland Fling

The cunning Irish centuries ago devised a way of dancing in tight cottage corners. For the Scots, dancing is reserved for the village hall or the ballroom. Many of the traditional dances, including the famous Highland Fling, call for the raising of the arms to depict the antlers of the red deer. Popular formations like the *Eightsome Reel* and *The Dashing White Sergeant* also involve much whirling around in large groups.

Like the accordion-pumped music that fires these breath-sucking scenes, Scottish dancing has its more rarified moments. There are country dance societies where members dance with the

kind of practised precision that must have been essential at the earliest Caledonian balls.

In the 1980s and 1990s, Scottish rock began to sit up and notice its Celtic heritage, with folk-rock bands such as Runrig and Wolfstone, all-electric but hitched to ancient Gaelic themes. In songwriting, too, folk music has made its mark in the rock venues. The leading singer-songwriters, such as Dougie MacLean, Rab Noakes and the brilliant Dick Gaughan, have found eager new audiences there, and their influence can be heard in the music of contemporary rock groups. One such group is Capercaillie, whose charismatic lead singer, Karen Matheson, comes from Oban and whose musical roots lie much closer to their Hebridean origins than most. ❏

GAMES HIGHLANDERS PLAY

A traditional Highland Gathering, with the skirl of
pipes, tartan-clad dancers and muscular athletes, is
a wonderfully colourful – and noisy – experience

Highland Gatherings, which are sometimes described as "Oatmeal Olympics", are much more than three-ring circuses. As the gathering gets going, a trio of dancers are on one raised platform; a solitary piper is on another; a 40-piece pipe band has the attention, if not of all eyes, at least of all ears; the "heavies" are tossing some unlikely object about; two men are engaged in some strange form of wrestling; a tug-of-war is being audibly contested and an 880yd/metre race is in progress.

Track events are the least important part of these summer games – but don't tell the runners. The venue has been chosen for its scenic beauty rather than its "Tartan" track. At the Skye Games, milers literally get dizzy as they run round and round the track's meagre 130yds/117 metres.

Pipers and dancers

Everywhere the sound of pipes can be heard. It is not only the piper playing for the dancers, another solitary piper playing a mournful dirge in the individual piper's competition, or the 40-strong pipe band being judged in the arena. Behind marquees, under trees, those still to compete are busy rehearsing.

The solo pipers are undoubtedly the aristocrats of the games, and the highest honour – and the biggest prize – is awarded to the pibroch winner. There are three competitions for solo pipers: pibrochs (classical melodies composed in honour of birthdays, weddings and the like), marches (military music); and strathspeys and reels (dance music). While playing a pibroch the piper marches slowly to and

fro, not so much in time to the music, but in sympathy with the melody. On the other hand, when playing dance music, the pipers remain in one position tapping their foot; and, understandably, when playing a march, they stride up and down the platform.

King Malcolm Canmore is credited with being responsible for one of the more famous dances seen at the games. In 1054 he slew one of King Macbeth's chieftains and, crossing his own sword and that of the vanquished chieftain, performed a *Gille Calum* (sword dance) before going into battle. The touching of either sword with the feet was an unfavourable omen.

The origin of the Highland Fling is curious. A

LEFT: hammer-throwing at a Highland Gathering.
RIGHT: taking a band-break.

grandfather was playing the pipes on the moors and his young grandson was dancing to them. Two courting stags were silhouetted against the horizon. The grandfather asked the lad: "Can ye nae raise yer hands like the horns of yon stags?" And so originated the Highland Fling. The dance

> Most of the tartan-clad dancers who take part in Highland Gatherings are female, although a thorn may appear among the roses. Seldom are any girls older than 18, and competitions are even held for three- and four-year-olds.

Olympic strength

Hurling the hammer and putting the shot are similar, yet different, to those events as practised at the Olympics. At the "Oatmeal Olympics" the hammer has a wooden shaft rather than a chain; the "shot", a 56lb (25kg) weight on the end of a short chain, is thrown with one hand; the length of weight and chain must not exceed 18ins (45cm). In this event it is not distance but height that counts. The competitor stands below and immediately in front of a bar with his back to it. Holding the weight in one hand, he swings it between his legs and throws it up and, with luck, over the bar. A correct throw will

is performed on one spot, because the Scot, like the stag, does not run after his women, he expects them to come to him. Another explanation is that it was originally danced on a shield. In the dance called *Sean Truibhas* – the Gaelic for old trews (trousers) – the performer's distaste for his garb is expressed. This dance originated after Culloden when the wearing of the kilt was proscribed.

One of the original aims of the games was to select the ablest bodyguards for the king or chieftain, and this is perpetuated in today's heavy events. The objects used have evolved from what would be found in any rural community, such as a blacksmith's hammer or even a stone in the river bed.

just miss the thrower on its way down, while a bad throw is liable to cause untold mischief.

The most spectacular event is tossing the caber, a straight, tapered pine-tree trunk shorn of its branches. It weighs about 125lbs (57kg) and is about 19ft (6 metres) long. The diameter at one end is about 9ins (23cm) and at the other about 5ins (13cm). Two men struggle to carry the caber to a squatting competitor. They place it vertically with the narrow end in his cupped hands. The competitor gingerly rises and, with the foot of the caber resting against his shoulder, and the remainder towering above, starts to run. Finally, at a suitably auspicious moment, the competitor stops dead, lets out an almighty roar, and thrusts his hands upwards. The wide end of the caber hits the ground; now is the moment of truth: will the quivering pole tumble backwards towards the hopeful competitor or will it stand up, turn over and fall away?

But why does an empty-handed, puffing judge trot alongside the competitor? Tossing the caber is judged not on distance but on style. An imaginary clockface is involved, and the athlete is presumed to be standing at the figure 6 when he makes his throw. A perfect throw lands at 12. Naturally, the athlete will attempt, after throwing, to swivel his feet so that his throw appears perfect. Hence the puffing judge. Caber-tossing

with the green of the grass and the purple of the heather to produce a muted palette.

Highland Games are very much in vogue, and new venues are constantly announced. Currently, more than 90 gatherings are held during the season, which extends from May until mid-September. In spite of the spectacular appeal of the great gatherings (Braemar, Cowal, Oban), you might find the smaller meetings (Ceres, Uist in the Hebrides) more enjoyable. These have an authentic ambience, and competitors in the heavy events are certain to be good and true Scots and not professionals from foreign parts. And you may not even have to pay admission. ❑

is believed to have evolved from throwing tree trunks into the river after they had been felled. They would then float to the sawmill. It was important to throw the trunks into the middle of the river or they would snag on the banks.

Colour codes

Colour is the keynote of the games. All dancers and musicians are dressed in full Highland regalia, as are many of the judges and some spectators. Competitors in the heavy events all wear the kilt. The reds of the Stuarts, the greens of the Gordons and the blues of the Andersons all mingle

LEFT: a display of strength and stamina at the Highland Games. **ABOVE:** Scottish dancers sit it out.

ROYAL CONNECTIONS

The Highlands of Scotland are famous for their games. Some claim that games were first held in 1314 at Ceres in Fife, when the Scottish bowmen returned victorious from Bannockburn. Others believe that it all began even earlier when King Malcolm organised a race up a hill called Craig Choinnich. The winner received a *baldric* (warrior's belt) and became Malcolm's foot-messenger. A race up and down Craig Choinnich became a feature of the Braemar Gathering, which is the highlight of the circuit. However, this isn't so much because of the calibre of the competition but because, since the time of Queen Victoria, it is often attended by the royal family.

A FONDNESS FOR FESTIVALS

The Scottish calendar is bursting with local festivals, very different from each other in origin but all offering an excuse to celebrate in spectacular style

Until the middle of the 20th century puritanical Scotland completely ignored Papist Christmas: offices, shops and factories all functioned as usual on 25 December. The great event in the Scottish calendar was the night of 31 December (Hogmanay) and New Year's Day (which was called *Nollaig Bheag* – Little Christmas – in many parts of the Highlands).

Traditionally, as the bells struck midnight, the crowds gathered around the focal points of towns would join hands and sing *Auld Lang Syne* and then whisky bottles would be passed around before all dispersed to go first-footing. It is important that the first-foot (the first person to cross a threshold in the new year) should be a tall, dark-haired male who brings gifts of coal and salt which ensure that the house won't want for fire or food in the coming year. Also, the first-foot will normally carry a bottle of whisky.

Warding off evil spirits

Fiery New Year processions that will drive out and ward off evil spirits have been held for centuries at Comrie, Burghead and Stonehaven. At the Comrie Flambeaux procession, locals walk through the town carrying burning torches; at Stonehaven, participants swing fireballs attached to a long wire and handle. Some suggest that the swinging of fireballs is a mimetic attempt to lure back the sun from the heavens during the dark winter months.

The Burning of the Clavie at Burghead is held on 11 January. (This is when Hogmanay falls according to the Old Style calendar, which was abandoned in 1752 but which still holds sway

LEFT: a Robert the Bruce lookalike.
RIGHT: captivated festival-goers.

when deciding the date of many celebrations.) The ceremony begins with the Clavie King lighting a tar-filled barrel, which is then carried in procession through the town and from which firebrands are distributed. Finally, the Clavie is left to burn on the summit of Doorie Hill before being rolled down the hill.

More recent in origin is the torchlight procession on Edinburgh's Princes Street on 31 December, the highlight of a five-day Hogmanay extravaganza. However, by far the greatest and most spectacular fire ceremony is Up-Helly-Aa, held at Lerwick in the remote Shetland Islands on the last Tuesday in January. Up-Helly-Aa (compare the old Scots name for

Twelfth Night, *Uphaliday*) begins with the posting of "The Bill", a 10ft (3-metre) high Proclamation, at the Market Cross, and the displaying of a 30ft (9-metre) model longship at the seafront.

Come evening, and with the Guizer Jarl magnificently dressed in Viking costume at the steering oar, the longship is followed by team after team of *guizers*, each clad in glorious or grotesque garb and all carrying blazing torches, to the ceremonial burning site. Here the Guizer Jarl leaves the longship, a bugle sounds, and everyone throws their torch onto the boat to set it on fire.

At Kirkwall, capital of Orkney, those who survived the Hogmanay celebrations gather on New Year's Day at the Mercat Cross for the "Ba' Game". Two teams attempt to carry a leather ball, about the size of a tennis ball, against all opposition, to their own end of the town. A giant scrum forms, becoming so torrid that steam rises from its centre. A good game lasts for several hours.

Later in the month, Burns Night (25 January) honours the birth of the national poet. In villages and cities throughout the land, Burns clubs and others toast the haggis *(see page 122)*.

A different kind of game, Whuppity Scoorie, can be seen at Lanark on 1 March. The church bells peal out and the children of Lanark, armed with home-made weapons of paper balls

THE RIDING OF THE MARCHES

Throughout the early summer months the clippity-clop of horses' hoofs is heard on the cobblestones of Border towns. The Riding of the Marches, introduced in the Middle Ages, is the custom of checking the boundaries of common lands owned by the town.

In some cases, the Riding of the Marches also commemorates local historical events, which invariably involved warfare between the English and the Scots during the Middle Ages. The festivities often last for several days and are always stiff with protocol.

The Selkirk Gathering, held in June, is the oldest, the largest and the most emotional of the Ridings. It concludes with the Casting of the Colours, which commemorates Scotland's humiliating defeat at the Battle of Flodden. At the "casting", flags are waved in proscribed patterns while the band plays a soulful melody.

Each town – including Dumfries, Duns, Galashiels, Jedburgh, Hawick, Langholm and Lauder – has its own variation of the Riding ceremonies; all have other activities, which include balls, concerts, pageants and sporting events, going on at the same time.

In Annan, the Riding of the Marches has been ridden since the town was created a Royal Burgh over 600 years ago. At Peebles, the Riding incorporates the Beltane Fair, which is the great Celtic festival of the sun and marks the beginning of summer.

on strings, race three times around the church, beating each other over the head as they go. Town officials then throw coins for which the children scramble. Some say the festival rids the town of evil spirits. A more mundane explanation is that it symbolises the coming of spring.

In April, students at St Andrews University stage the Kate Kennedy pageant, in which they play the parts of distinguished figures associated with the university or the town. Lady Kate, a niece of the university's founder, was a great beauty to whom the students are said to have sworn everlasting allegiance. Women are banned and Kate is played by a first-year male student.

Summer festivals

Traditional summer fairs are held throughout the country. Farm employees who wished to change their jobs used to seek out new employers at Feeing Markets, and one such market, enlivened with Highland dancing, country music and other entertainments, is still held in June at Stonehaven. Later in the month, a similar event, the Maggie Fair, is held at Garmouth: it commemorates the landing of Charles II at nearby Kingston after he had been proclaimed king of Scotland following the execution of his father.

The Beltane Festival, held on Edinburgh's Calton Hill on Midsummer's Eve, revives one of the major events of the Celtic calendar. Weirdly costumed, and often largely naked, revellers wielding flaming torches make this a dramatic welcome for the season of plenty.

The first day of August is Lammas Day, or Lunasdal – the feast of the sun god, Lugh – and was formerly a popular day for local fairs. Such fairs are still held in August, although not on the first day, at St Andrews and Inverkeithing. Also at this time a bizarre ritual occurs on the day before the South Queensferry Ferry Fair. A man, clad head to toe in white flannel, is covered with an infinite number of burrs until he becomes a moving bush. Bedecked with flowers and carrying two staves, this strange creature makes his way from house to house receiving gifts. One theory for this strange practice equates the Burryman with the scapegoat of antiquity.

The Highland Festival is centred on Inverness, but many of its musical, artistic and theatrical performances are staged throughout the region.

LEFT: a torch-lit procession in Shetland.
RIGHT: burning a Viking galley at Up-Helly-Aa.

Horses for courses

In late August, the ancient west-coast burgh of Irvine holds its Marymass Fair, which dates from the 12th century. Horse races, very much a part of this fair, are said to be even older and include Clydesdale carthorses.

"Horses" of a different kind are involved in a mid-August festival on the island of South Ronaldsay in Orkney. The "horses" are young boys or girls dressed in spectacular costumes. Pulling beautifully wrought miniature ploughs, often family heirlooms, and guided by boy ploughmen, these "horses" compete to turn the straightest furrows on a sandy beach.

Hallowe'en, on 31 October, is popular with children, who dress up as witches and ghouls in order to frighten off the "real" evil spirits abroad at All-Hallows Eve. The imported American custom of "trick or treat" is threatening to reduce the charm of this ancient ritual. On 5 November, towns and villages commemorate with bonfires and firework displays the anniversary of the Gunpowder Plot in 1605, when Guy Fawkes tried to blow up the Houses of Parliament in London.

St Andrew's Day (30 November), the national day, is mostly ignored. It does offer excuses for society types to dress in their finery, attend balls, toast the haggis, and imbibe unwise quantities of whisky. So, inexorably, the festive year rushes headlong towards another Hogmanay.   ❏

THE LURE OF THE GREEN TURF

To play on the hallowed ground of Scotland's ancient golf courses is the ambition of amateur and professional golfers alike, especially since it all began here so many centuries ago

Visit the 19th hole at any of Scotland's 400 golf courses and you're almost certain to hear a heated argument, over a dram or two, as to where the game of golf originated. The discussion doesn't involve geography but rather topography: the "where" refers to *which* part of Scotland. All know that, in spite of the Dutch boasting about a few old paintings that depict the game, it all began in Scotland centuries ago, when a shepherd swinging with his stick at round stones hit one into a rabbit hole. Little did the rustic know the madness he was about to unleash when he murmured to his flock: "I wonder if I can do that again?"

Scottish links

Few courses have the characteristics of the quintessential Scottish course. Such a course, bordering the seashore, is called a links. It is on the links of Muirfield, St Andrews, Troon and Turnberry that the British Open – or "the Open" – is often played.

The word links refers to that stretch of land which connects the beach with more stable inshore land, and a links course is a sandy, undulating terrain along the shore. One feature of such a course is its ridges and furrows, which result in the ball nestling in an infinite variety of lies. Another feature is the wind, which blows off the sea and which can suddenly whip up with enormous ferocity. A hole which, in the morning, was played with a driver and a 9-iron can, after lunch, demand a driver, a long 3-wood and a 6-iron.

Summer days in Scotland are long, and the eager beaver can tee off at 7am and play until

10pm – easily enough time for 54 holes, unless you're prone to slice, hook or pull. But the rough of gorse, broom, heather and whin is insatiable, and much time can be lost searching for balls.

Most golfers will immediately head for St Andrews. They will be surprised to find that the Old Course has two, rather than the customary four, short holes and only 11 greens. Yet it is categorically an 18-hole course: seven greens are shared. This explains the enormous size of the greens, on which you can find yourself facing a putt of almost 100yds/metres. Remember it is the homeward-bound player who has the right of way on these giant double greens.

Don't be too distressed if you fail to obtain a

LEFT: stuck in a bunker at St Andrews.

RIGHT: teeing off at Stuart Castle Golf Links.

starting time on the Old; the New Course is even more difficult, but St Andrews still has five others to choose from *(see Travel Tips, page 352)*.

Ancient as the Royal and Ancient Golf Club of St Andrews is, it must bow to the Honourable Company of Edinburgh Golfers, which was formed in 1774 and is generally accepted as the oldest golf club in the world. Its present Muirfield course – which is at Gullane (pronounced *Gillun*), 13 miles (21km) east of Edinburgh – is considered to be the ultimate test of golf. The rough here is ferocious, and if, on looking around, you lose your partner, don't panic: they will merely be out of sight in one of nearly 200 deep pot-bunkers which litter the course.

If you can't play at Muirfield, the tiny village of Gullane is also the home to three more challenging courses (simply called 1, 2 and 3) and to Luffness New. The latter is "New" because, by Scotland's standards, it is just that, having been founded as recently as 1894.

Capital courses

Back in the city of Edinburgh are more than a score of courses, two of which are home to very ancient clubs. The Royal Burgess Golfing Society claims to be even older than the Hon. Coy, while the neighbouring Bruntsfield Links

Golfing Society is only a few years younger.

On the road from Gullane to Edinburgh you pass through Musselburgh, where golf is known to have been played in 1672 and, most probably, even before that. Was this where Mary Queen of Scots was seen playing a few days after the murder of Lord Darnley, her second husband?

Glasgow, never to be outdone by Edinburgh, has nearly 30 courses. Outstanding among these are Killermont and Haggs Castle. The latter is less than 3 miles (5km) from the city centre. While golfers thrill over birdies and eagles at Haggs, their non-playing partners can enthuse over the renowned Burrell Collection, which is less than half a mile (1km) away. Even closer to the Burrell is the excellent Pollok course. Further afield at

Luss, 23 miles (37km) northwest of the city, by the bonnie banks of Loch Lomond is a course designed by Tom Weiskopf and Jay Morrish. Ranked in the top 20 courses in Britain, the Loch Lomond Golf Club is renowned worldwide.

Troon, 30 miles (48km) south of Glasgow and frequently the scene of the Open, is the kingpin in a series of nearly 30 courses bordering the Atlantic rollers. Here, you can play for almost 30 miles (48km). Troon itself has five courses.

To the north is Barassie with one, and Gailes with two courses. South of Troon are three at Prestwick – scene of the first Open in 1860 – and Ayr, also with three courses. Fifteen minutes further down the "course" are the exclusive Arran and Ailsa links of Turnberry. There's an excellent one at Brunston Castle, justs to the southeast,

Over on the east coast is another remarkable conglomerate of courses, with St Andrews as its kingpin. About 30 miles (48km) to the north, across the Tay Bridge, are the three Carnoustie courses. The Medal course here, also the scene of many Opens, has been called brutal, evil and monstrous.

Then, 20 miles (32km) south of St Andrews and strung, like a priceless necklace, along the north shore of the Firth of Forth, are the Elie, Leven, Lundin Links and Crail golf courses. The Crail course is claimed by golf-storians to be the seventh-oldest in the world.

Other glittering gems are found in the northeast. Here are Balgownie and Murcar, two of Aberdeen's half a dozen courses; nearby is Cruden Bay; Nairn, which is close to Inverness; and Dornoch, which stands in splendid isolation in the extreme northeast. The Balgownie and Cruden Bay clubs are both 200 years old; the founders of the latter are probably turning in their graves at the new name of their club – the Cruden Bay Golf and Country Club.

Dornoch is, even for a Scottish course, underplayed and may be Britain's most underrated course. Authorities believe that this course, all of whose holes have a view of the sea, would be on the Open rota if it were closer to a town.

Down at the extreme southwest of the country is Machrihanish, another underrated, underplayed links. Its turf is so naturally perfect that "every ball is teed, wherever it is". And if the

LEFT: on the banks of Loch Lomond.
RIGHT: a triumphant Colin Montgomerie in St Andrews has his hand shaken by a fan.

views from here, which include Ireland and the Inner Hebrides, seduce you, then you might wish to make your way over the seas to Islay, which is renowned for its Machrie course.

New additions

Scotland, home of golf, also has some superb inland courses. Many aficionados consider the King's at Gleneagles to be the best inland course in Britain. Certainly nowhere in the world can there be a championship course set in such dramatically beautiful scenery. In 1993, it was joined by the PGA Centenary Course, which is from the drawing board of

Jack Nicklaus and has the flavour of an American rather than a Scottish course. These are just two of the four courses, which make up the luxurious Gleneagles complex.

A mere 30 miles (48km) to the north is Blairgowrie with its fabled Rosemount course. Here, among parasol pines, larches, silver birch and evergreens, you will come upon lost golf balls, partridges, pheasants and otters.

New courses are still being created: the 18-hole par 72 Spey Valley Championship Golf Course opened in 2006 in Aviemore and was designed by Ryder Cup player, Dave Thomas, and the American billionaire Donald Trump is in the process of creating the Trump International Golf Links north of Aberdeen. ❑

HUNTING, SHOOTING AND FISHING

The natural assets of Scotland are eagerly exploited by wealthy proprietors, satisfying the continuing demand for up-market sports; as a result conservation is a main priority

While Scotland may have been blessed with more deer, grouse, salmon and trout than most small European countries, a significant proportion of these assets are controlled by a small number of wealthy estates, whose owners may live a long way from Scotland. This means that "field sports" such as deer stalking, salmon fishing and grouse shooting are touchy political issues, bound up with memories of the Highland Clearances and the ownership and use of the land.

Ownership of large Highland estates varies from local aristocrats who have been there for centuries to southern financiers, European entrepreneurs and oil-rich Arabs. While "traditional" estate owners retain a paternalistic approach, some of the newer proprietors arrive with little or no knowledge of the Scottish way of life, and try to recoup their investment any way they can, often at the expense of local interests.

Working together

Rights enjoyed and shared by local people can suddenly vanish. This happened when the then North of Scotland Hydroelectric Board (now Scottish Hydro-Electric) sold its fishing rights on the River Conon north of Inverness to a City of London financier for a reputed £1.5 million. He promptly divided the river into weekly time-share "beats" which were sold at up to £15,000 per person per week. Not unnaturally, locals who had long fished the river, but who could not afford such prices, were incensed.

There have also been problems in the past with estates covering large areas of prime hill-walking country trying to deny access to walkers and climbers during the shooting seasons.

However, the situation has eased considerably, thanks to greater cooperation between the various factions. In 1996, a national Access Forum was set up by Scottish Natural Heritage, to draw up a "Concordate on Access" recognising both the needs of the estates and the ambitions of walkers. Subsequently, the Land Reform (Scotland) Act 2004 now gives the public statutory rights to Scotland's mountains, moorlands, lochs and rivers. Based on the premise of "responsible access", the act aims to balance the interests of land managers with conservationists and recreations such as hill walking. In sensitive areas, a "Hillphone"

PRECEDING PAGES: grouse shooting, Moorfoot Hills. **LEFT:** stream fishing on the Borders. **RIGHT:** leaping salmon.

system operates under which walkers can phone a recorded message which tells them where stalking or grouse shooting is taking place.

Conservation concerns

The health of Scotland's field sports depends heavily on the state of the ecology, so environmental groups and estate owners can have similar concerns. Uneasy bedfellows in the past, they are now working together on such matters as scientific studies into the reasons for the dramatic decline in grouse numbers in many areas. Other common concerns include acid rain and the damage caused by tributyltin, a

marine pesticide, to salmon and sea trout. Over-enthusiastic conifer-planting of large areas has, happily, been reined in, with many areas now being replanted with native tree species.

Chasing the deer

Stalking the magnificent red deer is one of Scotland's prime attractions for wealthy foreign sportsmen. According to the Deer Commission for Scotland, there are 300,000–350,000 red deer in Scotland, most of them north of the "highland line" between Helensburgh and Stonehaven. Since 1950, numbers have more than doubled, the increase in recent

EXPENSIVE PURSUITS

The "Glorious Twelfth" is the popular name for 12 August, the day the red grouse season opens. It has been less than glorious in recent years, with a sharp decline in grouse numbers due to predation and disease. There are about 500 grouse moors in Scotland and northern England, and their management is carefully arranged to provide the best heather conditions for the birds.

Like deer stalking, grouse shooting doesn't come cheap. Drive grouse (shot with the aid of teams of beaters) can cost around £100 a brace: even estate-reared pheasants can cost the shooter up to £40 a brace.

years being partly due to more animals living in woodland – the cover is opening up as forests reach maturity. The annual cull, necessary to maintain a sustainable population level, is based on estimates of the numbers and density of deer herds.

The vast majority of the shooting is by professional stalkers, foresters or sporting parties under professional guidance who come from all over Britain, Europe and North America for the stag season (1 July to 20 October). When it ends, hind culling, though not for sport, continues until February.

Stag hunting isn't cheap. A week's stalking (six days) can cost £2,000–£3,000, and only the trophy (the head) belongs to the hunter; the venison will be sold by the estate. Accommodation is extra.

There are between 200,000 and 400,000 roe deer in Scotland, and shooting roe deer bucks (males), often from high seats fixed in the trees, is becoming more popular. It is less expensive, costs being roughly between half and two-thirds of those for a red deer stag shoot.

Seeking the salmon

The up-market sport par excellence has to be salmon fishing in one of Scotland's great salmon rivers such as the Dee, the Spey, the Tay, the Tweed or the Conon. One survey estimated that it cost the affluent angler over £2,000 to land an Atlantic salmon from a prime stretch of a Scottish river. Certainly, a week's fishing on a good stretch (called a "beat") at the height of the season (July to September) on one of the classier rivers is likely to set the fisherman back between £1,500 and £2,000.

Yet demand is so high that a number of specialist firms, and even some estates, have taken to operating salmon beats on a "time-share" basis. It works like this. The company buys a decent stretch of a good salmon river for a very large sum of money. The river is then divided into beats, and on each beat a week's fishing is sold "in perpetuity" for up to £30,000 (depending on when the slot occurs in the season and the quality of the fishing). All this is much against the wishes of those, like the Scottish Campaign for Public Angling (SCAPA), who believe that everyone should have the right to fish where they want and that no waters should be closed to the public.

With so much money at stake, it is little wonder that river proprietors have grown anxious as they have seen salmon stocks decline. Some commentators believe stocks of wild salmon could even be wiped out in a matter of decades. The drop has been attributed to net fishing at river mouths, river and sea pollution, global warming, intensive salmon farming and declining fertility in the fish.

The net fishing has almost died out, thanks partly to the efforts of the Atlantic Salmon Conservation Trust, set up in 1986. The trust rapidly raised several million pounds and acquired the rights to many net fishing operations, then closed them down. However, problems still exist. Drift

netting continues in the far North Atlantic, off Greenland, Iceland and the Faroe Islands, and poachers are still busy on the rivers.

While salmon fishing may be the glamour end of the sport, many anglers feel that too much is made of it. They argue that there is better sport in brown trout fishing, for far less outlay, on many

> *Angling is worth millions of pounds a year to the Scottish economy, and this figure is bound to grow as the hitherto secret delights of the upland rivers and lochs become better known.*

Scottish lochs, particularly on the west coast and in the northern Highlands, where the salmon are not abundant. Some remote lochs are still only visited by a few enthusiasts, and 100 fish in a day on two rods from a boat is not just a dream.

Trout are tops

Tourist authorities promote this valuable resource through schemes whereby a single ticket will get the angler access to a variety of waters during a holiday. Who knows, you might get lucky and snag a ferocious ferox trout, found in the West Highlands. They can weigh up to 20lbs (9kg) and are cannibals, but as one angler said, "a hell of an exciting fish to get on the end of your line". And a great tale for the pub. ❑

LEFT: take aim, then fire.
RIGHT: salmon fishing in the Highlands.

A WEE DRAM

While many dispute the secret of the unique taste of Scotch whisky, few deny the pleasures to be had from the "water of life" or "mountain dew"

At the end of sophisticated dinner parties in London, guests are invariably offered a choice of brandy or port but seldom a glass of Scotch. Familiarity, perhaps, has produced contempt for the native product – or, the Scots would argue, the English are showing their customary ignorance of all things Scottish.

The prejudice is an ill-founded one because good malt whiskies have a wider range of flavour and aroma than brandy and – an extra bonus – they are less likely to make the over-indulger's head throb the morning after. However, Scotland's unique drink has never quite managed to cultivate the exclusive image of cognac.

For one thing, there's a lot more of it on the international market. Scotch is one of Britain's principal export items, substantially contributing to the balance of trade: even the Vatican, on one recent annual reckoning, bought 18,000 bottles. More than 2,500 brands of Scotch whisky are sold around the world with the major export markets being the United States and Japan. And China and the Far East are catching up fast, showing a spectacular growth in sales.

Toddler's tipple

In the 18th century, Scotch whisky was drunk as freely as the water from which it was made, by peasants and aristocrats alike. A spoonful was given to newborn babies in the Highlands, and even respectable gentlewomen might start the day with "a wee dram". The poorest crofter could offer the visitor a drink, thanks to the home-made stills which made millions of bottles of "moun-tain dew" in the remote glens of the Highlands.

Yet something as easy to make cannot be made authentically outside Scotland. Many have tried, and the Japanese have thrown the most modern technology at the problem; but the combination of damp climate and soft water flowing through the peat cannot be replicated elsewhere.

Some historians believe that the art of distilling was brought to Scotland by Christian missionary monks. But it is just as likely that Highland farmers discovered for themselves just how to distil spirits from their surplus barley. The earliest known reference to whisky occurred in 1494, when Scottish Exchequer Rolls record that Friar John Cor purchased a

---

PRECEDING PAGES: the Macallan, a fine single malt. **LEFT:** the unusually-named Sheep Dip. **RIGHT:** the brass and glass spirit-safe.

large quantity of malt "to make aquavitae".

These days there are two kinds of Scotch whisky: *malt*, made from malted barley only; and *grain*, made from malted barley with unmalted barley, maize or other cereals. Most popular brands are blends of both types of whisky – typically 60 percent grain to 40 percent malt.

A single malt is becoming an increasingly popular drink, thanks largely to the aggressive marketing by William Grant & Sons of their Glenfiddich brand. In fact, the industry's most expensive whiskies have experienced such a boom in sales that new distilleries are being built and others upgraded.

Making whisky

So automated are Scotland's 100-plus distilleries that visitors, sipping an end-of-tour glass of the product they have watched being manufactured, are left with an image of the beautifully proportioned onion-shaped copper stills and a lingering aroma of malted barley – but not with any clear idea of how water from a Highland stream turns into *uisgebeatha*, the water of life.

What happens is this: to make malt whisky, plump and dry barley sits in tanks of water for two or three days. It is then spread out on a concrete floor or placed in large cylindrical drums and allowed to germinate for between eight and 12 days. It is dried in a kiln, which ideally should be heated by a peat fire. The dried malt is ground and mixed with hot water in a huge circular vat called a mash tun. A sugary liquid, "wort", is drawn off from the porridge-like result, leaving the remaining solids to be sold as cattle food. The wort is fed into massive vessels containing up to 9,900 gallons (45,000 litres) of liquid, where living yeast is stirred into the mix in order to convert the sugar in the wort into crude alcohol.

After about 48 hours, the "wash" (a clear liquid containing weak alcohol) is transferred to the copper pot stills and heated until the alcohol turns to vapour. This rises up the still to be condensed by a cooling plant into distilled alcohol, which is then passed through a second still.

Tricks of the trade

The trick is to know exactly when the whisky has distilled sufficiently. Modern measuring devices offer scientific precision, but the individual

---

TASTE THE DIFFERENCE

Despite the claims of distillers that each whisky blend has a unique taste, the truth is that most people, if taking part in a blind tasting, would be hard-pressed to say whether they were drinking Bell's, Teacher's, Dewar's, Johnnie Walker or J&B. Pure malt whiskies, on the other hand, are more readily identifiable.

The experienced Scotch drinker can differentiate between Highland malts, Lowland malts, Campbeltown malts and Islay malts, and there is certainly no mistaking the bouquet of a malt such as Laphroaig, which is usually described as tasting of iodine or seaweed.

So which is the best whisky, you may ask? Whole evenings can be whiled away in Scotland debating and

researching the question with no firm conclusions being reached. It all comes down to individual taste – after all, in the words of Robert Burns: "Freedom and Whisky gang thegither [together]."

However, the one point of agreement is that a good malt whisky should not be drunk with a mixer, which would destroy the subtle flavour. Yet, although it is said there are two things that a Highlander likes naked, connoisseurs may be permitted to add a little water to their single malt.

After dinner, malts are best drunk neat, as a liqueur. Blended whisky, in contrast, is refreshing in hot weather when mixed with soda and ice.

judgement of an experienced distiller is hard to beat. Once distilled, the liquid is poured into oak casks which, being porous, allow air to enter. Evaporation takes place, removing the harsher constituents of the new spirit and enabling it to mellow. Legally it can't be sold as whisky until it has spent three years in the cask, and a good malt will stay casked for at least eight years.

It wasn't until the 1820s that distilling began to develop from small family-run concerns into large manufacturing businesses. What accelerated the change was the invention in 1830 by Aeneas Coffey of a patent still. This was faster and cheaper than traditional methods; more

deliver the verdict that both drinks were equally wholesome and could call themselves whisky.

The industry's future, however, lay in the marriage between malt and grain whiskies. Blending tiny amounts of 30 or 40 malt whiskies with grain whisky, distillers found, could produce a palatable compromise between taste and strength. What's more, an almost infinite variety of combinations was possible.

Old favourites

In sales terms, it's estimated that more than 35 bottles of whisky are sold each second, while more Scotch is sold in one month in France than

importantly, it did not need the perfect mix of peat and water, but could produce whisky from a mixture of malted and unmalted barley mashed with other cereals.

But was the resulting grain whisky a real Scotch? Some dismissed it as flavourless surgical spirits; others approved of it as "lighter-bodied". The argument rumbled on until 1905, when one of London's local authorities decided to test in the courts whether pubs could legally sell the patent still (as opposed to the pot still) product as "whisky". Even the courts couldn't agree. It was left to a Royal Commission to

LEFT: the gleaming interior of a distillery.
ABOVE: the Scottish Whisky Experience, Edinburgh.

cognac in a year. The Scots themselves tend to favour Glenmorangie, which is matured in old Bourbon casks, charred on the inside, for at least 10 years to produce a smooth spirit with hints of peat smoke and vanilla. The most popular malt in the United States is The Macallan, which is produced on Speyside and matured in 100 percent sherry casks seasoned for two years in Spain with dry oloroso sherry; connoisseurs argue that the 10-year-old is a better drink than the more impressive-sounding 18-year-old.

To decide on your own favourite, you need only take one of the many distillery tours on the Scotch Whisky Trail or enjoy the Spirit of Speyside Whisky Festival held each spring and autumn (*see page 348*). ❑

PORRIDGE, HAGGIS AND COCK-A-LEEKIE

Cooked breakfasts, high teas and smoked salmon for supper
with something sweet to follow: traditional Scottish
food satisfies the heartiest of appetites

Scotland, as the writer H.V. Morton once remarked, is the best place in the world to take an appetite. No doubt his appetite was coaxed by the abundance of fresh food and the freshness of the air, which in the Highlands (and even the Lowlands) remains remarkably pure.

Scots cuisine, uninspired and uninspiring for many years, has been largely transformed in recent years. Some of Britain's top chefs now produce award-winning food in Scotland, relying on top-quality, locally produced fresh meat and fish prepared with an international twist – particularly Mediterranean flavours and the exotic tastes of Asian and Eastern food, which the Scots have long had a penchant for.

The Scottish diet also has its hazards, however. Local tastes, especially the love of fried food, are held to be a major contributory factor to the Scots' appalling level of heart disease. This is the home of the deep-fried Mars bar and the Scotch egg, a more traditional fast-food snack consisting of a hard-boiled egg wrapped in sausage meat, coated in breadcrumbs and then fried.

Scottish roots

Despite the recent rise in international influences, Scottish cookery still has its roots in the soil, especially in some of those isolated hotels and restaurants far from the main cities. There, real Scottish cuisine is something the proprietors are genuinely proud of serving, notably the "traditional full Scottish breakfast". This generally starts with kippers (smoked herring) or porridge made from oats. Traditionalists take it with salt, but many prefer it with sugar. This

LEFT: the perfect breakfast to start the day.
RIGHT: traditional Scottish fare in Edinburgh.

is followed by bacon, egg, sausage, and perhaps black pudding (a variety of sausage made with blood). Expect also an array of breads, rolls, oatcakes and scones, topped off with an assortment of (often home-made) jams and conserves.

Scottish bakery can often be really delectable, but can sometimes be stodgy, heavy and mass-produced. Not too long ago in Scotland, there were fewer restaurants than tearooms. Here, people ate not only lunch and afternoon tea but also "high tea", which usually consisted of fish and chips and a generous selection of scones and cakes. High teas are still on offer in some hotels.

It is also significant that biscuit-making – the renowned shortbread – remains an extensive and popular industry in both Edinburgh and Glasgow and as far north as Kirkwall in Orkney (where the oatcakes are arguably the best in the land). Dundee is renowned for its eponymous cake and for orange marmalade, its gift to the world's breakfast and tea tables – though the theory that the name "marmalade" derives from the words *Marie est malade* (referring to the food given to Mary Queen of Scots when she was ill) must be considered rather far-fetched.

Flavoursome fish and meat

Kippers, too, are a treat. The best of them are from Loch Fyne, where their colour emerges

When buying Scottish salmon, ask for "wild" as it's more flavoursome than the farmed variety. However, farmed fish is generally preferred for the production of justifiably renowned smoked salmon and trout, to ensure uniformity.

properly golden, not dyed repellent red as they are in so many places. Arbroath smokies or finnan-haddies (types of smoked haddock) are a tasty alternative, simmered gently in milk and butter. Salmon and trout are just as likely to come from some west-coast or northern fish farm as fresh from the river, but the standard remains high.

The beef of the Aberdeen Angus cattle remains the most famous in the world. Good Scottish meat, the experts claim, should be hung for at least four weeks or even for eight and should never be sliced less than 1¼in (3cm) thick.

Venison, pheasant, hare and grouse are also established features of the Scottish kitchen. Admittedly, the romance of eating grouse after it has been ritually shot on or around the glorious 12 August should be tempered (if you are honest with yourself) by this bird's depressing fibrous toughness, which makes grouse shooting seem, at least to a gourmet, an unutterable waste of time.

The national dish

As for haggis – though it, too, is hardly a gourmet delight – it does offer a fascinating experience for brave visitors. Scotland's great mystery dish is really only a sheep's stomach stuffed with minced lamb and beef, along with onions, oatmeal and a blend of seasonings and spices. After being boiled, the stomach is sliced open, as spectacularly as possible, and the contents served piping hot.

Butchers today often use a plastic bag instead of a stomach; this has the advantage that it is less likely to burst during the boiling process, resulting in the meat being ruined. But no haggis devotee would contemplate such a substitute.

The tastiest haggis, by popular acclaim, comes from Macsween's of Edinburgh, who also make a vegetarian haggis. (That's progress, as the Orkney poet George Mackay Brown would cynically say.) Small portions of haggis are sometimes served as starter courses in fashionable Scottish restaurants, though the authentic way to eat it is as a main course with chappit tatties (potatoes), bashed neeps (mashed turnips) and a number of nips (Scotch whisky, preferably malt). This is especially so on Burns Night (25 January), when the haggis is ceremonially piped to table, and supper is accompanied by poetry reading, music and Burns's own *Address to the Haggis*; or on St Andrew's Night (30 November).

Colourful cuisine

Many of Scotland's national dishes have names as rugged as Scottish speech. Soups such as Scotch broth (made with mutton stock, vegetables, barley, lentils and split peas), cock-a-leekie (made from chicken and leeks, but authentic only if it also contains prunes) and cullen skink (soup made from smoked haddock, cream and potatoes) are widely available, as are mutton pies (minced lamb in pastry) and the Forfar Bridie (a meat and onion pasty). But other dishes may be harder to track down: hugga-muggie (Shetland fish haggis, using the fish's stomach), crappit heids (haddock heads stuffed with lobster), partan bree (a soup

> The best places to eat in Scotland are members of "A Taste of Scotland" with more than 500 establishments where you will be served good quality, fresh Scottish produce.

A return to real cheese

Real cheese, at last fighting back against the marketing board's anonymous mass production, has been making progress in Scotland. Lanark Blue, handmade from unpasteurised sheep's milk, has been a success and is worth looking out for in go-ahead restaurants. Popular, too, is Cairnsmore, a hard ewe's-milk cheese from Wigtownshire, and Bonnett, made in Ayrshire from goat's cheese, while Island Cheese on Arran also finds favour with many a palate. Crowdie, Scotland's original creamed cottage cheese, has evolved into Caboc from the Highlands; with its original oatmeal coating, it is almost

made from giant crab claws, cooked with rice), stovies (potatoes cooked with onion), carageen mould (a Hebridean dessert), cranachan (a mixture of cream, oatmeal, sugar and rum), delicious with fresh Scottish raspberries, or hattit kit (an ancient Highland sweet made from buttermilk, milk, cream, sugar and nutmeg).

If you're in the southwest, Moffat toffees with a sherbert centre are a favourite, and, in Selkirk, the rich fruit bun eaten at Christmas, called a bannock. Plus there is an enormous variety of puddings and desserts, usually served with lashings of butterscotch sauce.

as creamy as France's crème fraîche. Pentland and Lothian cheeses are Scotland's answer to Camembert and Brie.

Cheese before pudding, as a running order, reflects Scotland's Auld Alliance with France, as does the large amount of fine claret to be found on the wine lists of good restaurants. But pudding before savoury is also an admirable tradition and is showing signs of a revival.

Hot savouries have always tended to have mysterious, sometimes misleading names. Scotch woodcock, for instance, is no more a bird than Welsh rarebit is a rabbit; it is a portion of anchovies coated with scrambled eggs and served on small slices of toast. It rounds off a meal most piquantly as an after-dinner savoury. ❑

LEFT: a plate of Scotch woodcock.
ABOVE: a tempting seafood platter.

Scotland

0   20 km
0   20 miles

N

ATLANTIC OCEAN

NORTH SEA

Unst
Yell
Papa
Stour
Mainland
Shetland
Foula
Lerwick
Sumburgh

Fair Isle

Westray
Sanday
Rousay
Stronsay
Orkney
Shapinsay
Mainland
Kirkwall
Stromness
Orkney
Hoy
Islands
South
Ronaldsay

Pentland Firth

Flannan Islands

Butt of Lewis
Port of Ness
Cape Wrath
Durness
Dunnet Head
Thurso
John O'Groats
Duncansby Head

Tongue
Melvich
Ben Hope
927
Wick
Scourie
Eddrachillis Bay
Aitnaharra
Loch Shin
Lybster

Stornoway
Lewis
Enard Sound
Ben More Assynt
998
Helmsdale

The Minch

Westeray

Harris
Ullapool
Lairg
Dornoch
North Uist
Gairloch
Garve
Tarbat Ness
Lochmaddy
Uig
Achnasheen
Dingwall
Cromarty
Moray Firth
Elgin
Banff
Kinnaird Head
Fraserburgh

Benbecula
Loch Maree
Nairn
Moray
Buckie
Macduff
Keith
Peterhead

South Uist
Dunvegan
Inverness
Spey
Huntly
Lochboisdale
Portree
Skye
Kyle of Lochalsh
Loch Ness
Grantown-on-Spey
Ellon
Inverurie

Barri
Castlebay
Canna
Armadale
Fort Augustus
Aviemore
Cairngorm Mountains
Don
Aboyne
Aberdeen

Rum
Eigg
Mallaig
Highland
Kingussie
Ben Macdhui
1309
Ballater
Braemar
Dee
Aberdeenshire
Banchory
Stonehaven

Muck
Lochailort
Glenfinnan
S C O T L A N D
Cairngorm National Park

Coll
Ben Nevis
1344
Dalwhinnie
Angus
Inverbervie

Tobermory
Loch Shiel
Fort William
Blair Atholl
Pitlochry
Brechin
Montrose

Tiree
Lochaline
Ben Lawers
1214
Perthshire and Kinross
Forfar
Blairgowrie
Arbroath

Fionnphort
Mull
Bridge of Orchy
BRAMPIAN MOUNTAINS
Loch Tay
Dundee

Oban
Crianlarich
Perth
St Andrews
Fife Ness
Crail

Colonsay
Inveraray
Loch Awe
Crieff
Stirling
Ochil Hills
Earlsferry

Argyll and Bute
Loch Lomond and the Trossachs National Park
Glenrothes
Fife
Kirkcaldy
Firth of Forth

Lochgilphead
Helensburgh
Stirling
Falkirk
Dunfermline
North Berwick
Dunbar

Jura
Greenock
Clydebank
Airdrie
East Lothian
Haddington
St Abb's Head

Kennacraig
Dumbarton
Paisley
Livingston
Edinburgh
Berwick-upon-Tweed

Islay
Glasgow
East Kilbride
Motherwell
Lanark
Peebles
Galashiels
Lindisfarne or Holy I.
Embleton

Ardrossan
Irvine
Lanarkshire
Selkirk
Borders
Melrose
Coldstream

Brodick
Arran
Troon
Prestwick
Kilmarnock
East Ayrshire
Hawick
Jedburgh
Kelso
Wooler
Alnwick

Campbeltown
Rathlin Island
Ayr
Sanquhar
Abington
SOUTHERN UPLANDS
Moffat
Langholm
Otterburn

Mull of Kintyre
Girvan
Kirkoswald
South Ayrshire
Dumfries and Galloway
Dumfries
Gretna Green
Brampton
Newcastle upon Tyne
South Shields

Coleraine
Ballantrae
Cairnryan
Newton Stewart
Castle Douglas
Carlisle
Hexham
Penrith
Durham

Derry
Stranraer
Gatehouse of Fleet
Solway Firth
Workington
ENGLAND

NORTHERN IRELAND

Lough Neagh
Bangor
Newtownards
Belfast
Wigtown Bay
Mull of Galloway

PLACES

A detailed guide to Scotland and its islands,
with principal sites clearly cross-referenced
by numbers to the maps

Scotland has something to suit all tastes. Whether you want the peace of wide open spaces or the excitement of dynamic cities, you can find it here. Even the unpredictable weather cannot dull Scotland's charm, as the wildest Highland storm only enhances the magnificence of the hills.

Edinburgh, a majestic capital city and home to the Scottish Parliament, enchants effortlessly, its castle towering over it on a rugged crag as a daily reminder of its turbulent history. Just 40 miles (64km) away, Glasgow, by contrast, is Britain's great unknown city, still suffering from an outdated image of industrial grime and urban decay. Yet it remodelled itself to become European City of Culture in 1990, and now has better shopping and nightlife than the capital.

Outside the two great cities lies an astonishingly varied landscape. To the southwest are the moorlands, lochs and hills of Dumfries and Galloway, haunt of Scotland's national poet Robert Burns; to the southeast, the castles, forests and glens of the Borders; to the west, the rugged splendour of the West Highlands, the jumping-off point for Skye and the Western Isles; to the northeast, the farms and fishing villages of Fife and on up along the North Sea coast through Dundee towards the granite city of Aberdeen, Scotland's oil capital. To the north are the elusive monster of Loch Ness, the splendour of the Highlands, and the islands of Orkney and Shetland, more Norse than Scottish.

Scotland's greatest appeal is to people who appreciate the open air, from rambling across moors to arduous hill-walking and hair-raising rock climbs and mountain bike trails. Or you can ski, canoe, surf, fish for salmon or play golf in the country that invented the game.

And the people? They have a reputation for being dour – but, as long as you avoid saying anything that could be taken as even faintly complimentary about the English, you are likely to find that the Scots character often contains a carefully concealed warmth.   ❏

PRECEDING PAGES: Loch Ba on misty Rannoch Moor; the magnificent Linlithgow Palace; the Royal Edinburgh Military Tattoo.
TOP: Isle of Skye. **ABOVE LEFT:** Fyrish Monument. **ABOVE RIGHT:** walking up Cairngorm Summit.

EDINBURGH

Set among a series of volcanic hills, Edinburgh is a stunning confection of late medieval tenements and neoclassical terraces, whose new status is supported by grand building projects

Main attractions

Not for nothing was that great parable of the divided self, *Dr Jekyll and Mr Hyde*, written by an Edinburgh man, Robert Louis Stevenson. He may have set the story in London, but he conjured it out of the bizarre life of a respectable Edinburgh tradesman. More than one critic has taken the Jekyll and Hyde story as a handy metaphor for the city of Edinburgh itself: something at once universal yet characteristically Scottish. Where else does a semi-ramshackle late medieval town glower down on such Georgian elegance? What other urban centre contains such huge chunks of sheer wilderness within its boundaries? Does any other city in Europe have so many solid Victorian suburbs surrounded by such bleak housing estates? Stevenson himself was inclined to agree. "Few places, if any," he wrote, "offer a more barbaric display of contrasts to the eye."

Just as Edward Hyde "gave an impression of deformity without any nameable malformation", so the meaner side of Edinburgh tends to lurk unnoticed in the beauty of its topography and the splendour of its architecture. Even the weather seems to play its part. "The weather is raw and boisterous in winter, shifty and ungenial in summer, and downright meteorological purgatory in spring," Stevenson wrote of his home town. But the Jekyll and Hyde metaphor can be stretched too far. For all its sly duality and shifty ways, Edinburgh remains one of Europe's most beautiful and amenable cities.

Living theatre

To the south the city is hemmed in by the Pentland Hills – some of which are almost 2,000ft (600 metres) high – and to the north by the island-studded waters of the Firth of Forth. In 1878 Stevenson declared himself baffled that "this profusion of eccentricities,

LEFT: busking on the Royal Mile.
RIGHT: the Edinburgh Tattoo.

Edinburgh

0 ____ 200 m
0 ____ 200 yds

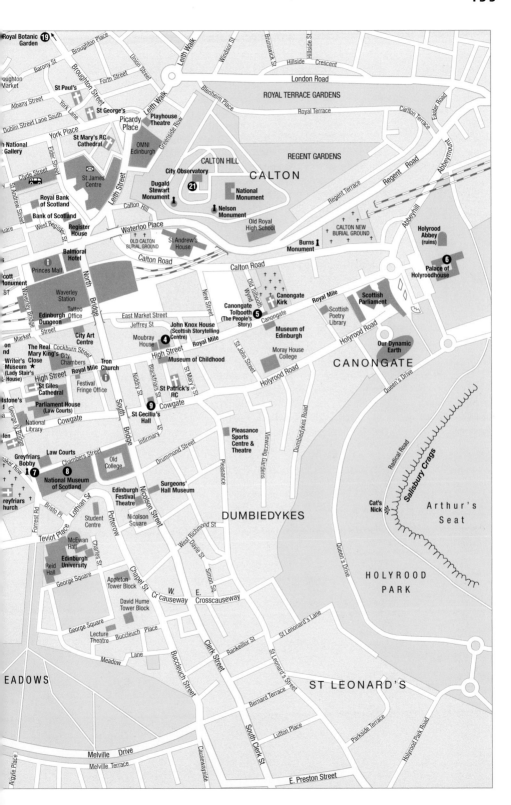

The Scotsman newspaper, published in Edinburgh, is still arguably the most influential piece of media north of the border, acting as a kind of noticeboard for the Scottish Establishment.

this dream in masonry and living rock is not a drop-scene in a theatre, but a city in the world of everyday reality".

Which, of course, it is. At the last count, Edinburgh contained just under half a million people rattling around in 100 sq miles (39 sq km) on the south bank of the Firth of Forth. While the city's traditional economy of "books, beer and biscuits" has been whittled away by the ravages of recession and change, there is a powerful underpinning of banking, insurance, shipping, the professions (especially the law), universities, hospitals, and, of course, government bureaucracies (local and central). By and large, the North Sea oil boom passed Edinburgh by, although some of the city's financiers did well enough by shuffling investment funds around, and for a while Leith Docks was used as an onshore supply base, to coat pipes and to build steel deck modules.

And like every other decent-sized city in the western hemisphere, Edinburgh thrives on a rich cultural mix. The "base" population is overwhelmingly Scots with a large Irish content (much of it from Northern Ireland),

but there are also communities of Poles, Italians, Ukrainians, Jews, Pakistanis, Sikhs, Bengalis, Chinese and, of course, English.

In 2004, one aspect of Edinburgh's heritage was celebrated when it was named as Unesco's first City of Literature. Its current residents include Ian Rankin, creator of Inspector Rebus, J.K. Rowling, begetter of Harry Potter, and Alexander McCall Smith, the prolific writer whose books include the successful *44 Scotland Street* series set in Edinburgh.

Capital city

In 1999 Edinburgh once again became a capital city with a parliament (initially meeting at the Church of Scotland Assembly Hall, at Holyrood). Following a strong endorsement from the Scottish people in the referendum of September 1997, the devolved parliament signalled a significant start to the new millennium.

The new Scottish Parliament was elected by a form of proportional representation (unlike elections to Westminster, which uses a traditional "first

BELOW: Edinburgh Castle dominates the skyline.

past the post" system) and it administers a wide range of local matters, although major areas such as defence and foreign policy are still dealt with by the United Kingdom Parliament in London. A Secretary of State for Scotland still represents Scotland's interests in the UK Parliament, but many regard this as an increasingly redundant post.

Even before the parliament was set up, Edinburgh wielded more power and influence than any British city outside of London. It has long been the centre of the Scots legal system, home to the Court of Session (the civil court) and the High Court of Justiciary (criminal court), from which there is no appeal to the House of Lords: Edinburgh's decision is final.

Edinburgh is also the base of the Church of Scotland (the established church), whose General Assembly every May floods Edinburgh with sober-suited Presbyterian ministers. And anyone seeking to consult the records of Scotland (land titles, company registration, government archives, lists of bankrupts, births, marriages, deaths) must make a pilgrimage to the city.

The early days

No one is quite sure just how old Edinburgh is, only that people have been living in the area for more than 5,000 years. But it seems certain that the city grew from a tiny community perched on the "plug" of volcanic rock which now supports **Edinburgh Castle**. With steep, easily defended sides, natural springs of water and excellent vantage points, the Castle rock was squabbled over for hundreds of years by generations of Picts, Scots, British (Welsh) and Angles, with the Scots (from Ireland) finally coming out on top. It was not until the 11th century that Edinburgh settled down to be the capital city of an independent Scotland, and a royal residence was built within the walls of Edinburgh Castle.

But Edinburgh proved to be a strategic liability in the medieval wars with the English. It was too close to England. Time after time, English armies crashed across the border laying waste the farmlands of the southeast, and burning Edinburgh itself. It happened in 1174 (when the English held Edinburgh Castle for 12 years), in 1296, in

TIP

For an introduction to Edinburgh's colourful past, you can join one of the excellent guided tours around the Castle or the Old Town. Alternatively, download a free Literary Trail from www.cityofliterature.com. Produced by Unesco City of Literature they cover the places in the books of Alexander McCall Smith, J.K. Rowling, Ian Rankin, Robert Louis Stevenson and many more.

BELOW:
the view of the city from Edinburgh Castle.

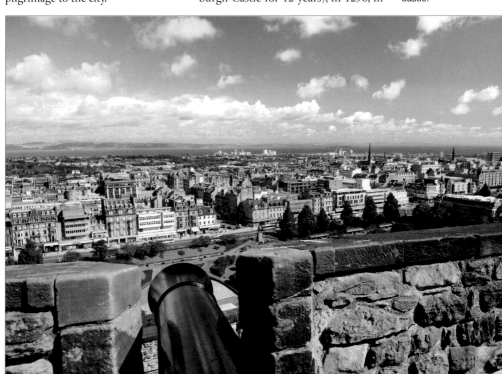

The concentration of talent in 18th-century Edinburgh led John Amyat, the king's chemist, to remark that he could stand at the Mercat Cross and "in a few minutes, take 50 men of genius by the hand".

BELOW: performing on the Royal Mile.

1313 (during the Wars of Independence), in 1357, in 1573, in 1650, and as late as 1689, when the duke of Gordon tried, and failed, to hold Edinburgh Castle against the Protestant army of William of Orange.

The hammering of Edinburgh by the English came to an end in 1707 when the Scottish Parliament, many of whose members had been bribed by English interests, voted to abandon the sovereignty of Scotland in favour of a union with England. "Now there's an end of an auld sang," the old earl of Seafield was heard to mutter as he signed the act. But in fact, power and influence had been haemorrhaging out of Edinburgh ever since the Union of the Crowns in 1603 when the Scottish King James VI (son of Mary Queen of Scots) became the first monarch of Great Britain and Ireland.

Stripped of its royal family, courtiers, parliament and civil service, 18th-century Edinburgh should have lapsed into a sleepy provincialism. But the Treaty of Union guaranteed the position of Scots law and the role of the Presbyterian Church of Scotland. With both these powerful institutions entrenched in Edinburgh, the city was still a place where the powerful and influential met to make important decisions.

The Scottish Enlightenment

In fact, for reasons that are still not clear, 18th-century Scotland became one of Europe's intellectual powerhouses, producing scholars and philosophers like David Hume, Adam Smith and William Robertson, architect-builders like William Adam and his sons Robert and John, engineers like James Watt, Thomas Telford and John Rennie, surgeons like John and William Hunter, and painters like Henry Raeburn and Allan Ramsay.

That explosion of talent became known as the Scottish Enlightenment, and one of its greatest creations was the **New Town** of Edinburgh. Between 1767 and 1840 a whole impeccable new city – bright, spacious, elegant, rational and symmetrical – was created on the land to the north of the **Old Town**.

It was very quickly occupied by the aristocracy, gentry and "middling" classes of Edinburgh, who left the Old Town to

the poor and to the waves of Irish and Highland immigrants who flooded into Edinburgh from the 1840s onwards.

Like most British (and European) cities, Edinburgh's population burgeoned in the 19th century, from 90,786 in 1801 to just over 413,000 in 1901. There was no way that the Old Town and the New Town could house that kind of population, and Victorian Edinburgh became ringed by a huge development of handsome stone-built tenements and villas in suburbs such as **Bruntsfield**, **Marchmont**, **The Grange** and **Morningside**, which in turn became ringed about by 20th-century bungalows and speculative housing.

Beginning in the 1930s, the Edinburgh Corporation (and later the Edinburgh District Council) outflanked the lot by throwing up an outer ring of huge council-housing estates.

Although the Old Town had been allowed to deteriorate in a way that is nothing short of disgraceful, it is steadily being revived. Serious efforts have been made to breathe new life into its labyrinth of medieval streets, wynds and closes. As a way of rescuing Edinburgh's

many architectural treasures, the city fathers have almost been giving away buildings (along with handsome grants) to private developers. Restored 17th-century tenements and also converted 19th-century breweries now provide up-market city-centre living.

The Old Town

Even after two centuries of neglect, Edinburgh's Old Town packs more historic buildings into a square mile than just about anywhere in Britain. Stevenson, again, provides the reason. "It [the Old Town] grew, under the law that regulates the growth of walled cities in precarious situation, not in extent, but in height and density. Public buildings were forced, whenever there was room for them, into the midst of thoroughfares; thoroughfares were diminished into lanes; houses sprang up storey after storey, neighbour mounting upon neighbour's shoulder, as in some Black Hole in Calcutta, until the population slept 14 to 15 deep in a vertical direction."

In this late medieval version of Manhattan, the aristocracy, gentry, merchants and commoners of Edinburgh

Ready for visitors at Edinburgh Castle: after London, Edinburgh is the UK's most popular tourist destination.

BELOW: historic Victoria Street.

Pub signs recall Edinburgh's royal history: this one depicts Mary Queen of Scots.

BELOW RIGHT:
Camera Obscura is full of optical experiences.

lived cheek by jowl. Often they shared the same "lands" (tenements), the "quality" at the bottom and hoi polloi at the top. They rubbed shoulders in dark stairways and closes, and knew one another in a way that was socially impossible in England. Any Lord of Session (High Court judge) whose verdict was unpopular could expect to be harangued or even pelted with mud and stones as he made his way home.

Not that life in the Old Town was entirely dominated by mob rule. Until the end of the 18th century the Old Town was the epicentre of fashionable society, a tight little metropolis of elegant drawing rooms, modish concert halls, dancing academies, and a bewildering variety of taverns, *howffs* (meeting places), coffee houses and social clubs. "Nothing was so common in the morning as to meet men of high rank and official dignity reeling home from a close in the High Street where they had spent the night in drinking," wrote Robert Chambers, a lively chronicler.

The heady social life of the Old Town came to an end at the turn of the 19th century, when it was progressively abandoned by the rich and the influential, whose houses were inherited by the poor and the feckless. "The Great Flitting" it was called, and crowds used to gather to watch all the fine furniture, crockery and paintings being loaded into carts for the journey down the newly created "earthen mound" (now called **The Mound**) to the New Town.

The Royal Mile

The spine of the Old Town is the **Royal Mile** a wide road that runs down from the Castle to the **Palace of Holyroodhouse**, and comprises (from top to bottom) Castlehill, Lawnmarket, the High Street and the Canongate. This street was described by the author of *Robinson Crusoe*, Daniel Defoe (who lived in Edinburgh in the early 18th century), as "perhaps the largest, longest and finest Street for Buildings, and Number of Inhabitants, not in Britain only, but in the world".

The **Castle** ❶ (tel: 0131-225 9846; www.edinburghcastle.gov.uk; daily 9.30am–6pm, Oct–Mar 9.30am–5pm; charge) is well worth a visit, if only for the views over the city. Many of the buildings are

The Rule of the Mob

Politicians, aristocracy and Church leaders came under close scrutiny of the citizens of Edinburgh during the 18th century. When the Scottish Parliament voted itself out of existence by approving the Treaty of Union with England in 1707, the Edinburgh mob went on the rampage trying to track down the "traitors" who, they felt, had sold Scotland out to the "Auld Enemy" (the English). The Edinburgh mob was a formidable political force. The Porteous Riot of 1737, involving a crowd of 4,000, showed how strong feelings in Scotland could be, and the government in London was sufficiently alarmed that it decided to demolish the Nether Bow Port in order to make it easier for its troops to enter Edinburgh in the event of further rebellions. (It is an episode that is described in vivid detail in the opening chapters of Sir Walter Scott's novel *The Heart of Midlothian*.)

For many years the Edinburgh mob was led by a certain "General" Joe Smith, a bow-legged cobbler who believed passionately in the inferiority of women (his wife had to walk several paces behind him) and who could drum up a crowd of thousands within a few minutes. With the mob at his back, Joe Smith could lay down the law to the magistrates of Edinburgh, and ran a kind of rough justice against thieving landlords and dishonest traders. His career came to an abrupt end in 1780 when, dead drunk, he fell to his death from the top of a stagecoach.

18th- and 19th-century, although the tiny Norman chapel dedicated to the saintly Queen Margaret dates to the 12th century. Go into the **National War Museum**, **Great Hall** (which has a superb hammerbeam roof), and the **Crown Room**, which houses the Regalia (crown jewels) of Scotland; these were lost between 1707 and 1818 when a commission set up by Sir Walter Scott traced them to a locked chest in a locked room in the castle. Also here is Scotland's symbolic coronation seat, the Stone of Destiny, returned from London in 1996 after a 700-year absence. If you're there at lunch time you can see the master gunner fire the famous One o' Clock gun (not on Sundays).

Just below the Castle esplanade, on **Castlehill**, are an iron fountain marking the spot where, between 1479 and 1722, Edinburgh burned its witches; **Ramsay Garden**, the tenements designed by the 19th-century planning genius Patrick Geddes; and a **Camera Obscura** ❷ (tel: 0131-226 3709; www. camera-obscura.co.uk; daily July–Aug 9.30am–7.30pm, Apr–June, Sept–Oct

9.30am–6pm, Nov–Mar 10am–5pm; charge) built in the 1850s.

Across the road is **The Scotch Whisky Experience** (tel: 0131 220 0441; www.whisky-heritage.co.uk; daily June–Aug 9.30am–6.30pm; Sept–May 10am–6pm, charge), where visitors can learn about the drink's origin from an audiovisual show and by travelling in a whisky barrel through 300 years of history. The shop sells a good selection of whiskies.

Next door, Tolbooth Kirk, where the city's Gaelic speakers used to worship, has reopened as **The Hub** (Edinburgh's Festival Centre; tel: 0131-473 2015; www.thehub-edinburgh.com), with a booking office, exhibition area, shop and café-bar.

On the north side of the Lawnmarket is **Gladstone's Land** ❸ (tel: 0844-493 2120; daily Apr–Oct 10am–5pm; July–Aug until 6.30pm; charge), a completely restored six-storey 17th-century tenement now owned by the National Trust for Scotland (NTS), which gives some insight into 17th-century Edinburgh life (dirty, difficult and malodorous). Next door is Lady Stair's House,

TIP

You could do worse than start a visit to Edinburgh at the Cannongate Tolbooth: home to the People's Story museum (tel: 0131-529 4057; Mon–Sat 10am–5pm, also Sun 12–5pm in Aug; free), the exhibition gives a good insight into ordinary Edinburgh folk from the late 18th century to the present.

BELOW LEFT: signs to the castle. **BELOW:** have a taste of the Scotch Whisky Experience.

John Knox House. Even though it's doubtful that John Knox, the Protestant Reformer, actually lived in the house that bears his name, it is likely that he preached from its window.

BELOW: Canongate Tolbooth. **BELOW RIGHT:** statue of Robert Fergusson, poet, outside Canongate Kirk.

now the **Writers' Museum** (tel: 0131-529 4901; Mon–Sat 10am–5pm, Aug Sun noon–5pm; free), dedicated to Robert Burns, Sir Walter Scott and Robert Louis Stevenson; and **Deacon Brodie's Tavern**, named after William Brodie, the model for the Jekyll and Hyde story.

Further along, on what is now **High Street**, are **Parliament House** (now the Law Courts); the **High Kirk of St Giles** (tel: 0131-225 9442; www.stgiles cathedral.org.uk; Mon–Sat 9am–5pm, Sun 1–5pm; free); the **Mercat Cross**, from which kings and queens are proclaimed; and the **City Chambers**, which was one of the first buildings in the great drive to "improve" Edinburgh in the late 18th century. Below, visitors can explore haunted **Mary King's Close** (tel: 0845-070 6244 for bookings; www. realmarykingsclose.com; Apr–Oct daily 10am–7pm, Nov–Mar Sun–Thur 10am–5pm, Fri–Sat 10am–9pm; charge). The lower part of the High Street contains the 15th-century **Moubray House**, which is probably the oldest inhabited building in Edinburgh; **John Knox House** ❹ (tel: 0131-556 9579; www.

scottishstorytellingcentre.co.uk; Mon–Sat 10am–6pm, July and Aug also Sun noon–6pm; charge), which is home to the **Scottish Storytelling Centre**; and the **Museum of Childhood** (tel: 0131-529 4141; Mon–Sat 10am–5pm, Sun noon–5pm; free) with displays of historical toys, dolls and books.

Across the road in **Trinity Church** in **Chalmer's Court** enthusiasts can make rubbings of rare Scottish brasses and stone crosses in the **Brass Rubbing Centre** (tel: 0131-556 4364; Apr–Nov Mon–Sat 10am–5pm; free, charge to make a rubbing).

Canongate buildings

Further east, **Canongate** is particularly rich in 16th- and 17th-century buildings. These include the **Tolbooth** ❺ *(see margin page 141)*; **Bakehouse Close**; the **Museum of Edinburgh**, the city's main museum of local history (tel: 0131-529 4143; Mon–Sat 10am–5pm, Aug also Sun noon–5pm; free); **Moray House**, the most lavish of the aristocracy's town houses; the Dutch-style **Canongate Church**; **White Horse Close** (once a coaching

inn); and the 17th-century **Acheson House**. Beyond the Canongate Church is the "**mushroom garden**", a walled garden laid out in the 17th-century manner, almost completely unknown.

The **Palace of Holyroodhouse ❻** (tel: 0131-556 5100; www.royalcollection. org.uk; daily 9.30am–4.30pm with exceptions; charge) began as an abbey in the 12th century, grew into a royal palace in the early 16th century and was much extended in the late 17th century for Charles II, who never set foot in it. Mary Queen of Scots witnessed the butchery of her Italian favourite, David Rizzio, here in 1558.

The new **Scottish Parliament** building (tel: 0131-348 5000; www.scottish. parliament.uk; daily times subject to parliamentary business; free) opened its doors at Holyrood in 2004 at a final cost of £431 million. Barcelona architect Enric Miralles's innovative architecture was described by one critic as being "like a cluster of boats, a sweeping of leaves, a collection of seaside shells, a Pandora's box of architectural motifs laced together ingeniously, this side of pandemonium". Opposite is

a stunning, tented tourist attraction, **Our Dynamic Earth** (tel: 0131-550 7800; www.dynamicearth.co.uk; Apr–Oct daily 10am–5.30pm, July–Aug until 6pm; charge). This is a family-oriented audiovisual "experience" of the formation and evolution of the planet.

South of the Royal Mile

Close to the Royal Mile, on George IV Bridge, are the **National Library of Scotland** (a UK copyright library; tel: 0131-623 3700) and the little bronze statue of **Greyfriars Bobby ❼**, the devoted Skye terrier immortalised by Walt Disney. In Chambers Street is the **National Museum of Scotland ❽** (tel: 0131-225 7534; www.nms. ac.uk; daily 10am–5pm; free), incorporating the Royal Museum, which houses a dazzling collection of 19th-century machinery, scientific instruments and natural history, plus the preserved remains of Dolly the sheep (1996–2003), the world's first cloned mammal. Currently about half of the museum is closed while the Royal Museum building is transformed, but will reopen in all its glory in 2011.

Holyrood Palace.

BELOW: inside the Scottish Parliament.

On the corner of Chambers Street and the South Bridge lies Robert Adam's **The Old College**, the finest of Edinburgh University's buildings.

Running roughly parallel with the Royal Mile to the south are the **Grass-market** – lined by cosy pubs and once the site of riots and public executions – and a long and rather dingy street called the **Cowgate**, which in the 19th century was crammed with Irish immigrants fleeing the Great Famine. The Irish Catholic nature of the Cowgate is testified to by the huge but inelegant bulk of **St Patrick's Roman Catholic Church**. A more interesting building is **St Cecilia's Hall** ❾, which now belongs to Edinburgh University, but was built by the Edinburgh Musical Society as a concert hall in 1762, modelled on the opera house at Parma.

A landmark of Europe

"A sort of schizophrenia in stone" is how the novelist Eric Linklater once described **Princes Street**, going on to contrast the "natural grandeur solemnised by memories of human pain and heroism" of the Castle rock with the tawdry commercialism of the north side of the street. Thanks to the developers and retailers of the 20th century it is no longer one of Europe's more elegant boulevards. Just about every decent building has been gouged out of the north side of the street and replaced by some undistinguished piece of modern architecture. Fortunately, on the south side **Princes Street Gardens** ❿ remain as the "broad and deep ravine planted with trees and shrubbery" that so impressed the American writer Nathaniel Willis in 1834. Furthermore, with Princes Street packed with visitors throughout the year, rumblings continue of pedestrianising the famous thoroughfare.

With the exception of the superb **Register House** by Robert Adam at the far northeast end of the street, and a few remaining 19th-century shops (such as Jenners, which is now owned by House of Fraser), everything worthwhile is on the south side of the street. The most startling edifice, which may be ascended for splendid views, is the huge and intricate Gothic **monument to Sir Walter Scott** ⓫ (Apr–Sept Mon–Sat 10am–

BELOW: a summer's evening in Princess Street Gardens.

7pm, Oct–Mar Mon–Sat 9am–4pm, Sun 10am–4pm; charge) erected in 1844 and designed by a self-taught architect called George Meikle Kemp. The unfortunate Kemp drowned in an Edinburgh canal shortly before the monument was completed, and was due to be buried in the vault under the memorial until some petty-minded member of Scott's entourage persuaded the Court of Session to divert the funeral.

Connected art galleries

Much more typical of Edinburgh are the two neoclassical art galleries at the junction of Princes Street and The Mound. Since the completion of a multi-million pound project in 2004, both the **Royal Scottish Academy** ⓬ (tel: 0131-225 6671; www.royalscottishacademy. org; Mon–Sat 10am–5pm, Sun noon–5pm; free) and the **National Gallery of Scotland** ⓭ (tel: 0131-624 6200; www. nationalgalleries.org; daily 10am–5pm, Thur until 7pm; free) have been connected by an underground passageway (Weston Link), accessed off Princes Street Gardens East. Both buildings were designed by William Playfair between 1822 and 1845. The space surrounding the galleries has long been Edinburgh's version of London's Hyde Park Corner, and is heavily used by preachers, polemicists and bagpipers.

Exhibitions at the Royal Scottish Academy come and go, but the National Gallery of Scotland houses the biggest permanent collection of Old Masters outside London. There are paintings by Raphael, Rubens, El Greco, Titian, Goya, Vermeer and a clutch of superb Rembrandts. Gauguin, Cézanne, Renoir, Degas, Monet, Van Gogh and Turner are well represented, and the gallery's Scottish collection is unrivalled. There are important paintings by Raeburn, Ramsay, Wilkie and the astonishing (and underrated) James Drummond.

At the southwest end of Princes Street is a brace of fine churches, **St John's** ⓮ (Episcopalian) and **St Cuthbert's** (Church of Scotland). St John's supports a lively congregation that is forever decking the building out with paintings in support of various Developing World causes and animal rights. The church, a Gothic Revival building designed by William Burn

BELOW LEFT: the National Gallery of Scotland.

A Wee Dram – or Real Ale?

E dinburgh's scores of "watering holes" suggest its 478,000 residents are spoilt for choice. Yet it is an extraordinary fact of Edinburgh life that there is not one pub on the whole length of Princes Street. But affluent George Street and workaday Rose Street, a narrow and once infamous thoroughfare that runs just behind it, make up for it.

The more diverting Rose Street hostelries are the **Kenilworth** (which has a lovely ceramic-clad interior), **Dirty Dick's** and the **Abbotsford**. A favourite Edinburgh sport has been to try to get from one end of Rose Street to the other, downing half a pint of real ale or a dram in every pub and still remain standing. In Rose Street you will also find a *howff* (meeting place) called **Milnes Bar**, which was once the haunt of 20th-century Edinburgh literati – writers like Hugh MacDiarmid and Norman MacCaig and jazz musicians such as Sandy Brown.

Live music is heard in many Edinburgh pubs today, particularly during the annual Edinburgh Jazz Festival. And the main August Festival transforms the city's pubs, which are granted extended licences to cope with the increased custom in these summer weeks. Not that drinkers here usually have a problem: ever since the relaxation of licensing regulations in 1976 genteel Edinburgh has been one of the easiest places in Britain in which to buy a drink, with bars open well into the "wee sma' hours".

TIP

During the weeks of the Festival in August many of Edinburgh's attractions have longer opening hours.

in 1816, has a fine ceiling which John Ruskin thought "simply beautiful".

The New Town

What makes Edinburgh a truly world-class city, able to stand shoulder to shoulder with Prague, Amsterdam or Vienna, is the great neoclassical New Town, built in an explosion of creativity between 1767 and 1840. The New Town is the product of the Scottish Enlightenment. And no one has really been able to explain how, in the words of the historian Arthur Youngson, "a small, crowded, almost medieval town, the capital of a comparatively poor country, expanded in a short space of time, without foreign advice or foreign assistance, so as to become one of the enduringly beautiful cities of Western Europe".

It all began in 1752 with a pamphlet entitled *Proposals for carrying on certain Public Works in the City of Edinburgh*. It was published anonymously, but was engineered by Edinburgh's all-powerful Lord Provost (Lord Mayor), George Drummond. He was determined that Edinburgh should be a credit to the Hanoverian-ruled United Kingdom which he had helped create, and should seek to rid itself of its reputation for overcrowding, squalor, turbulence and Jacobitism.

To some extent the New Town is a political statement in stone. It is Scotland's tribute to the Hanoverian ascendancy. Many of the street names reflect the fact, as witnessed in their names: **Hanover Street**, **Cumberland Street**, **George Street**, **Queen Street**, **Frederick Street**.

The speed with which the New Town was built is still astonishing, particularly given the sheer quality of the building. Built mainly in calciferous sandstone from Craigleith Quarry, to a prize-winning layout by a 23-year-old architect/planner called James Craig, most of the more important New Town buildings were in place before the end of the century: **Register House** (1778), the north side of **Charlotte Square** (1791), the **Assembly Rooms and Music Hall** (1787), **St Andrew's Church** (1785), most of **George Street**, **Castle Street**, **Frederick Street** and **Princes Street**.

The stinking Nor' Loch (North

BELOW: Bute House, the official residence of the First Minister of Scotland.

Loch) under the castle rock was speedily drained to make way for the "pleasure gardens" of Princes Street. By the 1790s the New Town was the height of fashion, and the gentry of Edinburgh were abandoning their roots in the Old Town for the Georgian elegance on the other side of the newly built North Bridge.

Inside a New Town house

Some idea of how the gentry lived can be seen in the **Georgian House** ⑮ (tel: 0844-493 2118; daily Apr–Oct 10am–5pm, Mar, Nov, Dec 11am–3pm; charge) at 7 Charlotte Square (on the block designed by Robert Adam). The house has been restored by the National Trust for Scotland. It is crammed with the furniture, crockery, glassware, silver and paintings of the period, and even the floorboards have been dry-scrubbed in the original manner. The basement kitchen is a masterpiece of late 18th-century domestic technology.

Also in Charlotte Square is **West Register House** (part of the Scottish Record Office; tel: 0131-535 1400), which was built by Robert Reid in 1811 and began life as St George's Church. Just along George Street are the **Assembly Rooms and Music Hall** ⑯ (tel: 0131-220 4348; www.assemblyroomsedinbrugh.co.uk), built in 1787 and once the focus of social life in the New Town, and still a top venue during the festival. Across the road is the **Church of St Andrew and St George** (1785), whose oval-shaped interior witnessed the "Great Disruption" of 1843. The Church of Scotland was split down the middle when the "evangelicals", led by Thomas Chalmers, walked out in disgust at the complacency of the Church "moderates" who were content to have their ministers foisted on them by the gentry (the custom in England). Chalmers went on to form the Free Church of Scotland, proclaiming a sterner but more democratic form of Presbyterianism.

Parallel to George Street lies **Queen Street**, whose only public building of interest is an eccentric Doge's Palace housing the **Scottish National Portrait Gallery** ⑰ (www.nationalgalleries.org; closed for restoration, due to reopen autumn 2011), well stocked with pictures of generations of Scots worthies.

Although St Andrew Square at the

Register House was built especially to store public records: its thick stone walls guard against the risk of fire.

BELOW: the lush view at the Royal Botanic Gardens.

Edinburgh's Money Men

Charlotte Square, Edinburgh's financial district, is still going strong despite the blows of the last decade's recession

Edinburgh is the second biggest financial centre in the UK outside the City of London and one of the largest financial hubs in Europe. Until the world recession of 2008–9, Scottish investment houses managed over £500 billion in funds and one in 10 people in Scotland was employed in financial services. The huge bail out by the British taxpayer and scandal surrounding the collapse of the Royal Bank of Scotland, resulting in the largest loss in corporate history, has given the industry a serious knock, one from which it is only slowly beginning to recover.

However, this reduced community of bankers, investment fund managers, stockbrokers, corporate lawyers, accountants and insurance executives still have to be "serviced", even if now in a diluted form. This was all nice business for Edinburgh's glossier advertising agencies, public relations firms, design studios and photographers – not to mention restaurants, wine bars and auction houses.

Just as "the City" is shorthand for London's vast financial community, so Edinburgh's was known as "Charlotte Square" until the 1990s, as the square and connecting George Street were the centre of the financial district. Many of the finance houses relocated to the Exchange Office district west of Lothian Road when they had difficulties upgrading the listed buildings, but George Street retains plush restaurants and shops, and Bute House in Charlotte Square is the official residence of Scotland's first minister. The result of the recession, however, has been unemployment and massive falls in profits, making the role of Edinburgh's money men decidedly shaky.

A right to print money

Edinburgh's star role in the financial world can be traced back to the enthusiasm of the Scots for making and then keeping money. The Scots have always been among the modern world's best and canniest bankers. This is why the Scottish clearing banks, including Clydesdale Bank and the Royal Bank of Scotland, have a statutory right (dating from 1845) to print their own distinctive banknotes. This is a right the Scottish banks relish, particularly as the English banks were stripped of it following a string of bank failures in the 19th century; the Scots are remarkably attached to their Edinburgh-based banks.

Probably the biggest fish in Edinburgh's financial pond are the giant Scottish insurance companies, although they too saw profits reduced by the recession. The most important is the Standard Life Assurance Company, with its prominent position off Lothian Road and offices all over Britain, Ireland and Canada. Like most of the Edinburgh insurance companies, the Standard Life is a vintage operation (1825). Some are even older, with full names that have a satisfyingly old-fashioned ring, like the Scottish Widows Fund and Life Assurance Society or the Scottish Provident Institution for Mutual Life Assurance.

It was with money from Scottish investment trusts that much of the American West was built. In the 19th century, Charlotte Square was heavily into cattle-ranching, fruit-farming and railways in the United States. Nowadays, it prefers to sink its "bawbees" into the high-tech industries. While Edinburgh as a whole benefited little from North Sea oil, parts of Charlotte Square did very nicely. It is time now, perhaps, for the Edinburgh financiers to exercise caution and to return to the days of thrift and Presbyterian principles in rebuilding the respect and trust of the Scottish people.   ❏

LEFT: environmentalists clash with the RBS (Royal Bank of Scotland).

east end of George Street has been knocked about a bit, it is still recognisable, with the most noteworthy building in the square being the head office of the Royal Bank of Scotland. Originally built in 1774 as the town house of Sir Laurence Dundas, it was remodelled in the 1850s, when it acquired a quite astonishing domed ceiling with glazed star-shaped coffers. The 150ft (45-metre) high monument in the centre of St Andrew Square is to Henry Dundas, 1st Viscount Melville, who was branded "King Harry the Ninth" for his autocratic (and probably corrupt) way of running Scotland.

Georgian elegance

To the north of the Charlotte Square/ St Andrew Square axis lies a huge acreage of Georgian elegance, which is probably unrivalled in Europe. Most of it is private housing and offices. Particularly worth seeing are **Heriot Row**, **Northumberland Street**, **Royal Circus**, **Ainslie Place**, **Moray Place** and **Drummond Place**. **Ann Street** ⑱ near the Water of Leith is beautiful but atypical, with its gardens and two- and three-storey buildings. Nearby **Danube Street** used to house Edinburgh's most notorious whorehouse, run by the flamboyant Dora Noyes (the house has reverted to middle-class decency).

The **Stockbridge** area on the northern edge of the New Town is an engaging bazaar of antique shops, curiosity dealers, picture framers and secondhand bookstores, with a sprinkling of decent restaurants and pubs. The **Royal Botanic Garden** ⑲ (tel: 0131-552 7171; daily 10am–dusk; free, charge for glasshouse), half a mile (0.8km) north of Stockbridge, comprises 70 acres (28 hectares) of woodland, green sward, exotic trees, heather garden, rockeries, rhododendron walks, elegant zoned plant houses and a Victorian glasshouse.

Also in this area, on Belford Road, is the **Scottish National Gallery of Modern Art** ⑳ (tel: 0131-624 6200; daily 10am–5pm, Thur until 7pm; free), with a fine permanent collection of 20th- and 21st-century art, including works by Matisse and Picasso, Magritte and Hockney. The **Dean Gallery** (daily 10am–5pm, Thur until 7pm; free), in a lovely 19th-century building across the

Ann Street was the creation of the painter Henry Raeburn, who named it after his wife. It was described by the English poet Sir John Betjeman as "the most attractive street in Britain".

BELOW: take time to reflect at the Dean Gallery.

The rules drawn up by the Honourable Company of Edinburgh Golfers at Leith Links in 1774 still form the basis of golf today.

BELOW: the Dugald Stewart Monument on top of Calton Hill.

road features the Paolozzi Collection of modern art donated by the Edinburgh sculptor, major Dada and Surrealist works and temporary exhibitions.

Pleasure seekers

Stevenson's Edward Hyde lurks in the New Town, too. The designers of the New Town provided it with a plethora of handsome "pleasure gardens" which range in size from small patches of grass and shrubbery to the three **Queen Street Gardens**, which cover more than 11 acres (4.5 hectares). All three are closed to the public and accessible only to the "key-holders" who live nearby. You may often see puzzled tourists shaking the gates, at a loss to understand why they are barred from ambling round the greenery.

Between 1815 and 1840 another version of the New Town grew beyond the east end of Princes Street and Waterloo Place. **Regent Terrace**, **Royal Terrace**, **Blenheim Terrace** and **Leopold Place** were its main thoroughfares.

This eastward expansion also littered the slopes of **Calton Hill** with impressive public buildings, which probably

earned Edinburgh the title "Athens of the North" (although a comparison between the two cities had been made in 1762 by the antiquarian James Stuart). On the hill are monuments to Dugald Stewart, the 18th/19th-century philosopher, and Horatio Nelson, whose memorial in the shape of a telescope may be climbed for great views; and the old **City Observatory** ㉑ where the city's Astronomical Society conducts public meetings most Friday evenings.

The oddest of the early 19th-century edifices on Calton Hill is known as "Scotland's Disgrace". It is a war memorial to the Scots killed in the Napoleonic Wars, which was modelled on the Parthenon in Athens. The foundation stone was laid with a great flourish during George IV's visit to Edinburgh in 1822, but the money ran out after 12 columns were erected and it remains incomplete to this day.

Beyond Calton Hill, on Regent Road, are the former **Royal High School** (called "the noblest monument of the Scottish Greek Revival"), the **Robert Burns Monument**, modelled on the Choragic Monument of Lysicrates in Athens, and the **Old Calton Burial Ground**, with 18th- and 19th-century memorials (including one honouring the philosopher David Hume), in the lee of the empty, semi-derelict **Governor's House** of the Old Calton Jail.

Maritime Edinburgh

Although more ships now sail in and out of the Firth of Forth than use the Firth of Clyde, maritime Edinburgh has taken a terrible beating since the 1980s. Edinburgh's port of **Leith** ㉒ was, until recently, one of the hardest-working harbours on the east coast of Britain (the city's coastline on the Firth of Forth is studded with former fishing villages: **Granton**, **Newhaven**, **Portobello**, **Fisherrow**, and, further east, **Cockenzie**, **Port Seton** and **Prestonpans**). Ships from Leith exported coal, salt fish, paper, leather and good strong ale, and returned with (among much else) grain, timber, wine, foreign foods

and Italian marble. The destinations were Hamburg, Bremen, Amsterdam, Antwerp, Copenhagen and occasionally North America and Australia.

Right up to the mid-1960s at least four fleets of deep-sea trawlers plied out of Leith and the nearby harbour of **Granton**, and the half-Scottish, half-Norwegian firm of Christian Salvesen was still catching thousands of whales every year into the 1950s (which is why there is a Leith Harbour in South Georgia, which was then the world's largest whaling centre). The 2-mile (3km) stretch of shore between Leith and Granton was once littered with shipyards, ship repair yards and dry docks. The streets of Leith itself were full of shipping agents, marine insurance firms, grain merchants, ships' chandlers, plus a burgeoning "service sector" of dockside pubs, clubs, doss-houses, bookies and whores.

A reinvented Leith

But most of this has gone. The trade has shifted to the container ports on the east coast of England, and Leith now has uneasy neighbours in the older, deprived residential areas and the increasingly up-market Shore, with "yuppy" flats, offices and restaurants. The whole area continues to be under siege by private developers with old warehouses, office buildings, lodging houses and at least one veteran cooperage converted into high-priced flats and houses. Leith is also now home to the gigantic Scottish Executive building (with, opposite, a row of smart new restaurants). In all, the port hosts a cluster of fashionable restaurants, an art gallery and, in a conversion of one of the dock-gate buildings, the successful Waterfront Wine Bar.

Meanwhile, Scottish Enterprise and the local authorities have been spending millions restoring the exteriors of some of Leith's handsome commercial buildings, such as the old **Customs House**, the **Corn Exchange**, the **Assembly Building** and **Trinity House** in the Kirkgate. In Bangor Road is **Scotland's Clan Tartan Centre** (tel: 0131-553 5161; daily 9am–5.30pm; free) where with the assistance of computers, you can learn that you too are a clan member.

TIP

After a visit to the Royal Yacht Britannia, visit Ocean Terminal, one of Edinburgh's flagship shopping and leisure centres designed by Sir Terence Conran. Shops are open 10–7pm most nights and the restaurants, bars and cinema are open until midnight.

BELOW: the waterfront at Leith.

The walk from Dean to Stockbridge takes you past St Bernard's Well, whose natural spring inspired the creation in the 18th century of a Roman temple with a statue of Hygeia, the Greek goddess of health.

Resident in Leith docks is the **Royal Yacht** *Britannia* (tel: 0131-555 5566; www.royalyachtbritannia.co.uk; visitor centre and yacht tours daily, July–Sept 9.30am–4.30pm, Jan–June, Oct–Dec 10am–3.30pm; charge). Now decommissioned, it was used by the royal family for 44 years for state visits and royal holidays and is fascinating to see.

The old port is still worth a visit, too, if only for its powerful sense of what it used to be. And many of the buildings on **Bernard Street**, **Commercial Street**, **Constitution Street** and **The Shore** are handsome and interesting. Leith has an intriguing constitutional history, first part of Edinburgh, then a separate burgh, and then swallowed up by Edinburgh again (in 1920). Halfway up the street known as **Leith Walk** is a pub called the Boundary Bar, through which the municipal border between Edinburgh and Leith used to run.

Newhaven

If ever a village has been killed by conservation it must be the little port of **Newhaven ㉓**, a mile west of Leith. Into the 1960s this was a brisk community, with a High Street and a Main Street lined with shops and other small businesses, through which trams and later buses used to trundle. But now that the picturesque houses have been "restored" there is hardly a shop left in the place, the once-crowded Main Street is a ghostly dead end, and Newhaven harbour is occupied by a few pleasure yachts.

All of this is a great pity. Newhaven is one of Edinburgh's more interesting corners. The village was founded in the late 15th century by James IV to build the *Great Michael*, then the biggest warship on earth and destined to be the flagship of a new Scottish navy. But like many such grandiose schemes – particularly those hatched in Scotland – the *Great Michael* was never a success. After the ruin of the Scots army (and the death of James IV) at Flodden in 1513, the great ship, which was the pride of Newhaven, was sold to the French, who left her to rot in Brest.

The villages

Like most other cities sprawling outwards, Edinburgh has enveloped a number of villages. The most striking

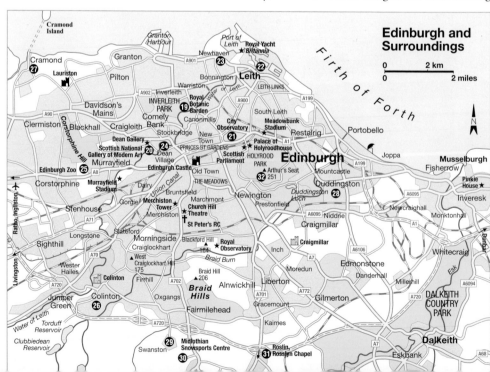

is probably **Dean Village** ㉔, a few minutes' walk from the West End of Princes Street. Now one of Edinburgh's more fashionable corners, Dean Village is at least 800 years old, and straddles the Water of Leith at a point that was once the main crossing on the way to Queensferry. The Incorporation of Baxters (bakers) of Edinburgh once operated 11 watermills and two flour granaries here. Its most striking building is **Well Court**, an unusual courtyard of flats built in the 1880s as housing for the poor by John Findlay, proprietor of *The Scotsman* newspaper.

Other villages that have been swallowed by the city include **Corstorphine** to the west, where the capital keeps its famous **Edinburgh Zoo** ㉕ (tel: 0131-334 9171; www.edinburghzoo.org.uk; daily Apr–Sept 9am–6pm, Oct and Mar 9am–5pm, Nov–Feb 9am–4.30pm; charge), with a fine collection of penguins in the world's largest enclosure, plus endangered species such as the white rhino.

Colinton ㉖, in the south, features an 18th-century parish church and a wooded dell beside the Water of Leith.

Cramond ㉗, on the Firth of Forth, used to sport an ironworks and was once the site of a Roman military camp.

Duddingston ㉘ is another interesting village, tucked under the eastern flank of Arthur's Seat, beside a small loch which is also a bird sanctuary. It has a fine Norman-style church and a 17th-century house which was used by Bonnie Prince Charlie in 1745. On the northern slopes of the Pentland Hills lies **Swanston** ㉙, a small huddle of white-painted cottages, near where the Stevenson family used to rent Swanston Cottage as a summer residence for the sickly Robert Louis Stevenson. For some odd reason, the gardens of Swanston are adorned with statuary and ornamental stonework taken from the High Kirk of St Giles when it was being "improved" in the 19th century.

The hills of Edinburgh

If there is such a creature as the urban mountaineer, then Edinburgh must be his or her paradise. Like Rome, the city is built on and around seven hills, none of them very high, but all offering good stiff walks and spectacular views of the

TIP

You can enjoy fish and chips at their best at the famous Harry Ramsden's restaurant on Newhaven's harbour-side.

BELOW LEFT: Edinburgh Zoo.
BELOW RIGHT: Dean Village.

Stained-glass window in Rosslyn Chapel.

city. They are, in order of altitude, Arthur's Seat (823ft/251 metres), Braid Hill (675ft/205 metres), West Craiglockhart Hill (575ft/173 metres), Blackford Hill (539ft/162 metres), Corstorphine Hill (531ft/159 metres), Castle Hill (435ft/131 metres) and Calton Hill (328ft/98 metres).

In addition, Edinburgh is bounded to the south by the **Pentland Hills**, a range of amiable mini-mountains that almost (but not quite) climb to 2,000ft (600 metres). Here, too, is the **Midlothian Snowsports Centre 30** (tel: 0131-445 4433; daily 9.30am–7pm), the longest artificial ski and snowboarding slope in Britain. Non-skiers can take the lift and then a short walk to Caerketton Hill for magnificent panoramic views.

In the village of Roslin is **Rosslyn Chapel 31** (tel: 0131-440 2159; www.rosslynchapel.org.uk; Mon–Sat 9.30am–5pm, Sun noon–4.45pm; charge). It is claimed that it contains the Holy Grail and other religious relics. This theory appears in Dan Brown's best-selling book, *The Da Vinci Code*, and has led to an increase in visitors. The interior is decorated with remarkable carvings including the **Apprentice Pillar**, so called because it

was carved by an apprentice stonemason while the master mason was absent. So jealous was the older mason that he killed the apprentice with a mallet.

Of the "city-centre" hills, Calton Hill at the east end of Princes Street probably offers the best view of Edinburgh. But it is **Arthur's Seat 32**, that craggy old volcano in the Queen's Park, which must count as the most startling piece of urban mountainscape. It is one of the many places in Britain named after the shadowy (and possibly apocryphal) King Arthur. The area around the city was a British (Welsh) kingdom before it was overrun by the Angles and Scots.

The outer city

Although Edinburgh may not have an "inner city" problem, it certainly has had its "outer city" difficulties. It is ringed with sprawling council estates, places like **Craigmillar** and **Niddrie**, **Alton**, **Muirhouse** and **Wester Hailes**. Some of the people who live here were "decanted" there the High Street, Cowgate and Leith, and perhaps many would return if only they could find affordable housing. ❏

The World's Biggest Arts Festival

Edinburgh is the only place to be when the Festival is on and the cream of artistic talent – present and future – flocks to the city

When the Edinburgh International Festival and Festival Fringe explode into life every August, the city, as the *Washington Post* once pointed out, becomes "simply the best place on Earth". Certainly the display of cultural pyrotechnics is awesome. Every concert hall, basement theatre and church hall in the centre of Edinburgh overflows with dance groups, theatre companies, string quartets, puppeteers, opera companies and orchestras. And for three weeks the streets of Edinburgh are awash with fire-eaters, jugglers, bagpipers, clowns, warblers, satirists and theatrical hopefuls of every shape, size and colour.

All of which is a distant cry from the dead and dreary days after World War II when the idea for an arts festival was hatched by Sir John Falconer, then Lord Provost of Edinburgh, Harry Harvey Wood of the British Council, and Rudolf Bing, the festival's first artistic director. The notion, said the novelist Eric Linklater, was "the triumph of elegance over drab submission to the penalties of emerging victorious from a modern war".

A sensual and visceral assault

In 2009 alone, almost 400,000 tickets were issued for the "highbrow" International Festival. Of course, it's not all plain sailing. During the 1980s, the artistic director Frank Dunlop sounded off regularly about upstart arts festivals trying to "poach" Edinburgh's hard-won commercial sponsors. Today, International Festival director Jonathan Mills must continue to juggle financial and artistic priorities and, with the box office generating over £2.5 million in 2009, one could argue that such a festival is a welcome sensual and visceral assault.

Edinburgh's "alternative" festival, the Festival Fringe (which also began in 1947), has become a behemoth – so big, in fact, that it threatens to outgrow the city. It's now the largest arts festival in the world. In 2009, the Fringe offered nearly 35,000 performances in over 250 venues. Of 2,100 different shows, around 200 were free. The Fringe has grown to eclipse its more staid official brother, selling over 1.8 million tickets in 2009.

A larger Fringe

Over the years it's been a nursery for new talent: Maggie Smith, Tom Stoppard (*Rosencrantz and Guildernstern Are Dead* was premiered here), Rowan Atkinson, Billy Connolly and Emma Thompson all made their entrance into the business on the Festival Fringe. Every year the cream of artistic talent makes its way to Edinburgh, and the Fringe has grown into arguably the largest showcase for performers in the world. In 2008 the Fringe faced crisis when the computer ticketing system failed and the director was forced to resign to be replaced by Kath Mainland in a newly appointed position as chief executive.

Throughout the year a "fringe" of the Fringe (as it were) has evolved, which includes about 10 other festivals, including the International and Fringe, referred to as "Edinburgh Festival". The stunning spectacle of the Edinburgh Military Tattoo, part of the wider Edinburgh Festival, celebrated its Diamond Jubilee in 2010.	❏

RIGHT: street performers draw a crowd at the Edinburgh Festival.

OLD AND NEW TOWN ARCHITECTURE

Declared a Unesco World Heritage Site in 1995, the centre of Edinburgh is a fascinating juxtaposition of medieval confusion and classical harmony

Architecturally, Edinburgh's Old and New Towns are utterly disparate. In the Old, everything is higgledy-piggledy; in the New – now more than 200 years old – order and harmony prevail.

The Old Town lies to the south of Princes Street Gardens. Its backbone is the Royal Mile, described by the writer Daniel Defoe in the 1720s as "perhaps the largest, longest and finest Street for Buildings, and Number of Inhabitants...in the world". Then it was lined with tall, narrow tenements, some with as many as 14 storeys, where aristocracy, merchants and lowly clerks all rubbed shoulders in friendly familiarity in dark stairways, and through which ran a confusing maze of wynds (alleys), courts and closes.

A New Order

In 1766 James Craig, an unknown 23-year-old, won a competition for the design of the New Town. His submission was a "gridiron" consisting of two elegant squares – Charlotte and St Andrew – linked by three wide, straight, parallel streets: Princes, George and Queen. Robert and John Adam, Sir William Chambers and John Henderson, premier architects of the day, all contributed plans for glorious Georgian buildings. During the first part of the 19th century, the New Town was extended by the addition of an extraordinary grouping of squares, circuses, terraces, crescents and parks, all maintaining the neoclassical idiom and permitting the New Town to boast the largest area of Georgian architecture in all Europe.

LEFT: the French-style Tolbooth, in the Old Town's Canongate, is the oldest remaining building here, dating from 1591.

ABOVE: the Royal Society of Edinburgh has been based in this fine Italianate classical building, with its distinctive cupola, since 1907.

STEPPING INSIDE THE PAST

Two of the finest examples of Edinburgh's Old and New Towns have been restored to their former glory and are open to visitors, thanks to the National Trust for Scotland (NTS), a charity founded in 1931 to promote the conservation of landscape and of historic buildings.

The Georgian House in Charlotte Square *(right and bottom right)* evokes elegant living in the New Town: it has been beautifully furnished to show how a wealthy family lived in the 18th century. Gladstone's Land on the Old Town's Royal Mile is a skilful restoration of a merchant's house. The six floors behind its narrow frontage were once occupied by five families, an example of a 17th-century Edinburgh skyscraper. The arcaded ground floor has been restored to its original function as a shopping booth.

ABOVE: imposing Dundas House, the registered office of the Royal Bank of Scotland, was designed in 1774 and constructed at the peak of Edinburgh's Georgian elegance.

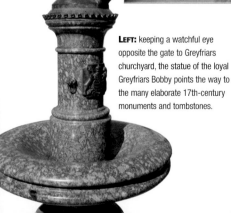

LEFT: keeping a watchful eye opposite the gate to Greyfriars churchyard, the statue of the loyal Greyfriars Bobby points the way to the many elaborate 17th-century monuments and tombstones.

LEFT AND BELOW: the attention's in the detail on Charlotte Square. New Town architecture reached its apotheosis with Robert Adam's superb design for Charlotte Square. The north frontage – the most magnificent – houses Bute House, official residence of the First Minister, and the Georgian House. On the west side is West Register House which has a green dome. The statue in the centre of the Square is of Prince Albert, consort to Queen Victoria.

GLASGOW

A city of noble character, handsome buildings and invincible spirit, Glasgow accommodates no neutrality: it is either loved or loathed by native Scots and admired or avoided by visitors

Glasgow is a city for connoisseurs. It always has been, from the days when one of its earliest tourists, the 18th-century writer Daniel Defoe, described it as "the cleanest and beautifullest and best built city in Britain", to its more recent endorsement by Bill Bryson, author of *Notes from a Small Island*. Yet there are few places in Europe that have been more publicly misunderstood and misrepresented than this monstrous, magnificent citadel to the worst and the best of commerce and capitalism, to the price and the prizes of Empire and the Industrial Revolution. And few cities can have inspired more furious conflicts of opinion of its worth, or ignited so much controversy.

Invincible spirit

Yet even in the darkest days of its reputation, when Glasgow slums and Glasgow violence were the touchstone for every sociologist's worst urban nightmares, it was still a city for connoisseurs. It appealed to those who were not insensitive to the desperate consequences of its 19th-century population explosion, when the combination of cotton, coal, steel and the River Clyde transformed Glasgow from elegant little merchant city to industrial behemoth; and who were not blind to the dire effect of 20th-century economics which, from

World War I onwards, presided over the decline of its shipbuilding and heavy industries; but who were nevertheless able to uncover, behind its grime and grisliness, a city of nobility and invincible spirit.

Its enthusiasts have always recognised Glasgow's qualities, and even at the height of its notoriety they have been able to give Glasgow its place in the pantheon of great Western cities. Today, it is fashionable to describe the city of Glasgow as European in character, for the remarkable diversity

Main attractions
PEOPLE'S PALACE
BOTANIC GARDENS
KELVINGROVE PARK
BURRELL COLLECTION
THE TALL SHIP
GLASGOW SCIENCE CENTRE
CLYDE WALKWAY
GALLERY OF MODERN ART
GLASGOW SCHOOL OF ART
HUNTERIAN ART GALLERY
GLASGOW CATHEDRAL
BARRAS MARKET

PRECEDING PAGES: the Clyde Arc. **LEFT:** Glasgow Cathedral at night. **RIGHT:** time for a chat in Buchanan Street.

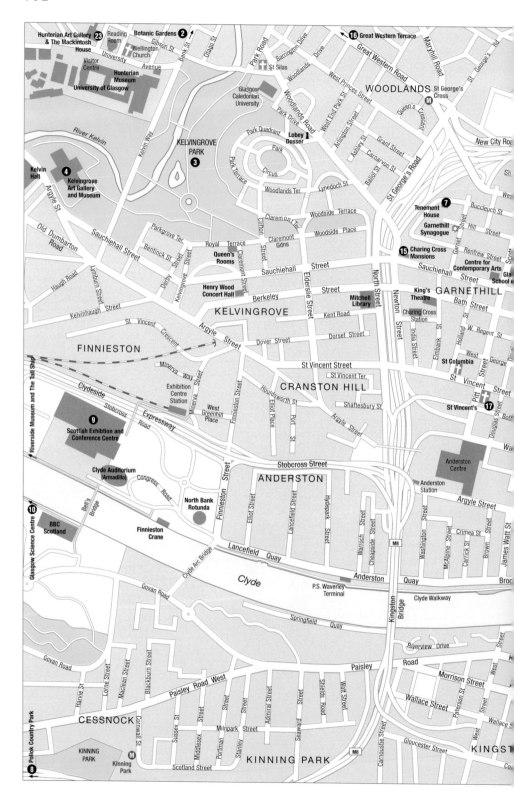

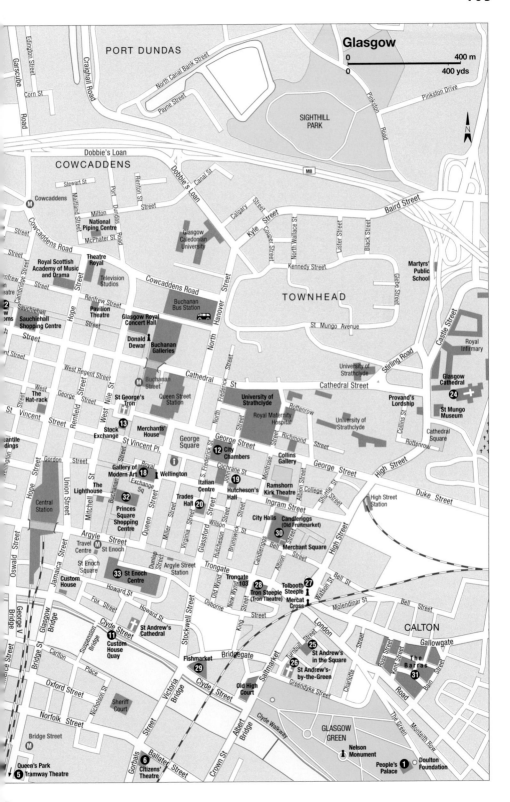

Glasgow

0 _____ 400 m
0 _____ 400 yds

PORT DUNDAS

North Canal Bank Street

Payne Street

SIGHTHILL PARK

Pinkston Drive

Pinkston Road

Dobbie's Loan

M8

COWCADDENS

Stewart St

Renton St

Canal St

Calgary Street

Kyle Street

Couper Street

Baird Street

Milton

National Piping Centre

McPhater St

Glasgow Caledonian University

TOWNHEAD

Maitland Street

Port Dundas Street

Dobbie's Loan

Kennedy Street

North Wallace St

Lister Street

Black Street

Glebe Street

Martyrs' Public School

Cowcaddens Road

Royal Scottish Academy of Music and Drama

Theatre Royal

Television Studios

Cowcaddens Road

Hanover Street

North Hanover Street

St Mungo Avenue

Stirling Road

Castle Street

Royal Infirmary

Renfrew Street

Pavilion Theatre

Buchanan Bus Station

Cathedral St

Cathedral Street

Glasgow Cathedral **24**

Sauchiehall Shopping Centre

Hope Street

West Regent Street

Glasgow Royal Concert Hall

Donald Dewar

Buchanan Galleries

University of Strathclyde

St Mungo Museum

Provand's Lordship

The Hat-rack

West George Street

West Nile Street

St George's Tron

Buchanan Street

Queen Street Station

Frederick Street

Royal Maternity Hospital

Rottenrow

University of Strathclyde

Cathedral Square

West Vincent Street

Renfield Street

Stock Exchange **13**

Merchants' House

George Street

George Square

Richmond Street

Collins St

Rottenrow

High Street

Gordon Street

Gallery of Modern Art **18**

Wellington

City Chambers **12**

S. Frederick St

Collins Gallery

George Street

mercantile buildings

Mitchell Street

The Lighthouse

Exchange Sq

Royal

Italian Centre

Cochrane St

Hutcheson's Hall **19**

Montrose

Ramshorn Kirk Theatre

Albion College St

Duke Street

High Street Station

Union Street

Central Station

Princes Square Shopping Centre **32**

Trades Hall **20**

Miller Street

Virginia Street

Wilson

City Halls

Candleriggs (Old Fruitmarket) **30**

Ingram Street

Bell Street

Argyle Street

Travel Centre

St Enoch **M**

St Enoch Square

Queen Street

Dunlop Street

Argyle Street Station

Glassford

Hutcheson

Brunswick St

Merchant Square

Candleriggs

Albion

Bell St

Jamaica Street

Custom House

St Enoch Centre **33**

Howard St

Old Wynd

New Wynd

Trongate

Trongate 103 **28**

Tron Steeple (Tron Theatre)

Tolbooth Steeple **27**

Mercat Cross

Watson St

Bell Street

CALTON

Gallowgate

Glasgow Bridge

George V Bridge

Suspension Bridge

Clyde Street

Fox Street

St Andrew's Cathedral **11**

Custom House Quay

Osborne Street

King Street

London Road

St Andrew's in the Square **25**

St Andrew's-by-the-Green **26**

Turnbull Street

Charlotte

Ross Street

Kent Street

The Barras

Bain

Molendinar St

Stockwell Street

Oxford Street

Carlton Place

Nicholson Street

Sheriff Court

Fishmarket **29**

Bridgegate

Victoria Bridge

Old High Court

Greendyke Street

Clyde Street

Albert Bridge

Clyde Walkway

GLASGOW GREEN

Nelson Monument

People's Palace **1**

Doulton Foundation

Monteith Row

The Green

Norfolk Street

Bridge Street **M**

Queen's Park **5**
Tramway Theatre

Gorbals Street

Ballater Street

Crown St

Citizens' Theatre **6**

Opened in 1983, the Burrell Gallery became the icon of the Glasgow renaissance.

BELOW RIGHT: the Finnieston Crane on the Clyde.

of its architecture and a certain levity of heart, or to compare it with North America for its gridiron street system and wisecracking street "patter".

But these resonances have long been appreciated by experienced travellers. In 1929, at a time when social conditions were at their worst, the romantic but perceptive travel writer H.V. Morton found "a transatlantic alertness about Glasgow which no city in England possesses" and – the converse of orthodox opinion – was able to see that "Edinburgh is Scottish and Glasgow is cosmopolitan".

And in 1960, the "British placetaster" Ian Nairn discovered, with quite a sense of shock, that "Glasgow was without doubt the friendliest of Britain's big cities", noting particularly that "any Glasgow walk is inflected by a multitude of human contacts – in shops, under umbrellas (there *is* a good deal of rain in Glasgow), even from policemen – and each of them seems to be a person-to-person recognition, not the mutual hate of cogs in a machine who know their plight but cannot escape it".

Culture city

Glasgow today is visibly, spectacularly, a city in transformation. It hasn't allowed its "hard, subversive, proletarian tradition" to lead it into brick walls of confrontation with central government. The result? A city which has massively rearranged its own environment; which sees its future in the service industries, in business conferences, exhibitions and indeed in tourism; which has already achieved some startling coups on its self-engineered road to becoming "Europe's first postindustrial city"; and which has probably never been more exciting to visit since, at the apogee of its Victorian vigour, Glasgow held the International Exhibition of Science and Art more than 100 years ago.

Glaswegians allow themselves a sly smile over their elevation to the first rank of Europe's cultural centres. (It was European City of Culture in 1990 and UK City of Architecture and Design in 1999, and it is to host the 2014 Commonwealth Games.) But the smile becomes a little bitter for those who live in those dismal areas of the

Fists of Iron

The Glaswegian comedian Billy Connolly said of Glasgow:"There's a lightness about the town, without heavy industry. It's as if they've discovered how to work the sunroof, or something." Yet Glaswegians themselves will admit that their positive qualities have a negative side. Even today, mateyness can turn to menace in certain dismal pubs where too much whisky is chased by too much beer. The working man's tipple here has traditionally been "a wee hauf and hauf" – a measure of whisky pursued by a half pint of beer, often replaced today by a lethal mixture of vodka and cheap wine. Religious bigotry, the obverse of honest faith, simmers below the surface, spilling out onto the streets and football terraces. And Glasgow's legendary humour, made intelligible even to the English through the success of comedians like Billy Connolly but available free on every street corner, is the humour of the ghetto. It is dry, sceptical, irreverent and often black. The Glasgow writer Cliff Hanley compares it to American-Jewish humour in its fast pace, but places it in "the hard, subversive proletarian tradition of the city".

city as yet untouched by the magic of stone-cleaning, floodlighting or even modest rehabilitation.

Defenders of the new Glasgow argue that their turn will come; that you can't attract investment and employment to a city, with better conditions for everyone, unless first you shine up its confidence on the inside and polish up its image on the outside.

Hills and water

Like the other four Scottish cities, Glasgow is defined by hills and water. Its suburbs advance up the slopes of the vast bowl that contains it, and the pinnacles, towers and spires of its universities, colleges and cathedral occupy their own summits within the bowl. It is, therefore, a place of sudden, sweeping vistas, with always a hint of ocean or mountain just around the corner.

Look north from the heights of **Queen's Park** and you will see the cloudy humps of the Campsie Fells and the precipitous banks of Loch Lomond. Look west from **Gilmorehill** to the great spangled mouth of the Clyde and you will sense the

sea fretting at its fragmented littoral and the islands and resorts that used to bring thousands of Glaswegians "doon the watter" for their annual Fair Fortnight.

The antiquity of this July holiday – Glasgow Fair became a fixture in the local calendar in 1190 – gives some idea of the long-term stability of the town on the Clyde. But for centuries Glasgow had little prominence or significance in the history of Scotland. Although by the 12th century it was both a market town and a cathedral city (with a patron saint, St Mungo) and flourished quietly throughout the Middle Ages, it was largely bypassed by the bitter internecine conflicts of pre-Reformation Scotland and the running battles with England.

Most of Scotland's trade, too, was conducted with the Low Countries from the east coast ports. But Glasgow had a university, now five centuries old, and a distinguished centre of medical and engineering studies, and it had the River Clyde. When trade opened up with the Americas across the Atlantic, Glasgow's fortune was made.

Today, the names of the streets of 18th-century Glasgow – like Virginia Street and Jamaica Street – tell something of the story which turned a small town into the handsome fief of tobacco barons, and hint at a shameful "profit" from the slave trade.

BELOW:
the Mitchell Library holds the Glasgow City Archives.

Exotic blooms thrive in the glasshouses of the Botanic Gardens.

The tobacco trade with Virginia and Maryland brought the city new prosperity and prompted it to expand westwards from the medieval centre of the High Street. (Little of medieval Glasgow remains.) In the late 18th century the urbanisation of the city accelerated with an influx of immigrants, mainly from the West Highlands, to work in the cotton mills with the new machines that had been introduced by merchants who had been forced to desert the tobacco trade. The Industrial Revolution had begun, and from then on Glasgow's destiny – grim and glorious – was fixed.

Instant city

The deepening of the Clyde up to the Broomielaw, near the heart of the city, in the 1780s and the coming of the steam engine in the 19th century consolidated a process of such rapid expansion that Glasgow has been called an "instant city". In the 50 years between 1781 and 1831 the population of the city quintupled, and was soon to be further swelled by thousands of Irish immigrants crossing the Irish Sea to

BELOW: inside the Botanic Gardens.

escape famine and seek work. The Victorians completed Glasgow's industrial history and built most of its most self-important buildings, as well as the congested domestic fortifications which were to become infamous as slum tenements. Since World War II, its population has fallen below the million mark to fewer than 600,000, the result of policies designed to decant citizens into "new towns" and the growing appeal of commuting from "green-belt" villages and towns.

An endearing name

One translation of the original Celtic is that the city's name, Glasgow, means "dear green place". Other translations include "dear stream" and "greyhound" (which some say was the nickname of St Mungo), but the green reference is most apt, for Glasgow has, after all, more than 70 parks – "more green space per head of population than any other city in Europe", as the tour bus drivers will proudly tell you.

The most unexpected, idiosyncratic and oldest of its parks, in fact, the oldest public park in Britain, is **Glasgow**

Green, once the common grazing ground of the medieval town and acquired by the burgh in 1662. To this day Glaswegians have the right to dry their washing on Glasgow Green, and its Arcadian sward is still spiked with clothes poles for their use, although there are few takers. Municipal Clydesdale horses, used for carting duties in the park, still avail themselves of the grazing, and the eccentricity of the place is compounded by the proximity of Templeton's Carpet Factory, designed in 1889 by William Leiper, who aspired to replicate the Doge's Palace in Venice. (The factory is now a business centre.)

Here, too, you will find the **People's Palace ❶** (tel: 0141-276 0788; Tue–Thur, Sat 10am–5pm, Fri, Sun 11am–5pm; free), built in 1898 as a cultural centre for the East End community, for whom its red sandstone munificence was indeed palatial. It's now a museum dedicated to the social and industrial life of the 20th-century city.

The most distinguished of the remaining 69-odd parks include the **Botanic Gardens ❷** (tel: 0141-276

1614; daily 7am–dusk; free) in the heart of Glasgow's stately West End, with another palace – the **Kibble Palace** – the most enchanting of its two large hothouses. It was built as a conservatory for the Clyde coast home of a Glasgow businessman, John Kibble, and shipped to its present site in 1873. The architect has never been identified, although legend promotes Sir Joseph Paxton, who designed the Crystal Palace in London.

Green and pleasant parks

Kelvingrove Park ❸, in the city's West End, was laid out in the 1850s and was the venue of Glasgow's principal Victorian and Edwardian international exhibitions, although that function is now performed by the modern Scottish Exhibition and Conference Centre on the north bank of the Clyde (see page 169). It is a spectacular park, traversed by the River Kelvin and dominated on one side by the Gothic pile of **Glasgow University** (this seat of learning was unseated from its original college in the High Street and rehoused on Gilmorehill in 1870) and by the

The much-loved Kelvingrove Art Gallery and Museum is the largest civic museum and art gallery in the UK, attracting over 1 million visitors a year.

BELOW:
hanging heads at the Kelvingrove Art Gallery.

A Cultural Explosion

After the decline of the shipbuilding industry, Glasgow turned its mind to creating a more refined city of culture, winning loud applause

Glasgow's elevation to the position of European City of Culture in 1990 (a title bestowed by the ministers of culture of the 12 member states of the European Community) was received with a mixture of astonishment and amusement in Edinburgh, which had long perceived itself as guardian of Scotland's most civilised values.

But, ever so quietly, Glasgow had been stealing the initiative. Edinburgh had been trying to make up its mind for nearly 30 years about building an opera house, but Glasgow went ahead and converted one of its general-purpose theatres, the Theatre Royal, into a home for the Scottish Opera and regular venue for Scottish Ballet. The city is also home to two major orchestras and the Royal Scottish Academy of Music and Drama.

Besides its traditional theatres – the King's and the Pavilion – Glasgow has the cavernous **Tramway Theatre ❺**, the former home of the city's trams and today an internationally acclaimed contemporary visual and performing arts theatre.

Peter Brook inaugurated the theatre in 1988 when he staged his ambitious, nine-hour epic *Mahabharata*, contributing to the cultural explosion that would lead to the city's prestigious title in 1990.

Studio theatres include the Tron, founded in 1979, the Mitchell Theatre, housed in an extension of the distinguished Mitchell Library, and two small theatres in the multimedia complex of the dynamic Centre for Contemporary Arts on Sauchiehall Street. However, Glasgow's most distinctive stage is the innovative **Citizens' Theatre ❻** started in 1943.

Each year, it seems, Glasgow adds a new festival to its calendar. The West End Festival, the city's biggest, has been followed by international jazz, cabaret and piping festivals, each held during successive months of the summer to keep visitors coming.

Distinguished art galleries

The turning point in Glasgow's progress towards cultural respectability came with the opening, in 1983, of the striking new building in Pollok Country Park to house the Burrell Collection, bequeathed to the city in 1944. Until recently, the enormous popularity of the Burrell Collection has tended to overshadow Glasgow's other distinguished art galleries and museums: Kelvingrove, at the western end of Argyle Street, which has a strong representation of 17th-century Dutch paintings and 19th-century French paintings as well as many fine examples of the work of the late 19th-century Glasgow Boys; the Gallery of Modern Art (GOMA), opened in 1996; the university's Hunterian Museum and Art Gallery; and the St Mungo Museum of Religious Life and Art. The McLellan Galleries, built in 1856, are currently closed.

Architecture and design

In 1999, The Lighthouse, designed by Charles Rennie Mackintosh and formerly the offices of the *Glasgow Herald*, reopened as an architecture and design centre, with displays on the work of Mackintosh, and exhibition galleries. Other museums of note are Haggs Castle, a period museum, on the South Side and the charming miniature repository of social history, the red sandstone **Tenement House ❼** (Mar–Oct daily 1–5pm; charge) a two-room-and-kitchen flat in an 1892 tenement in Garnethill, wonderfully preserved. The Museum of Transport has closed to make way for the exciting Riverside Museum on the Clyde, due to open in spring 2011. ❑

LEFT: a night at the opera.

elegant Victorian precipice of **Park Circus** on the other side.

The **Kelvingrove Art Gallery and Museum** ❹ (tel: 0141-276 9599; www. glasgowmuseums.com; Mon–Thur, Sat 10am–5pm, Fri, Sun 11am–5pm; free) includes a major collection of European paintings and extensive displays on the natural history, archaeology and ethnology of the area. It has a magnificent organ, which is regularly used for recitals, and a World War II Spitfire hangs in the main hall.

Victoria Park, near the north mouth of the Clyde Tunnel, has a glasshouse containing several large fossil trees of some 350 million years' antiquity.

Pollok Country Park ❽ on the city's south side (those who live south of the Clyde consider themselves a separate race of Glaswegian) has a well-worn path beaten to the door of the **Burrell Collection** (tel: 0141-287 2500; www.glasgowmuseums.com; Mon–Thur, Sat 10am–5pm, Fri, Sun 11am–5pm; free), where there are more than 9,000 exhibits, from artefacts of ancient civilisations to Impressionist paintings. Also in the park is the 18th-century

Pollok House, designed by William Adam (tel: 0844-493 2202; gardens and house all year daily, house 10am–5pm; charge). It, too, is an art gallery, with works by El Greco, Murillo, Goya and William Blake. The windows look out on a prizewinning herd of Highland cattle and Pollok Golf Course.

Also on the city's south side, south of Queen's Park in Cathcart, stands **Holmwood House** (tel: 0844-493 2204; Easter–Oct Thur–Mon 10am–5pm; charge), the best domestic example of the work of Alexander "Greek" Thomson, Glasgow's most famous Victorian architect. It was built in 1857–8 for a paper manufacturer, James Couper.

Old and new by the Clyde

Stobcross Quay on the north bank is the site of the ultramodern **Scottish Exhibition and Conference Centre** (SECC) ❾ and the Clyde Auditorium, known as **The Armadillo**, a 3,000-seater concert venue designed by Lord Foster. You can also marvel at the industrial colossus of the **Finnieston Crane** and **The Tall Ship** (tel: 0141-222 2513; daily Mar–Oct 10am–5pm,

The Glasgow Harbour project is an ambitious, multi-million-pound residential and leisure development transforming the banks of the Clyde.

BELOW LEFT: entrance to the Burrell Collection. **BELOW:** the Tall Ship at Glasgow Harbour.

Glasgow District Subway, opened in 1896, was one of the earliest underground train systems in Britain and the only one in the country that is called, American-style, "the Subway".

Nov–Feb 10am–4pm; charge), a three-masted Clyde-built barque (1896), with adjoining Pumphouse visitor centre and exhibition gallery.

Across Bell's Bridge is the **Glasgow Science Centre**  (tel: 0141-420 5000; www.glasgowsciencecentre.org; daily 10am–5pm; charge), a collection of futuristic buildings that includes Scotland's only **IMAX Cinema**, with an 80ft (24-metre) wide screen; the **Science Mall**, a hands-on extravaganza where visitors can explore, create and invent; and the **Glasgow Tower**, the tallest free-standing structure in Scotland and the only one in the world that will rotate through 360 degrees; the views are spectacular. To the west, beyond Stobcross Quay and adjacent to Glasgow Harbour, the £74-million futuristic **Riverside Museum**, dedicated to transport, is opening in spring 2011 and is to be The Tall Ship's new home.

A river walk

Stobcross Quay is also a terminus of the **Clyde Walkway**, an area that's part of a £1-billion 9-year-long "Clyde Waterfront Regeneration" scheme

BELOW RIGHT: taking a stroll by the River Clyde.

introducing new residential and leisure developments to the once heavily industrialised banks of the Clyde. It is possible to walk from the quay through the centre of the city past Glasgow Green to the suburb of **Cambuslang**.

Before you reach George V Bridge and Central Station's railway bridge, you come to the **Broomielaw**, an area rich in sailing history and being regenerated into the rapidly expanding financial services district with new offices and hotels. It was once the departure point for regular services to Ireland, North America and the west coast towns and islands of Scotland. You can sail "doon the watter" from here on the world's last sea-going paddle steamer, the *Waverley*, which cruises during the summer to the Firth of Clyde and the Ayrshire coast.

Custom House Quay , which looks across to the delicately restored Georgian facades of Carlton Place on the south bank, is also the subject of a major regeneration project.

The central section of the walkway is the most interesting, taking in the city's

Death on the Clyde

The old adage that "the Clyde made Glasgow and Glasgow made the Clyde" can not be taken as a true description of the relationship today. In his book *In Search of Scotland*, H.V. Morton describes the launching of a ship on the Clyde in a passage that brings tears to the eyes: "Men may love her as men love ships… She will become wise with the experience of the sea. But no shareholder will ever share her intimacy as we who saw her so marvellously naked and so young slip smoothly from the hands that made her into the dark welcome of the Clyde". That was written in 1929 – at a time when the Clyde's shipbuilding industry was on the precipice of the Great Depression from which it never recovered.

Soon another writer, the novelist George Blake, was calling the empty yards and silent cranes "the high, tragic pageant of the Clyde", and today that pageant is nothing more than a side-show. Not even the boost of demand during World War II, nor replacement orders in the 1950s, not even the work on supply vessels and oil platforms for the oil industry in the 1970s could rebuild the vigour of the Clyde. Today Glasgow no longer depends on the river for its economic survival. Developments like the Clyde Walkway, the Glasgow Science Centre and the Riverside Museum show a new future for the river in the leisure industry.

more distinguished bridges and many of the buildings associated with its maritime life. (The architectural historians Gomme and Walker identify only two bridges, the pedestrian **Suspension Bridge** and the **Victoria Bridge**, as being worthy of notice, dismissing the others as "a sorry lot".) The Victoria Bridge was built in 1854 to replace the 14th-century Old Glasgow Bridge, and the graceful Suspension Bridge was completed in 1871, designed by Alexander Kirkland, who later became the Commissioner of Public Buildings in Chicago.

There is also new life on the inner-city banks of the Clyde, as cranes and wharves are replaced by modern residential apartments. On the south bank, near Govan, up-market apartments have been built at the old **Prince's Dock**, the £20-million Clyde Arc links the Finnieston Quay with the new BBC Scotland complex on the south bank, and the massive Rotunda at the north of the old Clyde Tunnel, designed for pedestrians and horses and carts, has been restored as a restaurant complex.

Other opportunities to get on the river are offered by Seaforce, which runs powerboat trips from beside The Tall Ship, and the Clyde Waterbus, a river taxi between the Broomielaw and Braehead.

Rough sentimentalism

"Rough, careless, vulnerable and sentimental." That's how the Scottish poet Edwin Morgan, who died in August 2010 aged 90, described Glaswegians, and they are certainly qualities that Glaswegians have brought to their environment. The city has been both brutal and nostalgic about its own fabric, destroying and lamenting with equal vigour. When the city fathers built an urban motorway in the 1960s they liberated Glasgow for the motorist but cut great swathes through its domestic and commercial heart, and were only just prevented from extending the Inner Ring Road, which would have demolished in the process much of the Merchant City. But the disappearance of the last trams in the 1960s has been regretted ever since, even though Glaswegians have grown to love the "Clockwork Orange" – the violently coloured underground transport system.

But to Morgan's list of adjectives might have been added "pretentious" and "aspirational", two sides of the architectural coin that represents Glasgow's legacy of magnificent Victorian buildings. They aren't hard to find: the dense gridiron of streets around George Square and westwards invites the neck to crane at any number of soaring facades, many bearing the art of the sculptor and all signifying some chapter of the city's 19th-century history.

Victorian splendour

George Square is the heart of modern Glasgow. Like most Scottish squares, it contains a motley collection of statues, commemorating 11 people who seem to have been chosen by lottery. The 80ft (24-metre) column in its centre is mounted by the writer Sir Walter Scott, gazing southwards, so they say, to the land where he made all his money. But

TIP

Hampden Park, in the south of the city, has been redeveloped as Scotland's National Football (soccer) Stadium, with a museum of Scottish football (daily; charge).

BELOW: the Clyde Arc, locally known as the Squinty Bridge.

Glasgow City Chambers, the staircase. Sir John Betjeman, an architectural enthusiast as well as the Poet Laureate from 1972–84, described Glasgow as the "greatest Victorian city in Europe".

BELOW: George Square and Glasgow City Chambers.

the square is more effectively dominated by the grandiose **City Chambers** 🄬 (tel: 0141-287 4018; guided tours Mon–Fri at 10.30am and 2.30pm; free) designed by William Young and opened in 1888. The marble-clad interior is even more opulent and self-important than the exterior. The pièce de résistance is the huge banqueting hall, 110ft (33 metres) long, 48ft (14 metres) wide and 52ft (16 metres) high; it has a glorious arched ceiling, leaded glass windows and paintings depicting scenes from the city's history. The south wall is covered by three large murals, works of the Glasgow Boys *(see pages 87)*.

George Square's other monuments to Victorian prosperity are the former Head Post Office on the south side (now the main **Tourist Information Centre**) and the noble **Merchants' House** on the northwest corner (now home to the Glasgow Chamber of Commerce). Its crowning glory is the gold ship on its dome, drawing the eye ever upwards – a replica of the ship on the original Merchants' House.

Just off Buchanan Street is **Nelson Mandela Place** (its name having been changed from St George's Place in tribute to the South African political leader). Here you will find the **Glasgow Stock Exchange** 🄭, designed in the 1870s by John Burnet, whose reputation was to be eclipsed by his celebrated son J.J. Burnet; and the **Royal Faculty of Procurators** (1854).

Nearby are examples of the work of another distinguished Glasgow architect, the younger James Salmon, who designed the **Mercantile Buildings** 🄮 (1897–8) in Bothwell Street and the curious **Hat-rack** in St Vincent Street, named for the extreme narrowness and the projecting cornices of its tall facade. Further west, J.J. Burnet's extraordinary **Charing Cross Mansions** 🄯 of 1891, with grandiloquent intimations of French Renaissance style, were spared the surgery of motorway development which destroyed many 19th-century buildings around Charing Cross.

Magnificent terraces

On the other side of one of these motorways are the first buildings of the **Park Conservation Area**. These

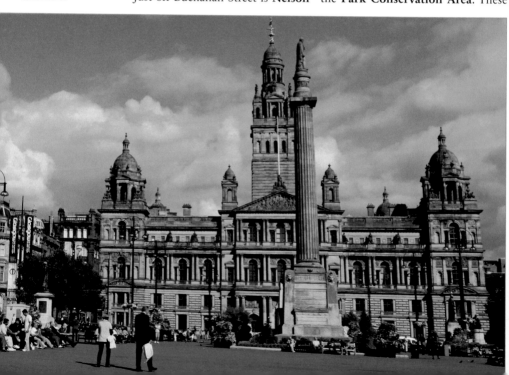

buildings have given rise to the statement that Glasgow is the "finest piece of architectural planning of the mid-19th century". Take a stroll upwards through this area to a belvedere above Kelvingrove Park and marvel at the glorious vistas.

The belvedere is backed by **Park Quadrant** and **Park Terrace**, which are probably the most magnificent of all the terraces in the Park Conservation Area. Still in the West End, in Great Western Road, you will find **Great Western Terrace** ⓰, one of the best surviving examples of the work of Alexander "Greek" Thomson, the architect who acquired his nickname as a result of his passion for Classicism.

Back towards the city centre in St Vincent Street is Thomson's prominent **St Vincent Street Church** ⓱. It is fronted by an Ionic portico, with sides more Egyptian than Greek and a tower that wouldn't have been out of place in India during the days of the Raj. Here the streets rise towards **Blythswood Square**, which was once a haunt of prostitutes but now, with its surroundings, provides a graceful

mixture of late Georgian and early Victorian domestic architecture.

Art and architecture

In Buchanan Street is the **Glasgow Royal Concert Hall**, a purpose-built venue that regularly attracts top artists and orchestras. Behind **St Vincent Place** is **Royal Exchange Square**, which is pretty well consumed by the city's **Gallery of Modern Art** ⓲ (tel: 0141-287 3050; www.glasgowmuseums.com; Mon–Sat 10am–5pm, Thur until 8pm, Sun 11am–5pm; free). The glorious building in which it is housed began life as the 18th-century mansion of a tobacco lord, and has since been a bank, the Royal Exchange, and more recently a public library and extensive archive.

Among the city centre's most distinguished Georgian buildings are **Hutcheson's Hall** ⓳, in Ingram Street, designed by David Hamilton; and, in nearby Glassford Street, **Trades Hall** ⓴, which, despite alterations, has retained the facade designed by the great Robert Adam.

But any excursion around Glasgow's

No. 7 Blythswood Square was where Madeleine Smith poisoned her French lover in 1858. She later moved to London, entertained George Bernard Shaw and married a pupil of the designer William Morris.

BELOW: busy shoppers along Buchanan Street.

Mackintosh's startling design for the School of Art was not expensive to build, thanks to its lack of ornamentation.

architectural treasures must include the work of the city's most innovative genius, Charles Rennie Mackintosh, who overturned the Victorians in a series of brilliant designs between 1893 and 1911. Mackintosh's influence on 20th-century architecture, along with his leading contribution to Art Nouveau in interiors, furniture and textile design, has long been acknowledged and celebrated throughout Europe, although all his finest work was done in and around Glasgow.

Mackintosh favourites

His sometimes austere, sometimes sensuous style, much influenced by natural forms and an inspired use of space and light, can be seen in several important buildings: his greatest achievement, designed in 1896, the **Glasgow School of Art ㉑** (tel: 0141-353 4526; www.gsa.ac.uk; guided tours, times vary so prior booking advisable; charge;) in Renfrew Street; **Scotland Street School**, on the South Side, opened in 1904 and now a Museum of Education (daily; free); and the **Martyrs' Public School** (tel: 0141-287 0500; Tue–Thur,

BELOW: Rennie Mackintosh detail in House for an Art Lover.

Sat 10am–5pm, Fri, Sun 11am–5pm; free), perched above a sliproad to the M8 motorway near Glasgow Cathedral, and now housing Glasgow Museum's Conservation Department.

In Sauchiehall Street the facade of his **Willow Tea Rooms ㉒** (1903) remains, and a room on the first floor has been turned over to teatime again, with reproduction Mackintosh furniture. But more stunning examples of his interior designs can be seen at the **Mackintosh House** at the University of Glasgow's **Hunterian Art Gallery ㉓** (tel: 0141-330 5431; www.hunterian.gla.ac.uk; Mon–Sat 9.30am–5pm; gallery free, house charge) on Gilmorehill. There, rooms from the architect's own house have been reconstructed and exquisitely furnished with original pieces of his furniture, watercolours and designs.

Also worth a visit are the **House for an Art Lover** (tel: 0141-353 4770; times vary, check first; charge) in Bellahouston Park, erected long after his death, but to his exact specifications; the **Queen's Cross Church** (tel: 0141-946 6600; Mon–Fri 10am–5pm, Mar–Oct Sun only 2–5pm; charge) in Garscube Road; and **The Lighthouse** (tel: 0141-221 6362; Mon, Wed–Sat 10.30am–5pm, Tue 11am–5pm, Sun noon–5pm; charge) in Mitchell Lane near Central Station, now a Mackintosh study centre as well as a broad-based architecture and design centre.

St Mungo's resting place

There's not much left in Glasgow that is old by British standards. The oldest building is **Glasgow Cathedral ㉔** (Mon–Sat 9.30am–5.30pm, Sun 1–5.30pm, Oct–Mar until 4.30pm; free), most of which was completed in the 13th century, though parts were built a century earlier by Bishop Jocelyn. It was completed by the first bishop of Glasgow, Robert Blacader (1483–1508). The only pre-Reformation dwelling house is **Provand's Lordship** (tel: 0141-552 8819; Mon–Thur, Sat 10am–5pm, Fri, Sun 11am–5pm; free), built in

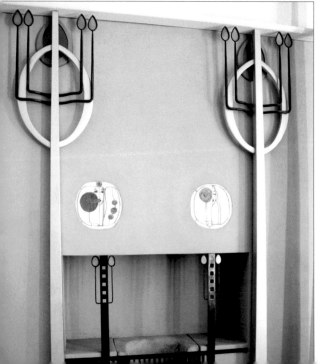

1471 as part of a refuge for poor people and extended in 1670. It now contains a museum of medieval material.

Both old buildings stand on **Cathedral Street**, at the top of the High Street – the cathedral on a site that has been a place of Christian worship since it was blessed for burial in AD 397 by St Ninian, the earliest missionary recorded in Scottish history. A severe but satisfying example of early Gothic, it contains the tomb of St Mungo.

Behind the cathedral, overseeing the city from the advantage of height, are more tombs – the intimidating Victorian sepulchres of the **Western Necropolis**. This cemetery is supervised by a statue of John Knox, the 16th-century reformer, and among the ranks of Glaswegian notables buried here is one William Miller, "the laureate of the nursery", who wrote the popular bedtime jingle, *Wee Willie Winkie*.

A cream-coloured Scottish baronial building in front of the cathedral is home to the **St Mungo Museum of Religious Life and Art** (tel: 0141-276 1625; Mon–Thur, Sat 10am–5pm, Fri, Sun 11am–5pm; free), which has a Japanese Zen garden. Don't miss the comments on the visitors' board.

The two oldest churches in Glasgow, other than the cathedral, are **St Andrew's Parish Church** ㉕, which contains some spectacular plasterwork, and the Episcopal **St Andrew's-by-the-Green** ㉖, once known as the Whistlin' Kirk because of its early organ. Both were built in the mid-18th century and both can be found to the northwest of Glasgow Green, in the Merchant City.

17th-century steeples

There you will also find two remnants of the 17th century, the **Tolbooth Steeple** ㉗ and the **Tron Steeple** ㉘. The Tolbooth Steeple, at Glasgow Cross (where the Mercat Cross is a 20th-century replica of a vanished one) is a pretty substantial remnant of the old jail and courthouses, being seven storeys high with a crown tower. The Tron Steeple was once attached to the Tron Church, at the Trongate, and dates back to the late 16th and early 17th centuries. The original church was burned down in the 18th century and the replacement now accommodates the

BELOW LEFT: Trongate, Glasgow's artistic centre.
BELOW: the Mercat Building.

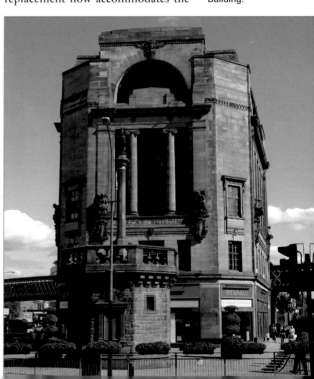

lively Tron Theatre. Just to the west is the new **Trongate 103**, an art resource venue and centre of artistic creativity housed over six storeys.

Market forces

Heavy industry has come and gone, but Glasgow still flourishes as a city of independent enterprise – of hawkers, stallholders, street traders and marketeers. Even the dignified buildings of its old, more respectable markets – fish, fruit and cheese – have survived in a city that has often been careless with its past, and have now become part of the rediscovery of the Merchant City area, which stretches from the **High Street** and the **Saltmarket** in the east to **Union Street** and **Jamaica Street** in the west. It contains most of the city's remaining pre-Victorian buildings.

The old **Fishmarket** ㉙ in Clyde Street is in fact Victorian, but it accommodates a perpendicular remnant of the 17th-century Merchants' House that was demolished in 1817. Known as the Briggait, a corruption of Bridgegate, it is now home to the Wasps Artists' Studios.

In **Candleriggs** ㉚, slightly to the

north, the old Fruitmarket now houses a variety of cafés, restaurants and shops, while Glasgow's market celebrity still belongs to the **Barras** ㉛ (Sat and Sun 10am–5pm), a thriving flea market in the Gallowgate to the east, where both repartee and bargains were once reputed to rival those of Paris's flea market and London's Petticoat Lane. Founding queen of the Barras was Mrs McIver, who started her career with one barrow, bought several more to hire out on the piece of ground she rented in the Gallowgate, and was claimed to have retired a millionaire.

Commercial interests

Argyle Street, traversed by the railway bridge to Central Station, **Sauchiehall Street** and the more up-market **Buchanan Street**, with the Buchanan Galleries complex, are Glasgow's great shopping thoroughfares, while the cosmopolitan café culture area round **Byres Road**, in the West End, is a centre for interesting bric-a-brac and boutiques. **West Regent Street** has a Victorian Village (small antique shops in old business premises) and the area around the **Italian Centre** in the Merchant City is alive with stylish café-bars.

Glaswegians have always spent freely, belying the slur on the open-handedness of Scots, and the city's commercial interests seem to believe that the appetite for shopping is insatiable. Just off Buchanan Street, up-market **Princes Square Shopping Centre** ㉜ is worth visiting even for those who don't wish to shop or eat.

The site of the demolished St Enoch Railway Station and hotel (one of Glasgow's major acts of vandalism) is now occupied by the **St Enoch Centre** ㉝, a spectacular glass-covered complex of shops, a fast-food "court", ice rink and car park. A popular "leisure and retail" development is the huge waterside **Braehead Centre**, at Renfrew on the western edge of the city.

"Edinburgh is the capital," as the old joke goes, "but Glasgow *has* the capital." And it flaunts it.   ❏

BELOW: bargains galore at Barras Market. **RIGHT:** a statue of Donald Dewar watches over Buchanan Street.

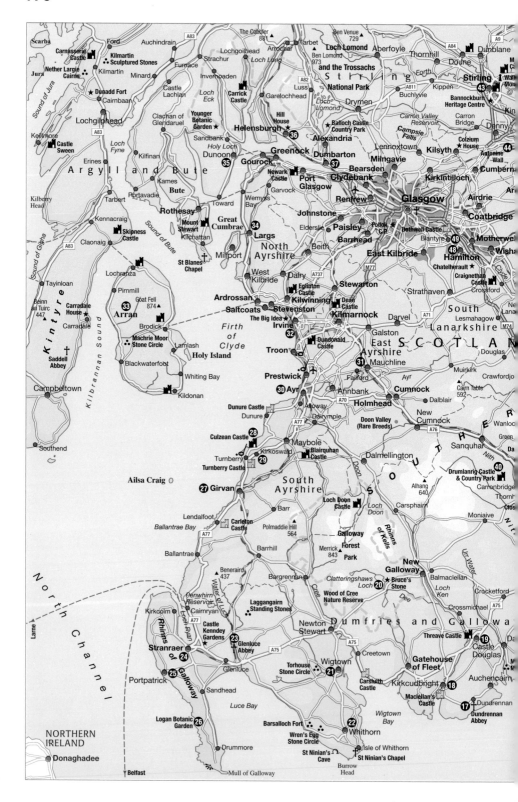

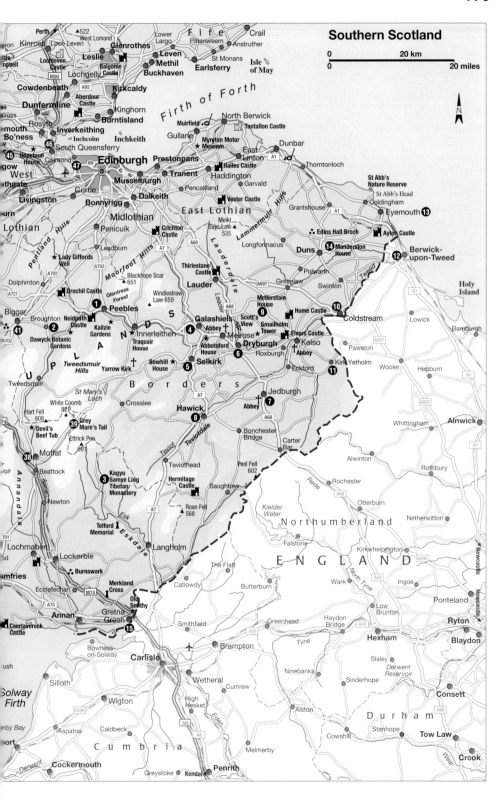

Southern Scotland

THE BORDERS

Castles, ruined abbeys, baronial mansions and evidence of past turbulent struggles against the English give the green, rolling hills of the Borders a romance all of their own

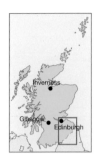

There's a mistaken assumption that, compared with all those northerly lochs and glens, rushing rivers and barren moors, the Borders have only borderline appeal. In reality this area of proud rugby-loving communities enjoys stunning scenery and a reputation for world-class mountain biking and fishing. Administratively, the Borders include the four "shires" of Peebles and Berwick in the north (though Berwick-upon-Tweed is in England) and Selkirk and Roxburgh in the south.

Quiet beginnings

Directly south of Edinburgh, the town of **Peebles ❶** owes much of its charm to its Tweedside location. Here the river already runs wide and fast. Peebles' central thoroughfare is equally wide but much more sedate. Peebles was never renowned for its hustle and bustle; an 18th-century aristocrat coined an ungenerous simile: "As quiet as the grave – or Peebles." This is no longer appropriate, for each June things liven up considerably with the week-long "Riding of the Marches" Beltane festival *(see page 102)*.

The **Cross Kirk** was erected in 1261 after the discovery of a large cross on this site. The remains include a 15th-century tower and foundations of a cloister and monastic buildings. St Andrew's Collegiate Church, the forerunner of the Cross Kirk, sits in a cemetery on the Glasgow Road. Here, too, only a tower remains; the remainder was burned by the English at the time of the sacking of the four great Border abbeys. At the bottom of Peebles High Street, the Gothic outline of Peebles Parish Church adds to the town's air of sobriety.

The **Chambers Institute**, Peebles' civic centre and home of the Tweeddale Museum, was a gift to the town

Main attractions
DAWYCK BOTANIC GARDEN
TRAQUAIR HOUSE
BOWHILL HOUSE & COUNTRY PARK
ABBOTSFORD HOUSE
DRYBURGH ABBEY
MELROSE
JEDBURGH
HAWICK
KELSO
FLOORS CASTLE
MELLERSTAIN HOUSE
BERWICK-UPON-TWEED

PRECEDING PAGES: the Hawick Common-Riding. **LEFT:** the Eildon Hills.
RIGHT: crossing the Tweed into Peebles.

Robert Smail's Printing Works in Innerleithen (Apr–Oct Thur–Mon noon–5pm, Sun 1–5pm) is a working museum, on the A72, with early 20th-century machinery and equipment, including a restored waterwheel. Visitors can watch the printer at work and can try their hand at typesetting.

from William Chambers, a native of the place and the founding publisher of Chambers Encyclopedia.

Following the Tweed

Just a few minutes out of Peebles (west on the A72), perched high on a rocky bluff overlooking the Tweed, **Neidpath Castle** is a well-preserved example of the many medieval tower houses in the region. Wordsworth visited in 1803 and wrote a famous poem lamenting the desolation caused in 1795 when the absentee landowner, the 4th duke of Queensberry, cut down all the trees for money to support his extravagant London lifestyle. Wordsworth would have been happier had he journeyed 8 miles (13km) southwest of Peebles on the B712 to the **Dawyck Botanic Garden** (tel: 01721-760 254; Feb–Nov daily from 10am, closure varies according to the season; charge), an out station of Edinburgh's Royal Botanic Garden, containing some of the oldest and tallest trees in Europe.

Continue via the B712 to **Broughton ❷**, the site of **Broughton Place**, an imposing 20th-century castellated

house that looks much older. John Buchan, author of the classic *The Thirty-Nine Steps*, grew up in this village, and just to the south is the **John Buchan Centre** (tel: 01899-221 050; www.johnbuchansociety.co.uk; Easter and May–mid-Oct daily 2–5pm; charge), a small museum dedicated to the man who eventually became governor general of Canada.

Buchan frequented the **Crook Inn**, just outside **Tweedsmuir**, 15 miles (24km) south of Broughton (at the time of writing the pub was closed, at the centre of a planning dispute). One of the oldest Border coaching inns, it has strong literary associations. Robert Burns was inspired to write his poem *Willie Wastle's Wife* in the kitchen (now the bar, with the original flagstone floor). Sir Walter Scott also visited, as did his lesser-known contemporary James Hogg, the poet known locally as "The Ettrick Shepherd".

Step southwards outside the Borders towards Eskdalemuir, and you'll be greeted by a real surprise: the **Kagyu Samye Ling Tibetan Monastery ❸** (tel: 01387-373 232; daily). Founded in

BELOW RIGHT: tranquility reigns at the Kagyu Samye Ling Tibetan Monastery.

Border Country

The River Tweed has inspired romantic Borders ballads for hundreds of years and was held by Sir Walter Scott to be the most precious river in the world. Its source is just a few miles south of the village of Tweedsmuir, and the river cuts through three of the most important Border towns: Peebles, Melrose and Kelso. Here, too, you will find rugged moorland and craggy terrain, reminiscent of the Scottish Highlands. The two highest points in the Borders, Broad Law and Dollar Law, rise to more than 2,750ft (840 metres) and 2,680ft (820 metres) respectively.

Draw a line between Hawick and Broughton and then stay south of it and you'll see the best the Borders have to offer. A popular route is the side road out of Tweedsmuir up to the Talla and Megget Reservoirs. Steep slopes and rock-strewn hillsides provide a stunning panorama as you twist and turn down to the A708, where you come to St Mary's Loch, the only loch in the Borders. If you love a good hike, follow the Southern Upland Way alongside the loch north across the moors to Traquair House, or south to the valley of Ettrick Water.

1967 for study, retreat and meditation, it's the first and largest Tibetan centre and Buddhist monastery in the West. Visitors, regardless of faith, can join free tours (booking in advance essential) around the centre's facilities.

East of Peebles on the road to Innerleithen, you will find **Kailzie Gardens** (tel: 01721-720 007; Apr–Oct daily 11am–5.30pm, Nov–Mar wild garden and woodland walks only during daylight hours; charge) adding to the beauty of the Tweed Valley with a formal walled garden, greenhouses and woodland walks. There is also a Chicken Village featuring some lovely rare breeds.

At Innerleithen on the A72 is **Traquair House** (tel: 01896-830 323; www.traquair.co.uk; daily June–Aug 10.30am–5pm, Apr, May and Sept noon–5pm, Oct 11am–4pm, Nov Sat–Sun 11am–3pm; charge), Scotland's oldest continually inhabited house (since 1107), where Mary Queen of Scots stayed with her husband Darnley in 1566. Its full history dates from the 12th century. After Bonnie Prince Charlie visited in 1745, the 5th earl of Traquair closed the Bear Gates after him and swore they would not open until a Stuart king had been restored to the throne. The wide avenue from the house to the gates has been disused ever since. The surrounding gardens include a hedge maze, crafts shops and a tearoom.

Heart of the Borders

Though it has little to tempt today's visitor, **Galashiels ❹** has played a pivotal role in the Borders' economy as a weaving town for more than 700 years. The School of Textiles and Design, founded in 1909, has helped to cement the reputation of the tartans, tweeds, woollens and other knitted materials sold in the mills here.

It is not only Galashiels that lets you sample the Borders' textiles. **Selkirk ❺** became a textile centre in the 19th century when the growing demand for tweed could no longer be met by the mills of Galashiels. Visit **Lochcarron of Scotland** at the Waverley Mill in Dundsdale Road (tel: 01750-726 100; Mon–Sat 9am–5pm; conducted mill tours Mon–Thur 10.30am, 11.30am, 1.30pm and 2.30pm;

TIP

Just 1 mile (1.6km) east of Peebles, the forests of Glentress are riddled with purpose-built mountain biking tracks (www.thehubintheforest.co.uk).

BELOW:
Traquair House.

Sir Walter Scott wrote all the Waverley *novels at Abbotsford House, but only admitted to being the author late in life, feeling that it wasn't "decorous" for a Clerk of Session to be seen writing novels.*

BELOW: the impressive collection of armoury at Abbotsford House.

charge). Other than shopping, there are several interesting places to visit, including the 18th-century **Halliwell's House Museum** (tel: 01750-20096; Easter–Oct Mon–Sat and Sun am; free), a former old ironmongers which now tells the story of Selkirk in entertaining detail.

Nearby is **Sir Walter Scott's Courtroom** (tel: 01750-20096; Easter–Sept Mon–Fri 10am–4pm, Sat 11am–5pm, May–Aug also Sun 11am–3pm, Oct Mon–Sat noon–3pm; free) where the great writer dispensed justice during his 35 years as sheriff here.

Scott's stamping ground

Don't leave the locality without visiting **Bowhill House and Country Park** (tel: 01750-22204; www.bowhill. org; house tours July daily 11am–5pm, Aug daily 2–3.30pm; country park weekends and bank holidays Apr–June 10am–5pm; charge). Bowhill is the home of the Scotts of Buccleuch and Queensberry, once one of the largest landowners of all the Border clans. More than 300 years of discerning art collecting has amassed

works by great painters such as Canaletto, Guardi, Raeburn, Reynolds and Gainsborough.

If the Borders have a sort of visitors' Mecca, then **Abbotsford House** (tel: 01896-752 043; www.scottsabbotsford. co.uk; June–Sept daily 9.30am–5pm, Mar–May and Oct Mon–Sat 9.30am–5pm, Sun 11am–4pm; charge), home of Sir Walter Scott from 1811 to 1832, undoubtedly lays claim to that title. Scott spent £50,000 and the rest of his life turning a small farm into an estate befitting his position as a Border laird.

Scott was buried at **Dryburgh** ❻, one of the four great 12th-century abbeys in the Borders (tel: 01835-822 381; daily 9.30am–5.30pm, Oct–Mar until 4.30pm; charge). While the ruins at Jedburgh, Kelso and Melrose lie near the edge of their respective towns, Dryburgh, founded by Hugh de Morville for monks from Alnwick in Northumberland, is tucked away in an idyllic location among trees by the edge of the Tweed.

Dryburgh's setting is no match for **Scott's View** on the B6356, from where there is a magnificent sweeping view

of the unmistakable triple peaks of the **Eildon Hills** (reputed to be the legendary sleeping place of King Arthur and his knights) and a wide stretch of the Tweed Valley. Scott came here many times to enjoy the panorama.

Melrose Abbey

The town of **Melrose**, between Dryburgh and Galashiels, escaped much of the industralisation that affected Selkirk, Hawick and Galashiels. **Melrose Abbey** (tel: 01896-822 562; daily 9.30am–5.30pm, Oct–Mar until 4.30pm; charge) seals the town's pedigree. The abbey was founded in 1136 by King David I, who helped to found all four of the great Border abbeys, and this was the first Cistercian monastery in Scotland. Tragically, it lay in the path of repeated English invasions long before Henry VIII made his presence felt in the 16th century. An attack in 1322 by Edward II prompted Robert Bruce to fund its restoration. The heart of King Robert I is believed to have been buried in the abbey.

Also in Melrose is **Priorwood Garden** (Apr–Oct Mon–Sat 10am–5pm, Sun 1–5pm; charge), a walled garden specialising in plants suitable for drying, and the **Trimontium Exhibition** outlining the Roman occupation of the area. Melrose is the starting point of the 60-mile (100km) **St Cuthbert's Way** walk to Lindisfarne (Holy Island) and, every April, hosts the Melrose (rugby) Sevens Tournament.

North of Melrose, on the outskirts of **Lauder**, is **Thirlestane Castle** (tel: 01578-722 430; www.thirlestanecastle.co.uk; Jul–Aug Sun–Thur 10am–3pm, May–June and Sept Sun, Wed–Thur, Oct–Mar grounds close at 5pm; charge), once the seat of the Earls of Lauderdale and still owned by their descendants. It is one of Scotland's oldest castles and has renowned 17th-century plaster ceilings.

Roman reminders

Historically, **Jedburgh** ❼ is the most important of the Border towns. It was also strategically important; as the first community across the border it often bore the full brunt of invading English armies. Earlier invaders came from even further afield: 2 miles (3km) north of Jedburgh one can follow the course of

The heart of Robert the Bruce was said to be buried near the high altar in Melrose Abbey, but excavations have failed to locate any trace of it.

BELOW: the ruins of Dryburgh Abbey.

Contrary to popular belief, the word "tweed" does not come from the river; in fact, it was originally a misprint – by an English publisher – for "tweels", the Border name for woollen fabrics.

Dere Street, the road the Romans built in southern Scotland more than 1,900 years ago.

The oldest surviving building, **Jedburgh Abbey** (tel: 01835-863 925; daily 9.30am–5.30pm, Oct–Mar until 4.30pm); charge), was founded in 1138 by Augustinian canons from northern France. Stonework in the abbey's museum dates from the first millennium AD and proves that the site had much older religious significance. Malcolm IV was crowned here, and Alexander III married his second wife in the abbey in 1285. Their wedding feast was held at nearby Jedburgh Castle, which occupied a site in Castlegate. It was demolished in 1409 to keep it out of English hands. In 1823 the **Castle Gaol** (tel: 01835-864 750; Easter–Oct Mon–Sat 10am–4.30pm, Sun 1pm castle's foundations; its museum of social history is well worth a visit.

Mary Queen of Scots

Near the High Street, displays in **Mary Queen of Scots' House** (tel: 01835-863 331; Mar–Nov Mon–Sat 10am–4.30pm, Sun 11am–4.30pm; charge) tell a short but crucial chapter in Scotland's history. It was in this house in late 1566 that Queen Mary spent several weeks recovering from a serious illness after her renowned dash on horseback to Hermitage Castle to see her injured lover James Hepburn, earl of Bothwell. Her ride resulted in a scandal that was made all the worse by the murder of her husband Darnley the following February. From then on, her downfall was steady. Years later, during her 19 years of imprisonment, Mary regretted that her life hadn't ended in the Borders: "Would that I had died in Jedburgh."

Cashmere and tweed

If you decide to retrace Mary's journey to Hermitage Castle, you're likely to pass through **Hawick** ❽ (pronounced *Hoik*). The Borders' textile industry is all around you here, not least at the Cashmere Visitor Centre (01450-371 221; Mon–Sat 9.30am–5pm). At the **Hawick Museum** in **Wilton Lodge Park** (tel: 01450-373 457; Easter–Sept Mon–Fri 10am–noon, 1–5pm, Sat–Sun 2–5pm, Oct–Mar Mon–Fri noon–

3pm, Sun 1–3pm; free) a fascinating collection of exhibits picks up older sartorial threads.

Still retaining its cobbled streets leading into a spacious square, **Kelso** is one of the most picturesque Border towns. Close to the town centre is **Kelso Abbey**, once the largest and richest of the Borders' abbeys. It suffered the same fate as those at Melrose, Jedburgh and Dryburgh and is today the least complete of all of them.

It is ironic that, while the English destroyed Kelso's abbey, the Scottish were responsible for the much greater devastation of the town of **Roxburgh** and its castle. Roxburgh had grown up on the south bank of the Tweed around the mighty fortress of Marchmount. An important link in the chain of border fortifications, Marchmount controlled the gateway to the north. In the 14th century the English took Roxburgh and its castle and used it as a base for further incursions into Scottish territory. In 1460 James II of Scotland attacked Marchmount but was killed by a bursting cannon. His widow urged the Scottish troops forward.

On achieving victory they destroyed Roxburgh's castle (to make sure it stayed out of enemy hands for good) with a thoroughness that the English would have found hard to match. Today, on a mound between the Teviot and the Tweed just west of Kelso (the plain village of Roxburgh a few miles on is no direct relation of the ancient town), only fragments of Marchmount's walls survive.

Flamboyant Floors

On the north bank of the Tweed, Kelso thrived, however. **Floors Castle** (tel: 01573-223 333; Easter–Oct daily 11am–5pm; charge) was designed by Robert Adam and built between 1721 and 1726. It owes its present flamboyant appearance to William Playfair, who remodelled and extended the castle between 1837 and 1845. An outstanding collection of German, Italian and French furniture, Chinese and Dresden

porcelain, paintings by Picasso, Matisse and Augustus John, and a 15th-century Brussels tapestry are some of the many glittering prizes that give Floors an air of palatial elegance. There is also a licensed restaurant and coffee shop.

Saved by a ballad

Smailholm Tower (tel: 01573-460 365; daily 9.30am–5.30pm, Oct–Mar 9.30am–4.30pm; charge) stands gaunt and foreboding 6 miles (10km) northwest of Kelso (B6404). Walter Scott made a deal with the owner of this superb 16th-century peel tower: in exchange for saving it, Scott would write a ballad – *The Eve of St John* – about it. Today, the stern-faced fortress is a museum of costume figures and tapestries relating to Scott's *Minstrelsy of the Borders*.

Northwest from Kelso on the A6089 is **Mellerstain House** ❾ (tel: 01573-410 225; www.mellerstain.com; July–Aug Sun, Mon, Wed and Thur 12.30–5pm, Easter weekend, May, June and Sept Sun, Wed, bank holidays 12.30–5pm, grounds open at 11.30am; charge), one of Scotland's finest Georgian

Floors Castle is the largest inhabited castle in Scotland.

BELOW:
Floors Castle.

TIP

Berwick-upon-Tweed retains its medieval street plan and has several steep, cobbled streets that are worth exploring if you are feeling energetic.

mansions and the product of the combined genius of William Adam and his son Robert. Externally it has the dignity, symmetry and well-matched proportions characteristic of the period. Inside there is furniture by Chippendale, Sheraton and Hepplewhite; paintings by Gainsborough, Constable, Veronese and Van Dyck; and some exquisite moulded plaster ceilings, doorheads and light fittings. As if all this weren't enough to impress, formal Italian gardens were laid out in 1909 to create a series of gently sloping terraces, and the house became a popular venue for fashionable dances.

Border crossings

East of Kelso the Tweed marks the natural boundary between England and Scotland. **Coldstream** ❿, one of the last towns on this river before Berwick, has little to offer the visitor other than history. The town's name was taken by the famous regiment of Coldstream Guards that was formed by General Monck in 1659 before he marched south to support the restoration of the

Stuart monarchy. The regiment today loans material to the **Coldstream Museum** (tel: 01890-882 630; Easter–Sept Mon–Sat 10am–4pm, Sun 2–4pm, Oct Mon–Sat 1–4pm; free), set up in a house that was Monck's headquarters.

Nearly 150 years earlier, in 1513, James IV of Scotland crossed the Tweed at Coldstream to attack the English with a much larger force. Though Henry VIII was at that time fighting in France (James IV's invasion was a diversion intended to aid the French) an English army was sent north to meet the threat. The encounter, which took place near the English village of Branxton but was known as the Battle of Flodden, was a military disaster for Scotland: the king, his son, and as many as 46 nobles and 9,000 men were slain.

Happier endings are to be had at **Kirk Yetholm** ⓫, just 1 mile (1.6km) away from the English border. Overlooking the village green, the Border Hotel bills itself as the "End of the Pennine Way". A few miles outside **Linton Kirk**, said to be the oldest building in continuous use for Chris-

BELOW: magnificent Manderston House.

tian worship in the area, sits proudly on a hummock of sand in a picturesque valley.

Berwick – a confusion

When it comes to identifying precise border lines, **Berwick-upon-Tweed** **12** can be forgiven for feeling a little confused. Boundaries around here lack a sense of fair play: Berwick is not part of Berwickshire. And although the town takes its name from a river that has its source in the Scottish Borders, Berwick-upon-Tweed is not part of Scotland. It's in Northumberland, England. It wasn't always like that. The town changed hands 13 times between 1147 and 1482 (when it was finally taken for England by Richard, duke of Gloucester – later Richard III).

Historically Berwick is very much a part of the Borders. The town's castle, built in the late 12th century by Henry II, once towered high above the Tweed. Much of it was demolished in 1847 to make space for the railway station, which bears an appropriate inscription by Robert Stevenson: "The Final Act Of Union". Berwick's town wall, built on the orders of Edward I, has fared better and is one of the most complete of its kind in Britain.

Situated in Scotland, along the coast just north of Berwick, **Eyemouth** **13** is a small working fishing town whose **museum** (tel: 01890-750 678; Apr–Oct Mon–Sat 10am–5pm, Sun noon–3pm; charge) vividly outlines Eyemouth's long tradition as a fishing port. The museum's centrepiece is the Eyemouth Tapestry, made by local people in 1981 to commemorate the disaster of 1881 when 189 fishermen were drowned, all within sight of land, during a storm.

A few miles north, **Coldingham's Medieval Priory** and **St Abb's Head Nature Reserve** (tel: 0844-493 2256; all year daily; free) are two further justifications for making this detour off the A1 to Edinburgh. An alternative route to Edinburgh is the A6105/A697. If you do go this way, stop at **Manderston House** **14** (tel: 01361-882 836; www.manderston.co.uk; mid-May–Sept Thur and Sun, house 1.30–5pm, gardens 11.30am–dusk; charge), just outside Duns, to enjoy "the finest Edwardian country house in Scotland". ❑

Each of the 36 bells in the servants' quarters of Manderston House has a different tone: the cacophony must have been deafening when the servants were summoned to clean the silver staircase, the only one in the world.

BELOW:
Berwick bridge spans the River Tweed.

HISTORIC CASTLES AND ABBEYS

An Englishman's home may be his castle, but for centuries and, in some instances, even today, a Scotsman's castle has been his home

Dotted throughout the Scottish landscape are more than 2,000 castles, many in ruins but others in splendid condition. The latter, still occupied, do not fulfil the primary definition of "castle" – a fortified building – but rather meet the secondary definition: a magnificent house, such as Fyvie.

Either way, all are not merely part of Scottish history: they are its essence. Many carry grim and grisly tales. Thus, Hugh Macdonald was imprisoned in the bowels of Duntulm Castle and fed generous portions of salted beef, but he was denied anything – even whisky – to drink.

In 1746 Blair Castle was, on the occasion of the Jacobite uprising, the last castle in the British Isles to be fired upon in anger. Today, the duke of Atholl, the owner of Blair Castle, is the only British subject permitted to maintain a private army, the Atholl Highlanders. Prior to the siege, Bonnie Prince Charlie slept here (visitors might be excused for believing there are few castles in Scotland where the Bonnie Prince and Mary Queen of Scots did not sleep). You, too, can sleep in Scottish castles. Culzean, Dalhousie (both Queen Victoria and Sir Walter Scott visited here) and Inverlochy all have rooms to let. And, for those eager to become a laird, don the kilt and own a castle, several are invariably on the market.

LEFT: stained glass at Stirling Castle, once called "the key to Scotland" because of its strategic position between the Lowlands and Highlands. It became a favourite residence of Stuart monarchs. Nowadays it is also the home of the regimental museum of the Argyll and Sutherland Highlanders.

ABOVE: this tranquil view of 15th-century Blackness Castle belies its formidable past. Garrison fortress and former state prison, it served to protect the port and Royal Burgh of Linlithgow.

BELOW: completed in 1511, the Great Hall of Edinburgh Castle was designed for ceremonial use but was relegated to a barracks after Oliver Cromwell's invasion of 1650. It was finally restored in 1880

SCOTTISH BORDER ABBEYS

Scotland, especially the Borders, is full of abbeys that now lie ruined but were once powerful institutions with impressive buildings. During the reign of David I (1124–53), who revitalised and transformed the Scottish Church, more than 20 religious houses were founded. Outstanding among these is a quartet of Border abbeys – Dryburgh (Premonstratensian), Jedburgh (Augustinian), Kelso (Tironensian) and Melrose (Cistercian). All have evocative ruins, though perhaps it is Jedburgh *(above and below)*, with its tower and remarkable rose window still intact, that is Scotland's classic abbey.

It was not the Reformation (1560) that caused damage to these abbeys but rather the selfishness of pre-Reformation clergy, raids in the 14th–16th centuries by both English and Scots, the ravages of weather and activities of 19th-century restorers. The concern of the Reformation, spearheaded by firebrand John Knox, was to preserve, not to destroy, the churches they needed.

Monasteries continued to exist as landed corporations after the Reformation. Why upset a system that suited so many interests? After all, the Pope, at the king's request, had provided priories and abbeys for five of James V's bastards while they were still infants.

OVE: nestling in the beautiful Perthshire countryside, Blair Castle he ancient seat of the Dukes and Earls of Atholl. Now a top itor attraction, its long history stretches back to the 13th century.

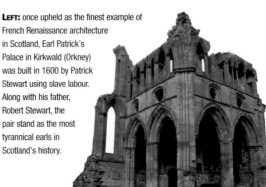

LEFT: once upheld as the finest example of French Renaissance architecture in Scotland, Earl Patrick's Palace in Kirkwald (Orkney) was built in 1600 by Patrick Stewart using slave labour. Along with his father, Robert Stewart, the pair stand as the most tyrannical earls in Scotland's history.

THE SOUTHWEST

The Southwest is gentle country, with scattered farms and villages and a dense concentration of literary associations. Its colourful and sometimes brutal history belies the comeliness of the land which sweeps down to a beautiful coastline

In the landscape and seascapes of Southwest Scotland, in the pretty villages of Dumfries and Galloway and the hill farms of South Lanarkshire, in the industrial townships of Ayrshire and the ports and holiday resorts of the Clyde coast, you will find something of the rest of Scotland. All that is missing, perhaps, is the inspiring grandeur of the West Highlands. The **Galloway Hills** are lonely, lovely places in their own right, but none rises to more than 2,800ft (850 metres).

Yet travellers from England often bypass the pastoral hinterland of the Solway in their scamper up the M74 to points north and the Highlands, hesitating only at a place which is legendary for just one reason. **Gretna Green** ⑮, just over the border (until the boundary between England and Scotland was agreed in 1552, this area was known simply as the Debatable Land), became celebrated for celebrating marriages. It was the first available community where eloping couples from England could take advantage of Scotland's different marriage laws.

Many a makeshift ceremony has been performed at the **Old Blacksmith's**, which is now a visitor centre (tel: 01461 338 441; daily 9am–5pm; free), with exhibits telling the story of the town's claim to fame and you

can still tie the knot here, like many a romantic bride and Gretna FC football fan, who still choose to be married at Gretna Green today.

The Burns legend

A few miles to the north is **Ecclefechan**, where the pretty white **Arched House** (tel: 0844-493 2247; May–Sept Fri–Mon 1.30–5.30pm; charge), in which the man of letters Thomas Carlyle was born in 1795, is now a modest literary shrine. But the Southwest is more inescapably identified with the poet Robert

Main attractions
DUMFRIES
KIRKCUDBRIGHT
GALLOWAY FOREST PARK
ISLE OF WHITHORN
CULZEAN CASTLE
BURNS NATIONAL HERITAGE PARK
SCOTTISH MARITIME MUSEUM
ARRAN
ISLAND OF BUTE
DRUMLANRIG CASTLE
NEW LANARK

PRECEDING PAGES: Culzean Castle. **LEFT:** Threave Castle. **RIGHT:** wedding day at Gretna Green.

TIP

End your tour of Burns country with a drink at the Globe Inn (est. 1610) in Dumfries, where you can sit in the poet's favourite chair.

Burns, whose short life and legend remains an integral part of the Scottish tourist scene.

The urban centres of the Burns industry are Dumfries and Ayr. **Dumfries ⑯** is also "the Queen of the South", an ancient and important Border town whose character survives the unsightly housing estates and factories on its periphery, and which is within easy reach of the haunting, history-rich Solway coast. Burns, the farmer-poet, took over Ellisland Farm some 6 miles (10km) outside the town in 1788, built the farmhouse and tried to introduce new farming methods. His venture collapsed and he moved to Dumfries to become an exciseman, but **Ellisland** (tel: 01387-740 426; Apr–Sept Mon–Sat 10am–1pm, 2–5pm, Sun 2–5pm, Oct–Mar Tue–Sat 2–5pm; charge), where he wrote *Tam o'Shanter* and *Auld Lang Syne*, is now a museum. So is **Burns House** (tel: 01387-255 297; Apr–Sept Mon–Sat 10am–1pm, 2–5pm, Sun 2–5pm; Oct–Mar Tue–Sat 2–5pm; free) in Mill Vennel (now Burns Street), Dumfries, where he died in 1796 at the age of 37.

To bring it all together, visit the stone mill on the River Nith. This is home to the **Robert Burns Centre** (tel: 01387-253 374; Apr–Sept Mon–Sat 10am–1pm, 2–5pm, Sun 2–5pm; Oct–Mar Tue–Sat 2–5pm; free).

Around Dumfries

The handsome waterfront of the **River Nith**, with its 15th-century bridge, and the red sandstone dignity of nearby **St Michael's Church**, in whose churchyard Burns is buried, give Dumfries its distinctive character. Its environs have just as much to offer. On opposing banks of the Nith estuary, where it debouches into the Solway, are **Caerlaverock Castle** (tel: 01387-770 244; daily 9.30am–5.30pm, Oct–Mar 9.30am–4.30pm; charge), the **Wildfowl and Wetlands Trust Reserve** (tel: 01387-770200; daily 10am–5pm; charge) – a winter haunt of wildfowl – and **Sweetheart Abbey** (tel: 01387-850 397; Apr–Sept daily 9.30am–5.30pm, Oct until 4.30pm, Nov–Mar Mon–Wed, Sat–Sun 9.30am–4.30pm; charge).

The castle is strikingly well preserved, dates back to the 13th century

BELOW: plaques at Burns House.
BELOW RIGHT: one of the Glenkiln sculptures at Shawhead.

and was the seat of the Maxwell family, later earls of Nithsdale – one of the most powerful local dynasties. It was besieged by Edward I during the Wars of Independence and in 1640 fell to a 13-week siege mounted by the Covenanters *(see page 34)*.

The graceful ruin of Sweetheart Abbey, in the pretty village of New Abbey, is a monument to the marital devotion of the noble Devorgilla Balliol, who not only founded this Cistercian abbey in 1273 but founded Balliol College, Oxford, in memory of her husband. She also carried his heart around with her until her own death in 1290, when she and the heart were buried together in front of the high altar.

The shallow estuary of the Solway is noted for the speed of its tidal race and the treachery of its sands, but the hazardous areas are well signposted, and if you follow the coastal roads from River Nith to **Loch Ryan** you will find an amiable succession of villages, yachting harbours, attractive small towns and good beaches, not to mention many secret coves and snug, deserted little bays.

Ancient Galloway

This is the ancient territory of Galloway, whose people once fraternised with Norse raiders and whose lords preserved a degree of independence from the Scottish crown until the 13th century. Many of Scotland's great names and great causes have seen action among these hills and bays. At **Dundrennan Abbey** ⓱ (tel: 01557 500262; Apr–Sept daily 9.30am–5.30pm, Oct–Mar Sat–Sun 9.30am–4.30pm); charge), 7 miles (11km) southeast of Kirkcudbright on the A711, Mary Queen of Scots is believed to have spent her last night in Scotland, on 15 May 1568, sheltering in this 12th-century Cistercian house on her final, fatal flight from the Battle of Langside to her long imprisonment in England.

Kirkcudbright ⓲ (pronounced *Kir-koo-bree*), at the mouth of the River Dee, has the reputation of being the most attractive of the Solway towns, with a colourful waterfront (much appreciated and colonised by artists) and an elegant Georgian town centre. Little remains of the Kirkcudbright

The Tolbooth at Kirkcudbright once entertained John Paul Jones, who was imprisoned for the manslaughter of his ship's carpenter. Jones restored his reputation in later life by laying the foundations of the American navy.

BELOW:
the ruins of
Dundrennan Abbey.

Castle Douglas serves as a market centre for a large tract of Galloway's rich hinterland, giving it some of the best food shops in the south of Scotland – particularly butchers.

BELOW: take the boat to Threave Castle.

which took its name from the vanished Kirk of Cuthbert, but it has a **Market Cross** of 1610 and a **Tolbooth** from the same period.

Broughton House (tel: 0844-493 2246; Easter–Oct daily noon–5pm; charge) in Kirkcudbright was the home of E.A. Hornel, one of the Glasgow Boys (*see page 87*), and has a major gallery of his paintings. Don't miss the wonderful Japanese-style garden, inspired by his visit to Japan in 1893.

Ten miles (16km) northeast from Kirkcudbright is another neat and dignified little town, **Castle Douglas** ⓲, on the small loch of Carlingwark, where you will find a formidable tower stronghold. **Threave Castle** (tel: 07711-223 101; Apr–Sept daily 9.30am–5pm; charge) was built towards the end of the 14th century by the wonderfully named Archibald the Grim, third earl of Douglas. It has associations with the Covenanters, who seized it in 1640 and vandalised the interior. **Threave Garden** (tel: 0844-493 2245; Apr–Oct daily 10am–5pm, check for other times of year; charge) has superb flower, plant and

tree displays all year. It is possible to visit the baronial Threave House by guided tour only.

Villages of Galloway

In Galloway you will find pretty villages, whose characteristic whitewashed cottages with black-bordered doors and windows look as if they have taken their colour scheme from the black and white Belted Galloway cattle.

Many of the most pleasant villages – **New Galloway**, **Balmaclellan**, **Crossmichael** – are in the region of long, skinny **Loch Ken**, which feeds the River Dee. To the west, shrouding the hills to the very shoulders of the isolated **Rhinns of Kells**, a tableland of hills around 2,600ft (800 metres), lies the massive Galloway Forest Park, 150,000 acres (60,000 hectares) crisscrossed by Forestry Commission walking and mountain biking trails and the Southern Upland Way.

Among the trees you will find **Clatteringshaws Loch** ⓴, 12 miles (19km) northeast of Newton Stewart (a "planned town" built in the late 17th century by a son of the earl of Galloway) on the A712. This is the site of the **Clatteringshaws Forest Wildlife Centre** (tel: 01671-402 420; Apr–Oct daily 10.30am–5pm, Sept–Oct 10.30am–4.30pm; free) and a fascinating introduction to the range of the area's natural history.

Nearby, **Bruce's Stone** represents the site of the Battle of Rapploch Moss, a minor affair of 1307 but one in which the energetic Robert the Bruce routed the English. There are, in fact, two Bruce's Stones in **Galloway Forest Park**, which creeps within reach of the coast at Turnberry, where Robert may have been born. The second stone – reached only if one backtracks from Newton Stewart and then travels northwest for 10 miles (16km) on the A714 before taking an unmarked road to the east – is poised on a bluff above Loch Trool and recalls the stones hefted down the hill by the hero in another successful wrangle with the English.

About 4 miles (6km) away is a sombre landmark: the **Memorial Tomb** of six Covenanters murdered at prayer. It is a simple stone that records their names and the names of their killers.

Saints and stones

Back on the coast, the A75 between benign **Gatehouse of Fleet** and **Creetown**, which hugs the sea below the comely outriders of the distinctive hill, **Cairnsmore of Fleet**, was said by Thomas Carlyle to be the most beautiful road in Scotland. It has good views across **Wigtown Bay** to the flat green shelf, which was the cradle of Scottish Christianity. The **Creetown Gem Rock Museum** (tel: 01671-820 357; www.gemrock.net; daily Apr–Sept 9.30am–5.30pm, Oct–Mar 10am–4pm; charge) has a wide range of precious stones on display.

On the other side of the bay is the pleasant town of **Wigtown** ㉑, whose **Martyrs' Monument** is one of the most eloquent testaments to the Covenanters, who were heroically supported in the Southwest – the site of the stake where in 1685 two women,

one elderly and one young, were left to drown on the estuary flats.

On the promontory south of Wigtown, the coast becomes harsher and the villages bleaker, as if it indeed required the gentling influence of Christianity. **Whithorn** ㉒ is the birthplace of Christianity in Scotland, and the **Whithorn Story Visitor Centre** (tel: 01988-500 508; Easter–Oct daily 10.30am–5pm; charge), in the town centre, is on the site of the first known Christian church in Britain, built by St Ninian around the year 400. Next to the centre is the **Priory** where Mary Queen of Scots once stayed. Here you will find the Latinus Stone of 450, the earliest Christian memorial in Scotland, as well as a significant collection of early Christian crosses and stones.

Four miles (6km) away is the misnamed **Isle of Whithorn**, which is a delightful town built around a busy yachting harbour and with more St Ninian connections: there is the ruined **St Ninian's Chapel**, which dates from 1300 and may have been used by overseas pilgrims; and along

TIP

Portpatrick is the start of the Southern Upland Way, a coast-to-coast route across southern Scotland which runs for 212 miles (340km) to Cockburnspath on the Berwickshire coast.

BELOW: Bruce's stone at the entrance to Glen Trool.

The Ploughman Poet

Robert Burns is Scotland's national treasure, keeping the home fires burning across the world with his poems and ideals, even in Russia

Few poets could hope to have their birthday celebrated in the most unexpected parts of the world 200 years after their death. Yet the observance of Burns Night, on 25 January, goes from strength to strength. It marks the birth in 1759 of Scotland's national poet, Robert Burns, one of seven children born to a poor Ayrshire farmer. It was an unpromising beginning, yet today Burns's verses are familiar in every English-speaking country and are especially popular in Russia, where Burns Night is toasted with vodka. Millions who have never heard of Burns have joined hands and sung his words to the tune of that international anthem of good intentions, *Auld Lang Syne* (dialect for "old long ago"):

Should auld acquaintance be forgot,
And never brought to mind?
Should auld acquaintance be forgot,
And days o' auld lang syne?

This was one of many traditional Scottish songs

which he collected and rewrote, in addition to his original poetry. He could and did write easily in 18th-century English as well as in traditional Scots dialect (which, even in those days, had to be accompanied by a glossary). His subjects ranged from love songs (*Oh, my luve's like a red, red rose*) and sympathy for a startled fieldmouse (*Wee, sleekit, cowrin', tim'rous beastie*) to a stirring sense of Scottishness (*Scots, wha hae wi' Wallace bled*) and a simple celebration of the common people (*A man's a man for a' that*).

An amorous laddie

The key to Burns's high standing in Scotland is that, like Sir Walter Scott, he promoted the idea of Scottish nationhood at a time when it was in danger of being obliterated by the English. His acceptance abroad, especially in Russia, stems from his championing of the rights of ordinary people and his satirical attack on double standards in Church and State.

An attractive and gregarious youth, Burns had a long series of amorous entanglements and, once famous, took full advantage of his acceptance into Edinburgh's high society. Finally, he married Jean Armour, from his own village, and settled on a poor farm at Ellisland, near Dumfries. No more able than his father to make a decent living from farming, he moved to Dumfries in 1791 to work as an excise officer. It was a secure job, and riding 200 miles (320km) a week on horseback around the countryside on his duties gave him time and inspiration to compose prolifically. His affairs continued: the niece of a Dumfries innkeeper became pregnant, but died during childbirth. Four years later, in 1796, Burns too was dead, of rheumatic heart disease. He was 37.

International fame

The 612 copies of his first edition of 34 poems sold in Kilmarnock in 1786 for the sum of three shillings (15p); today each copy will fetch around £10,000. Almost 100,000 people in more than 20 countries belong to Burns clubs, and the poet's popularity embraces the unlikeliest locations. The story is told, for example, of a local man who rose to propose a toast at a Burns Night supper in Fiji. "You may be surprised to learn that Scottish blood flows in my veins," he declared. "But it is true. One of my ancestors ate a Presbyterian missionary." ❑

LEFT: Burns, pictured at Alloway.

the coast is **St Ninian's Cave**, which is believed to have been used by the saint as an oratory.

Just inland from the undistinguished shoreline of Luce Bay, playground of the Ministry of Defence, are some relics of the Iron Age and Bronze Age, including **Torhouse Stone Circle**, a ring of 19 boulders standing on a low mound. The most impressive sight in this corner, however, is **Glenluce Abbey** ㉓ (tel: 01581-300 541; Apr–Sept daily 9.30am–5.30pm; charge), a handsome vaulted ruin dating from the 12th century.

Rhinns of Galloway

From Glenluce the traveller crosses the "handle" of that hammer of land called the **Rhinns of Galloway**, the southwest extremity of Scotland terminating in the 200ft (60-metre) high cliffs of the Mull of Galloway, from which Ireland seems within touching distance.

At the head of the deep cleft of **Loch Ryan** is the port of **Stranraer** ㉔, market centre for the rich agricultural area, modest holiday resort and Scotland's main seaway to Northern Ireland. The Rhinns' other main resort is **Portpatrick** ㉕, and

among the somewhat limited attractions of this remote peninsula are two horticultural ones: the subtropical plants of **Logan Botanic Garden** ㉖ (tel: 01776-860 231; daily Apr–Sept 10am–6pm, mid-Mar–Oct 10am–5pm; charge) and the great monkey puzzle trees of **Castle Kennedy Gardens**, near Stranraer (tel: 01776-702 024; Easter–Sept daily 10am–5pm; charge).

Stranraer's trunk roads are the A75, infamous for the volume of heavy traffic disembarking from the ferries from Ireland, which strikes east to Dumfries and points south and blights Thomas Carlyle's "loveliest stretch" between Creetown and Gatehouse of Fleet; and the A77, which takes you north past the cliffs of **Ballantrae** (*not* the Ballantrae of R.L. Stevenson's novel) to the mixed pleasures of Ayrshire and, ultimately, to the edge of the Glasgow conurbation.

En route is the pleasant resort of **Girvan** ㉗, first of a series of resorts interspersed with ports and industrial towns, stretching to the mouth of the Clyde. About 10 miles (16km) offshore is a chunky granite monolith over 1,000ft (300 metres) high – the uninhabited

The picturesque waterfront at Portpatrick.

BELOW: the Portpatrick Hotel.

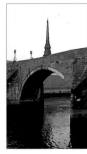

According to Burns, Ayr was unsurpassed "for honest men and bonnie lasses".

BELOW: the clifftop Culzean Castle.

island of **Ailsa Craig**, sometimes called Paddy's Milestone for its central position between Belfast and Glasgow.

Here, too, you begin to see more clearly the mountains of Arran and the lower line of the Kintyre peninsula, while at **Turnberry**, a Mecca for golfers and site of some castle ruins, promoted as the birthplace of Robert the Bruce, there is a choice of roads to Ayr.

On the trail of Burns

The coast road (A719) invites you to one of the non-Burnsian showpieces of Ayrshire – **Culzean Castle** (tel: 0844-493 2149; www.culzeanexperience.org; castle Mar–Oct daily 10.30am–5pm; charge; country park daily all year 9.30am–sunset; free), magnificently designed by Robert Adam and built between 1772 and 1792 for the Kennedy family. Now owned by the National Trust for Scotland, it has a country park of 560 acres (226 hectares) – the first in Scotland. A few miles beyond Culzean, the road entertains drivers at the **Electric Brae**, where an optical illusion suggests you are going downhill rather than up.

The inland road (A77) takes you

through **Kirkoswald** , where Burns went to school, and the first of the cluster of Burns shrines and museums: **Souter Johnnie's Cottage** (tel: 0844-493 2147; Apr–Sept Fri–Tue 11.30am–5pm; charge), once the home of the cobbler who was the original Souter Johnnie in *Tam O'Shanter*. The B7024 then leads to the Mecca of Burns pilgrims, the village of **Alloway**, where he was born.

Here, within the **Burns National Heritage Park** (tel: 01292-443 700; www. burnsheritagepark.com), you can visit **Burns Cottage** (daily Apr–Sept 10am–5.30pm, Oct–Mar 10am–5pm; charge); **Alloway Kirk** (where his father is buried and which features in *Tam O'Shanter*); the pretentious **Burns Monument** (a neoclassical temple) and the 13th-century **Brig o' Doon**, whose single span permitted Tam o' Shanter to escape from the witches. There is also the **Burns Museum** (times as Burns Cottage) and the audiovisual **Tam O'Shanter Experience** (daily Apr–Sept 10am–5.30pm, Oct–Mar 10am–5pm; charge). The park has been undergoing major redevelopment with a new museum, the **Robert Burns Birthplace Museum** (times as Burns Cottage).

You are now on the doorstep of **Ayr** , a bustling resort associated not only with Burns but also with the warrior-patriot William Wallace, who is thought to have been born in **Elderslie**, near Paisley, and who was once imprisoned in Ayr.

Inland from Ayr, to the west and north, is another clutch of Burns associations: the village of **Mauchline** , where he married Jean Armour and where their cottage is now yet another museum (tel: 01290-550 045; Tue–Sat 10am–4pm; charge); and **Poosie Nansie's Tavern** (still a pub), which inspired part of his cantata *The Jolly Beggars*. Nearby at **Failford** is Highland Mary's Monument, which allegedly marks the spot where Burns said farewell to his doomed fiancée Mary Campbell; and then there is the sprawling town of **Kilmarnock**, where the first edition of his poems was published in 1786. A hun-

dred years afterwards the town built a monument in his honour.

Coasts and islands

The A77 from Kilmarnock takes you straight into Glasgow. But if you are island or Highland bound, you should return to the coast for ferries to the Cowal peninsula and Clyde islands. **Irvine** ❷ is the home of the **Scottish Maritime Museum** (tel: 01294-278 283; www.scottishmaritimemuseum.org; Apr–Oct daily 10am–5pm; charge). Visitors can board various well-restored vessels, including the steam yacht *Carola*, tour a restored, 1920s' shipyard worker's tenement flat and relax in Puffers Coffee Shop. Nearby is the **Magnum Centre**, one of Scotland's largest leisure centres. South of Irvine are two golfing resorts, **Troon** and **Prestwick**.

Ardrossan serves the island of **Arran** ❸, the ferries disembarking passengers and cars at **Brodick**, the capital. Arran is popular with walkers and climbers (the sharp profile of the Arran ridge, which reaches 2,866ft/874 metres at the rocky summit of Goatfell, provides stunning views). Yet the 2-mile (3km) walk from

Brodick's attractive harbour to **Brodick Castle** (tel: 0844-493 2152; Easter–Oct Sat–Wed 11am–4pm; country park daily all year 9.30am–sunset; charge), is congenial and effortless. The castle parts of which date from the 14th century, is the ancient seat of the dukes of Hamilton. It contains paintings and objets d'art from their collections, and has an excellent tearoom serving traditional food.

Other villages include **Lochranza**, **Blackwaterfoot**, **Whiting Bay** and **Lamlash**, where precipitous **Holy Island** spans the mouth of the bay. St Molaise, once lived in a cave on its west coast. It is now a Buddhist retreat.

Bute *(see box below)*, another Clyde island, with the attractive, ancient capital of **Rothesay**, was a premier destination for day-trippers on the Clyde paddle steamers taking Glaswegians "doon the watter", as was the little island of **Great Cumbrae** with its family resort of **Millport**. This is reached from **Largs** ❹, the most handsome of the Clyde resorts and the scene, in 1263, of a battle that conclusively repelled persistent Viking attempts to invade Scotland. The **Vikingar!** centre (tel: 01475-689 777; daily

The woodland garden of Brodick Castle is justly claimed to be one of the finest rhododendron gardens in Britain.

BELOW LEFT: the home of the village shoemaker, John Davidson.

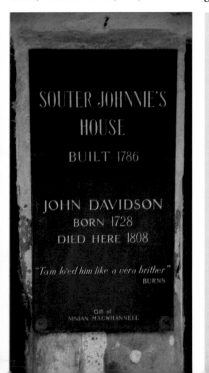

The Island of Bute

Bute is a comely island, especially at its northern end where the narrow Kyles of Bute almost close the gap with the Cowal peninsula (ferry). Rothesay, Bute's capital, is a royal burgh which gives the title of duke to the Prince of Wales. Its unusual moated ruined castle with four round towers dates back to the early 13th century, when it was stormed by Norsemen, soon to be routed at Largs. Its Winter Garden (with a Discovery Centre) and elegant promenade are especially busy in summer. It's worth spending a penny to see the restored Victorian toilets at the pierhead.

Mount Stuart (tel: 01700-503 877; www.mountstuart.com; May–Sept daily, times vary; charge) 3 miles (5km) south of Rothesay, is an astonishing Gothic fantasy pile, with humorous details. It reflects the 3rd marquis of Bute's fascination with astrology, mythology and religion. Its extensive grounds are enchanting.

Two sandy beaches at Ettrick Bay and Kilchattan Bay, on the east coast, are popular spots. However, it's easy to escape to the hills: the view from Canada Hill once won the award for the best view in Britain.

The Grey Mare's Tail waterfall near Moffat drops 200ft (60 metres) from a hanging valley.

Apr–Sept 10.30am–5.30pm, Oct, Mar 10.30am–3.30pm, Nov, Feb Sat–Sun 10.30am–3.30pm; charge) dramatically traces the history of the Vikings in Scotland. The ferry to Bute is from **Wemyss Bay**, between Largs and Gourock. From Gourock you can also board a ferry for Dunoon and the Cowal peninsula.

Escaping the city

For many people in West Central Scotland, the Cowal peninsula represents Highland escapism. It has a new population of second-home owners from the Glasgow conurbation, which makes it busy during weekends and holidays, despite the time it takes to negotiate its long fissures of sea lochs (**Loch Fyne** to the west and **Loch Long** to the east, with several others in between).

Dunoon ⑤ is its capital, another ancient township turned holiday resort, with a 13th-century castle, of which only remnants remain on **Castle Hill**, where you will again meet Highland Mary.

East of Gare Loch, the Clyde begins to be compressed between the once great shipbuilding banks of **Clydeside**, with its first resort town on the north bank

at **Helensburgh** ㊱, now a stately dormitory for Glasgow. Those smitten with Charles Rennie Mackintosh will enjoy **Hill House** (tel: 0844-493 2208; Easter–Oct daily 1.30–5.30pm; charge), his finest domestic commission.

Industrial **Dumbarton** ㊲ is even closer to the city and its name confirms it has been there since the days of the Britons. Its spectacular lump of rock was their fort, and supports a 13th-century castle which has close connections with – inevitably – Mary Queen of Scots.

Hidden treasures

The eastern edge of Southwest Scotland is dominated by the M74, the frenzied highway that is Glasgow's access to the Borders and England. It carves through some of the shapeliest hills in Scotland, with some lovely, lonely places and unexpected treasures tucked away.

A detour brings you to **Moffat** ㊳, an elegant former spa town with the broadest main street in Scotland. Northwest of Moffat is the **Devil's Beef Tub**, a vast, steep, natural vat in the hills where Border raiders used to hide stolen cattle. Northeast of Moffat on the A708 is the spectacular **Grey Mare's Tail** ㊴ waterfall. Further north is **Tibbie Sheil's Inn**, the meeting place of the circle of writer James Hogg (the "Ettrick Shepherd").

On either side of the M74, a few miles driving will take you to the highest villages in Scotland: **Leadhills** and **Wanlockhead**. Once centres of mining, an idea of their past can be seen at the **Wanlockhead Museum of Lead Mining** (tel: 01659-74387; Apr–Oct daily 11am–4.30pm, July–Aug 10am–5pm; charge). Here, too, are Drumlanrig Castle, the historic market town of Lanark and the lush orchards and dramatic falls of the River Clyde.

Drumlanrig Castle and Country Park ㊵ (tel: 01848-331 555; www.drumlanrig.com; Apr–Aug daily 11am–4pm; charge) is at the bottom of the precipitous **Dalveen Pass**, a natural stairway between the uplands of South Lanarkshire and the rolling pastures and woodland of Dumfriesshire. It is a palace of

pink sandstone fashioned in late 17th-century Renaissance style on the site of an earlier Douglas stronghold and near a Roman fort. Its rich collection of French furniture and Dutch paintings (Holbein and Rembrandt) includes interesting relics of Bonnie Prince Charlie.

The A73 to **Lanark** skirts **Tinto Hill**, the highest peak in Lanarkshire and the site of Druidic festivals. Lanarkshire schoolchildren traditionally carry stones up to add to its enormous cairn.

Hiding place for Wallace

Biggar ❹ is a lively little town, with museums focusing on local history as if in defiance of the greater celebrity of its big neighbour, **Lanark**. The high, handsome old royal burgh was already important in the 10th century, when a parliament was held there, but is more closely identified with William Wallace. It is said that he hid in a cave in the Cartland Craigs, just below the town, after killing an English soldier in a brawl.

Lanark was also a Convenanting centre and is still a place of great character, much of it due to its weekly livestock market and the steep fall of the Clyde

below the town at **New Lanark** ❷, Scotland's most impressive memorial to the Industrial Revolution and a World Heritage Site. Here, between 1821 and 1824, a cotton spinning village became the scene of the pioneering social and educational experiment of Robert Owen. The handsome buildings have been regenerated and feature an imaginative Visitor Centre (tel: 01555-661 345; www.newlanark.org; daily 11am–5pm; charge).

Nearby, the cataracts of the **Falls of Clyde Nature Reserve** are the preface to one of the river's prettiest passages, its last Arcadian fling among the orchards and market gardens of Kirkfieldbank, Hazlebank and Rosebank before it reaches industrial North Lanarkshire.

Near the pastoral village of **Crossford**, is one of Scotland's best-preserved medieval castles. **Craignethan Castle** (tel: 01555-860 364; Apr–Sept daily 9.30am–5.30pm, Nov–Mar Sat–Sun 9.30am–4.30pm; charge), was built between the 15th and 16th centuries not far from the Clyde, and was a stronghold of the Hamiltons, friends of Mary Queen of Scots. It claims to be the original Tillietudlem in Sir Walter Scott's *Old Mortality*. ❑

The first duke of Queensberry, for whom Drumlanrig Castle was built, was so horrified by its cost that he spent only one night in it.

BELOW: Corra Linn (waterfall) in full flow.

FORTH AND CLYDE

Standing strategically as the gateway to the
Highlands, the ancient town of Stirling is a focal
point for any visit to Central Scotland and the
waterways of the Forth and Clyde

For centuries, Stirling's Old Bridge
has given access to the north
across the lowest bridging point
of the River Forth, while the 250ft
(75-metre) volcanic plug, which supports the castle, was the natural fortress that made **Stirling ⓭** significant
from the 12th century onwards.

The **Castle** (tel: 01786-450 000; www.
stirlingcastle.gov.uk; daily 9.30am–6pm
Oct–Mar 9.30am–5pm; charge) – every
bit as impressive as Edinburgh Castle
– was the favourite residence of the
Stuart monarchy and is one of Scotland's Renaissance glories (see box on
page 212). Nearby is the **Royal Burgh
of Stirling Visitor Centre** (tel: 01786-
479 901; daily Apr–Oct 9.30am–6pm,
Nov–Mar 9.30am–5pm; free), which
vividly describes the long history of the
castle and the city.

City transformation

One of Scotland's oldest and most
atmospheric towns, Stirling became
Scotland's newest city in 2002 to
mark Queen Elizabeth II's Golden
Jubilee. Its city status owes much to
its excellent university, a new national
park on its doorstep, a huge regeneration project, a growing population
and a good quality of life.

Stirling's historic past is well docu-
mented but it is its modern attitudes
that make it a great destination in
which to spend some time, owing to
its cutting-edge culture and first-class
art venues. You can take the historic
Old Town Walk one day, then mingle
with the locals in the excellent shopping areas, or take in an evening at the
theatre, the next.

One of the top art venues of the
city is the **Stirling Smith Art Gallery and Museum** (Dunbarton Road;
tel: 01786-471 971; www.smithartgallery.
demon.co.uk; Tue–Sat 10.30am–5pm,

Main attractions
STIRLING
WALLACE MONUMENT
ALLOA TOWER
FALKIRK WHEEL
LINLITHGOW PALACE
SOUTH QUEENSFERRY
INCHCOLM ABBEY
DEEP SEA WORLD
HOPETOUN HOUSE
CRAMOND
CHATELHERAULT
BOTHWELL CASTLE

PRECEDING PAGES: the Forth Rail Bridge.
LEFT: barges on the Forth and Clyde Canal.
RIGHT: Robert the Bruce with the Wallace
Monument.

Adjacent to the palace of Linlithgow is the Church of St Michael, Scotland's largest pre-Reformation parish church; the abstract golden crown was mounted on its tower in 1964.

Sun 2–5pm; free), which is a cultural centre with not only an important collection of artefacts, an exhibition space for contemporary art, photography and ceramics, but also a venue for music and drama.

The medieval **Church of the Holy Rood** (St John's Street, Castle Wynd; Easter–Sept 11am–4pm; admission by donation) is one of Scotland's finest churches with an original 15th-century hammerbeam roof. **The Old Town Jail** (St John Street; tel 01786-450 050; www. oldtownjail.com; June–Oct daily 10am–5pm; charge) offers the experience of a live prison tour, complete with incarcerated characters.

Heroes of the past

The achievements of both Wallace and Bruce are recalled around Stirling. On the rock of **Abbey Craig**, above the site where Wallace camped, is the ostentatious **Wallace Monument** (tel: 01786-472 140; www.nationalwallacemonument. com; daily July, Aug 10am–6pm, Jan–Mar, Nov–Dec 10.30am–4pm, Apr–June, Sept, Oct 10am–5pm; charge), home of the hero's two-handed sword.

From its elevation at the top of 246 spiral steps, you can see the leaping ramparts of the **Ochil Hills**, while to the southeast, the Forth spreads across its flat plain to the spectacular flare-stacks of **Grangemouth**.

The Ochil Hills

The Ochils are a range of hills extending from the Bridge of Allan, north of Stirling, tailing off eastwards to the south side of the Firth of Tay at Newburgh. These hills not only provide wonderful views of Stirling and its castle, they offer great opportunities for walkers and some fine panoramas for motorists.

Taking the minor Sheriffmuir Road out of Stirling up from the university, after about a mile (1.5 km) there are opportunities to pull off the road and look down on the city. For those wishing to walk, for an even better view take the path up to Dumyat. The starting point, on the right-hand side of the road opposite the sheep pens, is just north of the electricity cables, which cross the road. The path to the beacon – keeping to the left – is around

Stirling Castle

The impressive bulk of Stirling Castle was a formidable challenge to any invaders. It had its most active moments during Scotland's Wars of Independence: surrendered to the English in 1296, it was recaptured by the warrior-patriot William Wallace after the Battle of Stirling Bridge (not today's stone bridge, built around 1400, but a wooden structure). It became the last stronghold in Scotland to hold out against Edward I, the "Hammer of the Scots". Eventually, it went back to the English for 10 years, until Robert the Bruce retook it in 1314 after the Battle of Bannockburn, which decisively secured Scotland's independence.

The Stuarts favoured Stirling Castle as a royal residence: James II and V were born in it, Mary Queen of Scots was crowned there at the age of nine months, and its splendid collection of buildings reflects its history as palace and fortress. Perhaps the most striking feature is the exterior facade, with ornate stonework that was largely cut by French craftsmen. The Great Hall, or Parliament House (before 1707 this was a seat of the Scottish Parliament), also has exquisite carving and tracery, which has recently been carefully reconstructed. A programme of major restoration has also included the kitchens of the castle, which now recreate the preparations for a sumptuous Renaissance banquet given by Mary Queen of Scots for the baptism of her son, the future James VI.

2 miles (3km) long and although it's only a climb of some 850ft (260 metres) the view from there is superb.

To the west, not far from Stirling, lies Scotland's first national park, the **Loch Lomond and the Trossachs National Park**, which was officially opened by the Princess Royal in 2002, and covers four distinct areas: the Argyll Forest in the west on the Cowal Peninsula, Loch Lomond, The Trossachs, east of Callander and the northern peaks around Crianlarich (*see page 262*).

The Battle of Bannockburn

The site of the Battle of Bannockburn, a few miles south of Stirling, has been more or less consumed by a housing estate. No one is precisely sure where the battle was fought, but the rotunda beside the heroic bronze equestrian statue of Bruce is said to mark his command post. The **Bannockburn Heritage Centre** (tel: 0844-493 2139; daily Apr–Sept 10am–5.30pm, Mar, Oct 10am–5pm; charge) gives an audiovisual account of the matter. Also close to Stirling is the **Alloa**

Tower (tel: 0844-493 2129; Apr–Oct daily 1–5pm; charge), the superbly restored former home of the earls of Mar, built in the late 15th century with dungeon, medieval timber roof and an impressive rooftop parapet walk with fine views.

Stirling is almost equidistant from Edinburgh and Glasgow. If you take the M9 to Edinburgh, you stay roughly parallel to the broadening course of the Forth. There are rewarding diversions to be made on this route. Just outside Falkirk is the **Falkirk Wheel** (tel: 08700-500 208; Mar–Oct daily 10am–5.30pm; free). Opened in June 2002, this spectacular feat of engineering is a unique rotating boatlift that carries boats between the Forth & Clyde and Union canals. You can see the lift in action and take a ride on amphibious boats (charge).

Also near Falkirk are four good sections of the **Roman Antonine Wall** ㊹, which the Emperor Antoninus Pius had built between the Firths of Clyde and Forth around AD 140; while the motorway itself has opened up a distracting view of the loch and the late 15th-cen-

BELOW:
the magnificent
ruins of Linlithgow
Palace.

Most of the original 18th-century furniture and wall coverings can still be seen at Hopetoun House.

tury **Linlithgow Palace** ⑮ (tel: 01506-842 896; daily Apr–Sept 9.30am–5.30pm, Oct–Mar 9.30am–4.30pm; charge), the well-preserved ruins of Scotland's most magnificent palace and birthplace of Mary Queen of Scots.

From the M9, you can also visit the village of **South Queensferry** ⑯ on the southern bank of one of the Forth's oldest crossings, where river becomes estuary. Until the **Forth Road Bridge** was built, ferries had plied between South and North Queensferry for 900 years. Today, South Queensferry huddles between and beneath the giant bridges that provide such a spectacular contrast in engineering design – the massive humped girders of the 1890 rail bridge and the delicate, graceful span of the suspension bridge, which took six years to complete and was opened in 1964.

At South Queensferry, you can take a boat excursion to the island of **Inchcolm** in the Forth and visit the ruined abbey (tel: 01383-823 332; daily Apr–Sept 9.30am–5.30pm, Oct–Mar 9.30am–4.30pm; charge), monastic buildings and gardens. Be

aware that adverse weather conditions could make the crossing impossible. Cross the Forth Road Bridge or take the train to North Queensferry to visit the huge aquarium at **Deep Sea World** (tel: 01383-411 880; www.deepseaworld.com; Mon–Fri 10am–5pm, Sat–Sun 10am–6pm; charge).

Near South Queensferry are **Hopetoun House** (tel: 0131-331 2451; Easter–Oct daily 10am–4.30pm; charge), home of the earls of Hopetoun, magnificently situated in parkland beside the Forth and splendidly extended by William Adam and his son John between 1721 and 1754; and **Dalmeny House** (tel: 0131-331 1888; June–July Mon, Tue, Sun guided tours at 2.15pm, 3.30pm; charge), home of the earls of Rosebery, with a fine collection of paintings.

The Forth and Clyde

You can walk beside the Forth through the wooded Rosebery estate to the **River Almond**, where a little rowing-boat ferry transports you across this minor tributary to the red pantiles and white crowstep gables of

BELOW: spectators at Deep Sea World.

Cramond **47**. Still very much its own 18th-century village, Cramond has a harbour that was used by the Romans. Its **Roman Fort**, whose foundations have been exposed, was built around AD 142, and may have been used by Septimius Severus.

Scotland's pre-eminent river, the **Clyde**, undergoes more personality changes than any other in its progress to the western seaboard. The limpid little stream, which has its source 80 miles (130km) southeast of Glasgow, moves prettily through the orchards and market gardens of Clydesdale before watering the industries of North Lanarkshire and welcoming the ships and shipyards of Glasgow.

Strathclyde Country Park

The lower reaches of the Clyde valley have been colonised by the city's satellites, and by a clutter of hill towns: Wishaw, Motherwell and Hamilton. Once drab coal and steel towns, they are attempting to recover their dignity and vitality: witness the creation of **Strathclyde Country Park**, a huge recreational area with a 200-acre

(80-hectare) loch, formed by diverting the Clyde, and subsuming part of the old estate of the dukes of Hamilton.

Hamilton 48 has associations with Mary Queen of Scots, Cromwell and the Covenanters, who were defeated by Monmouth at nearby Bothwell Bridge in 1679. Immediately south of Hamilton is **Chatelherault** (tel: 01698-426 213; visitor centre Mon–Sat 10am–5pm, Sun noon–5pm; house Mon–Thur 10am–4.30pm; free), a glorious restored hunting lodge and kennels built in 1732 for the duke of Hamilton by William Adam.

Bothwell Castle (tel: 01698-816 894; Apr–Sept daily 9.30am–5.30pm, Oct daily 9.30am–4.30pm, Nov–Mar Sat–Wed 9.30am–4.30pm; charge), perhaps the finest 13th-century castle in Scotland, was fought over by the Scots and English.

Memories of more recent times can be found in adjacent **Blantyre 49**, birthplace of explorer David Livingstone, whose life is recalled at the **David Livingstone Centre** (tel: 0844-493 2206; Apr–Dec Mon–Sat 10am–5pm, Sun 12.30–5pm; charge). ❏

Crammond Inn, a sign to stop and linger over lunch.

BELOW: a cycle ride round Crammond.

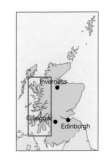

THE WEST COAST

Mountain and moor, heather and stag, castle and loch – and a magical seaboard of isolated villages and small ports – are all to be found on the glorious west coast of Scotland

Map on page 220

From the long finger of Kintyre to the deep fissure of Loch Broom, the west coast is the part of Scotland that most perfectly conforms to its romantic image. Nowhere else in Scotland (outside Caithness and Sutherland) is a physical sense of travelling more thrillingly experienced; and few other areas provide such opportunities for solitude and repose, as well as the slightly awesome impression that this dramatic landscape is not to be trifled with.

The longest peninsula

It all begins gently enough at the Clyde estuary, where the deep penetration of the sea at **Loch Fyne** has created Scotland's longest peninsula, which is 54 miles (87km) from Crinan to the Mull of Kintyre and never wider than 10 miles (16km). This mighty arm is nearly bisected by West Loch Tarbert into the two regions of Knapdale and Kintyre, and its isolated character makes it almost as remote as any of the islands.

Here there are rolling hills rather than mountains, rough moors and forests in Knapdale, grassy tops in Kintyre and a coast that is most interesting on its west side, with a close view of the island of Jura from **Kilberry Head ❶** (where you can also view a fine collec-

tion of medieval sculptured stones). **Tarbert ❷** is a port popular with yachties. Once a thriving herring fishing base, it's now the annual host of dozens of yachts during May's Brewin Dolphin Scottish Sailing Series. There are several cosy pubs and, for accommodation, seek out the tourist office by the harbour-side.

Further south is **Tayinloan ❸**, from where you can take the 20-minute ferry ride across to the tiny island of Gigha, noted for the fine **Achamore Gardens**, and south again is the vast beach

Main attractions

LOCH FYNE
TARBERT
MULL OF KINTYRE
INVERARAY
CRUACHAN POWER STATION
ARDUAINE GARDEN
SCOTTISH SLATE ISLANDS HERITAGE TRUST CENTRE
OBAN
ARDNAMURCHAN POINT
GLEN COE
EILEAN DONAN CASTLE
INVEREWE GARDEN

PRECEDING PAGES: wildlife spotting off Seil Island. **LEFT:** Oban harbour. **RIGHT:** the Glenfinnan Viaduct.

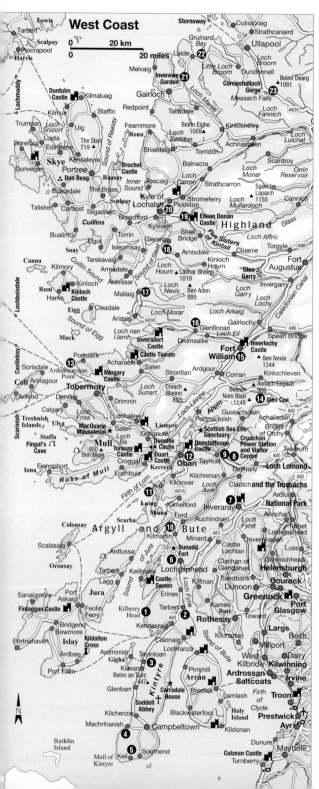

West Coast

of **Machrihanish ❹**. Few have kind words for the Kintyre "metropolis" of **Campbeltown**. However, from here it is only a short drive to the tip of the peninsula, the **Mull of Kintyre** itself (now an RSPB bird reserve). The Northern Ireland coast is only 12 miles (19km) away, and legend has it that St Columba first set foot in Scotland at **Keil ❺**, near the holiday village of Southend. You can see his "footprints" imprinted on a flat rock near a ruined chapel.

Kintyre's east coast

From the great lighthouse on the Mull, first built in 1788 and remodelled by Robert Stevenson, grandfather of Robert Louis, there is nowhere else to go. You can retreat back up the secondary road (B842) of Kintyre's east coast, which has its own scenic drama in the sandy sweep of **Carradale Bay** and the view across the water to the mountains of Arran, reached by car ferry from Claonaig. The hump behind Carradale is **Beinn an Tuirc**, Kintyre's highest hill (1,490ft/447 metres). The name means Mountain of the Boar, from a fearsome specimen said to have been killed by an ancestor of the Campbells. You can take in the ruined walls and sculptured tombstones of **Saddell Abbey**, a 12th-century Cistercian house, and **Skipness Castle and Chapel**.

From **Lochgilphead ❻** – close to where, at Ardrishaig, the 9-mile (15km) Crinan Canal crosses the neck of the peninsula and connects Loch Fyne to the Atlantic Ocean – you have a choice of two main routes to the handsome port and resort of Oban. The longer route, up Loch Fyne by Inveraray to Loch Awe (A83 and then A819) is the more dramatic, although the shorter route (A816) keeps you close to the coast and its vistas of those low-lying islands, which are the floating outriders of the mountains of Jura and Mull.

Inveraray castle

Both routes are punctuated by places of interest. The most celebrated castle in the area is **Inveraray ❼** (tel: 01499-302

203; www.inveraray-castle.com; Apr–Oct daily 10am–5.45pm; charge), the seat of the chiefs of Clan Campbell, the dukes of Argyll, for centuries. The present building – Gothic Revival, famous for its magnificent interiors and art collection – was started in 1743, when the 3rd duke also decided to rebuild the village of Inveraray. The result is a dignified community with much of the orderly elegance of the 18th century. The castle is the venue for the Inveraray Highland Games held annually in July. By means of wax figures, commentary and imaginative displays, **Inveraray Jail** (tel: 01499-302 381; www.inveraray-jail.co.uk; daily Apr–Oct 9.30am–5pm, Nov–Mar 10am–5pm; charge) brings to life a courtroom trial and what it was like in the cells in the 19th century. You can interact with costumed characters, meet the warder, experience courtroom trials and even sample the punishments.

Two very different museums call for a visit. Moored at the pier in Inveraray is the 1910-built *Arctic Penguin*, a former lightship packed with seafaring exhibits and now managed by the **Inveraray**

Maritime Museum (tel: 01499-302 213; Apr–Sept daily 10am–4pm; charge). Some 5 miles (8km) south is **Auchindrain Township Museum** (tel: 01499-500 325; Apr–Oct daily 10am–5pm; charge), whose dwellings and barns of the 18th and 19th centuries were once a communal-tenancy Highland farm, paying rent to the duke.

A mighty mountain

Loch Awe, where the road takes you past the fallen house of the Breadalbane dynasty – the romantic ruin of **Kilchurn Castle** (contact Loch Awe boats; tel: 01866-833 256) on a promontory on the water – is the longest freshwater loch in Scotland. At its northwest extremity, where it squeezes past the mighty mountain of Ben Cruachan and drains into Loch Etive through the dark slit of the Pass of Brander, it's as awesome as its name promises.

Almost a mile inside Ben Cruachan is the **Cruachan Power Station ⑧** (tel: 01866-822 618; www.visitcruachan.co.uk; Easter–Oct daily 9.30am–4.45pm, Feb–Mar, Nov–Dec Mon–Fri 10am–3-.45pm; charge), a pumped-storage

The Pass of Brander is so steep and narrow that legend claims it was once held against an army by an old woman wielding a scythe.

BELOW:
Kilchurn Castle, with views down Loch Awe.

hydroelectric power station located in an artificial cavern, which you can view on an electric bus. The 30-minute guided tour takes you deep inside the mountain and gives you a chance to view the huge generators.

The road continues through **Taynuilt** , a village of more than passing interest. One of the earliest monuments to Nelson was erected here when locals dragged an ancient standing stone into the village and carved an inscription on it. It can still be seen, near the church. The main attraction, however, is the **Bonawe Iron Furnace** (tel: 01866-822432; Apr–Sept daily 9.30am–5.30pm; cha rge). Founded in 1753 by a North of England partnership, it is the most complete charcoal-fuelled ironworks in Britain. A little nearer to Oban, the road passes by the Connel Bridge, under which are the foaming **Falls of Lora**, a remarkable waterfall that appears in a series of dramatic cataracts as Loch Etive drains into the sea at ebb tide.

Coastal sights

If you take the A816 from Lochgilphead to Oban by the coast, you will pass one of the ancient capitals of Dalriada, the kingdom of the early Scots. The striking eminence of **Dunadd Fort** (*c.* AD 500–800) sets the mood for a spectacular group of prehistoric sites around the village of **Kilmartin** : standing stones, burial cairns and cists are all accessible. Start with the collection of sculptured stones in the churchyard.

As you drive north, the coast becomes more riven, while the natural harbours of the sea lochs and the protective islands of **Shuna**, **Luing** (noted for its slate) and **Seil** attract the yachting fraternity. Here, too, is **Arduaine Garden** (tel: 01852-200 366; www.arduaine-garden.org.uk; Apr–Sept daily 9.30am–4.30pm; charge), a 20-acre (8-hectare) promontory owned by the National Trust for Scotland and renowned for superb rhododendrons, azaleas and magnolias.

Seil and its neighbours were supported by a vigorous slate industry until a great storm in 1881 flooded the quarries deep below sea level and efforts to pump them out failed. You can see vivid evidence of those days on Seil at the **Scottish Slate Islands**

BELOW RIGHT:
Oban dominated by the folly, McCaig's Tower.

Seaway to the Hebrides

Ringed by wooded hills and clasped within the sheltered bay, Oban has the finest harbour on the Highland seaboard. Here even a landlocked traveller feels the pull of the islands: there are regular ferries to Mull, Barra, South Uist and Colonsay, as well as the nearby islands of Kerrera and Lismore. Oban is the focal point for tourists throughout the whole of Argyll, but also serves as the shopping centre for the rural population of the region, so it's likely to be busy all year round. In August there is the added attraction of the Argyllshire Highland Gathering, with displays of traditional dancing and folk music.

Hotels and boarding houses abound – a far cry from 1773 when Dr Johnson had to content himself with a "tolerable inn". However, modern tourism hasn't been so kind to the dignity of its high street; it lost the delightful Victorian buildings of its railway station in an act of institutionalised vandalism. But the town still has atmosphere – mostly centred on the busy harbour. Pulpit Hill is Oban's best viewpoint – and there is also the extraordinary folly of McCaig's Tower. John Stuart McCaig was an Oban banker who financed this strange enterprise on a hill above the town centre to give work to the unemployed and provide himself with a memorial. The tower was raised between 1890 and 1900, but McCaig's grand plan was never completed. What remains looks like an austere Scottish Colosseum.

Heritage Trust (tel: 01852-300 449; Apr–Oct daily 10.30am–1pm, 2–5pm; charge). Seil itself is so close to the mainland that it's reached by the single stone arch of the 1791 Clachan Bridge, the "bridge over the Atlantic".

Island hopping from Oban

Every facility for visitors can be found in **Oban** ⑫, whose only beach, **Ganavan Sands**, is 2 miles (3km) north of the town. Whisky-making is explained at **Oban Distillery** (tel: 01631-572 004; July–Sept Mon–Fri 9.30am–7.30pm, Sat–Sun 9.30am–5pm, Easter–June Mon–Sat 9.30am–5pm, Oct Mon–Sat 9.30am–5pm, Nov, Mar–Easter Mon–Fri 10am–5pm, Dec, Feb Mon–Fri 12.30–4pm ; charge) and there are castles to be visited: the scant fragment of **Dunollie** on its precipitous rock and, at Connel, the fine 13th-century fortress of **Dunstaffnage** (tel: 01631-562 465; Apr–Sept daily 9.30am–5.30pm, Oct daily 9.30am–4.30pm, Nov–Mar Sat–Wed 9.30am–4.30pm; charge).

Oban is a great place for island-hopping. **Mull** is just a 40-minute ferry ride away, as is the long fertile island of **Lismore**, whose name means "great garden". In Oban Bay is pretty little **Kerrera**, reached by a small foot ferry. A walk round the island takes you past the dramatic ruin of **Gylen Castle** at its southern tip, commanding a spectacular view of sea, coastline and islands.

North from Oban, the A828 crosses the Connel Bridge to reach the lovely landscapes of Benderloch and Appin. Just past Benderloch you'll find the **Scottish Sea Life Sanctuary** (tel: 01631-720 386; www.sealsanctuary.co.uk; daily from 10am – closing times vary, check in advance; charge) with a walk-through aquarium, touch tanks, seal pond and otter sanctuary with underwater viewing. In all, some 30 natural marine habitats can be observed, containing anything from octopus to sharks. Adorable seal pups can be seen at the nursery where the sick or injured young are cared for every year. Close by is **Barcaldine Castle** (tel: 01631-720 598) also known as the **Black Castle**, now an up-market accommodation option complete with secret stairs, bottle dungeon and resident ghost.

Continuing north leads you through

The Scottish Sea Life Sanctuary near Barcaldine includes all kinds of marine life, from small crustaceans to seals and even sharks.

BELOW: sample a wee dram at Oban Distillery.

"Yesterday we went up Ben Nevis," wrote the poet John Keats in 1818. "I am heartily glad it is done – it is almost like a fly crawling up a wainscot."

BELOW: the dramatic landscape of Glen Coe.

Appin, a name which evokes romantic tragedy. In a historical incident made famous by Robert Louis Stevenson in *Kidnapped*, James Stewart of the Glens was wrongly hanged for the murder of Colin Campbell, the "Red Fox" and government land agent, following the Jacobite Rising of 1745. Further north still, at **Corran**, you can cross **Loch Linnhe** on a five-minute ferry ride to **Ardgour** and the tortuous drive to isolated **Ardnamurchan Point** ⑬, the most westerly point of the Scottish mainland.

Power of Glen Coe

Once across the Ballachulish Bridge, the full grandeur of the West Highlands lies before you. To the east is the sublime mountain scenery of perhaps the most famous glen in Scotland, though for the wrong reason: **Glen Coe** ⑭, where in a savage winter dawn in February 1692, 40 members of the Clan Donald were slaughtered by government soldiers to whom they had given shelter and hospitality. The landscape here exerts a great deal of power and even the unimaginative must feel a shiver up their spine as they follow the A82

between the dark buttresses of **Buachaille Etive Mor**, **Bidean nam Bian** and the **Aonach Eagach**. These mountains are notorious: they are among Britain's supreme mountaineering challenges, and nearly every winter they claim lives. The National Trust for Scotland owns most of Glen Coe and exhibitions at its **Glen Coe Visitor Centre** (tel: 0844-493 2222; Mar–Oct daily 10am–5pm, Nov–Feb Thur–Sun 10am–4pm; charge) near the foot of the glen tell its story.

Some 15 miles (24km) north of Ballachulish on the A82 is **Fort William** ⑮. The fort itself was demolished, not by the Jacobites but by the railway. A secret portrait of Bonnie Prince Charlie, and his bed, are among the Jacobite relics in the **West Highland Museum** (tel: 0139-702 169; July–Aug daily 10am–5pm, June and Sept Mon–Sat 10am–5pm, Oct–May 10am–4pm; charge).

The highest mountain

Despite its fine position between the mountains and Loch Linnhe and proximity to world-class mountain biking at Nevis Range (www.nevisrange.co.uk), busy Fort William has little to com-

mend it beyond its proximity to **Ben Nevis** and glorious Glen Nevis. Britain's highest mountain (4,406ft/1,344 metres) looks a deceptively inoffensive lump from below, where you can't see its savage north face. But the volatile nature of the Scottish climate should never be underestimated when setting out on any hill walk: the "Ben" is a long, tough day, and you should take advice from the visitor centre at its foot in Glen Nevis.

The road to the Isles

From Fort William, turn west on the A830, taking the "road to the Isles" to Mallaig, another ferry port for the Hebrides (particularly the "Small Isles" of Canna, Rum, Eigg and Muck). At **Corpach** you will find **Treasures of the Earth** (tel: 01397-772 283; www.treasuresoftheearth.co.uk; daily July–mid-Sept 9.30am–7pm, Mar–June, mid-Sept–Oct 10am–5pm, Nov–Feb restricted hours, phone for details; charge), an intriguing geology-based exhibition of gemstones and rare minerals.

In summer the **Jacobite Steam Train** (tel: 0845-128 4681) runs through the spectacular scenery from Fort William to Mallaig. This was the track that accommodated the Hogwart's Express in the movie version of *Harry Potter and the Chamber of Secrets*.

The road continues past Loch Eil to **Glenfinnan** ⓰. In August 1745 Charles raised the white-and-crimson Stuart banner here to the cheers of 5,000 men who had rallied behind the charismatic young prince's impetuous adventure, which was to cost the Highlands dear. A monument was raised on the spot in 1815; the National Trust for Scotland's **Glenfinnan Visitor Centre** (tel: 0844-493 2221; daily July–Aug 9.30am–5.30pm, Easter–June, Sept–Oct 10am–5pm; charge) tells the story convincingly.

Prince Charlie's escape

The prince had landed from his French brig at **Loch nan Uamh**, a few miles further west. Just over a year later, after the disaster of Culloden, he left from the same place, having fled pursuing government troops for months around the Highlands and islands: despite a price of £30,000 on his head – a for-

The Glenfinnan Monument marks the place where Bonnie Prince Charlie raised his standard at the beginning of the Jacobite Rising of 1745.

BELOW: Mallaig fishermen splicing their ropes.

A short diversion from Kyle of Lochalsh takes you to the popular holiday village of Plockton, where, because of its sheltered position, palm trees flourish.

BELOW: looking out across Loch Maree.

tune for the time – he was never once betrayed. A memorial cairn on the shore of Loch nan Uamh marks his final exit from Scotland.

From **Arisaig** the road passes between the silver sands of **Morar** and the deep **Loch Morar** (said to be the home of Morag, another water monster) and comes to an end at **Mallaig** ⓱, an important landing place for white fish and shellfish. You can take a car ferry across the Sound of Sleat to **Armadale** on Skye or enjoy a cruise to the great, roadless mountain wilderness of **Knoydart** with its two long sea lochs, **Hourn** and **Nevis** – said to be the lochs of heaven and hell. Land at Inverie for a dram or pint at The Old Forge (tel: 01687-462 267), Britain's remotest mainland pub.

The alternative from Fort William is to continue on the A82 and at **Invergarry** turn west on the A87 to climb past a spectacular road side viewpoint looking down Glen Garry, and then drop to the head of Glen Shiel, with the famous peaks of the **Five Sisters of Kintail** soaring above on your right. At Shiel Bridge, a minor road turns

left over the Mam Ratagan pass to reach **Glenelg** ⓲, worth a visit not only for its beauty but also for **Dun Telve** and **Dun Troddan**, two superb brochs – circular Iron Age towers with double walls which still stand over 30ft (9 metres) high. Here, too, are the remains of **Bernera Barracks**, quartered by Hanoverian troops during the 18th century.

Eilean Donan Castle

Go back to Shiel Bridge and continue on the A87 along lovely Loch Duich to reach **Eilean Donan Castle** ⓳ (tel: 01599-555 202; www.eileandonancastle. com; daily July–Aug 9am–6pm, Mar–June, Sept–Oct 10am–6pm; charge), a restored Mackenzie stronghold on an islet reached by a causeway and probably the most photographed castle in Scotland. The road runs on to Kyle of Lochalsh and the bridge across to Skye.

From **Kyle of Lochalsh** ⓴, mainland travellers continue north, and you can take the coast road via Duirinish for 6 miles (10km) to **Plockton**, one of the most picturesque loch-side villages in Scotland. Continue to the

lovely **Loch Carron**, leaving Inverness-shire for the tremendous mountain massifs of **Wester Ross**. Here, on the isolated peninsula of **Applecross** and among the mighty peaks of **Torridon** with their views to the Cuillins of Skye and the distant, drifting shapes of the Outer Hebrides, is some of Europe's most wild and spectacular scenery.

More gentle pursuits can be found in **Poolewe** village, where the road through Gairloch passes between Loch Ewe and **Loch Maree**, possibly the most sublime inland loch in Scotland. The loch's particular features are the old Scots pines along its shores and the impressive presence of **Slioch**, the "mountain of the spear", on its eastern shore.

Inverewe Garden

Inverewe Garden ㉑ (tel: 0844-493 2225; visitor centre daily May–Aug 10am–6pm, Apr, Sept 10am–5pm, Oct 10am–4pm; charge) provides a sumptuous collection of subtropical plants, growing – thanks to the mild climate created by the North Atlantic Drift – on the same latitude as Siberia. The gardens were begun in 1862 by Osgood Mac-kenzie, further developed by his daughter Mrs Mairi Sawyer, and given to the National Trust for Scotland in 1952.

A few miles further north is the glittering 4-mile (6km) scoop of **Gruinard Bay ㉒**, with coves of pink sand from the red Torridon sandstone, nearly 800 million years old. The road then takes you round **Little Loch Broom**, below the powerful shoulders of **An Teallach** ("The Forge", 3,483ft/1,062 metres), the highest of these mighty peaks and a mountain which, said W.H. Murray, made "most Munros of the South and Central Highlands seem tame by comparison". (A Munro is a Scottish mountain of over 3,000ft/900 metres, named after the man who collated them. There are 284 in all, of which nine rise higher than 4,000ft/1,200 metres.)

You are now within easy reach of **Loch Broom** and the substantial fishing port and tourist centre of Ullapool (*see page 294*). On your way, stop at the **Measach Falls ㉓**, 10 miles (16km) before Ullapool, to admire the 120ft (35-metre) drop into the spectacular **Corrieshalloch Gorge**, crossed by a swaying Victorian suspension bridge.❏

TIP

From Glenelg you can cross the water of Loch Duich to Kylerhea in Skye, as Dr Johnson and Boswell did, although the little car ferry (tel: 01599-522 273) runs only in the summer. Alternatively, use the Skye Bridge at Kyle of Lochalsh.

BELOW: Eilean Donan Castle.

SKYE

Arguably the most magnificent of the dozens of Scottish islands, Skye is a romantic, misty isle of dramatic sea lochs, rocky peaks and breathtaking views

So deep are the incisions made by the sea lochs along the coast of Skye that, although the island is about 50 miles (80km) long and 30 miles (50km) wide, no part is more than 5 miles (8km) from the sea. The population, unlike that of most Scottish islands, is on the increase – mainly due to immigrants, many of whom are from south of the border.

Dominating the "Misty Island" are the jagged **Cuillin Hills**, on a sharp winter's day providing as thrilling a landscape as any in Nepal or New Zealand. Strangely, these, the greatest concentration of peaks in Britain, are referred to as "hills" rather than mountains; although they attain a height of not much more than 3,000ft (900 metres), they spring dramatically from sea level.

Garden of Skye

Most visitors now reach Skye by driving over the road bridge which spans the **Kyleakin Narrows** between Kyle of Lochalsh and **Kyleakin ❶**. Alternative car ferry routes are from Glenelg to Kylerhea and from Mallaig to Armadale. The former, a ferry (www.skyeferry.co.uk) accommodating a mere handful of cars, runs only during the summer – never on a Sunday – while the latter becomes a passenger-only ferry in the winter.

Overlooking Kyleakin harbour are the scanty ruins of **Castle Moil**, once a stronghold of the Mackinnons and a lookout post and fortress against raids by Norsemen. Six miles (10km) out of Kyleakin, turn south on the A851 and, after 17 miles (27km), you will come to **Armadale ❷** and its ruined castle. **Armadale Castle Gardens and Museum of the Isles** (tel: 01471-844 305; www.clandonald.com; Apr–Oct daily 9.30am–5.30pm; charge) was formerly the home of the MacDonalds, who were once one of Scotland's most powerful clans and Lords of the Isles.

Main attractions

THE CUILLIN HILLS
ARMADALE CASTLE GARDENS
LOCH SCAVAIG
PORTREE
AROS EXPERIENCE
TROTTERNISH PENINSULA
STAFFIN
SKYE MUSEUM OF ISLAND LIFE
DUNVEGAN CASTLE
COLBOST FOLK MUSEUM
LOCH BRACADALE
TALISKER DISTILLERY

PRECEDING PAGES: bridge at Sligachan, Isle of Skye. **LEFT:** the Storr rock face. **RIGHT:** sailing to shore.

Many British mountaineers who have challenged Everest and other great peaks of the world did part of their serious training on the Cuillin Hills.

BELOW: the natural harbour at Portree.

The **Clan Donald Trust**, which was formed in the 1970s and now has members throughout the world, has turned one wing of the ruined castle into a museum with audiovisual presentations. The old stables house an excellent restaurant, a good bookshop, gift shop and luxurious self-catering accommodation. There's a ranger service and guided walks through the grounds where there are many mature trees and rhododendrons. Further exploration of this area, called **Sleat** (pronounced *Slate*), reveals why it bears the sobriquet "Garden of Skye".

Return north to reach **Broadford**, from where a diversion southwest on the B8083 leads, after 14 miles (22km), to the scattered village of **Elgol** ❸. It was from here on 4 July 1746 that the Young Pretender, after being given a banquet by the Mackinnons in what is now called **Prince Charles's Cave**, finally bade farewell to the Hebrides. The view of the **Black Cuillins** from here is one of the most splendid in all Britain.

In summer, motorboats go from Elgol across wide **Loch Scavaig**, past schools of seals, to land passengers on the rocks from where they can scramble upwards to **Loch Coruisk** in the very heart of the Cuillins. The scene was much painted by Turner and other Romantics and written about by Sir Walter Scott.

Crofters' rebellion

Backtrack once more to the A87 and, after 7 miles (11km) with the Red Cuillins to the left – they are much more rounded and much less dramatic than the Black Cuillins – you arrive at **Luib**, a crofting township once at the centre of the crofters' grievances *(see pages 236–7)*. Skye was the scene of some of the most intense fight-backs by crofters threatened with eviction during the Clearances. The Battle of the Braes (1882) was the last such "battle" fought in Britain.

The road continues on through **Sligachan** ❹, a base for serious climbers of the Black Cuillins, and then descends into **Portree** ❺, the island's capital, an attractive town built around a natural harbour and with neat and brightly painted houses rising steeply from the water. In 1773, when they visited Portree, Dr Johnson and James Boswell dined in

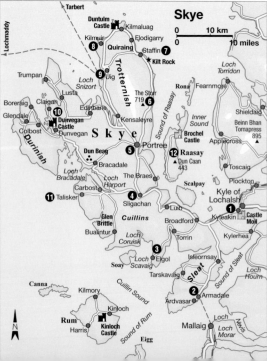

the Royal Hotel, then called McNab's Hostelry, believing it was "the only inn on the island". A quarter of a century before that, Prince Charlie had bade farewell to Flora MacDonald at McNab's. Just south of Portree is the **Aros Experience** (tel: 01478-613 649; www.aros.co.uk; daily 9am–5.30pm; charge for exhibition), where the story of the island is told from 1700 to the present day. There are also attractive woodland walks.

Old Man of Storr

Magnificent rock scenery and breathtaking views can be enjoyed by driving north from Portree on the **Trotternish peninsula**. Seven miles (11km) out along the A855 is **The Storr ❻**, a 2,360ft (719-metre) peak which is shaped like a crown and offers a stiff two-hour climb; to its east is the **Old Man of Storr**, an isolated 150ft (45-metre) pinnacle of rock. Further north is **Kilt Rock**, a sea cliff that owes its name to columnar basalt strata overlying horizontal ones beneath, the result bearing only the most fanciful relationship to a kilt.

A further 2 miles (4km) leads to **Staffin ❼**, immediately beyond which

is **The Quiraing**, so broken up with massive rock faces that it looks like a range in miniature rather than a single mountain. The various rock features of the Quiraing – the castellated crags of **The Prison**, the slender, unclimbed 100ft (30-metre) **Needle** and **The Table**, a meadow as large as a football field – can be appreciated only on foot and can be reached readily by a path from a glorious minor road which cuts across the peninsula from Staffin to Uig.

However, to take this road rather than to loop around Trotternish peninsula is to forego some historic encounters. The annexe of the **Flodigarry Hotel** was Flora MacDonald's first home after her marriage in 1750 to Captain Allan MacDonald. Nearby is **Kilmuir churchyard ❽**, where Flora lies buried, wrapped in a sheet from the bed in which the fugitive prince had slept. On a clear day there are fine views from here of the Outer Hebrides, from where Charlie and Flora fled to Skye.

Then, at the northwest tip of the peninsula, is the ruined **Duntulm Castle**, an ancient MacDonald stronghold commanding the sea route to the

A Celtic cross marks the spot where Flora MacDonald is buried in Kilmuir.

BELOW: the Storr with the Black Cuillins in the distance.

TIP

Sabhal Mor Ostaig, on the Sleat peninsula, is Skye's Gaelic College, offering courses in many aspects of Gaelic life, language and culture.

Outer Hebrides. South of the castle is the **Skye Museum of Island Life** (tel: 01470-552 206; www.skyemuseum. co.uk; Apr–Oct Mon–Sat 9.30am–5pm; charge), whose seven thatched cottages show how the crofters lived. And so, after a few miles, to **Uig ❾**, from where the ferry departs for Lochmaddy on North Uist and Tarbert on Harris. The A87 south from Uig returns to Portree, but turn right at the junction with the A850 and travel westwards to Dunvegan 19 miles (30km) further on.

To the south you'll see **Macleod's Tables**, which dominate the **Duirinish peninsula**. Their flatness is attributed to the inhospitality shown Columba when he preached to the local chief: in shame the mountains shed their caps so that the saint might have a flat bed on which to lie.

Legendary castle

No other castle in Scotland can claim so long a record of continuous occupation by one family as **Dunvegan Castle ❿** (tel: 01470-521 206; Apr–Oct daily 10am–5.30pm; charge), which has been home to the MacLeods for

the past 700 years. Set on a rocky platform overlooking Loch Dunvegan, its stuccoed exterior lacks the splendour of at least a dozen other Scottish castles. Its interior, however, is another matter, with a wealth of paintings and memorabilia, including a painting of Dr Johnson by Sir Joshua Reynolds and a lock of Bonnie Prince Charlie's hair.

Best known, though, is the "Fairy Flag", a torn and faded fragment of yellow silk spotted with red. Some say a fairy mother laid it over her half-mortal child when she had to return to her own people: others, more prosaic, that it was woven on the island of Rhodes in the 7th century and that a MacLeod captured it during the Crusades. Whatever its origins, the Fairy Flag is said to have three magic properties: when raised in battle it ensures a MacLeod victory; when spread over the MacLeod marriage bed it guarantees a child; and when unfurled at Dunvegan it charms the herring in the loch. The flag should be flown sparingly: its powerful properties will be exhausted when used three times. So far, it has twice been invoked.

Three miles (5km) before the town of

BELOW: Dunvegan Castle towers above Loch Dunvegan.

Dunvegan, take the secondary B886 and travel northwards for 8 miles (13km) to **Trumpan** where, in 1597, the "Fairy Flag" was unfurled. A raiding party of MacDonalds from the island of Uist landed and set fire to a church packed with worshipping MacLeods. The alarm was raised: the MacDonalds were unable to escape as a falling tide had left their longboats high and dry and they were slain. The bodies were laid out on the sands below the sea wall, which was then toppled to cover them.

Primitive justice once practised on Skye is seen in the **Trumpan churchyard** in the shape of a standing stone pierced by a circular hole. The accused would be blindfolded and, if he could put his finger unerringly through the Trial Stone, was deemed innocent.

Local crafts

A few miles west of Dunvegan are Colbost, Glendale and Boreraig. The **Colbost Folk Museum** (tel: 01470-521 296; Easter–Oct daily 10am–6pm; charge) is very atmospheric, with a peat fire on the floor of the "black house" waiting to cook a stew and a box bed uncomfortable enough to be genuine. Behind the house an illicit whisky still is no longer in use, but the restored 200-year-old watermill at **Glendale** is operating

The **Borreraig Park Museum** (tel: 01470-511 311; daily 9am–6pm; charge) is a local history museum, plus a shop selling crafts made by some 50 local craftspeople. A small display portrays the MacCrimmon family, the hereditary pipers to the MacLeods.

Heading south from Dunvegan, the A863 follows the shores of **Loch Bracadale**, one of the most magnificent fjords of the west coast, with the black basalt wall of **Talisker Head** away to the south. At **Dun Beag**, near Bracadale, is a well-preserved broch (circular Iron Age fortified building). A left turn onto the B885 before reaching **Talisker ⓫** leads back to **Portree**. Alternatively, remain on the A863 and at the head of **Loch Harport**, take the B8009, and cut back left into wooded **Glen Brittle** and more

glorious views of the Black Cuillins. The B8009 continues to **Carbost** and the **Talisker Distillery** (tel: 01478-614 308; July,–Aug Mon–Sat 9.30am–5pm, Sun 11am–5pm, Apr–June, Sept–Oct Mon–Sat 9.30am–5pm, Nov–Mar Mon–Fri 10am–5pm; tours throughout the day but booking advisable; charge) where you can see how the "water of life" at Skye's sole whisky distillery is made.

Raasay – a prince's shelter

Some say that the sole purpose of Skye is to protect the small lush island of **Raasay ⓬**, just to the east. In the 18th century the English burned all Raasay's houses and boats because the laird had sheltered Bonnie Prince Charlie after Culloden. Today the island has a population of about 200. **Dun Caan**, an extinct volcano, dominates the centre. Visitors can see the ruined **Brochel Castle**, home of the MacLeods of Skye and the grounds of Raasay House, now an outdoor pursuits centre (despite a major fire in 2009 it is still open). When Boswell stayed at the house with Dr Johnson, he danced a jig on top of the 1,456ft (443-metre) high Dun Caan ridge. ❑

With a distinctive peaty flavour all its own, the whisky from the Talisker Distillery has been described by one expert as having "all the uncertainties of the Skye weather".

BELOW: Neist Point Lighthouse on the northwest tip of Skye.

A Crofter's Rugged Life

Almost 18,000 crofts in the Scottish Highlands keep people on the land, but they function more as a traditional way of living than as a source of income

The word "croft" derives from the Gaelic *croit*, meaning a small area of land. Often described as "a piece of land fenced around with regulations", the croft is both much cherished and highly frustrating. Its emotive power comes from its origins. In the aftermath of the 19th-century Highland Clearances, groups of local men banded together to protect their families from being swept overseas to make way for sheep. At the time they were entirely at the whim of often absentee landowners.

By standing their ground despite all the odds – particularly at the so-called Battle of the Braes, in Skye – these men were rewarded in 1886 by an Act of Parliament which gave them security of tenure. It also regulated rents and entitled them to compensation for any improvements made to their properties. In May 2010 MPs at Holyrood backed a controversial Crofting Reform Bill to tackle the problems of absentee landlords and neglect of croft land.

CROFTING TOWNSHIPS TODAY

A croft is usually a combination of a house and a handful of barren, boggy acres for the crofter to cultivate or on which to graze livestock. The crofting community – commonly called a township – acts together in such activities as fencing, dipping or hiring a bull. Problems of remoteness are gradually being overcome as increasing numbers of crofters are replacing the tweed loom in the shed with a computer keyboard in the living room.

Only around 3,600 crofts are owner-occupied. The rest are tenanted, although the rental they pay their landlord is minimal. In Scotland it's estimated there are just under 18,000 crofts and 12,000 crofters, with 33,000 people residing in crofting households.

ABOVE: making hay the traditional way, island of Yell, Shetland. Crofting may be a small player in terms of agricultural production but it has proven an effective stewardship of the land as it is – without it, whole communities would simply pack up and leave.

BELOW: every crofting township used to have a blacksmith, as evidenced by this furnace workshop. Even today, crofters have to be self-sufficient and able to mend practically everything.

LEFT: Highland cow.

A Tradition that Ties up the Land

The most common criticisms of crofting are that it ties up land in segments too small ever to be economically viable, that most crofters are too old to cope, and that too many crofts are left to run down by absentee tenants – these are all problems faced by government body the Crofters' Commission. Certainly, as far as agricultural production is concerned, crofting is a very small player, with estimates suggesting that some two-thirds of crofts are not actively farmed at all. But alternative agricultural projects have been shown to provide little employment, and would alter the landscape radically.

Crofting has lately been redefined to include any economic activity, so it can also cover such enterprises as running a B&B establishment. In Assynt and on the island of Eigg, crofters banded together to become land-owners themselves, raising millions with internet appeals and the help of charities supporting traditional land use. There have been similar takeovers on Gigha and at Inverie, Knoydart Peninsula, where the Old Forge serves fresh seafood and venison from the local red deer, which wander freely in the single street.

ABOVE: sheering sheep with hand clippers.

RIGHT: MP Angus MacNeil on his Barra croft.

RIGHT: when tenants get too old to work the croft themselves, they have the right to assign the croft to the next generation. Some percent do just that.

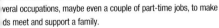

BELOW: crofting is often more a way of life than a viable means of living. A modern crofter has to have several occupations, maybe even a couple of part-time jobs, to make ends meet and support a family.

THE INNER HEBRIDES

The Inner Hebrides have a variety of pleasures to explore: the attractive landscape of Mull, the restored abbey on Iona and a host of smaller islands, some inhabited only by wildlife

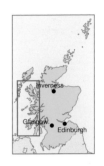

Visitors come to the volcanic island of **Mull ❶** for the contrasting scenery, wooded and soft to bleak and bare; for fishing in the lochs; and for walking. Increasingly, it's an island renowned for its sightings of rare wildlife, including the golden eagle. Visitors will find all types of terrain and weather; stroll on a wet day past Loch Scridain, through the boggy desolation of the **Ross of Mull**, or walk to the top of Mull's highest mountain, **Ben More**, a respectable 3,169ft (950 metres).

The island is not large, only 25 by 26 miles (40 by 41km), but don't be deceived: a drive on the mainly single-track roads, running mostly around the perimeter, is made even slower by Scotland's most feckless and fearless sheep, who regard roads as grassless fields.

Tobermory – a pretty port

Mull's trump card is **Tobermory**, the prettiest port in western Scotland, tucked in a wooded protected bay whose waters are almost invariably unruffled. Yet, in 1588, an explosion reverberated across the bay and the waters gurgled as the Spanish galleon *Florida* sank to the bottom. The exact spot, just 100 yds/metres) straight out from the pier, is well defined. And here, it is believed, a vast treasure of gold

awaits salvage. In 2007, yet another attempt was made to retrieve it.

The tall, brightly painted houses curving round the harbour go back to the late 18th century, when the British Fisheries Society planned a herring port. But the fish were fickle, and today Tobermory's sparkling harbour bobs with pretty pleasure yachts. Be sure to stop in at the small chocolate factory and shop, where the speciality is chocolate made with whisky.

The other towns – **Craignure** in the east where the Oban ferry docks, **Salen**

Main attractions

TOBERMORY
TOROSAY CASTLE
DUART CASTLE
IONA
FINGAL'S CAVE
COLL AND TIREE
COLONSAY
ISLANDS OF EIGG, RUM, MUCK AND CANNA
ISLAY WHISKEY
JURA
GIGHA

PRECEDING PAGES: St Edwards Church, Isle of Canna. **LEFT:** Tobermory, Isle of Mull.
RIGHT: local inhabitant on Iona.

Inner Hebrides

0   20 km

0   20 miles

at the narrow neck of the island, and **Dervaig** in the northwest – are neat, serviceable little places. Drive through Glen More, the ancient royal funeral route to Iona which bisects Mull from east to west, for some of the best scenery on the island. These 20 roads form part of the popular annual Tunnocks Mull Rally, held in October.

On the west, you will find **Calgary**, the silver-sand beach where, after the Clearances, despairing emigrant ships set sail for the New World. The beach held happy memories for one émigré: Colonel McLeod of the Northwest Mounted Police named a new fort in Alberta, Canada, after it.

Further proof, if it be needed, that Scotland's two main exports are whisky and brains can be found south of Calgary at **Loch Ba** near Salen. The **MacQuarie Mausoleum** houses the remains of Major General Lachlan MacQuarie, the first governor general of New South Wales, who is sometimes called the "Father of Australia".

The islanders' psyche

To understand what the 19th-century Clearances (*see page 236–7*) meant to all Hebrideans and to grasp the harshness of a crofting life visit the **Old Byre Heritage Centre** (tel: 01688-400 229; www.old-byre.co.uk; Easter–Oct Wed–Sun and bank holidays 10.30am–5.30pm; charge) at Dervaig. They help explain the islanders' fatalistic attitude to life. Some charitable outsiders think this attitude stems from the trauma of the Clearances, which still trouble the collective consciousness. But cynical mainlanders say the islanders are simply idle. When you find islanders – for many service jobs, particularly those to do with tourism, seem to be run by incomers – they say they work as hard as anyone. Crofting and fishing, they argue, just aren't understood by urbanised outsiders. The centre also has displays of Mull's habitat and the flora and fauna found within.

Two castles are open to the public, both on the east. **Torosay** (tel: 01680-

812 421; www.torosay.com; Apr–mid-Oct daily 10.30am–5pm, gardens all year 9am–sunset; charge), with 19th-century Scottish baronial turrets and crenellations, is near Craignure and is reached from there on a 1½-mile (2km) miniature steam railway. The castle is still lived in by the Guthrie-James family and is a friendly, non-imposing house. On wet days (frequent), you can leaf through old books in the drawing room or visit the separately owned weaving workshop in the grounds (daily; free). There is shapely Italian statuary in the large terraced grounds, fine clematis climbing on old brick walls and a sweet-smelling rock garden.

Across the bay, the 13th-century **Duart Castle** (tel: 01680-812 309; www.duartcastle.com; daily May–mid-Oct 10.30am–5.30pm, Apr Sun–Thur 11am–4pm; charge), on a dramatic headland overlooking the Sound of Mull, was the MacLeans' stronghold. Mull belonged to the clan until it was forfeited when the MacLeans supported young Prince Charles Edward, who was defeated at Culloden in 1746. The castle was deserted for almost 200 years, then restored by Sir Fitzroy MacLean early in the 20th century.

Mull is the jumping-off point for several islands: Iona, Staffa, the Treshnish Isles, Coll and Tiree.

Pilgrimage to Iona

You feel like a pilgrim as you board the serviceable little 10-minute shuttle for a day trip to **Iona ❷**. Near the ferry terminal at **Fionnphort**, on Mull's southwest tip, the **Columba Centre** (tel: 01681-700 640; Apr–Sept daily 10am–1pm, 2–5pm; free) provides an introduction to Iona's saint. Cars and big coaches line the road, as vehicles cannot be taken across to the Holy Island.

The main destination is the restored abbey (tel: 01681-700 512; daily Apr–Sept 9.30am–5.30pm, Oct–Mar 9.30am–4.30pm; charge) but the general store near the ferry has added bicycle hire to its varied services, so in theory there's time to see **Coracle Cove** where Columba landed in AD 563. From the abbey it is just 100 yds/metres to the cemetery of **Reilig Oran** *(see below)*.

Fingal's Cave on **Staffa ❸** is a big attraction; supposedly it inspired Men-

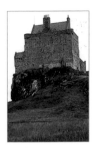

Sir Fitzroy MacLean of Duart Castle was a Hussar in the Light Brigade in the Crimea in 1854: his mementoes are displayed in the Grand Banqueting Room.

BELOW LEFT: the cloisters of Iona Abbey.

Holy Pilgrimage

Curiosity and a search for some intangible spiritual comfort draw well over half a million people from all over the world each year to the tiny 3-mile (5km) island of Iona. Here St Columba and 12 companions landed from Ireland in the 6th century to set up the mission that turned Iona into the Christian centre of Europe.

In 1773, Dr Samuel Johnson was impressed with the piety of Iona. The abbey, which had been suppressed at the Reformation, was still in ruins and there were not many visitors. In the 1930s, the low, sturdy building was restored by the Iona community, and the number of visitors has been growing ever since. Some of the best restoration is to be seen in the tiny cloister, especially the birds and plants on the slender replacement sandstone columns, which were meticulously copied from the one remaining medieval original.

Until the 11th century the Reilig Oran – or royal cemetery – was the burial place of Scottish kings, and there are said to be 48 Scottish rulers buried here, including Duncan, who was murdered by Macbeth in 1040. In addition, here lie the bodies of eight Norwegian, four Irish and two French kings. The cemetery is also the final resting place of John Smith, who was leader of Britain's Labour Party from 1992 until his untimely death in 1994.

delssohn to compose his overture. The experience of going into the cave, if the weather is good enough for landing, is well worth the 90-minute boat journey. The primeval crashing of the sea, the towering height of the cave and the complete lack of colour in the sombre rocks make a powerful impression. Even if the little 47ft (14-metre) partially covered passenger launch can't land, it's worth the journey just to see the curious hexagonal basalt rocks surrounding the gaping black hole of the cave. Birdwatchers, too, have plenty to enjoy.

Beyond Staffa are the uninhabited **Treshnish Islands** – a haven for puffins, kittiwakes, razorbills, shags, fulmars, gannets and guillemots.

Island rivalry

From Mull's northern flank, the Caledonian MacBrayne ferry can be seen going from Oban to Coll and Tiree. There's the usual rivalry between these sister islands, most distant of the Inner Hebrides. People from Tiree can't understand why anyone would want to get off the ferry at Coll. The people of Coll maintain that the inhabitants of Tiree are permanently

bent by the island's ceaseless wind.

Purists, or those against progress, feel **Coll ❹** is too civilised. A young cyclist, camping near the glorious west coast beaches, complained that the island's only hotel had gone suburban when it installed a sauna; while a 75-year-old resident of **Arinagour**, the only village, where most of the 230-strong population live, spoke with astonishment of the local café's transformation into a bistro.

Families go to Coll for a simple holiday, pottering on uncrowded beaches. Much of the coast can be reached only on foot – although bicycles can be hired. This isn't an island for antiquities, apart from the restored medieval castle of **Breachacha**, and an 18th-century castle where Samuel Johnson and James Boswell spent most of their time when they were stranded on Coll for 10 days during their Highland Tour. Johnson commented on the island's garden flowers but neither he nor Boswell climbed the giant dunes (100ft/30 metres) separating the beaches of Feall Bay and Crossapool Bay.

The Gaelic name for **Tiree ❺**, *Tir fo Thuinn*, means "land below the

waves". It's a good description of this flat, sunny island whose two hills are only 400ft (120 metres) high. One of the island's most eccentric visitors was Ada Goodrich Freer, who claimed telepathic gifts and an ability to receive messages through sea shells. She spent three weeks on Tiree in 1894 investigating Highland second sight. She spoke no Gaelic and was finally defeated, not by the language, but by the monotonous diet of tea, eggs, bread and jam provided by the Temperance Hotel.

Nowadays international windsurfers, who call Tiree the Hawaii of the North, are attracted to the island by the great Atlantic rollers that break on the long, curving silver beaches.

Excellent wildlife

Some people find **Colonsay** ❻, 40 miles (64km) southwest of Oban, too bland. But for others it is an antidote to the prettiness of Mull and the glowering Cuillins of Skye. It has its antiquities – seven standing stones and six forts – as well as excellent wildlife – birds, otters and seals. It also has good white beaches and isn't over-mountainous. Visitors are few as there are no organised day trips, and, even though the ferry calls six times a week (only three times in winter), accommodation has to be found either at the one hotel or with families providing bed and breakfast.

The island, 8 miles (12km) long and 3 miles (5km) wide, has a population of around 110 and is one of the largest British islands still in private hands. It is warmed by the North Atlantic Drift, and the gardens of **Colonsay House** have a variety of exotic plants.

At low tide it's possible to walk across muddy sands to tiny **Oronsay**, off the southern tip of Colonsay; alternatively there are boat trips. Oronsay is about 2 miles (3km) square and has a population of six. Its fine 14th-century priory is the biggest medieval monastic ruin in the islands, after Iona.

Island-hopping

The small islands of Eigg, Muck, Rum and Canna can be reached from Mallaig on the Sleat peninsula, at the end of the "Road to the Isles". There's not a great deal to do on the islands. Mostly people go for the wildlife, for a bit

It's said that the wild goats on Colonsay are descended from survivors of the Spanish Armada ships wrecked in 1588.

BELOW: Rum and Eigg from Morar.

A coastal cave was the scene of the most bloody episode in Eigg's history. It is said that a group of MacLeod men from Skye landed and raped some of the island women, for which they were seized, castrated and returned to their boats. When the MacLeods sought revenge, most Eigg folk took refuge in the cave, but the MacLeods lit a great fire in its mouth, suffocating almost all of the population.

BELOW: red deer on the lookout.

of esoteric island-hopping or for the superb walking, particularly on Rum.

The islands are all different, and, if you just want to see them without landing, take the little boat that makes the five- to seven-hour round trip six times a week in the summer, less often in winter. It's a service for islanders rather than a pleasure boat for visitors, and carries provisions, mail, newspapers and other essentials. Only those planning to stay are allowed to disembark. However, in summer, boarding the MV *Shearwater* at Arisaig, 8 miles (13km) before Mallaig, allows you to stop for several hours at either Eigg or Rum.

Eigg ❼ has had a chequered history in recent years. Owned first by Yorkshire businessman Keith Schellenberg and then by an eccentric German artist called Marum, it has now been bought by the Isle of Eigg Heritage Trust (www.isleofeigg.net), a partnership between the islanders and the Scottish Wildlife Trust with a large contribution from public subscriptions. The famous rock prow known as The Scurr (pronounced *Skoor*) can be climbed for magnificent views.

Muck ❽ is only 2 miles (3km) long and has neither transport nor shops. Visitors must bring provisions and be landed by tender. Eighty breeds of birds nest on Muck, whose name means "pig" (local porpoises were called sea pigs).

Fine birdwatching

An incongruous Greek temple stands on the rugged island of **Rum ❾**: the mausoleum of Sir George Bullough, the island's rich Edwardian proprietor. His castellated Kinloch Castle was used as a convalescent home during the Boer War just after it was built, and was for a time a hotel. The island is owned by Scottish Natural Heritage, although in April 2010 a significant area of land and property was transferred to the Isle of Rum Community Trust. There is fine birdwatching and hill walking.

Graffiti adorn the rocks near the landing stage at **Canna ❿**; they are at least 100 years old and record the names of visiting boats. The harbour's safe haven is one of the few deepwater harbours in the Hebrides. This sheltered island, the most westerly of the four, is owned by the National Trust for Scotland and is particularly interesting to botanists.

There are just two holiday cottages, each with enough room for four people.

Islay ⓫ is the place to go if you enjoy malt whisky. There are over half a dozen distilleries on this attractive little island, some with tours. Islay, where Clan Donald started, was once the home of the Lord of the Isles. A fascinating insight into its medieval history is to be found at the archaeological site of **Finlaggan** (www.finlaggan.com; Apr–Sept Mon–Sat 10.30am–4.30pm, Sun 1.30–4.30pm; charge). Islay also has some good beaches on the indented north coast.

Also on this side of the island is one of the best Celtic crosses in Scotland: the 9th-century **Kildalton Cross** stands in the churchyard of a ruined, atmospheric little chapel. **Port Askaig**, where the ferry from the Kintyre peninsula docks, is a pretty little place with a hotel, once a 16th-century inn, on the old drovers' road a few steps away from the ferry.

Orwell's solitude

Jura ⓬, Islay's next-door neighbour, is so close you can nip over for a quick inspection after dinner. Three shapely mountains, the Paps of Jura, 2,500ft (750 metres) high, provide a striking skyline. Although palms and rhododendrons grow on the sheltered east side, warmed by the North Atlantic Drift, it's a wild island inhabited by sheep and red deer and is much favoured by sportsmen, birdwatchers and climbers. It was to the island of Jura that George Orwell came in 1947, seeking seclusion while working on his novel *1984*.

A yachting haven

The tiny island of **Gigha** ⓭ has one of the nicest hotels in the islands – bright, spacious and beautifully neat and simple. There is no need to take a car on the 3-mile (5km) crossing from **Tayinloan** to this small green island which is popular with the yachting fraternity: no walk is more than 3 miles (5km) from the attractive ferry terminal at **Ardminish**, which is lined with sparkling white cottages.

The formal attraction on Gigha is **Achamore Gardens** (daily dawn to dusk; charge). Seals, barking amiably, cruise in the waters off the little used north pier. ❑

TIP

Tastings are available when you visit the distilleries of Laphroaig and Lagavulin at Port Ellen on Islay.

BELOW: the Paps of Jura.

THE OUTER HEBRIDES

The dramatic islands of the Outer Hebrides are relentlessly pounded by the fierce Atlantic Ocean. Visitors are either thrilled by their wild bleakness or find their remoteness disconcerting

The Outer Hebrides, 40 miles (64km) west of the mainland, are known locally as the Long Island. They stretch in a narrow 130-mile (208km) arc from the Butt of Lewis in the north to Barra Head in the south. Each island regards itself as the fairest in the chain. The people live mainly by crofting and fishing supplemented by tourism, with commercial fish farming – crabs and mussels as well as salmon and trout – and teleworking growing fast.

There are enormous flat peat bogs on Lewis and North Uist, and the islanders cut turf to burn rather than to export to the garden centres on the mainland. The men cut it during the summer and dry it *in situ*; then the women and children cart it home and stack it against the house for winter fires. A traditional blessing on Lewis is "Long may you live, with smoke from your house."

Fierce loyalty

These climatically hostile Western Isles of few trees and stark scenery are the Gaidhealtachd, the land of the Gael. When their Gaelic-speaking inhabitants change to English, as they politely do when visitors are present, they have virtually no accent and are among the easiest Scots for visitors to understand. They were fiercely loyal to Bonnie Prince Charlie. When, after the Battle of Culloden in 1746, the young man, with a £30,000 price on his head, dodged round the Outer Hebrides pursued by government forces, no one betrayed him.

Harris and the larger **Lewis** are really one island. Lewis is mostly flat moorland. Harris rises into high, rocky mountains with the peak of Clisham at 2,622ft (799 metres).

Turn north from the ferry terminal at **Tarbert** ❶ for Lewis, south for Harris. Ferries from Lochmaddy on North Uist and Uig on Skye dock in this sheltered port tucked into the hillside. There are a few shops selling

Main attractions
TARBERT
HARRIS BEACHES
TARANSAY ISLAND
HUSHINISH POINT
STORNOWAY
CALLANISH
BERNERAY ISLAND
VALLAY
BENBECULA
SOUTH UIST
ERISKAY ISLAND
BARRA ISLAND

LEFT: Borve beach, Isle of Harris.
RIGHT: the port of Tarbert.

Outer Hebrides

0   20 km
0   20 miles

N

Flannan Islands

Butt of Lewis
Port of Ness

Lewis

Arnol
North Tolsta
Shawbost
Barvas
Carloway Broch
Col
Callanish
Stornoway
Portnaguran
Uig
Crulivig
Achmore
Lewis Castle
Brenish
Balallan
Ranish
Loch Langavat
Scarp
Kebock Head
Western
Hushinish
Point
Hushinish
Ardvourlie
Clisham
Lemreway
Amhuinnsuidhe
799 ▲
▲ Beinn Mhor
Castle
571
Taransay
Isles
Luskentyre
Tarbert
Scalpay
Plocrapool
Shiant Islands
Harris
Pabbay
Manish
Berneray
Leverburgh
Boreray
Brove
Rodel
Vallay
Newtonferry
Duntulm
Castle
Kilmaluag
Balranald
Nature
Blashaval
Kilmuir
Staffa
Reserve
North Uist
Lochmaddy
Barpa Langass
Clachan
Trumpan
Loch
Shizort
Uig
Heisker or
Carinish
Monach
Culla
Trinity Temple
Lusta
The Storr
Rona
Islands
Beach
Ronay
Boreraig
719 ▲
Borve Castle
Benbecula
Wiay
Kensaleyre
Brochel
Eochar
Dunvegan
Raasay
Castle
Loch Bee
Dun Beag
Portree
Inner
Loch Druidibeg
Madonna
Bracadale
Skye
Sound
Nature Reserve
and Child
The
Scalpay
Howmore
620 ▲
Hecla
Carbost
Braes
Beinn Mhor
606
Talisker
Stigachan
Luib
Broadford
South Uist
Cuillins
Bualintur
Torrin
Pollachar
Lochboisdale
Soay
Elgol
Isleornsay
Ludag
Barra
Eriskay
Canna
Kilmory
Tarskavaig
Armadale
Kisimul
Castle
Ardvasar
Vatersay
Castlebay
Rum
Kinloch
Mallaig
Sandray
Harris
Kinloch
Rosinish
Castle
Cleadale
Arisaig
Mingulay
Eigg
Loch nan
Muck
Uamh
Castle Tioram
Ardnamurchan
Portuairk
Point
Acharacle
Sorisdale
Mingary
Salen
Coll
Castle
Tobermory
Loch
Arileod
Arinagour
Sunart
Caoles
Dervaig
Drimnin
Breachacha
Castle
Lochaline
Tiree
Scarinish
Treshnish
Ulva
MacQuarie
Salen
Barrapol
Islands
Mausoleum
Loch Ba
Hynish
Staffa
Ben
Oban
Fingal's Cave
950 ▲
More
Iona
Croggan
Fionnphort
Ross of Mull
Lochbuie
Firth of Lorn
Oban
Colonsay
Scarba
Scalasaig
Jura
Port
Ardlussa
Oronsay
Askaig

Flannan
Islands

Outer Hebrides

The Little Minch

The Minch

Ullapool

Sound of Raasay

Sound of Barra

Sea of the Hebrides

Inner Hebrides

Sound of Rum

Sound of Eigg

Cuillin Sound

Harris tweed, the Harris Hotel, a tourist office, a bank and some sheds.

A drive around South Harris (40 miles/64km) is rewarding. As you head south on the A859 along the west coast, you pass many glorious beaches – **Luskentyre, Scarista** – before reaching **Leverburgh**, with the remains of the buildings erected by the industrialist Lord Leverhulme (of Sunlight soap fame) for a projected fishing port. The main road ends at **Rodel ❷** with the 16th-century **St Clement's Church**, one of the best examples of ecclesiastical architecture in the Hebrides.

Superb seascapes

The single track road up the east coast offers superb seascapes and views across the Minch to Skye and you will pass tiny crofts from which you'll hear (as you will everywhere) the click-clack of crofters' looms producing tweed.

At Ardhasig, 2 miles (3km) north of Tarbert, you can take a boat (weather permitting) to the island of **Taransay** with some of the best beaches in the Hebrides and the location in 2000 for the BBC TV programme *Castaway*. Continuing north of Tarbert on the A859 after 4 miles (6km) turn onto the B887, which clings to the shore of **West Loch Tarbert**. The 16-mile (26km) drive from Tarbert to golden **Hushinish Point** is dramatic, particularly in the evening as the sun catches the peaks of Beinn Dhubh on Harris across the water.

The road goes straight through the well-maintained grounds of **Amhuinnsuidhe Castle** (pronounced *Avinsuey*), so close to the house you can almost see inside. This pale turreted castle, now a fishing lodge, was built in 1868, and James Barrie began his novel *Mary Rose* here. Close by, a salmon river runs into the sea.

From Hushinish, ferries cross to the small island of **Scarp**. In the 1930s, a new postal service was announced here. A special stamp was issued; the first rocket was fired, but it exploded, destroying both mail and project.

Return to the A859, which twists and turns past lochs and around mountains for 35 miles (56km) to **Stornoway ❸**, the capital of Lewis and the only town in the Western Isles. Here the **Museum nan Eilean** (tel: 01851-709 266; Apr–Sept Mon–Sat 10am–5.30pm, Oct–Mar Tue–Fri 10am–5pm, Sat 10am–1pm; charge) in Francis Street will give you some history of the islands. Most activity in this solid town of 9,000 inhabitants is at the harbour, where seals can often be seen. They give Stornoway its nickname of Portrona (Port of Seals). This is also where the ferry from Ullapool docks.

The best view of **Lewis Castle** is from the harbour. Lord Leverhulme bought it in 1918. In 1920 he purchased Harris, becoming Britain's largest landowner. His visions were admirable: to turn the islanders into a viable community not dependent on crofting but making their living from the sea. He failed only because of timing: today, fishing dominates the island's economy.

To explore Lewis's many antiquities, leave Stornoway on the A859 and, after a couple of miles, bear right onto the A858. **Callanish ❹** and its magnificent standing stones are 16 miles (26km) from Stornoway. The 13 ritual stones, some 12ft (3 metres) high, are set in a circle like Stonehenge. The **Callanish Visitor Centre** (tel: 01851-621 422; Apr–Sept Mon–Sat 10am–9pm, Mar and Oct Wed–Sat 10am–4pm; free, charge for exhibition) is close by.

Keeping to the A858, you soon reach the upstanding remains of the 2,000-year old **Carloway Broch** and **Arnol** with its **Blackhouse Museum** (tel: 01851-710 395; Mon–Sat 9.30am–5pm, until 4pm in winter; charge), which shows how the people of Lewis used to live. A different world unfolds if, just before Callanish, you take the B8011: it leads to **Uig** and its wondrous beaches.

The Uist archipelago

Lochmaddy ❺, where the ferry from Uig in Skye docks, is the only village on **North Uist**, and you are almost through it before you realise it's there. But to prove its status it has a hotel and a bank.

The Uist archipelago of low bright islands dominated by the glittering sea is 50 miles long and only 8 miles at its widest (80km by 13km) and is so peppered

Nobody knows why the Callanish stones are there. Once known as Nu Fir Breige – the false men – they have been claimed as a Viking parliament, a landing base for UFOs and a site for predicting eclipses.

BELOW LEFT: the Callanish standing stones.

Finding Your Way in Gaelic

The official tourist map of the Outer Hebrides is essential for the Uists. Even though only one main road links the three islands of North Uist, Benbecula and South Uist, most signposts are in Gaelic; the map gives them in English too. The Lochmaddy tourist office has a free sheet of English/Gaelic names put out by the Western Isles Council. To help preserve one of Europe's oldest languages, the council has put up Gaelic-only place names and signposts in the Outer Hebrides. In English-speaking Benbecula and in Stornoway on Lewis, the signs are also in English. Gaelic is a living language on these islands: local people often speak Gaelic among themselves and in the schools the children are taught in both English and Gaelic. And church services – on both the Protestant islands in the north and the Catholic islands in the south – are also usually held in Gaelic.

There are other problems to waylay the unsuspecting visitor: locals warn that roads in North Uist may be different from those on the map because the constant movement of the bog makes them change direction. Certainly at times the causeway road feels as springy as a dance floor.

Aiseag Scalpaigh

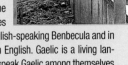
Ionad Fiosrachaidh Luchd-Turui Tourist Information

TIP

Rare species to be spied at the Balranald sanctuary include the corncrake, lapwing and barnacle goose. The visitor centre is open all year (tel: 01463-715 000).

with lochs that on the map the east coast around Benbecula looks like a sieve.

Rather than going south on the A865, which runs for 45 miles (72km) and which, because of the causeway and bridge, virtually makes North Uist, Benbecula and South Uist one island, travel around North Uist anticlockwise on the A867 and A865. On a 45-mile (72km) trip, you will pass superb beaches and antiquarian treasures.

The oldest pottery

The standing stones of **Blashaval** are 3 miles (5km) north of Lochmaddy and 3 miles (5km) further on, a turn-off on the right (B893) leads to **Newtonferry** and the new causeway to the island of **Berneray**, where Prince Charles occasionally recharges his batteries. Back on Uist, in the middle of the north shore, is the rocky islet of **Eilean-an-Tighe**, the oldest pottery "factory" in Western Europe, where quality items were produced in Stone Age times.

Still on the north coast is the superb beach of **Vallay** (actually an island reached on foot: beware of the tides). Round on the west coast, which is

greener than the east, is **Baleshare**, another island with a great beach joined to Uist by a causeway. Before reaching here, you pass the **Balranald Nature Reserve**, which was created to protect the breeding habitat of the red-necked phalarope, a small wader.

At **Clachan** the A865 turns south while the A867 runs northeast to return to Lochmaddy and the **Barpa Lanyass**, a 5,000-year-old squashed beehive tomb, 5 miles (8km) further along. Nearby is the **Pobull Fhinn** standing stone circle. Return to the A865; just before the causeway is **Carinish**, where Scotland's last battle with swords and bows and arrows took place. Not far away is the ruined 12th-century **Trinity Temple**.

Cross the North Ford by the 5-mile (8km) causeway to tiny **Benbecula**, whose eastern part is so pitted with lochs that most people live on the west coast. You can now go south for 5 miles (8km) to the southern tip of Benbecula or turn right onto the B892, which makes a 10-mile (16km) loop around the west of the island before rejoining the A865.

The loop road first passes the small airport and a Royal Artillery base before

BELOW:
a crofter's cottage on North Uist.

reaching **Culla Beach** – the best of many great beaches – and the ruins of **Borve Castle** with 10ft (3-metre) thick walls. The castle, one of the most important medieval ruins in the Outer Hebrides, was built in the 14th century and was the home of the MacDonalds of Clanranald, who once ruled Benbecula.

The South Ford, separating Benbecula and **South Uist**, is crossed by a ½-mile (800-metre) long single-track bridge. On **Loch Bee** there are hundreds of mute swans.

South Uist treasures

The main road runs down the west of the island for 22 miles (35km). To the west, are seascapes with yet more splendid beaches and, to the east, mountains and peat bogs are dominated by **Beinn Mhor** (2,034ft/620 metres) and **Hecla** (1,988ft/606 metres). After 4 miles (6km), atop **Rueval Hill**, "hill of miracles", is the modern pencil-like statue of **Madonna and Child**, which was paid for by worldwide donations. Just beyond this, still to the east, is the **Loch Druidibeg Nature Reserve**, home to corncrakes and greylag geese.

Next, to the west, is **Howmore**. Once the ancient ecclesiastical centre of the island, it is now a cluster of protected whitewashed cottages, one a youth hostel. Continue beyond Howmore to reach a superb beach. Further on is the renovated **Kildonan Museum** (tel: 01878-710 343; Apr–Oct Mon–Sat 10am–5pm, Sun 2–5pm; charge) with local history displays, crafts shops and a tearoom. Nearby is a bronze cairn honouring the birthplace of Flora MacDonald. At the end of the main road lies tiny **Lochboisdale ❻**, the main village of the south and the terminal for the Oban ferry.

At **Pollachar**, at the southwest tip, is a 3,000-year-old standing stone surrounded by wild orchids and clover, from where you can gaze across to Eriskay and Barra. There is now a causeway from nearby Ludag to Eriskay.

Eriskay, the subject of the hauntingly beautiful *Eriskay Love Lilt*, is disappointing, though for a fishing island only 2 by 3 miles (3 by 5km) with around 200 inhabitants, it has become very famous. Bonnie Prince Charlie landed on the long silver beach on the west side on 23 July 1745; 200 years later the *Politician*, a cargo ship laden with whisky, sank in the Eriskay Sound. Compton Mackenzie's *Whisky Galore* (known in America as *Tight Little Island*) was a hilarious retelling of the redistribution of the cargo.

Fishing has always dominated **Barra ❼**. In the 1880s, choice Barra cockles were eaten in London. By the 1920s Barra herrings were so important that girls came from as far away as Yarmouth in England to work 17 hours a day in **Castlebay**, the capital, to gut the silver darlings. Today Barra is primarily a crofting society with fishing restricted to white fish and shellfish.

The **Barra Heritage Centre** (tel: 01871-810 413; May–Aug Mon–Sat Mar–Apr and Sept Mon, Wed, Fri 10.30am–4.30pm; charge) tells the island's story. Also worth visiting is **Kisimul Castle**, the home of the MacNeils of Barra (tel: 01871-810 313; Apr–Sept daily 9.30am–5.30pm; charge). ❑

Kisimul Castle on the Isle of Barra.

BELOW:
Hebridean shores.

CENTRAL SCOTLAND

Perth is a superb centre for exploring the Central Highlands – the lochs of the Trossachs, romantic castles in the hills – as well as the ancient city of St Andrews and picturesque harbours along the Fife coast

Georgian terraces and imposing civic buildings line the riverside in the genteel city of **Perth ❶**, but principal streets are uncompromisingly Victorian. No dullness, though. "All things bright and beautiful" as the 36 bells of the handsome 15th-century **St John's Kirk** strike, heralding the hour – a contrast to John Knox's iconoclastic preaching here in the mid-16th century.

Behind the imposing portico and dome of the **Museum and Art Gallery** (George Street; tel: 01738-632 488; Mon–Sat 10am–5pm, May–Aug also Sun 1–4.30pm; free) is drama in Sir David Young Cameron's landscape *Shadows of Glencoe*, in the stuffed but still snarling wildcat, its bushy tail black tipped, and in Perth's link with space, the Strathmore Meteorite of 1917.

Scottish colourist

More art can be enjoyed in the roundhouse of the old waterworks, now the delightful **Fergusson Gallery** (Marshall Place; tel: 01738-783 425; Mon–Sat 10am–5pm, May–Aug also Sun 1–4.30pm; free) devoted to the life and works of the Perthshire painter J.D. Fergusson, one of the Scottish Colourists. *The Fair Maid of Perth*, Sir Walter Scott's virginal heroine, lived in **Fair Maid's House**, the setting for his novel of the time of the Battle of the Clans on the

meadow of the North Inch nearby.

Take a walk round the **Bells Cherrybank Gardens** (Glasgow Road; tel: 01738-627 330; May–Sept Mon–Sat and Sun pm; charge), with the National Heather Collection; or go for something more energetic at **Bell's Sports Centre** (tel: 01738-492 460), Scotland's largest sports facility. History and tradition take the stage in the **Perth Theatre** (High Street; tel: 01738-621 031), the longest established theatre in Scotland.

Splendid views over the city and River Tay can be enjoyed from the

PRECEDING PAGES: Kinross geese migrating.
LEFT: Abbot House, Dunfermline.
RIGHT: Blair Castle.

A guided tour of Falkland Palace includes an explanation of Royal Tennis, the game of kings (quite unlike modern tennis) that has been played on the court here since 1539.

top of **Kinnoull Hill** on the outskirts of the city, while **Branklyn Garden** (Barnhill, Tay Street; tel: 01738-625 535; www.branklyngarden.org.uk; Apr–Oct daily 10am–5pm; charge) has been described as "the finest two acres of private garden in the country".

Perth's castles

Perth is ringed with castles, some family homes, others romantic ruins like **Huntingtower Castle**, 3 miles (4km) west (tel: 01738-627 231; Apr–Oct daily 9.30am–5.30pm, Nov–Mar Sat–Wed; charge). An intriguing rooftop walk gives glimpses of hidden stairs and dark voids. James I had a year's imprisonment here.

Scone Palace (tel: 01738-552 300; www.scone-palace.net; Apr–Oct Mon–Fri 9.30am–5pm, Sat 9.30am–4pm; charge), 2 miles (3km) north of Perth, was Scotland's Camelot and home to the much-travelled Stone on which 40 kings of Scotland were crowned. Brought here in the 9th century and taken to London in 1296 by Edward I, it was stolen in 1950 from beneath the Coronation Chair in Westminster Abbey and recovered from Arbroath.

(It is now in Edinburgh Castle.) The earl of Mansfield's home offers such diverse charms as six generations of family photographs, Highland cattle, ornamental fowls and giant trees, as well as period furniture and interiors.

A lake for all seasons, **Loch Leven ②** is heaven for trout anglers and the chosen wintering ground for wild geese and other waterfowl. On an island and reached by ferry from the loch side is the ruined **Loch Leven Castle** (Castle Island; tel: 07767-651 566; daily Apr–Sept 9.30am–5.30pm, Oct 9.30am–4.30pm; charge), where the notorious Wolf of Badenoch and Mary Queen of Scots were once imprisoned.

Falkland Palace ③ (tel: 0844-493 2186; Mar–Oct Mon–Sat 11am–5pm, Sun 1–5pm; charge), sitting cosily in the main street of its old Royal Burgh, was the favourite retreat of the Stuart kings. Stone lintels that top many doors carry the incised initials of the couples the houses were built for in the 1600s, the date and a heart. Loving care is evident everywhere in the many manicured green spaces and carefully conserved weavers' houses.

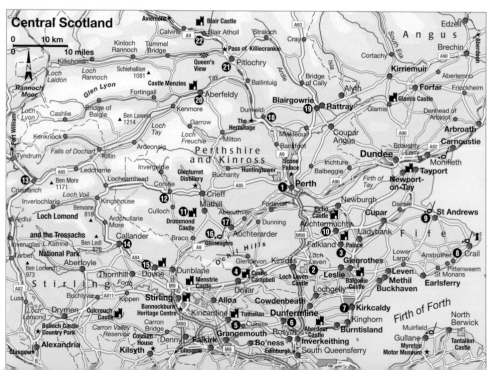

Castle Campbell ❹ (tel: 01259-742 408; Apr–Oct daily 9.30am–5.30pm, Nov–Mar Sat–Wed; charge) is rather impressively situated at the head of Dollar Glen, southwest of Perth. **Menstrie Castle** (tel: 0844-493 2130; Easter–Sept Wed and Sun 2–5pm; free), near Stirling, the birthplace of Sir William Alexander, James VI's lieutenant, links Scotland with Nova Scotia.

The kingdom of Fife

The M90 motorway that links Perth to Edinburgh does more than bypass Fife, thrust out into the North Sea between the Firth of Forth and the Tay. It bypasses an area rich in history, architecture and scenery. The kingdom's harbours nudge one another on a coast tilted towards Scandinavia, buildings reflecting the thriving trade it had in the 17th century with the Baltic and the Low Countries.

Culross ❺, where the Firth of Forth narrows, is a unique survival: a 17th- and 18th-century town that looks like a film set, and often is. Then it was a smoky, industrial town with coal mines and saltpans, manufacturing griddles and baking plates for oatcakes. Sir George Bruce, who took over where the mining monks left off in 1575, went on to such success that James VI made Culross a Royal Burgh. Today, the town's wealth of old buildings, with crow-stepped gables and red pantiled roofs, make it one of Scotland's finest showplaces.

Wynds, or pathways, lead past the 16th-century **Culross Palace** (tel: 0844-493 2189; house: June–Aug daily noon–5pm, Apr_May, Sept–Oct Thur–Mon; charge) – probably the finest gentleman's house of its period in Scotland – the "**Study**" (access by guided tour only), with a 17th-century Norwegian painted ceiling, and **Snuff Cottage** (1673). Past the house with the Evil Eyes are the church, the ruined abbey and the magnificent Abbey House. The clock tower of the **Town House** (access by guided tour only) dominates the waterfront and in the centre is the **Mercat Cross**, the tiny market place.

Although **Dunfermline** ❻ was for 600 years the capital of Scotland and burial place of kings, with a fine church and abbey (St Margaret Street; tel: 01383-739 026; Sat–Thur 9.30am–

An inscription on Snuff Cottage in Culross reads "Wha wad ha thocht it". The second line: "Noses wad ha bought it" is on a house in Edinburgh that was owned by the same snuff merchant.

BELOW: medieval Huntingtower Castle.

TIP

Near Crail you can visit
Scotland's Nuclear
Bunker (Mar–Oct daily
10am–5pm; tel:
01333-310 301;
www.secretbunker.co.
uk), which would have
been the government
headquarters for
Scotland in the event of
nuclear war.

BELOW RIGHT:
ice cream at St
Andrews.

5pm, except Thur pm and Sun am; charge), it owes its international fame to its humblest son, Andrew Carnegie. The great philanthropist opened the first of 3,000 free libraries here in 1881. The tiny cottage where he was born contrasts vividly with **Pittencrieff House** (tel: 01383-722 935; daily Apr–Sept 11am–5pm, Oct–Mar 11am–4pm; free), the mansion he left to the town on his death, which is now a museum with changing exhibitions on local history, costume and other period themes. The cut-out words "King Robert the Bruce" on the church tower advertise the king's burial here in 1329.

At **Leven**, behind the esplanade and the parked oil rigs, are marvellous shell gardens. Begun in 1914, the walls, menagerie and aviary are patterned with shells, broken china and Staffordshire figures.

Kirkcaldy's famous sons

Kirkcaldy's ❼ association with coal and floor coverings may not appeal, but the Lang Town, as it is often called, made important contributions to architecture, economics and litera-ture. Robert Adam and Adam Smith were born here and the **Kirkcaldy Museum** (tel: 01592-583 213; Mon–Sat 10.30am–5pm, Sun 2–5pm; free) has a superb collection of paintings by the Scottish Colourists, Sir Henry Raeburn and Sir David Wilkie, and the distinctive Wemyss Ware pottery can be viewed here as well.

Northwards along the coast there are some lovely fishing villages and sandy beaches. **Lower Largo**, its tiny harbour and inn stage-set beneath a viaduct, gave birth in 1676 to Alexander Selkirk, Daniel Defoe's "Robinson Crusoe". The original "Fifie" fishing boats were built at **St Monans**, but the shipyard now builds only pleasure craft. A path leads from the harbour to the 14th-century church, its feet on the rocky shore.

Pittenweem bustles with the business of fish. Nearby, **Anstruther** ❽, with the **Scottish Fisheries Museum** (tel: 01333-310 628; www.scotfishmuseum.org; Apr–Sept Mon–Sat 10am–5.30pm, Sun 11am–5pm, Oct–Mar Mon–Sat 10am–4.30pm, Sun noon–4.30pm; charge), and **Crail** end the run of picturesque harbours before Fife Ness is reached. The

Ancient and Royal

The Scots are so obsessed with golf that it is said that Mary Queen of Scots went off to play when her husband had just been assassinated. Wherever you are in Scotland there will be a golf course nearby. There are over 500 courses to choose from, and even tiny Highland villages have their own nine-hole courses. The game was developed as far back as the 15th century on the coastal courses known as "links", and you can still play on some of the world's oldest courses along the east coast of Scotland – though for a cheaper round it's best to avoid the Championship courses.

At St Andrews, golf qualifies as "ancient" as well as "royal": its Old Course was laid out in the 15th century and the Royal and Ancient Golf Club formed in 1754. There are no fewer than seven courses here. The Old Course is flanked by the New on the seaward and by the Eden on the inland side. Tucked between the New and the white caps of the North Sea is the shorter Jubilee Course. The Strathtyrum is an 18-hole course of modest length, while the Balgrove is a nine-hole beginners' layout. In 2008, the 18-hole Castle Course opened (www.standrews.org.uk).

oldest Royal Burgh in East Neuk, Crail's crow-stepped gables and red roofs ensure that artists outnumber fishermen.

There is a nice contrast in leaving the simplicities of Crail for the concentration of learning, religious importance and historical significance that is **St Andrews ❾**. Best known as the home of golf, with seven courses and a collection of memorabilia on display at the **British Golf Museum** (Bruce Embankment; tel: 01334-460 064; www.britishgolfmuseum.co.uk; daily Apr–Oct 10am–5pm, Nov–Mar 10am–4pm; charge).

The damage to the cathedral following John Knox's impassioned sermons started neglect that reduced it to ruins. **St Rule** nearby survives as a tower, and **St Andrews Castle** (The Scores; tel: 01334-477 196; daily 9.30am–4.30pm; charge) fared little better, though it has a wonderful dungeon. Elsewhere, the **West Port** spans a main street and steeples abound, but not for climbing, as Dr Johnson found.

At the **Aquarium** (tel: 01334-474 786; www.standrewsaquarium.co.uk; daily 10am–5pm; charge) all kinds of marine life can be seen in settings that resemble their natural surroundings. The **University**, whose buildings line North Street, is the oldest in Scotland.

Off the road back to Perth is **Hill of Tarvit** (tel: 0844-493 2185; grounds daily, house limited hours – call for times; charge), a superb mansion house remodelled by Sir Robert Lorimer with magnificent garden and grounds. Further on, **Auchtermuchty ❿** has surviving thatched cottages once used by weavers. The tea shop keeps the key to the Pictish, chimney-like church tower.

Lochs and mountains

Westward from Perth, roads follow rivers in the ascent to the lochs and watershed of the Grampians. At **Crieff** you can visit **Glenturret**, the oldest distillery in Scotland (tel: 01764-656 565; Mon–Sat 9.30am–6pm, Sun noon–6pm with exceptions, Jan Mon–Fri; charge), and glass, pottery and textile workshops. The romance of the **Drummond Arms** as the scene of Prince Charles Edward's council of war in 1746 endures, though it has been rebuilt. Five miles (8km) southeast of Crieff is the oldest public library in Scotland, the **Innerpeffray**

Innerpeffray Library, near Crieff, has a Treacle Bible, so called because "Is there no balm in Gilead?" is translated into "Is there no treacle in Gilead?"

BELOW: the crumbling remains of St Andrews Cathedral.

The cathedral and town of Dunkeld were fought over and the Highlanders defeated in 1689. Only the choir of the cathedral was restored and the main building is still roofless.

Library (tel: 01764-652 819; Wed–Sat 10am–12.45pm, 2–4pm, Sun 2–4pm; charge), founded in 1680. Also near Crieff, **Drummond Castle** ⓫ opens only its Italianate gardens (tel: 01764-681 433; www.drummondcastlegardens. co.uk; May–Oct daily 1–6pm; charge).

Comrie's ⓬ situation on the River Earn where two glens meet makes it an attractive walking centre. The town is on the Highland Boundary Fault and is known as "Scotland's Earthquake Centre". The road then leads on past Loch Earn, with magnificent mountain scenery, to **Lochearnhead**. Beyond here the high peaks have it – **Ben More**, **Ben Lui** and **Ben Bhuidhe** – until the lochs reach in like fingers from the coast.

Bonnie banks

Crianlarich ⓭ is a popular centre with climbers and walkers. For those on wheels, **Ardlui** is a beautiful introduction to **Loch Lomond**. The largest body of water in Britain, full of fish and islands, it is best known through the song that one of Prince Charlie's followers wrote before his execution. On the A82 southwards along the loch is the **Loch Lomond Shores Visitor Centre** and at the southern end in Balloch is the **National Park Gateway Centre**, the visitor centre for the **Loch Lomond and the Trossachs National Park** – 720 sq miles (1,865 sq km) of wonderful scenery (*see page 213*).

The road back to **Aberfoyle** traverses the Queen Elizabeth Forest Park and leads to the splendid wooded scenery of the **Trossachs**, best viewed on foot or from the summer steamer on **Loch Katrine**. Scott's *Lady of the Lake* and *Rob Roy* attracted flocks of Victorian visitors. **Callander** ⓮ found fame as the "Tannochbrae" of the 1960s' BBC TV series *Dr Finlay's Casebook*. Its **Toy Museum** (Main Street; tel: 01877-330 004; Easter–Oct Tue–Sun 11am–4.30pm; charge) includes Victorian tin soldiers.

Doune's 15th-century **castle** ⓯ (tel: 01786-841 742; Apr–Oct daily 9.30am–5.30pm, Nov–Mar Sat–Wed; charge) is remarkably complete, with two great towers and a hall between. Close by is **Dunblane**; the west front of its 13th-century cathedral was described by the Victorian writer Ruskin as a perfect example of Scotland's church architecture. The famous moorland courses of **Gleneagles** ⓰, 11 miles (18km) east of Dunblane, are a golfer's paradise.

North of the Ochil Hills, **Auchterarder** ⓱ is a starting point for the Mill Trail. Thanks to good grazing and soft water, Scotland's world-famous tweeds, tartans and knitwear have been produced here in the Hillfoots Villages since the 16th century. The trail leads from the Heritage Centre in Auchterarder, with the only surviving steam textile engine and Tillicoultry's handsome Clock Mill powered by a waterwheel, to the most modern mills in Alloa and Sauchie.

Moving north

From Perth, the road north bypasses **Bankfoot**'s raspberry canes and motor museum. At **Dunkeld** ⓲, cross Telford's fine bridge over the Tay's rocky bed for the charm and character of this old ecclesiastical capital of Scotland. A delightful museum in the cathedral's **Chapter House** introduces Niel Gow, the celebrated fiddler.

Romantics will feel at home at **The Hermitage**, west of the town. Built in 1758, this is the centrepiece of a woodland trail beside the River Braan, a folly poised over a waterfall. At the foot of the Highlands is **Blairgowrie ⓲**, which reserves its charm for anglers and lovers of raspberries and strawberries. At **Meikleour** the road to Perth is bordered by a beech hedge, over 120ft (36 metres) high and 1,804ft (550 metres) long, planted in 1746.

Along the Tay

Aberfeldy ⓴, easily reached from Dunkeld, is noted for the fine Wade Bridge across the Tay, built in 1733. A beautiful walk is through the **Birks of Aberfeldy** to the Moness Falls. To the west of Aberfeldy is **Castle Menzies** (tel: 01887-820 982; www.menzies.org; Apr–Oct Mon–Sat 10.30am–5pm, Sun 2–6pm; charge), a good example of a 16th-century Z-plan tower house. Beyond is glorious **Glen Lyon**, the longest and one of the most beautiful glens in Scotland, with the

village of **Fortingall**, where you can find Scotland's oldest tree, a yew over 3,000 years old. Nearby, **Loch Tay**, a centre for salmon fisheries, has **Ben Lawers** 3,984ft (1,214 metres) towering above it.

Seek out **Pitlochry ㉑** for spectacle. The Festival Theatre, magnificently situated overlooking the River Tummel, has an excellent summer programme of drama and music. But it's upstaged by the dam at the hydroelectric power station where in spring and summer thousands of migrating salmon can be seen through windows in a fish ladder (tel: 01796-473 152; Apr–Oct Mon–Fri 10am–5.30pm; free, charge for exhibitions). The Queen's View, 8 miles (13km) northwest of Pitlochry, is a truly royal vista up Loch Tummel, dominated by the cone-shaped Schiehallion (3,547ft/1,081 metres).

Beyond the **Pass of Killiecrankie** where Soldier's Leap recalls the battle of 1689, is **Blair Atholl ㉒**, key to the Central Highlands, and 13th-century **Blair Castle** (tel: 01796-481 207; www. blair-castle.co.uk; Apr–Oct daily 9.30am– 5.30pm; charge). ❑

Blair Castle is home to the duke of Atholl, the only person in Britain permitted to have a private army.

BELOW: a view from Luss, looking over Loch Lomond to Ben Lomond.

THE EAST COAST

The coast and countryside between the Firth of Tay and the sandy Moray Firth is a region of rare and subtle loveliness: here the scale is human and the history dense

Scotland's east coast and its hinterland are often bypassed by tourists, but the area has plenty of rewards that should not be missed. This is, after all, probably the most industrious (but not industrial) region of the country. Its ports and coastal villages have given Scotland its fishing industry. Its agriculture, from the rich croplands of Angus to the famous beef farms of Aberdeenshire – the largest stretch of uninterrupted farmland in Britain – has been hard won and hard worked.

"Our ancestors imposed their will on Buchan," says the writer John R. Allan of that flinty outcrop buffeted by the North Sea, "an idea imposed on nature at great expense of labour and endurance, of weariness and suffering."

The Scottish character

It is, therefore, the east coast of Scotland that most physically and visibly exemplifies that which is most dogged and determined (and perhaps dour) in the Scottish character; and which best knows how to exploit its assets.

The northeast port of Peterhead, for example, already Europe's busiest fishing harbour, turned itself into a major berth for North Sea oil-supply vessels; while the gentle, wooded valley of the River Spey is not only the centre of malt whisky production but, with its own "Malt Whisky Trail", has made tourist capital out of its celebrated local industry.

Along this coast you can learn to live without the majestic wilderness and Gothic melodrama of the West Highlands and their archipelago – although you will find echoes of their atmosphere in the Grampian glens of Angus and the outriders of the Cairngorms, which stretch into Aberdeenshire – and here you can explore the versatility of man's dealings with the land and the sea.

PRECEDING PAGES: the bright lights of Aberdeen Harbour. **LEFT:** Dunnottar Castle. **RIGHT:** hay bales and wind turbines.

Tale of two cities

The east coast cities are **Dundee** and **Aberdeen**, of comparable size (populations about 200,000 each) and separated only by 70 miles (110km). In recent years, Dundee, which long had the feel of a city down on its luck, has capitalised on its vigorous industrial past – rooted in textiles, shipbuilding and jute – and has transformed itself into a popular destination and a vibrant centre for arts, culture and discovery.

On the other hand, Aberdeen, the "Granite City", is as solid and unyielding as its nickname, a town of such accustomed prosperity and self-confidence that it assumed its new title of oil capital of Europe as though it were doing the multinationals a favour.

Naples of the North

Topographically, **Dundee** ❶ promises more than it fulfills. It has a magnificent position on the Tay estuary. It is dominated by an extinct volcano called the Law, and it has been fancifully called the Naples of the North. From the south side of the estuary, from the spectacular approaches of its road and rail bridges, you might be persuaded that its setting merits the comparison. There are other points of similarity. Like Naples, Dundee has had its share of slums and deprivation; like Naples, it is a port with a long maritime history (it was once the centre of the Scottish wine trade, and a leading importer of French claret). Unlike Naples, it has dealt its own history a mortal blow by destroying its past in a series of insensitive and sometimes shady developments.

"Perhaps no town in Scotland has been oftener sacked, pillaged and destroyed than Dundee," wrote an 18th-century historian, commenting on the fact that since the 11th century Dundee had the habit of picking the losing side in the various internecine and international conflicts that have plagued Scotland over the centuries.

Oil rig on Cromarty Firth.

Northern Scotland

0   20 km
0   20 miles

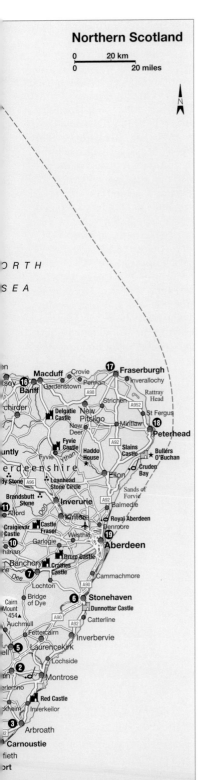

(map of Northern Scotland)

ORTH
SEA

Macduff — Crovie — ❶ Fraserburgh
Banff — Gardenstown — Penman — Inverallochy
chirder — Delgatie Castle — New Pitsligo — Rattray Head
New Deer — Strichen — St Fergus
Fyvie Castle — Mintlaw ⓲
untly — Fyvie — Haddo House — Slains Castle — Peterhead
erdeenshire — Ellon — Bullers O'Buchan
ly Stone — Loanhead Stone Circle — Cruden Bay
Brandsbutt Stone — Inverurie — Sands of Forvie
Alford — Kintore — Balmedie
Craigievar Castle — Castle Fraser — Royal Aberdeen
Garlogie — Westhill — Denmore
harian — Drum Castle — ⓳ Aberdeen
Banchory — Crathes Castle
Dee — Lochton — Cammachmore
Cairn — Bridge of Dye — ❻ Stonehaven
Mount 454▲ — Dunnottar Castle
Auchmull — Catterline
Fettercairn — Inverbervie
ell — ❺ Laurencekirk
Lochside
❷ — Montrose
erlenno
Red Castle
kheim — Inverkeilor
❸ — Arbroath
Carnoustie
fieth
rt

Climb on board Captain Scott's ship, RRS Discovery, at Discovery Quay.

BELOW: below deck on RRS Discovery.

The city's own fathers – and the **University of Dundee** – completed the process in the 20th century. A distinguished Scottish newspaper editor refused to set foot in Dundee after a graceful 17th-century town house was demolished to make way for the building of the **Caird Hall** (concerts and civic events) in the 1930s. Less controversial is the purpose-built **Dundee Contemporary Arts Centre** (Nethergate; tel: 01382-909 900; www.dca.org.uk; Mon–Sat 10am–midnight) by the River Tay.

Today, the future looks bright for the city of Dundee with big plans for a waterfront development, including a new museum, but this is expected to take a good many years to complete.

Building on the past

Little is left of antiquity for the history-conscious visitor: the 15th-century **Old Steeple**; the venerable **Howff graveyard**, which occupies land given to the city by Mary Queen of Scots; the **East Port**, rem-

nant of Dundee's fortified wall. But showing new initiative – and in the spirit of enterprise which is revitalising its economy through sunrise industries – Dundee is now capitalising on its maritime past.

The major attraction is **Discovery Point** (tel: 01382-309 060; Apr–Oct Mon–Sat 10am–6pm, Sun 11am–6pm; charge), which tells the story of Antarctic discovery and has displays on the "last wilderness" of Antarctica. Captain Scott's ship *Discovery*, built in Dundee, is moored here and may be boarded. In Victoria Dock is the restored HMS *Unicorn* (tel: 01382-200 900; www.frigateunicorn.org; Apr–Oct daily 10am–5pm, Nov–Mar Wed–Fri noon–4pm, Sat–Sun 10am–4pm; charge), the oldest British warship still afloat and one of only four frigates left in the world. Dundee had a high reputation for building clippers and whalers 100 years ago and sent its own fleet of whalers north to the Arctic. Their story is recalled at the **Broughty Castle Museum** (tel: 01382-436 916; Apr–Sept daily

10am–5pm, Oct–Mar Tue–Sun; free) in Broughty Ferry.

Another reminder of past glories is to be found at the award-winning **Verdant Works** (West Henderson's Wynd; tel: 01382-309 060; Nov–Mar Wed–Sun 10.30am–4.30pm; charge), a former jute mill in which an imaginative range of displays now tells the history of Dundee's important jute and textiles industries.

Looking more to the future, **Sensation Dundee** (Greenmarket; tel: 01382-228 800; www.sensation.org.uk; daily 10am–5pm; charge) is an innovative science centre that focuses on the five senses, with more than 80 hands-on interactive exhibits, and you can even have a go at keyhole surgery and meet some robots.

Land of the Picts

Outside Dundee, the county of Angus is an eloquent fusion of hill, glen, farmland, beach and cliff, and its towns and villages reach back into the dawn of Scottish history. **Brechin ❷** has a 12th-century cathedral and one of the only two Celtic round towers remaining

on the Scottish mainland. Set in the Brechin Castle Centre Country Park, **Pictavia Visitor Centre** (tel: 01356-626 241; www.pictavia.org.uk; Mar–Oct Mon–Sat 9am–5pm, Sun 10am–5pm, Nov–Feb Sat–Sun 10am–5pm; charge) tells the story of the Picts, the first known inhabitants of Scotland.

The twin Caterthun Hills near Brechin are ringed with concentric Iron Age ramparts and there are Pictish sculptured stones in the churchyard of **Aberlemno**, off the A90, while the former Royal Burgh of **Arbroath ❸**, a fishing port and holiday resort now moving into light industry, was once a Pictish settlement.

Arbroath Abbey (tel: 01241-878 756; Apr–Sept daily 9.30am–5.30pm, Oct–Mar 9.30am–4.30pm; charge), now a handsome ruin, dates back to 1178 and was the scene, in 1320, of a key event in the troubled history of Scotland: the signing of the Declaration of Arbroath. There, the Scottish nobles reaffirmed their determination to resist the persistent invasions of the English and to preserve the liberty and independence of their country.

Arbroath smokies are still produced in small family smokehouses in the fishing port of Arbroath.

BELOW: the innovative garden at Maggies Centre, Dundee.

Arbroath's red cliffs and harbour at the Fit o' the Toon (foot of the town) remain atmospheric, and its local cottage industry of smoking haddock continues to produce the celebrated Arbroath smokies. The **Signal Tower** complex, built in 1813 to serve the families of the keepers of the lonely Bellrock Lighthouse, now houses a **museum** (tel: 01241-875 598; Mon–Sat 10am–5pm, July and Aug also Sun 2–5pm; free) telling the story of the lighthouse and its keepers and the people of Arbroath.

Glamis Castle

Between Arbroath and Dundee is the resort of **Carnoustie**, which has a famous golf course and a lot of sand, while 13 miles (22km) to the north is the elegant town of **Montrose**, built at the mouth of a vast tidal basin, which is the winter home of pink-footed Arctic geese.

Inland, the country town of **Forfar** (where King Malcolm Canmore held his first parliament in 1057) is a striking point for the gloriously under-used and somehow secretive glens of Angus and lies close to what must be considered the county's star attraction, **Glamis Castle** ❹ (tel: 01307-840 393; Mar–Oct daily 10am–6pm, Nov–Dec 10.30am–4.30pm; charge), the exquisite fairy-tale home of the earls of Strathmore and Kinghorne and the childhood home of the late Queen Elizabeth the Queen Mother. It was claimed by Shakespeare to be the legendary setting for *Macbeth*. ("Hail Macbeth, Thane of Glamis!")

A group of 17th-century cottages in the village of Glamis have now been turned by the National Trust for Scotland into the **Angus Folk Museum** (tel: 0844-493 2141; July–Aug daily noon–5pm, Apr–June and Sept–Oct Sat–Sun only; charge), illustrating the nature of domestic and agricultural life over the past 200 years.

A visit to Glamis can be combined with a look at **Kirriemuir**, birthplace of the writer J.M. Barrie and the "Thrums" of his novels. The house in which the author of *Peter Pan* was born is a **museum** (tel: 01575-572 646; July–Aug daily 11am–5pm, Apr–June, Sept–Oct Sat–Wed noon–5pm, Sun 1–5pm;

BELOW: the distinctive Glamis Castle.

charge) where you can see Barrie's very first theatre.

Walking in the glens

Kirriemuir is also the gateway to **Glen Prosen** and **Glen Clova**, from where the committed walker can penetrate deep into the heart of the Grampians to **Glen Doll** and pick up the old drover roads over to Deeside. These routes were once used by armies, rebels and whisky smugglers, as well as cattle drovers. They look easy walking on the Ordnance Survey map, but can be treacherous.

To the southwest is **Glen Isla** and to the north **Glen Lethnot** (route of a "whisky road" formerly used by smugglers to outwit Revenue men). Here too is the graceful, meandering **Glen Esk**, which is reached through the pretty village of **Edzell ❺**, where **Edzell Castle** (tel: 01356-648 631; Apr–Oct daily 9.30am–5.30pm, Nov–Mar Sat–Wed 9.30am–4.30pm; charge), the ancestral home of the Lindsay family, has a magnificent walled Renaissance garden.

Dramatic cliffs

Edzell lies on the Angus boundary with Aberdeenshire, and here the countryside begins to alter subtly. It lies, too, on the western edge of the **Howe of the Mearns**, which means something special to lovers of Scottish literature. This is the howe, or vale, which nurtured Lewis Grassic Gibbon, whose brilliant trilogy *A Scots Quair* gave the 20th-century Scottish novel and the Scots language its most distinctive voice: *Sunset Song, Cloud Howe, Grey Granite*. His lilting, limpid prose sings in your ears as you cross these rolling fields of rich red earth and granite boulders to a coast that becomes ever more riven and rugged as you near **Stonehaven ❻** and the big skies, luminous light, spare landscape and chilly challenge of the northeast.

"The Highland Fault meets the sea at Stonehaven, and when you cross it you say goodbye to ease and ampli-

tude," writes John R. Allan, the northeast's most eloquent advocate. The A90 to Aberdeen bypasses Stonehaven, but this little fishing port-turned-seaside resort is worth a visit for the drama of its cliffs and **Dunnottar Castle** (tel: 01569-762 173; www.dunnottarcastle.co.uk; Apr–mid-Oct daily 9am–6pm, mid-Oct–mid-Apr Fri–Mon 10.30am–sunset; charge), standing on its own giant rock south of the town. In the dungeons of these spectral ruins Covenanters were left to rot, and the Scottish Regalia – the "Honours of Scotland" – were concealed in the 17th century from Cromwell's Roundheads. Today's brave souls may wish to take a dip in Stonehaven's Art Deco heated outdoor swimming pool, which is open throughout the summer.

From Stonehaven to Aberdeen is a clear, high, exhilarating run of 15 miles (24km) along the cliffs. But why not let the Granite City and the coast be the climax to your northeast tour and take, instead, the A957 to the lower Dee Valley? Called the Slug Road, from the Gaelic for a narrow passage, it takes you to **Crathes** where you

BELOW: boats moored at Stonehaven.

Originally looking for an estate further west, Queen Victoria and Prince Albert were advised that the climate near the River Dee in the east would be better for Albert's delicate constitution.

BELOW: rugged scenery on Rothiemurchas.

can visit the late 16th-century tower house and its renowned gardens (tel: 0844-493 2166; house June–Aug daily 10.30am–5pm, Apr–May, Sep–Oct Sat–Thur, Nov–Mar Sat–Sun only; gardens daily all year; charge). Nearby is the little town of **Banchory ❼**, where you can sometimes see salmon leaping at the **Bridge of Feugh**.

Royal haunts

The **Dee Valley** is justly celebrated for its expansive beauty and the pellucid, peat-brown grace of its salmon river. At the handsome village of **Aboyne**, between Banchory and Ballater, you begin to tread on the rougher hem of the Eastern Highlands. Deeside's royal associations make it the tourist honeypot of Aberdeenshire. **Ballater ❽** is where the royal family pops down to the shops (look for the "By Appointment" signs) while staying at **Balmoral** (tel: 013397-42534; www.balmoralcastle.com; grounds and exhibitions Apr–July daily 10am–5pm; charge). Since 1852 Balmoral has been a private royal residence, and in midsummer the Queen shares her gardens with the public and

her prayers with her subjects at nearby **Crathie** church.

On the A93, 8 miles (13km) west of Balmoral, is the village of **Braemar ❾**, much loved by Queen Victoria, and best enjoyed in September when the Highland Gathering brings people from all over the world. Fairy-tale **Braemar Castle**'s surprising charm and intimacy stem from being lived in (tel: 013397-41219; www.braemarcastle.co.uk; Sat–Sun 11am–5pm, also Wed July–Aug; charge).

From Banchory you can strike over to Donside (the valley of Aberdeen's second, lesser-known river), taking the A980 through the village of **Lumphanan ❿**, alleged to be the burial place of the doomed King Macbeth whose history has so often been confused with Shakespeare's fiction. But **Macbeth's Cairn** doesn't mark the grave of the king – it is a prehistoric cairn. (It has now been established that Macbeth, like so many of the early Scottish kings, was buried on Iona (*see page 243*). You can see at Lumphanan, however, one of Scotland's earliest medieval earthworks, the **Peel Ring of Lumphanan**.

Near the explosively named village of Echt is the magnificent **Castle Fraser** (tel: 0844-493 2164; July–Aug daily 11am–5pm, Apr–June and Sept–Oct Thur–Sun noon–5pm; charge). Completed in 1636, it has been the home of the Fraser chiefs ever since. Extensive walks can be taken in the grounds (all year daily).

Donside's metropolis is the little country town of **Alford** ⑪ where you can take a trip in the **Alford Valley Railway**'s narrow-gauge passenger steam railway (tel: 07879-293 934; www.alfordvalleyrailway.org.uk; May–Sept daily 11.30am–4pm with exceptions; charge), and visit the **Grampian Transport Museum** (tel: 01975-562 292; www.gtm.org.uk; daily Mar–Sept 10am–5pm, Oct 10am–4pm; charge); and nearby **Kildrummy Castle** (tel: 01975-571 331; Apr–Sept daily 9.30am–5.30pm; charge) a romantic and extensive 13th-century ruin which featured prominently in the 1715 Jacobite Rebellion.

Older history can be found at Oyne at the **Archaeolink** (tel: 01464-851 500; www.archaeolink.co.uk; Apr–Oct daily 10am–5pm; charge) a "pre-his-tory park" which takes you on a journey back in time.

Around the Cairngorms

The lonely, savage massif of the **Cairngorms**, which became Britain's biggest national park in 2003, dominates the Eastern Highlands. There is no direct route through its lofty bulk, but from Deeside and Donside you can pick up the road which circles around it for a thrilling journey.

At the hamlet of **Cock Bridge**, 32 miles (52km) west of Alford, beside the austere, curtain-walled **Corgarff Castle** (tel: 01975-651 460; Apr–Sept daily 9.30am–5.30pm, Oct–Mar Sat–Sun 9.30am–4.30pm; charge), the A939 becomes the **Lecht Road**, which rises precipitously to some 2,000ft (600 metres) before careering giddily down into the village of Tomintoul. In winter, the Lecht is almost always the first main road in Scotland to be blocked with snow, encouraging an optimistic ski development at its summit. A mile or so to the north of that summit, look out for the **Well of the Lecht**. Above a small natural spring, a white stone

The CairnGorm Mountain Railway is a funicular railway that runs through the Cairngorm ski area.

BELOW: a bottlenose dolphin in the Moray Forth.

*You can view
Strathspey in comfort
and style from the
Strathspey Railway:
the steam train runs
through the valley
during the summer.*

BELOW: rusting
boats in the
harbour.

plaque, dated 1745, records that five companies of the 33rd Regiment built the road from here to the Spey.

Speyside whisky trail

Tomintoul , at 1,600ft (500 metres), is one of the highest villages in Scotland and a pick-up point for the "Malt Whisky Trail" which can take you meandering (or perhaps reeling) through seven famous malt whisky distilleries in and around the Spey Valley. The **Glenlivet Distillery** (tel: 01340-821 720; www.theglenlivet.com; Apr–Oct daily 9.30am–4pm; free) was the first in Scotland to be licensed. From Glenlivet you can also enjoy the extensive walks and cycleway network on the Crown Estate.

Strathspey – *strath* means valley – is one of the loveliest valleys in Scotland, as much celebrated for the excellence of its angling as for its malt whisky industry. When you descend from the dark uplands of the Lecht passage through Tomintoul to the handsome granite town of **Grantown-on-Spey** , you see a land gradually tamed and gentled by natural woodland,

open pastures and the clear, comely waters of the River Spey itself. This pretty town is the focal point of the 935 sq mile (2,420 sq km) **Cairngorms National Park**, Britain's biggest national park, where you might see a golden eagle.

Grantown, like so many of the small towns and large villages in this area, was an 18th-century "new town", planned and built by its local laird. It makes a good centre for exploring Strathspey and it's also within easy reach of the Moray Firth, and the leading resort and former spa town of Nairn. The route from Grantown (the A939) takes you past the island castle of **Lochindorb** – once the lair of the Wolf of Badenoch, Alexander Stuart – the notorious outlawed son of Robert II, who sacked the town of Forres and destroyed Elgin Cathedral.

Nairn , when the sun shines – and the Moray Firth claims to have the biggest share of sunshine on the Scottish mainland – is a splendid place, even elegant, with fine hotels and golf courses, glorious beaches and big blue vistas to the distant hills on

the north side of the firth. Look out for the resident bottlenose dolphins; the best time to see them is between June and August.

On Nairn's doorstep is **Cawdor Castle** (tel: 01667-404 401; www.cawdorcastle.com; May–Oct daily 10am–5.30pm; charge), 14th-century home of the Thanes of Cawdor (more Macbeth associations); eastwards up the coast are the ghostly **Culbin Sands**; and on the Ardersier peninsula to the west is the awesome and still occupied **Fort George** (tel: 01667-460 232; daily Apr–Sept 9.30am–5.30pm, Oct–Mar 9.30am–4.30pm; charge) built to control and intimidate the Highlands after the 1745 Rebellion.

Battle of Culloden

The most poignant and atmospheric reminder of Charles Edward Stuart's costly adventure, however, is **Culloden Moor**, which lies between Nairn and Inverness. Culloden was the last battle fought on Britain's mainland, and here in April 1746 the Jacobite cause was finally lost to internal conflicts and the superior forces of the Hano-

verian army. Now owned by the National Trust for Scotland, it is a melancholy, blasted place – in effect, a war graveyard where the Highlanders buried their dead in communal graves marked by rough stones bearing the names of each clan. The new **Visitor Centre** (tel: 0844-493 2159; daily Apr–Oct 9am–6pm, Feb–Mar, Nov–Dec 10am–4pm; charge), complete with a "Battle Immersion Theatre", tells the gruesome story of how in only 40 minutes the prince's army lost 1,200 men to the king's 310. "Butcher" Cumberland's Redcoats even slaughtered some of the bystanders who had come out from Inverness to watch.

The coast and countryside to the east of Nairn is worth attention – a combination of fishing villages like **Burghead** and **Findhorn** (now famous for the Findhorn Foundation, an international "alternative" community whose life and work, based on meditation and spiritual practice, have turned the sand dunes into flourishing vegetable gardens). And there are pleasing, dignified inland towns built of golden sandstone, such as

In a great sandstorm in 1695, the Culbin Sands off Nairn finally overwhelmed the village of Culbin, which now lies buried beneath them.

BELOW:
peace and quiet on Culloden Moor..

Black Gold in the North Sea

The discovery of oil and natural gas in the North Sea has always been a controversial issue, but there is still more under the waves

The Scottish National Party (SNP) would argue otherwise, but the days when it was assumed that the North Sea's "black gold" would cure all Scotland's social and industrial ailments may be long gone. The huge oil revenues have disappeared into the maw of the British Treasury, and little has come back across the border. As one Scottish nationalist put it: "Scotland must be the only country on Earth to discover oil and become worse off."

Even after devolution, Scotland still has no access to the revenues, but it has acquired a mature, technologically advanced industry that employs thousands of people and underwrites a great many other jobs all over the country. The birth of the offshore oil industry partly compensated for the jobs lost in traditional heavy industries like coal, shipbuilding and steel.

Oil was discovered in the North Sea in the 1960s, and development proceeded rapidly. The early days between 1972 and 1979 were astonishing. Every week new schemes were announced for supply bases, refineries and petrochemical works. Scotland was galvanised. The SNP startled Britain by getting 11 members elected to parliament in 1974 on the crude but effective slogan "It's Scotland's Oil".

Heady days, but they didn't last. When the price of oil slumped in 1985–6 from $40 to less than $10 a barrel, recession struck the east coast. Nevertheless, recovery followed, and production reached a new peak of 2.95 million barrels per day in 1999. In 2007, North Sea crude oil was selling at over $60 a barrel.

Major world player

Minimal government regulation and free competition make the area attractive to the oil companies. The high quality of the oil, political stability and proximity to large European markets have made the area a major world player despite relatively high production costs.

Oil and gas flow from more than 100 oilfields off the east coast of Scotland. Though the UK is Europe's largest producer of oil and natural gas, the government estimates it will become a net importer of oil within a decade. Many oil platforms are in the deep, stormy waters of the East Shetland Basin, while others lie under the shallower seas east of Edinburgh.

The oil comes ashore in Scotland at three points: on the island of Flotta in Orkney, at St Fergus north of Aberdeen, and at Sullom Voe in Shetland. This last is Europe's largest oil and gas terminal, processing more than 500,000 barrels of crude oil per day. Its impact on the local environment is closely monitored by the Shetland Oil Terminal Environmental Advisory Group (SOTEAG) based at Aberdeen University. Aberdeen is the oil capital, where every oil company, exploration firm, oil-tool manufacturer and diving company has a foothold.

While the SNP continues to fight for Scotland's share of oil revenues, major oil companies are reapproving their North Sea oil activity as older fields become less productive. Nevertheless, the days of North Sea oil production are far from over, with an estimated 920 million tonnes of recoverable crude still remaining. Exploration reveals that an area west of Shetland and the Outer Hebrides may well produce viable returns in the future. ❑

LEFT: North Sea oil rig.

Forres, **Elgin** ⓰ and **Fochabers**, the ancient capital of Moray. Elgin's graceful cathedral, now in ruins, dates back to 1224 (tel: 01343-547 171; Apr–Oct daily 9.30am–4.30pm, Nov–Mar Sat–Wed; charge). With a medieval street plan still well preserved, Elgin is one of the loveliest towns in Scotland.

Monks clad in coarse white habits add a medieval touch to the giant **Pluscarden Abbey** (fax: 01343-890 258; www.pluscardenabbey.org; daily 4.30am–8.30pm; free), hidden in a sheltered valley 5 miles (8km) southwest of Elgin. The abbey, founded in 1230, fell into disrepair until, in 1948, an order of converted Benedictines started to rebuild it.

The mouth of the Spey

The **River Spey** debouches at wild and windy Spey Bay, which is the site of the **Tugnet Ice House** (tel: 01343-820 339; daily 10.30am–5pm, closed in winter; free) run by the Whale and Dolphin Conservation Society, a thick-walled house with a turf roof, built in 1830 to store ice for packing salmon and now housing an exhibition dedicated to the salmon fishing industry and wildlife of the Spey estuary. The Spey marks something of a boundary between the fertile, wooded country and sandy coast of the Moray Firth and that plainer, harsher land which pushes out into the North Sea. Hikers can pick up the **Speyside Way** from here, a trail that follows the river all the way to Aviemore, large parts of it along disused railway track.

Now the motoring tourist, with Aberdeen just in sight, is faced with a choice. You can cut the coastal corner by driving straight through the prosperous agricultural heartland of Aberdeenshire by way of **Keith, Huntly, Inverurie** and yet more Aberdeenshire castles – Huntly, Fyvie and Castle Fraser (*see page 275*), to name but three.

Fishing villages

Alternatively you can hug the forbidding littoral of Banffshire and Buchan and see for yourself John R. Allan's "stony fields and diffident trees", the workmanlike ports of **Buckie, Fraserburgh** and **Peterhead**, and that whole chain of rough-hewn fishing villages and harbours that has harnessed this truculent coast into something productive. Here you will find spectacular seascapes, rich birdlife and the enduring fascination of working harbours, fish markets and museums dedicated to the maritime history.

Banff ⓰ is a town of some elegant substance with a Georgian centre, while the 16th-century merchants' houses around **Portsoy** harbour have been agreeably restored.

This village is also distinguished for the production and working of Portsoy marble, while there is beauty and drama to be found in **Cullen**, with its striking 19th-century railway viaducts and its sweeping stretch of sand.

Between Macduff and Fraserburgh, where the coast begins to take a right-angle bend, tortuous minor roads link the precipitous villages of **Gardenstown, Crovie** and **Pennan**, stuck like limpets to the bottom of cliffs.

Aberdeenshire is said to have more castles, both standing and ruined, than any other county in Britain.

BELOW: ruins on Portsoy.

TIP

For a fascinating route along what was once the Herring Coast – recalling the more prosperous days of the British fishing industry – follow the Fishing Heritage Trail.

At **Fraserburgh** , is the **Museum of Scottish Lighthouses** (tel: 01346-511 022; www.lighthousemuseum.org.uk; Apr–Oct Mon–Sat 10am–5pm, Sun noon–5pm, Nov–Mar 10am–4pm, Sun noon–4pm; charge), which tells the story of the lights and keepers who manned them.

South of **Peterhead**, around the corner, the sea boils into the **Bullers O'Buchan**, a high circular basin of rocky cliff which in spring and summer is home to hundreds of thousands of sea birds.

Close by are the gaunt clifftop ruins of **Slains Castle**, said to have ignited the imagination of Bram Stoker and inspired his novel *Dracula*. It is certainly true that Stoker spent holidays at the golfing resort of Cruden Bay, where the craggy shore begins to yield to sand until, at the village of Newburgh and the mouth of the River Ythan, you find the dramatic dune system of the **Sands of Forvie** nature reserve. South from here, an uninterrupted stretch of sand dune and marram grass reaches all the way to Aberdeen. Britain's largest breed-ing colony of eider ducks is estab-lished here with around 6,000 flying in each summer. and 1,000 staying on for the winter.

Aberdeen – a granite city

Of all Britain's cities, **Aberdeen** is the most isolated. It comes as a shock to drive through miles of empty coun-tryside from the south and, breasting a hill, find revealed below you the great grey settlement clasped between the arms of the Dee and the Don, as if it were the simple, organic extension of rock and heath and shore instead of a complex human artifice. On the sea's horizon you might see a semi-submersible oil rig on the move; in the harbour, trawlers jostle with sup-ply vessels; and there are raw new ribbon developments of housing and warehousing to the north and south of the city. But otherwise Aberdeen, in its splendid self-sufficiency and glorious solitude, remains curiously untouched by the coming of the oil industry.

Aberdeen is largely indifferent to the mixed reception it receives from

BELOW: oil rig support ships in Aberdeen.

outsiders. Its infuriating complacency, however, has been its strength, and will almost certainly be its salvation when the North Sea oil wells run dry and the city refocuses on its own considerable resources of sea, land and light industry.

Much of historic Aberdeen remains, although most of its imposing city centre dates only from the 19th century, with the building of **Union Street**, its main thoroughfare, in the early 1800s and the rebuilding of **Marischal College**, part of the ancient University of Aberdeen, in 1891. The facade of Marischal College, which stands just off Union Street in Broad Street, is an extraordinary fretwork of pinnacles and gilt flags in which the unyielding substance of white granite is made to seem delicate. Occupying part of the college is an **archaeology and history museum** (tel: 01224-274 300), which is closed until 2011 due to building work.

Union Street's die-straight mile from Holborn Junction skirts the arboreal churchyard of St Nicholas, Aberdeen's "mither kirk", and terminates in the **Castlegate**, which remains almost unchanged since the 13th century. Its centrepiece is the 17th-century **Mercat Cross**, adorned with a sculptured portrait gallery of the Stuart monarchs. Castlegate has the best views of the city, looking over the square and down Union Street.

The cross is the focus of Aberdeen's long history as a major market town and import-export centre. For centuries fishwives from **Fittie**, the fishing village at the foot of the Dee, and farmers from the expansive hinterland brought their produce to sell round the cross, while more exotic products from Europe and the New World were hefted up the hill from the harbour by porters from the Shore Porters' Society, Britain's oldest company.

Historic sights

Aberdeen's oldest quarter and civic origins, however, lie to the northwest of the city centre on the banks of the River Don, whose narrow, sandy estuary was never developed as a harbour and port in the manner of its larger twin, the Dee. Although Aberdeen was

Marischal College, in Aberdeen, is the second largest granite building in the world – the largest is the Escorial near Madrid.

BELOW LEFT:
Robert Gordon University.

Stony Facade

The city of Aberdeen inspires strong emotions. You are either convinced that its own conceit is well deserved – the city's Book of Remembrance contains the sentiment, "Aberdeen to Heaven – nae a great step" – or you find its exposed interface with the North Sea and its granite austerity wintry of aspect and chilly of soul. Even those who affect to dislike it do so with ambivalence. The writer Lewis Grassic Gibbon, wrote: "It has a flinty shine when new – a grey glimmer like a morning North Sea, a cold steeliness that chills the heart… Even with weathering it acquires no gracious softness, it is merely starkly grim and uncompromising… One detests Aberdeen with the detestation of a thwarted lover. It is the one haunting and exasperatingly lovable city in Scotland."

To counteract its critics, the city's tourist board has tried hard to change the image of Aberdeen from Granite City to Rose City, lavishing attention on every flower bed in the town. Its efforts have been rewarded by regular victories in the "Britain in Bloom" award; after 10 wins the city was debarred from entering to give other places a chance.

*Writing in 1929,
H.V. Morton was
uncompromising in
his description of
Aberdeen: "A city of
granite palaces,
inhabited by people
as definite as their
building material.
Even their prejudices
are of the same hard
character."*

already a busy port when it was granted a royal charter in the 12th century by King William the Lion, its earliest settlement was to be found clustered around **St Machar's Cathedral** in Old Aberdeen, once an independent burgh. The cathedral, founded in the 6th century, is one of the oldest granite buildings in the city (although it has a red sandstone arch which is a remnant of an earlier building) and has colourful, jewel-like stained-glass windows. The cobbled streets and lamplit academic houses surrounding it are atmospheric and peaceful.

Here, too, is Aberdeen's first university, **King's College** (founded in 1495 by Bishop Elphinstone). **Provost Skerne's House** (Guestrow; tel: 01224-641 086; Mon–Sat 10am–5pm, Sun 1–4pm; free), dating from 1545, houses a series of period rooms furnished to show how people lived from the 17th to 19th centuries.

The **Tolbooth Museum** (Castle Street; tel: 01224-523 653; restricted hours, call to check) provides a unique experience in the form of its atmospheric 17th- and 18th-century cells,

original doors and barred windows. Displays include the blade of Aberdeen's 17th-century guillotine.

Aberdeen's history has often been self-protective; the city gave the duke of Cumberland, later to become infamous as "Butcher" Cumberland, a civic reception as he led his Hanoverian army north to confront Prince Charles Edward Stuart's Jacobites at Culloden. But it is to its credit that it offered protection to Robert the Bruce during Scotland's Wars of Independence in the 14th century. In return, Bruce gave the "Freedom Lands" to the city (which still bring it an income) and ordered the completion of the **Brig o' Balgownie** (bridge), whose building had been interrupted by the wars.

Present attractions

The vigorous **Art Gallery** (tel: 01224-523 700; www.aagm.co.uk; Tue–Sat 10am–5pm, Sun 2–5pm; free) on Schoolhill has an impressive collection of European paintings mainly from the 18th to the 20th centuries, with works by Toulouse Lautrec and

BELOW: the
headquarters of
BP's North Sea
operation.

Raeburn, as well as by contemporary Scottish artists, and a sculpture court. For anyone with a military bent, the **Gordon Highlanders Museum** (St Luke's, Viewfield Road; tel: 01224-311 200; www.gordonhighlanders.com; Apr–Sept Tue–Sat 10am–4.30pm, Sun 12.30–4.30pm; charge) is a must. This unique collection tells the story of one of the most celebrated fighting units in the British Army. There is also an award-winning **Maritime Museum** (Shiprow; tel: 01224-337 700; www.aagm.co.uk; Tue–Sat 10am–5pm, Sun 2–3pm; free) that recalls Aberdeen's long and fascinating relationship with the sea. Children of all ages make a beeline for **Satrosphere** (Constitution Street; tel: 01224-640 340; www.satrosphere.net; daily 10am–5pm; charge), a hands-on interactive science and technology centre.

Aberdeen offers excellent shopping with a good selection of individual shops, plus a thriving nightlife. A lively theatre and a succession of festivals provide entertainment to suit all tastes. Besides all of its more obvious attractions, the city confidently promotes itself as a holiday resort and is one of the few cities in Britain with a beach, giving it the nickname "The Silver City by the Gold Sands".

On Aberdeen's beach

Between the mouths of the two rivers the sands are authentically golden, though don't expect to sunbathe often or comfortably on them: Aberdeen's beach is open-backed and exposed to the bitter North Sea breezes. Its parks, however, are glorious, wonderfully well kept and celebrated, like many of the other open spaces, for their roses.

Further afield, **Hazelhead**, on the city's western edge, **Duthie Park**, with extensive winter gardens, and **Seaton Park** on the River Don are probably the best open spaces, but all have good play areas and special attractions for children in summer. At Maryculter in the Dee Valley, is one of the country's most attractive small "theme parks", **Storybook Glen** (tel: 01224-732 941; www.storybookslgenaberdeen.co.uk; daily Mar–Oct 10am–6pm, Nov–Feb 10am–4pm weather permitting; charge), with giant tableaux of childhood characters. ❏

A commemorative plaque in the city centre.

BELOW: statue of King Edward VII in Union Street.

THE NORTHERN HIGHLANDS

The remote landscape of the Northern Highlands has a wild and wonderful beauty that won't disappoint. But the mountains, lochs, glens and rugged coastline have a story to tell in the museums of the towns and villages

Main attractions

INVERNESS
AVIEMORE
CROMARTY
STRATHPEFFER
TAIN
DORNOCH
HELMSDALE
JOHN O' GROATS
DURNESS
ULLAPOOL

PRECEDING PAGES:
Lochinver backed
by Suilven. **BELOW:**
Inverness Castle.

Nowhere in Britain is the blood-ied hand of the past so heavily laid as it is in the Highlands. The pages of its history read like a film script – and have often served as one. There are starring roles for Bonnie Prince Charlie, Flora MacDonald, Mary Queen of Scots, Rob Roy, the Wolf of Badenoch and Macbeth, with a supporting cast of clansmen and crofters, miners and fisher folk, businessmen and sportsmen.

The cameras could find no better point at which to start turning than

Inverness , the natural "capital" of the Highlands. It is assured of that title by its easily fortified situation on the River Ness where the roads through the glens converge. Shakespeare sadly maligned the man who was its king for 17 years, Macbeth. His castle has disappeared, but from **Castlehill** a successor dating from the 1830s dominates the city: a pink cardboard cut-out, like a Victorian doll's house, that makes Flora MacDonald in bronze shield her eyes and her dog lift a paw. It is now the setting of the Castle Garrison Encounter, a costume re-enactment of the life of an 18th-century soldier.

A cultural tour

In the nearby **Inverness Museum and Art Gallery** (tel: 01463-237 114; http://inverness.highland.museum; Mon–Sat 10am–5pm; free), the death mask of Flora's bonnie prince shares cases with Mr Punch in his "red Garibaldi coat", Duncan Morrison's puppet figure that once delighted local children. Traditions are strongly represented in silversmithing, taxidermy, bagpipes and fiddles, and even a 7th-century Pictish stone depicting a wolf.

Preserved in front of the **Town House**, on busy High Street, uphill from the river, is the **Clach-na-Cuddain**, a stone on which women rested their tubs of washing. **Abertarff House**, on Church Street, is the city's oldest secular building, dating from 1593. It has one of the few remaining examples of the old turnpike stair and is home these days to small art galleries.

Inverness today is modern and go-ahead, a small city with busy streets that conceal a fine selection of pubs, restaurants and late-night venues. An important cultural venue is the **Eden Court Theatre**, though this is just one among several venues that host a varied events programme. The city is expected to become one of the fastest growing in the UK, with a 40 percent population growth estimated over the next two decades. The environment is very attractive, with Inverness a former "Britain in Bloom" award winner.

Dolphin-watching cruises run from Inverness harbour, out under the handsome Kessock Bridge, opened in 1982 to ease traffic from the North Sea oil firms in Easter Ross. The bridge replaced the ancient Kessock ferry between the city and the Black Isle.

Loch Ness

From an area of Inverness rich in industrial archaeology the **Caledonian Canal** climbs through six locks like a flight of stairs to the "Hill of Yew Trees", **Tomnahurich**. This highland waterway, which joins the North Sea and the Atlantic Ocean through the Great Glen, was predicted by a local seer a century before it was built: "Full-rigged ships will be seen sailing at the back of Tomnahurich." Now you can set sail here in summer for a trip on **Loch Ness**, and enjoy "a wee dram in the lingering twilight". The dram may assist you in spotting the monster, the lake's supposed ancient occupant. You can take a variety of combined bus and boat tours from Inverness all year.

Urquhart Castle ㉑ (tel: 01456-450 551; daily Apr–Oct 9.30am–6pm, Nov–Mar 9.30am–4.30pm; charge) is a picturesque ruin on the loch's edge (15 miles/24km south of Inverness on the A82) which bears the scars of having been fought over for two centuries.

At **Fort Augustus ㉒** (29 miles/48km further south), the canal descends down another flight of locks near the **Clansmen Centre** (tel: 01320-366 444; www.scottish-swords.com; Apr–Oct daily 10.30am–6pm; charge), which illustrates the glen's history from Pictish to modern times. The garrison, set up

TIP

If you fail to spot the real Loch Ness monster, you can always visit the two visitor centres at Drumnadrochit, where multimedia shows invite you to separate fact from fiction.

BELOW: legendary Loch Ness.

Real-life Highland folk recall days gone by at the Highland Folk Museum.

after the 1715 Jacobite Rising, later became a Benedictine abbey.

Turn right at **Invergarry** onto the A87 for the beauty of glen and mountain on the road to Kyle of Lochalsh and Skye *(see pages 231–5)*. Or, continuing south on the A82, stop at the "Well of the Heads" monument, which records the murder of a 17th-century chieftain's two sons and, as reprisal, the deaths of seven brothers, whose heads were washed in the well, then presented to the chief.

The A82 now crosses to the east bank of **Loch Lochy**. Six miles (10km) before Fort William is the **Nevis Range**, where gondolas whisk you in 12 minutes up to 2,150ft (645 metres), giving stunning views of Scotland's highest mountains. On the outskirts of **Fort William ㉓** *(see page 224)*, take the A830 and you will immediately reach "Neptune's Staircase", eight locks taking the Caledonian Canal to the sea, from where there are grand views of Ben Nevis.

Aviemore's attractions

From Inverness you can also head southeast towards **Aviemore ㉔** and the magnificent scenery and wild-

BELOW RIGHT:
a Siberian Tiger prowls around the Highland Wildlife Park.

life of the Cairngorms. Aviemore barely existed before the railway arrived on its way to Inverness in the 1880s. Today, and after a slump in fortunes in the 1990s, Aviemore is a thriving magnet for outdoor types with hiking in the summer and winter sports when the snows come. The centrepiece of the revamped centre is the impressive **Macdonald Aviemore Highland Resort** complete with golf course and spa (tel: 01479-815 300; www.aviemorehighlandresort.com).

Nearby, at Carrbridge, is the **Landmark Centre** (tel: 01479-841 613; www.landmarkpark.co.uk; daily 10am–5pm with exceptions; charge). The attractions at this heritage park include a tree top trail through the forest, horse-logging and a new "Runaway Timber Train" roller-coaster ride.

At Kincraig, 6 miles (10km) southwest of Aviemore, is the **Highland Wildlife Park** (tel: 01540-651 270; www.highlandwildlifepark.org; daily 10am–5pm with exceptions; charge). Here once indigenous animals, including wolves, boar and bison, run free and the newest arrival, a snow mon-

Aviemore's Expansion

It's doubtful if the Clan Grant, whose war cry was "Stand Fast Craigellachie", could have resisted the forces at work in Aviemore, below their rallying place. The quiet Speyside halt has been transformed into a year-round resort by the opening of roads into the Cairngorms and chairlifts for the skiers. In the 1960s, Brewers built the Aviemore Centre, recently extensively revamped to form the impressive Macdonald Aviemore Highland Resort at its centre. Shops along the main street cater for the mass of visitors, selling outdoor equipment for skiing and mountaineering.

The beginnings of Aviemore's expansion date back to the 1880s when the railway arrived here on its way to Inverness. Once an important junction, Aviemore had a branch line to Grantown-on-Spey and Forres. Today, Aviemore is still a central base from which to explore the spectacular mountains and moors and to enjoy the bounteous wildlife – you may even see a golden eagle – and, when the snows melt, the pretty alpine flowers. A relaxing way to experience the scenery can be had by wining and dining on a Highland Railway steam train, which runs in the summer months en route from Aviemore to Boat of Garten (tel: 01479-810 725). A year-round funicular railway carries skiers and sightseers to the summit of Cairn Gorm, which provides some breathtaking views of Rothiemurchus and Strathspey below (tel: 01479-861 336).

key called Bishoujo, is drawing a lot of attention. Part of the park is drive-through, part walk-through.

Further south at **Kingussie** is the **Highland Folk Museum** (tel: 01540-673 551; www.highlandfolk.com; daily Apr–Aug 10.30am–5.30pm, Sept–Oct 11am–4pm; charge). The museum has a whole replica "township" of Highland blackhouses from about 1700, faithfully reproduced from excavations throughout the north. Craftsmen keeping alive the ancient skills in building, furnishing and various types of thatching are on hand to explain their secrets.

Only a few miles from Kingussie, on the A86, is the village of Laggan and the enchanted countryside that inspired the BBC TV series *Monarch of the Glen*, chronicling the ups and downs of an impecunious young laird and his struggles to keep a Highland estate alive.

A Highland Gathering

Back in Inverness, the A9 crosses the neck of the **Black Isle**, which is neither an island nor black but forest and fertile farmland, and is bisected by roads serving the oil centres on the north shore of the Cromarty Firth.

Just before you reach Fortrose, the one-time fishing village of **Avoch**, still with a pretty harbour, was a focal point during the Scottish Wars of Independence. Half a mile west along the coast stands the great mound of **Ormond Castle** with only the slightest remains of its one-time bastion still visible. This was the base of a largely unsung Highland hero, Andrew De Moray, who raised a Highland army that cleared the north of the English invaders in a brilliant guerrilla campaign that drove them back through the Southern Highlands. Having disposed thus far of the Auld Enemy, he joined William Wallace to form a credible force for the notable victory at the Battle of Stirling Bridge. In May each year there is a procession of villagers to the top of the castle hill to commemorate the Highland Gathering, as it is known.

On the golf links at **Fortrose ㉕**, on the east shore, a plaque marks the spot where, in the 17th century, the Brahan Seer, accused of being a witch, was put to death in an oil barrel – but not before he had foretold the building of the Caledonian Canal, the demise of crofting and much more. The annual St Boniface's Fair is held in the square adjacent to the magnificent ruins of a 14th-century cathedral; the fair's traders and entertainers wear medieval costume.

Nearby, at Rosemarkie, is **Groam House Museum** (tel: 01381-620 961; www.groamhouse.org.uk; May–Oct Mon–Sat 10am–5pm, Sun 2–4.30pm, Mar–Apr, Nov–Dec Sat–Sun 2–4pm; free), a Pictish interpretive centre with a superb collection of sculpted stones, audiovisual displays and rubbings.

Cromarty ㉖, at the extreme tip of the Isle, lost face as a Royal Burgh through declining fortunes as a seaport and trading community, but has earned rightful popularity as a place where visitors can step back in time in the unspoilt old town. Taped tours point out some of the most beautiful late 18th-century buildings in Britain,

BELOW: Hugh Miller's cottage.

*Beinn Eighe is a
fascinating geological
"pudding" of old red
sandstone topped with
white quartzite.*

BELOW: Fyrish
Monument near
Alness.

such as the **Courthouse**, now a prize-winning museum (tel: 01381-600 418; www.cromarty-courthouse.org.uk; Sun–Thur 11am–4pm; charge), the thatched cottage where the 19th-century geologist Hugh Miller, Cromarty's most famous scholarly son, lived (tel: 0844-493 2158; May–Oct Sun–Wed 1–5pm; charge) and the **East Kirk**, with three wooden lofts.

A road leads to **South Sutor**, one of two precipitous headlands guarding the narrow entrance to the Firth of Cromarty, where numerous oil rigs are moored. Around the rigs swim the North Sea's only resident group of bottlenose dolphins, plus innumerable grey and common seals.

A natural spa

Though Scots had long known the local sulphur and chalybeate springs at **Strathpeffer ㉗**, it took a doctor who had himself benefited to give substance to "miracle" recoveries and, incidentally, recognise their profitable potential. Dr Morrison opened his pump room around 1820, and the new railway brought thousands to fill the hotels and, if they felt inclined, enjoy

a "low-pressure subthermal reclining manipulation douche". A couple of wars intervened and the spa declined, but, like all things Victorian, this elegant town is enjoying something of a revival as a resort of character. The old railway station is now a visitor centre. If you want a taste of the Strathpeffer waters, call in at the town's **Water Sampling Pavilion** (tel: 01997-421 415; Tue–Sat 10am–5pm).

On leaving Strathpeffer, join the A835, which, after **Garve**, winds through Strath Ben and **Achnasheen ㉘**. From here the southern leg (A890) through Glen Carron is the stuff of photomurals, with Kyle of Lochalsh at the end of the rainbow that leads across the sea to Skye. Achnasheen's northern leg (A832) leads to **Kinlochewe ㉙** at the head of **Loch Maree** (*see page 227*) and close to the National Nature Reserve of **Beinn Eighe**; buzzards fly above the pine forests, home to the elusive pine marten and rare and protected wildlife, and perhaps you might see a golden eagle; nature trails begin in the car park.

Alternatively, from **Dingwall** – was Macbeth really born here? – road (A9)

and rail cling to the east coast. **Evanton** has an abundance of accommodation, and there's a good chance of seeing seals on the shore walk. Near **Alness** ㉚, on a hill, is a replica of the Gate of Negapatam in India, which General Sir Hector Munro, hero of its capture, had built by local men. Today Alness is dormitory to **Invergordon** on Cromarty Firth, which offered shelter to Britain's navy through two world wars and suffered the closure of its naval base in 1956. The area has also seen dramatic changes since the choice of Nigg Bay for the construction of oil-rig platforms.

A taste of Glenmorangie

Memories at **Tain** ㉛ are older, going back to 1066, when it became a Royal Burgh. Though St Duthac was born and buried here, it didn't save the two chapels dedicated to him from disastrous fires – or guarantee sanctuary. Today visitors can call in at the **Glenmorangie Distillery** (tel: 01862-892 477; Mon–Fri 9am–5pm, June–Aug Sat also 10am–4pm, Sun noon–4pm; charge) to see how the famous malt whisky is made and to sample some.

From Tain, the A836 leads to **Bonar Bridge**, and motorists have to adjust to negotiate single-track roads and the sheep that share them. This is Viking country, more Scandinavian than Scottish, with spectacular views of heather-covered moor and loch. At **Invershin** is a superbly situated castle without a burden of history. Retainers, some heavy-laden, come and go beneath the towers and battlements with which it is over endowed. **Carbisdale Castle** was built as late as 1914 for the duchess of Sutherland and is now a youth hostel.

The nearby **Falls of Shin** offer glimpses of salmon ascending the cataracts as they migrate, while the visitor centre has educational wildlife events for children. The centre also accommodates the "Harrods of the North", as it is known locally, with products from the prestigious London store set up by its previous owner Mohamed Al Fayed, who is also the laird of the 65,000-acre (26,000-hectare) Balnagown Estate in Easter Ross. It sells mainly tourist souvenirs, but has a range of fine foodstuffs plus a restaurant and tearoom.

TIP

There are many single-track roads in this part of Scotland. Cautious drivers should use the passing places not only to let oncoming vehicles pass but also to allow faster traffic from behind to overtake. Beware of sheep on the roads.

BELOW: watch salmon leaping at the Falls of Shin.

Spectacular cliffs carved out by the sea at Duncansby Head.

BELOW: the gardens at Dunrobin Castle were inspired by those at Versailles.

Crofting country

"All roads meet at Lairg," so the saying goes. Sometimes in August it seems all the sheep in Scotland do as well. **Lairg** ㉜ is in the heart of Sutherland crofting country, and the lamb sales identify it as a major marketplace. Mirrored in the quiet waters of Loch Shin is an Iron Age hut circle on the hill above the village.

The eastern spoke (A839) from Lairg's hub reaches the coast at Loch Fleet and **Dornoch** ㉝, where some regard Royal Dornoch, opened in 1616, as offering better golf than the Old Course at St Andrews. Dornoch Castle's surviving tower has been a garrison, courthouse, jail, school and private residence. Now it's a hotel. The lovely cathedral is also a survivor: badly damaged in a 17th-century fire, it was largely restored in the 1920s. The last witch to be burned in Scotland, Janet Horne, was condemned to death in Dornoch in 1727, though her commemoration stone reads 1722.

More happily, the Dunfermline-born industrialist and philanthropist Andrew Carnegie, who made his money in the United States, bought nearby Skibo Castle (now a country club) in the 1890s and lived there until he died in 1919; he funded the town's Carnegie Library.

The Sutherland clan

To the north is **Golspie,** which lives in the shadow of the Sutherlands. An oversize statue of the controversial 1st duke looks down from the mountain; a stone in the old bridge is the clan's rallying point; and nearby is the duchess' **Dunrobin Castle** (tel: 01408-633 177; www.dunrobincastle.co.uk; Apr–Oct Mon–Sat 10.30am–4.30pm, Sun noon–4.30pm; charge), an improbable confection of pinnacles and turrets. The formal gardens are a riot of colour in summer. The prehistoric fort at **Carn Liath** a little further along the coast is a simple antidote.

The gold rush that brought prospectors to the burns of **Helmsdale** ㉞ in the 1860s was short lived. The town's main attraction today is the **Timespan Heritage Centre** (tel: 01431-821 327; www.timespan.org.uk; Mon–Sat 10am–5pm, Sun noon–5pm; charge), which brings the history of the Highlands to life; there is also a large garden with

a unique collection of medicinal and herbal plants. Intrepid travellers keep going north to **Caithness**, for centuries so remote from the centres of Scottish power that it was ruled by the Vikings. Trade links were entirely by sea, and in the boom years of the fishing industry scores of harbours were built. The fleets have gone, the harbours remain.

The A9 to **Berriedale** twists spectacularly past the ravines of the Ord of Caithness and on to **Dunbeath**, where a few lobster boats are a reminder of past glories. Here, too, is the **Laidhay Croft Museum** (tel: 01593-731 244; daily 10am–6pm; charge), a restored longhouse with stable, house and byre all under one roof. **Lybster** ❸ offers more bustle, but at **Mid Clyth** leave the road at a sign, "Hill o'Many Stanes", for a mystery tour. On a hillside are 22 rows, each with an average of eight small stones, thought to be Bronze Age.

Herring were the backbone of **Wick**'s prosperity and come to life again in the **Wick Heritage Centre** (tel: 01955-605 393; www.wickheritage.org; Easter–Oct Mon–Sat 10am–3.45pm; charge). More than 1,000 boats used to set sail to catch the "silver darlings". Now the near-empty quays give the harbour a wistful charm.

The end of the road

For cross-country record-breakers, **John O' Groats** ❸, at the end of the A99, has a natural attraction – although, contrary to popular belief, it is not the northernmost point in Britain. A Dutchman, Jan de Groot, came here in 1500 under orders from James IV to set up a ferry service to Orkney to consolidate his domination over this former Scandinavian territory. A mound and a flagstaff commemorate the site of his house.

Boat trips run from the harbour to Orkney and to **Duncansby Head**, 2 miles (4km) to the east, where many species of birds nest on the dramatic towering stacks. From here a road runs to the lighthouse. West of John O' Groats, on the A836, is the **Castle of Mey**, the late Queen Elizabeth the Queen Mother's home. **Dunnet Head** is the British mainland's most northerly point.

The approaches to **Thurso** ❸ are heralded by the Caithness "hedges" that line the fields, the flagstones that were once shipped from local quarries to every

Jan de Groot's response to requests from his eight sons as to who should succeed him was to build an octagonal house with eight doors and with an octagonal table in the middle so that each sat at the "head".

BELOW:
Thurso surf.

Welcoming the Wolves

A rather inventive way of protecting the ecosystem in the Highlands has been the suggestion of reintroduction of wild wolves (hunted to extinction in the 1700s) to control the number of red deer whose numbers poses a threat to plant and insect life. This project could lead to the regrowth of the forests of old, and winter nights reverberating with howling packs roaming the wilderness.

Public opinion in surrounding cities has been largely positive, with many wishing to see Scotland reverting back to traditional landscapes. However, proposals have met with objections from farmers who fear for their livestock, and have little time for scientific claims that wolves will not hunt down entire herds of cows or flocks of sheep.

Highland sheep on Ben Eighe.

BELOW: sailing into Ullapool harbour.

corner of the old empire. The streets of Calcutta were paved by Caithness. **Fisherbiggins**, the fishermen's old quarter, is a reproduction from 1940, but elsewhere there is pleasant Victorian town planning. **Scrabster** is Thurso's outport, with a ferry to Orkney. The site of Scotland's first nuclear power research station, now defunct, at **Dounreay** was partly chosen for its remoteness.

Wild Cape Wrath

It's an odd feeling: nothing between you and the North Pole except magnificent cliff scenery. At **Tongue** ❸ the sea loch pokes deep into the bleak moorland, and near **Durness** ❸, which has some huge expanses of wonderful beach, the Alt Smoo River drops from the cliff into the Caves of Smoo. From Durness, a combined ferry and bus service travels to **Cape Wrath** from where you can see Orkney and the Outer Hebrides. Look out for cooties, sea cockies, tammies and tommienoories (aka puffins).

The return to Lairg can be made south from Tongue on the lovely A836 through **Altnaharra** ❹, where crosses, hut circles and Pictish brochs (forti-

fied towers) abound. From Durness the A838 joins the western coast at **Scourie** ❹, where seals are mistaken for mermaids and palm trees grow.

Ullapool ❹, 52 miles (83km) south of Scourie, is a resort for all seasons, beautifully situated on Loch Broom facing the sunset. The **Ullapool Museum and Visitor Centre** on West Argule Street (tel: 01854-612 987; Apr–Oct Mon–Sat 10am–5pm, Nov–Mar by prior arrangement; charge) has displays on the history and people of the area. Today, a car ferry serves Stornoway in Lewis and trippers leave for the almost deserted but delightfully named **Summer Isles**. Smoking is good for you at **Achiltibuie** ❹, where fish and game are cured in spicy aromatic brines.

Another route south is through **Bettyhill**, where the 18th-century kirk is a museum of the Clan MacKay and the 19th-century Highland Clearances. Strathnaver, to the south, was the centre for this once-powerful clan, which raised thousands of mercenaries for campaigns in Europe. Proof of their warlike history is in the fact that Strathnaver has the remains of no fewer than 10 brochs. ❑

Peatland versus Profit

The world's largest bogland in the far north of Scotland has suffered many threats in its long history, but now common sense prevails

Travel throughout the far north of Scotland and you will be struck by the lack of people. It's hard to imagine that from Neolithic times until the controversial Highland Clearances of the 18th and 19th centuries, much of the wild landscape of Caithness and Sutherland was populated by scores of crofters and thriving coastal settlements.

Indeed, even the Flow Country, a rugged "wilderness" that encompasses almost 1 million acres (400,000 hectares) of habitat-rich peatland, once supported settlers. Today, this fragile ecosystem and site of the world's largest bogland is owned or managed by an array of private shooting estates and national conservation and land-management agencies including the Royal Society for the Protection of Birds (RSPB), Forestry Commission Scotland (FCS), Scottish Natural Heritage (SNH) and the Deer Commission for Scotland (DCS).

Incorporating more than 20 Sites of Special Scientific Interest, few doubt the ecological importance of the Flow Country, beloved by fishermen, walkers and twitchers alike. Indeed, ornithologists estimate more than 60 percent of Europe's greenshanks annually breed in the Flow Country, while the peatland's startling diversity of fauna and flora also supports rare mosses, short-eared owls, golden eagles, plovers and hen harriers.

Fragile ecosystem

However, until very recently the Flow Country was a watchword for controversy. Until common sense prevailed (and generous tax concessions for wealthy investors were removed) conservation bodies struggled throughout the 1980s to counter the excesses of misguided commercial forestry projects designed to maximise revenue by planting and selling for timber huge swathes of (non-indigenous) conifer trees.

To the dismay of the "green lobby", these ill-advised "job and profit" motivated ventures threatened to unbalance a very fragile ecosystem that had existed on the peatland bogs for thousands of years.

Fortunately, today's forestry masters have ensured a more enlightened approach has been adopted by formerly overzealous landowners. With more than 8 percent of Scotland's total land area under its control, the FCS is now actively involved in helping reverse some of the worst excesses of commercial land management that for decades blighted the Flow Country.

Finding a balance

According to Tim Cockerill, Forest District Manager for Dornoch: "We are now trying to find a balance [between sustainable forestry and conservation]. We accept that the process of afforestation in the past was a step too far and we are working with agencies such as the RSPB to identify forested areas where natural habitats can best be restored."

With more than 25,000 acres (10,000 hectares) of peatland and grassland under the RSPB's ownership, initiatives include helping to reintroduce waterfowl by restoring watercourses to more than 5,000 acres (2,000 hectares) of bog previously drained for forestry.

Though the scars of the Clearances remain, it could be argued that the Flow Country of Caithness and Sutherland will slowly recover from this more recent folly to befall the landscape.   ❏

RIGHT: the mountain Creag Mhor stands in the ancient forest of Mamlorn.

HIGHLAND FLORA AND FAUNA

The wilderness of northern Scotland may appear to be older than living memory, but humans have actually had a big impact on its natural history

The symbol of Scotland – the thistle – is not tough enough for the Highlands. Heather, bilberry, bog cotton, asphodel and sphagnum moss (a springy, water-retaining plant that eventually rots down into peat) are the plant survivors here.

But ranging across this unrelentingly bony land are a couple of other particularly resilient symbols of Scotland – golden eagles and red deer. Red deer in the Highlands are thought to number 330,000, a population that is barely restrained by the huge deer stalking industry. In the summer the herds are almost invisible to all but the hardiest walkers, but in the winter they descend into river valleys in search of food. The golden eagle is virtually invisible all year round, although the population is relatively stable in the mountains. Recent moves have re-established pairs of white-tailed sea-eagles on the island of Rum.

Causing concern is the capercaillie, a turkey-sized game bird with the mating call of a brass band. Although it is no longer hunted, it has never learned to cope with modern deer fences: flying low through woodland, it crashes straight into them at speed. Another distinctive Highland bird is also vanishing fast. The corncrake's unmistakable rasping call is only heard in remote corners of the outer Hebridean islands.

After years of lobbying by conservationists, controlled trials are now being conducted to reintroduce beavers into the wild in Scotland.

CURSED WEE BEASTIE

One thriving specimen of Highland natural history is often omitted from the brochures: the biting midge. Of Scotland's 34 species, only two or three attack humans, and *Culicoides impunctatus* (with distinctive speckled wings) does the lion's share. In the end, you have to laugh, or they'd drive you crazy. As they say, midges are compassionate creatures: kill one, and a couple of thousand arrive for the funeral.

ABOVE: the idea that deer are nomadic and range for great distances in search of food is a romantic misconception: most animals remain "hefted" to the couple of square miles where they were born.

BELOW: nocturnal mammal the pine marten nests in hollow trees. Their numbers were drastically reduced by the fur trade last century.

RETURN OF THE LONESOME PINE

Long ago, most of the now desolate areas of the Highlands were forested. Over the centuries the trees were felled for timber and to accommodate livestock. Deer and sheep are very effective grazers, and tree shoots don't stand a chance. Stop at a loch to compare the growth onshore with that of offshore islands and you will see how destructive grazing animals can be.

Several decades ago the Forestry Commission, a government body, set about fencing off areas of moorland for reforestation. To make the initiative economically viable they chose the fast-growing sitka spruce, which they planted in marching rows. The result is not particularly pleasing on the eye, and there has been controversy over the use of public money. There are also worries about the damage coniferisation causes to the unique habitats in many areas – like the areas of bogland in parts of Caithness.

Recently several initiatives to reforest large areas with native Scots pine *(above)* and deciduous trees have been started on privately purchased land by charitable organisations such as the Royal Society for the Protection of Birds, John Muir Trust and Scottish Woodlands Trust. It will be many years before these large-scale plantings start to show themselves on the landscape.

BELOW RIGHT: eagle pairs mate for life. A young eagle will stay with its parents for up to a year before setting off in search of new territory and a mate of its own.

ABOVE: the mountain hare, whose ordinarily russet brown coat turns to grey or white in winter.

RIGHT: the saxifrage is common in the Arctic, but regularly adds a splash of colour to Scottish moorlands.

FAR LEFT: the red grouse, a game bird tough enough to nest on open moorland, has suffered heavily from over-hunting by humans and by birds of prey.

ORKNEY

In few places in the world is the marriage of landscape and seascape so harmonious, or is there such a profusion of archaeological wonders and variety of wildlife

Six miles (12km) of sea separate the northeast corner of Scotland from an archipelago of 70 islands, 20 of which are inhabited. This is Orkney (the word means "seal islands" in old Icelandic), which extends over 1,200 sq miles (3,100 sq km). If you believe there are more islands it may be because you have drunk too well of the products of Orkney's two distilleries or are counting seals – both common and grey – which abound in these waters.

Norwegian links

The "ey" is Old Norse for islands, and so one should refer to Orkney and not "the Orkneys" or "the Orkney Islands". It also announces an ancient affiliation with Norway, an affiliation historical rather than geographical, for Norway lies 300 miles (480km) to the east. Orkney was a Norwegian appendage until the end of the 15th century, and the true Orcadian is more Norse than Scot. With a rich tradition of sagas, it is no surprise that 20th-century Orkney produced such distinguished literati as Edwin Muir, Eric Linklater and George Mackay Brown.

To Orcadians, Scotland is the "sooth" (south) and never the "mainland", for that is the name of the group's principal island: when inhabitants of the smaller islands visit the largest, therefore, they journey to **Mainland**, and when they travel to the UK they are off "sooth" to Scotland. Not that there are many of them to travel: the population is about 19,500, of whom one-quarter live in the capital, Kirkwall. Travel within the archipelago is by ferries or more often by planes. The Loganair flight between Westray and Papa Westray is the shortest commercial flight in the world. In perfect weather conditions it takes only two minutes.

Main attractions
KIRKWALL
STROMNESS
MAESHOWE
SKARA BRAE
HOY
ROUSAY
STRONSAY
NORTH RONALDSAY

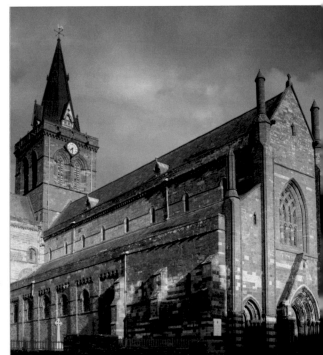

PRECEDING PAGES: Rackwick Bay, Hoy.
LEFT: the ruins of St Magnus Kirk, Egilsay.
RIGHT: St Magnus Cathedral in Kirkwall.

TIP

On average, every square mile (2.6 sq km) on Orkney has three recorded items of antiquarian interest. The key to these is often kept at the nearest farmhouse and payment is made by placing money in an honour box.

To wander these islands is, for the dedicated lover of archaeology, a taste of paradise. Orkney offers an uninterrupted continuum of mute stones from Neolithic times (about 4500 BC) through the Bronze and Iron ages to about AD 700, followed by remains from the days when the islands were occupied successively by the Celts and the Vikings.

Kirkwall ❶ is dominated by the 12th-century **St Magnus Cathedral** (tel: 01856-874 894; Mon–Sat 9am–6pm with exceptions; free). Construction began in the Norman style, but its many Gothic features attest to more than 300 years of building. Facing it is the ruined **Bishop's Palace** (tel: 01856-871 918; Apr–Sept daily 9.30am–5.30pm, Oct Sat–Wed 9.30am–4pm; charge), a massive structure with a round tower reminiscent of a castle. In the 13th century the great Norwegian king, Haakon Haakonsson, lay dying here while Norse sagas were read aloud to him.

Nearby is a third ancient building, the **Earl Patrick's Palace** (joint ticket with Bishop's Palace), a romantic gem of Renaissance architecture. It is roofless because in the 17th century its slates were removed to build the town hall.

Other Kirkwall attractions are the **Tankerness House Museum** (tel: 01856-873 191; Mon–Sat 10.30am–5pm; free), which presents the complete story of Orkney from prehistory to the present: and the **Orkney Wireless Museum** (tel: 01856-871 400; Apr–Sept Mon–Sat 10am–4.30pm, Sun 2.30–4.30pm; charge), which displays communications equipment from World War II. There is also a golf course and a sports and leisure centre.

Scapa Flow

South of Kirkwall is the great natural harbour of **Scapa Flow**. Here, the captured German fleet was anchored after World War I and eventually scuttled. Only six of the 74 ships remain on the bed of this deep, spacious bay, which is bliss for the scuba diver and a peaceful cornucopia for the deep-sea angler.

The island of **Flotta**, at the south of Scapa Flow, is a North Sea oil terminal. This is the Orcadians' only concession to black gold.

BELOW: one in six of all seabirds that breed in Britain nests in Orkney.

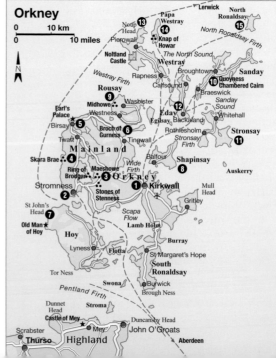

Orkney

0   10 km
0   10 miles

Fifteen miles (24km) west of Kirkwall is picturesque **Stromness ❷**, Orkney's second town. A well on the main street testifies that, in the 17th century, Stromness was developed by the Hudson Bay Company, whose ships made this their last port of call before crossing the Atlantic.

The **Pier Arts Centre** (tel: 01856-850 209; Mon–Sat 10.30am–5.30pm; free) has been renovated recently and in much improved surroundings houses a collection of 20th-century paintings and sculpture. Also of interest is the **Stromness Museum** (tel: 01856-850 025; Apr–Sept daily 10am–5pm, Oct–Mar 11am–3.30pm; charge), which has natural history exhibits, model ships and a display on the scuttling of the German Fleet at Scapa Flow. There is a golf course and indoor pool here, too.

Archaeological sites

Most of Mainland's major archaeological sites are to the north of Stromness. Crawl into awesome **Maeshowe ❸** (tel: 01856-761 606; daily 9.30am–5pm with exceptions; charge), the most magnificent chambered tomb in Britain, which dates from 3500 BC. Within is a spacious burial chamber built with enormous megaliths; on some of these are incised the world's largest collection of 12th-century Viking runes (symbols).

Near Maeshowe are the **Ring of Brodgar** and the **Standing Stones of Stenness**, the remains of two of Britain's most spectacular stone circles. When the former (whose name means "Circle of the Sun") was completed, about 1200 BC, it consisted of 60 standing stones set along the circumference of a circle about 340ft (103 metres) in diameter. Today, 27 stones, the tallest at 14ft (4 metres), still stand. The four giant monoliths of Stenness are all that remain of that particular circle of 12 stones, erected about 2300 BC.

Skara Brae ❹ (visitor centre and replica house; tel: 01856-841 815; daily 9.30am–5.30pm with exceptions; charge), Britain's Pompeii, sits on the Atlantic coast alongside a superb sandy beach. The settlement, remarkably well preserved, consists of several dwelling houses and connecting passages and was engulfed by sand 4,500 years ago after having been occupied for 500

One stone in Maeshowe is surely the forerunner of today's graffiti. It says simply: "Ingigerd is the sweetest woman there is."

BELOW: the neolithic Standing Stones of Stenness.

Brochs are Iron Age (100 BC to AD 300) strongholds built by the Picts. Unique to Scotland and ubiquitous in Orkney, they were circular at their base and their massive walls tapered gently inwards to a height of about 60ft (18 metres).

years. Skara Brae is a quintessential Stone Age site; no metal of any kind has been found.

Five miles (8km) north is **Birsay** ❺ with its 16th-century **Earl's Palace**. Opposite is the **Brough of Birsay**, a tiny tidal island (avoid being stranded); it is covered with rich remains of Norse and Christian settlements. A further 8 miles (13km) east, and guarding Eynhallow Sound, is the **Broch of Gurness** ❻ (tel: 01856-751 414; Apr–Sept daily 9.30am–5pm, Oct Sat–Wed 9.30am–4.30pm; charge).

The principal southern islands are South Ronaldsay, Burray, Lamb Holm, Hoy and Flotta. Technically, the first three are no longer islands, being joined to Mainland by the **Churchill Barriers**. These were built by Italian prisoners during World War II after a German submarine penetrated Scapa Flow and sank the battleship *Royal Oak*. On **Lamb Holm** enter some Nissen huts and be astonished at the beautiful chapel built with scrap metal by these prisoners.

Hoy, the second largest island of the archipelago, is spectacularly dif-

ferent. The southern part is low-lying, but at the north stand the heather-covered Cuilags (1,420ft/426 metres), from where all Orkney, except Little Rysa, can be viewed. A stroll along the 1,140ft (367-metre) high **St John's Head** ❼, which teems with seabirds (beware the swooping great skuas) and boasts some rare plants, is sheer delight for the geologist, ornithologist and botanist, or for those who just like to ramble.

Immediately south of St John's Head is Orkney's most venerable inhabitant, the **Old Man of Hoy**, who, sad to say, appears to be cracking up. This 450ft (135-metre) perpendicular sandstone column continues to challenge the world's leading rock climbers.

The northern islands

And so to the northern islands. Fertile **Shapinsay** ❽ is so near Mainland that it is called suburbia. Also near Mainland, but further west and readily reached by local ferry, are **Rousay** ❾ and **Egilsay**. Rich archaeological finds have earned the former the sobriquet "Egypt of the North". Visit the remarkable 76ft (23-me-

BELOW: the ornate chapel, on Lamb Holm, built by Italian prisoners during World War II.

tre) long Neolithic **Midhowe Chambered Cairn** (open access), aptly named the "Great Ship of Death", which has 12 burial compartments each side of a passage. Nearby is the magnificent **Midhowe Broch,** Rousay's finest archaeological site. Ascend Mansemass Hill and stroll to Ward Hill for superb views of **Eynhallow**, medieval Orkney's Holy Island, between Rousay and Mainland.

On **Egilsay** an unusual round church, which has affinities with similar buildings in Ireland, marks the 12th-century site of the martyrdom of St Magnus.

White sandy beaches

Low-lying **Sanday**, with its white beaches, has room for a golf course but not to the exclusion of archaeological remains. Most important is the **Quoyness Chambered Cairn ⑩** (open access), standing 13ft (3 metres) high and dating from about 2900 BC. It is similar to, but even larger than, Maeshowe. **Stronsay ⑪**, another low-lying island with sandy beaches, was formerly the hub of the prosperous Orkney herring industry. **Eday ⑫** may

be bleak and barren, yet it is paradise for birdwatchers and has the customary complement of archaeological edifices.

Westray, the largest northern island, is unique in that its population is increasing. This is largely because of a successful fishing fleet, which contradicts the assertion that the Orcadian is "a farmer with a boat". **Noup Head ⑬** is Westray's bird reserve and splendid viewpoint. The island also has a golf course and the ruined Renaissance **Notland Castle. North Hill Nature Reserve** on **Papa Westray ⑭** is home to Arctic terns and skuas. At **Knap of Howar** (open access) there are considerable remains of the earliest standing dwelling houses in northwest Europe (approximately 3000 BC). Their occupants, archaeologists have found, had "a strong preference for oysters".

On the most northerly island, **North Ronaldsay ⑮**, a dyke around the island confines sheep to the shore, leaving better inland pastures for cattle. Seaweed, the sole diet of these sheep, results in a dark meat with an unusually rich flavour – an acquired taste. ❏

The ruined Earl Patrick's Palace, Kirkwall (see page 302).

BELOW: Skaill Bay on the west coast of Orkney.

SHETLAND

Remote and mysterious, the Shetland Islands are a geologist's and birdwatcher's paradise, withstanding the pounding of the sea and – more recently – the invasion of oil companies

The writer Jan Morris called them "inset islands". In those two words she succinctly defined the mystery of the **Shetland Islands**, whose remoteness (200 miles/320km to the north of Aberdeen) means that, in maps of Britain, they are usually relegated to a box in the corner of a page.

The 15 inhabited islands – 85 or so more are uninhabited – are dotted over 70 miles (112km) of swelling seas and scarcely seem part of Britain at all. The tiny population of less than 22,000 doesn't regard itself as British, or even as Scottish, but as Norse: one of the nearest mainland towns is Bergen in Norway, Norwegian is taught in the schools and the heroes of myths have names like Harald Hardrada.

Heavy rainfall

Spring comes late, with plant growth speeding up only in June. Rainfall is heavy, mists are frequent and gales keep the islands virtually treeless. However, it's never very cold, even in mid-winter, thanks to the North Atlantic Drift; and in midsummer (the "Simmer Dim") it never quite gets dark.

The late January festival of Up-Helly-Aa is loosely based on a pagan fire festival intended to herald the impending return of the sun. It is an authentic fiesta primarily for islanders, who are excep-

tionally hospitable and talkative. When a Shetlander says, "You'll have a dram," it's an instruction, not an enquiry.

Two check-in counters confront passengers at **Sumburgh Airport** on the main island, **Mainland**. North Sea oil generates the traffic, and at one time threatened to overwhelm the islands. But the oil companies, pushed by a determined local council, made conspicuous efforts to lessen the impact on the environment and, although a large proportion of Britain's oil flows through the 1,000-acre (400-hectare)

Main attractions
JARLSHOF
LERWICK
YELL
UNST
FOULA
FAIR ISLE

PRECEDING PAGES: a puffin on the clifftop. **LEFT:** Viking festivities, part of the Up-Helly-Aa festival. **RIGHT:** sailing in Lerwick.

It's worth attending a folk concert in Shetland, as the islands are full of astonishingly well accomplished fiddlers.

Sullom Voe terminal on a strip of land at the northern end of Mainland, they seem to have succeeded beyond most islanders' expectations. Since the 16 crude oil tanks were painted mistletoe-green, 124 species of birds have been logged within the terminal boundary, and outside the main gates a traffic sign gives priority to otters.

A concentrated anthropological history of the islands is located at **Jarls-hof ❶**, a jumble of buildings near the airport. Settlers from the Stone, Bronze and Iron ages built dwellings here, each on the ruins of its predecessor. The Vikings built on top of that, and medieval farmsteads later buried the Viking traces. At the end of the 19th century the site was just a grassy mound, topped with a medieval ruin. Then a wild storm laid bare massive stones in a bank above the beach, and archaeologists moved in. Hearths were found where peat fires burned 3,000 years ago. Today old wheelhouses (so called because of their radial walls) have been revealed, and an **exhibition area** (tel: 01950-460 112; Apr–Sept daily 9.30am–5.30pm; charge) fleshes out Jarlshof's history.

En route to the capital, Lerwick, 27 miles (43km) to the north, the offshore island of **Mousa** is home to sheep and ponies, and also to a spectacularly well-preserved broch, a drystone tower more than 40ft (13 metres) high.

Lerwick – Shetland's capital

Lerwick ❷ looks no more planned than Jarlshof. The old town has charm, with intimate stone-paved alleys leading off the main street of granite houses and dignified shops (no chainstores here). The windows of the baronial-looking **town hall** were presented by Norway, Holland and Germany as thanks for Shetland's kindness to seamen.

The sea and rural landscapes dominate the **Shetland Museum and Archives** (tel: 01595-695 057; www. shetland-museum.org.uk; Mon–Sat 10am–5pm, Sun noon–5pm; charge), sited above the library in Hillhead. Its theme is the history of life in Shetland from prehistory to the present. It has a collection of 5,000-year-old beads, pots and pumice stones found when excavating Sumburgh airport.

Scalloway ❸, the old fishing port 6

Local Populations

Sheep outnumber people on Shetland by more than 10 to one. "They eat everything," says one islander. Shetland ponies are more loved. They were carefully bred to keep their legs short so that they could pull carts through Britain's coal mines, but these days they graze freely. But it's birds that dominate Shetland. Because of the lack of woodlands there are fewer than 50 breeding species, but no lack of numbers. Filling the sky and cliff ledges are around 30,000 gannets, 140,000 guillemots and 300,000 fulmars. Shetland supports more than 50 percent of the world's population of great skuas (bonxies). Puffins *(above)* begin to arrive in May, and before long there are 250,000 of them. Take a small boat round the islands and, as well as the birds, you can find seal colonies, porpoises and dolphins.

Shetland

0   10 km
0   10 miles

ATLANTIC OCEAN

Muckle Flugga
Hermaness
Haroldswick
Unst ❻
Baltasound
Belmont
Muness Castle
Gutcher
Fetlar
Isbister
Mid Yell
The Faither
Yell Sound
Yell ❺
Funzie
Esha Ness
Sullom
Voe
Ulsta
Hillswick
Toft
Out Skerries
St Magnus Bay
Brae
Vidlin
Shetland Islands
Muckle Roe
Papa Stour
Voe
Laxo
Symbister
Whalsay
Melby
S h e t l a n d
Mainland
Walls
Heglibister
Girlsta
NORTH SEA
Vaila
Tingwall ❹
Foula ❼
Veensgarth
Lerwick ❷
Isle of Noss
Ham
❸ Scalloway
Bressay
Hamnavoe
Easter Quarff
West Burra
Cunningsburgh
Mousa
Levenwick
Boddam
Sumburgh
Fair Isle ❽
❶ Jarlshof
Stromness, Aberdeen
Bergen

miles (10km) away, was once Shetland's capital. It features the gaunt ruins of an early 17th-century castle built for Earl Patrick Stewart, a nephew of Mary Queen of Scots (tel: 01856 -841 815; Mon–Sat 9.30am–5pm; free).

Deep voes (inlets) poke into the Shetland Islands like long fingers so that no part of the watery landscape is more than 3 miles (5km) from the sea. Arguably, Shetlanders were always more sailors than landlubbers, but clearly "matters of state" were held on dry land. It is said that a Norse parliament once stood by the loch of **Tingwall ❹**.

Remote places

Small ferries connect a handful of smaller islands to Mainland. **Yell ❺**, a peaty place, has the **Old Haa Visitor Centre** (tel: 01957-722 339; May–Sept Tue–Thur, Sat 10am–4pm, Sun 2–5pm; donations) which includes a display of the story of the wrecking of the German sail ship, the *Bohus*, in 1924, and a craft centre selling genuine rather than generic Shetland garments.

Unst ❻, the UK's most northerly island, has an important nature reserve at **Hermaness** with a visitor centre (tel: 01595-693 345; Apr–mid-Sept daily 9am–6pm; free). Puffins breed on the cliffs and rare red-throated divers nest on the moor, to name but a few. From the cliffs at Hermaness gaze out on rocky **Muckle Flugga**, the last land before the Arctic Circle. **Fetlar**'s name means "fat island", a reference to its fertile soil.

Whalsay is prosperous, thanks to its notably energetic fishermen. The **Out Skerries**, a scattered archipelago, has a thriving fishing fleet. The peacefulness and abundant wild flowers of **Papa Stour**, a mile of turbulent sea west of Mainland, once attracted a transient hippy colony.

Foula ❼, 14 miles (23km) to the west of Scalloway, must be Britain's remotest inhabited island and, most winters, is cut off for several weeks by awesome seas. The spectacular 1,200ft (370-metre) cliffs are home to storm petrels, great skuas and a host of other sea birds. **Fair Isle ❽**, 20 miles (32km) to the southwest, is the home of Fair Isle sweaters, whose distinctive geometric patterns can be dated back 2,000 years to Balkan nomads. ❑

BELOW: Mukkle Flugga Lighthouse, located on the northernmost tip of the Shetland Isles.

INSIGHT GUIDES TRAVEL TIPS

SCOTLAND

Transport

Accommodation

Eating Out

Activities

A – Z

Further Reading

T RANSPORT

GETTING THERE
AND GETTING AROUND

GETTING THERE

By Air

There are excellent services from London (Heathrow, London City, Gatwick, Luton and Stansted airports) and several English regional airports to Edinburgh, Glasgow, Aberdeen and Inverness. You will get the cheapest fare by booking well in advance. Airlines flying these routes include **British Airways** and **British Midland**.

Flying time from London to Edinburgh or Glasgow is about 70 minutes, and under two hours from London to Aberdeen or Inverness.

Ryanair and easyJet have very low-price, no-frills flights into Scotland. **EasyJet** flies from London (Gatwick, Luton and Stansted) to Edinburgh and Glasgow, to Inverness (from Gatwick and Luton) and to Aberdeen (Luton only), while **Ryanair** flies from London (Stansted) to Glasgow Prestwick, and

also from Dublin to Aberdeen and Edinburgh. **Aer Lingus** flies from Dublin to Glasgow and Edinburgh.

Glasgow International Airport is Scotland's busiest airport with more than 40 airlines serving 80 worldwide destinations. Glasgow receives non-stop flights from New York (**Continental**), Philadelphia and Orlando (**US Airways**), Toronto and Vancouver (**Canadian Affair**). It also receives non-stop flights from Amsterdam (**KLM**), Berlin and Geneva (**easyJet**), Copenhagen (**BMI**), Dubai (**Emirates**), Lahore (**Pakistan International Airlines**), Malaga (easyJet), Paris (easyJet) and Reykjavik (**Icelandair**).

Direct Ryanair flights from Riga, Dublin, Brussels, Paris, Gothenburg, Faro, Wroclaw, Milan, Rome, Pisa, Malaga and Barcelona all land at Glasgow Prestwick. Edinburgh airport handles non-stop flights from destinations including New York (**Continental Airlines**), Dublin (**Aer Lingus** and **Ryanair**), Faro (**Jet2.com, Ryanair**), Shannon (**Ryanair**), Milan

(**easyJet**), Amsterdam (**easyJet, KLM**), Barcelona (**Spanair**), Brussels (**BMI**), Chambery (**Jet2.com**), Copenhagen (**BMI**), Bergen (**Wideroe**), Frankfurt (**Lufthansa**), Geneva (**easyJet**), Oslo (**Norwegian Air Shuttle**), Paris (**Air France, easyJet, Ryanair**), Alicante (**easyJet, Ryanair**), Madrid (**easyJet**) and Zurich (**BMI**).

Direct flights into Aberdeen include from Amsterdam (**KLM**), Bergen (**Wideroe**), Copenhagen (**SAS**), Dublin (**Ryanair**) and Stavanger (**SAS**). Direct flights into Inverness include from Belfast (**Flybe**) and Bristol (**easyJet**).

By Rail

There are frequent InterCity services to Scotland from many mainline stations in England. On most trains the journey time from London (Euston or King's Cross) to Edinburgh is just over four hours and to Glasgow about 5½ hours.

Sleeper services run between London (Euston) and Edinburgh, Glasgow, Aberdeen, Inverness and Fort William. Try to avoid travel on Sundays when services are often curtailed, and engineering works mean that journeys can take much longer. A limited number of cheap fares, known as Apex fares, are available for those booking at least seven days in advance. For current fares and timetables, call National Rail Enquiries on 08457-484 950; www.nationalrail.co.uk.

By Road

There are good motorway connections from England and Wales. The M1/M6/A74 and M74 is the quickest route, though heavily congested at the

Airports

• **Edinburgh Airport** (tel: 0844-481 8989) is 8 miles (13km) west of the city centre with good road access and a useful Airlink bus service to the heart of town. A taxi will take approximately 20 minutes.
• **Glasgow International Airport** (tel: 0844-481 5555) is 8 miles (13km) west of the city centre alongside the M8 motorway at Junction 28. Various buses run between the airport and Buchanan Street bus station and Queen Street Railway Station, in the city centre, and take about 25 minutes.

• **Glasgow Prestwick Airport** (tel: 0844-481 6666) is 30 miles (48km) south of the city centre and easily reached by road or a 45-minute rail link to Central Station.
• **Aberdeen Airport** (tel: 0870-040 0006) is 7 miles (11km) west of the city centre with excellent road access (A96). A coach service runs between airport and city centre.
• **Inverness Airport** (tel: 01667-464 000) is about 10 miles (16km) east of the town. A bus link runs into the city centre.

southern end. The A1(M), a more easterly approach, is longer but may be a better bet if you plan to make one or two stopovers. Edinburgh and Glasgow are about 400 miles (650km) from London.

Bus Services

Scottish Citylink (tel: 08705-505 050) and National Express (tel: 0871-818 181) operate daytime and overnight coaches from England to Scotland. The journey takes about nine hours from London to Edinburgh or to Glasgow. Coach travel may not be as comfortable or as fast as the trains, but it is a good deal cheaper, unless you can get an Apex rail fare.

By Sea

There are three sailings a week, operated by Norfolk Line, leaving Zeebrugge in Belgium to make the 20-hour crossing to Rosyth, which is about 30 minutes by road from Edinburgh. In Scotland, tel: 08718-900 900; www.norfolkline.com.

GETTING AROUND

By Air

There is a network of regular air services, which is especially valuable if going to the islands. Barra, Benbecula, Campbeltown, Islay, Kirkwall (Orkney), Stornoway (Lewis), Sumburgh (Shetland) and Tiree are all serviced by Glasgow International Airport. Some of these destinations can also be reached from Inverness, Aberdeen and Edinburgh airports. Flying there saves a lot of time and can also give a different perspective on the countryside. The major carrier is Loganair (franchise partner of Flybe). The booking number for all services is 08717-002 000, or log on to www.loganair.co.uk.

By Rail

First ScotRail offers a wide variety of tickets that permit unlimited travel throughout Scotland. The Freedom of Scotland Travelpass permits unlimited travel on eight or 15 consecutive days or on four out of eight or 10 out of 15 consecutive days. Two other rover passes are available: a Central Scotland Rover ticket offers three days' unlimited travel out of seven; and the Highland Rover is valid for four out of eight consecutive days.
    Scottish Travelpasses permit

ABOVE: the former Forsinard railway station.

unlimited travel for eight or 15 consecutive days on ScotRail and most of the Caledonian MacBrayne west coast ferries. Together with discounts on the P&O ferries and many buses and postbuses, these are truly comprehensive Scottish travel tickets. Details can be obtained from First ScotRail, tel: 08457-550 033; www.scotrail.co.uk.
    A few routes to try are:
Glasgow to Fort William and Mallaig (164 miles/265km). Train enthusiasts head for the West Highland line, which operates regular trains from Fort William to the fishing port of Mallaig, from which a ferry departs for Skye. From Glasgow, the route passes alongside Loch Lomond, across the wild Rannoch Moor and over the majestic Glenfinnan Viaduct.
Glasgow to Oban (101 miles/ 163km). The train branches off the Fort William route at Crianlarich and heads past ruined Kilchurn Castle and the fjord-like scenery of the Pass of Brander to Oban, "gateway to the Inner Hebrides".
Perth to Inverness (118 miles/ 190km). The route, through forested glens and across the roof of Scotland, takes in Pitlochry, Blair Atholl and Aviemore. As well as being a ski centre, Aviemore is the departure point for steam trains on the 5-mile (8km) Strathspey Railway line.
Inverness to Kyle of Lochalsh (82 miles/132km). This twisting line with breathtaking scenery takes in lochs, glens and mountains from the North Sea to the Atlantic Ocean, and is especially dramatic towards Kyle of Lochalsh, from where the bridge leads over the water to Skye.
Inverness to Wick or Thurso (161 miles/260km). Passes by castles, across moorland and on to Britain's most northerly rail terminals.

Steam Trains

Railway preservation societies are alive and thriving in Scotland. Over half a dozen other lines operate steam trains of one sort or another.
    The **Northern Belle**, a luxury touring train operated by Orient-Express, offers day excursions and short breaks in Scotland. These trips include all meals served at seats, accommodation in hotels and off-train visits. Information from Northern Belle, 20 Upper Ground, London SE1 9PF; tel: 0845-077 2222; www.orient-express.com.
    The **Caledonian Railway,** Brechin, Angus, runs steam train rides every Saturday from July to August and every Sunday from May to September, from Brechin to Bridge of Don. Brechin station is also open on Saturdays. Enquire at Brechin Station, 2 Park Road, Brechin, Angus DD9 7AF; tel: 01356-622 922; www.caledonianrailway.com.
    The **Bo'ness & Kinneil Railway,** West Lothian, runs steam-hauled trains on most weekends April to August, daily in July and August, and Tuesday and Wednesday in June, on a 3-mile (5km) branch line to Birkhill for a visit to the Avon Gorge and the Fireclay Mine. Historic Scottish locomotives, rolling stock and railway buildings. Contact Bo'ness Station, Union Street, Bo'ness EH51 9AQ; tel: 01506-822 298; www.srps.org.uk.
    Strathspey Railway runs April to October and at Christmas for 5 miles (8km) from Aviemore (Speyside) through Boat of Garten to Grantown-on-Spey, providing good views of the Cairngorm Mountains. Enquiries to Aviemore Station, Dalfaber Road, Aviemore, Inverness-shire PH22 1PY; tel: 01479-810 725; www.strathspeyrailway.co.uk.
    The **Mull & West Highland**

Caledonian MacBrayne Ferries

An essential item for any visitor who intends to explore the island-studded west coast – the Hebrides and the islands of the Clyde – is the Caledonian MacBrayne timetable, which can be obtained from Ferry Terminal, Gourock, PA19 1QP; tel: 01475-650 100. Reservations: 0800-066 5000; www.calmac.co.uk.

Faced with a myriad of island destinations, the uninitiated may find CalMac's timetable daunting, though locals whip through it with ease. Summer booking is vital to avoid the nerve-racking, time-consuming "standby" queue.

Caledonian MacBrayne, a fusion of two companies, grew out of the 19th-century passenger steamers and now has a near monopoly on west-coast routes. Calling into over 30 ports throughout the west coast, its 31 vessels service 24 routes, from the Isle of Arran in the south to Lewis in the Outer Hebrides. The company sells various island-hopping tickets and, best value for visitors with cars, bicycles and motor homes, rover tickets, giving eight or 15 days' unlimited travel on most routes.

Railway has steam and diesel trains running April to mid-October on a narrow-gauge track for 1¼ miles (2km) through superb mountain and woodland scenery from the ferry terminal at Craignure to Torosoy Castle and Gardens on Mull. Enquiries on tel: 01680-812 494; www.mullrail.co.uk.

At the top end of the market is the **Royal Scotsman**, one of the world's most exclusive trains. This mobile hotel for just 32 passengers combines spectacular scenery with superb food and wine and impeccable service. A variety of two- and seven-night tours are available; highlights include Glamis Castle and the islands of Bute and Skye. Tours operate between April and October, departing from and returning to Edinburgh. Enquiries to The Royal Scotsman, 46a Constitution Street, Edinburgh EH6 6RS; tel: 0845-077 2222; www.royalscotsman.com.

The **Jacobite Steam Train** chugs its way from Fort William to the fishing port of Mallaig; its picturesque route, including crossing the Glenfinnan Viaduct, appears in the Harry Potter novels of the celebrated Scottish writer, J.K. Rowling.

The train runs from mid-May to mid-October (Mon–Fri) and daily throughout July and August. Contact the West Coast Railway Company on tel: 0845-128 4681; www.steamtrain.info.

Ferries

Scottish ferries are great. On long routes, like the five-hour Oban-to-Barra ferry, there are car decks, cabins, comfortable chairs, a restaurant and self-service cafeteria. On others, such as the seven-hour round trip to the tiny islands of Eigg, Muck, Rum and Canna, ferries are basic with wooden seats and minimal refreshments. These working boats, carrying goods and mail as well as passengers, are mainly used by islanders, with some birdwatchers and occasional curious visitors. Take note that unless you specify beforehand, disembarking for sightseeing is not allowed.

There are plenty of small private businesses on the west coast providing cruises from Arisaig on the mainland to Skye and Mull as well as to Eigg, Muck, Rum and Canna. Day trips to the National Trust for Scotland's island of Staffa with Fingal's Cave, to the bird island of Lunga and the uninhabited Treshnish Islands start from Ulva Ferry, Dervaig and Fionnphort, all of which are on Mull, while Staffa can also be reached from Iona. There is a 10-minute shuttle service from Fionnphort on the southwest tip of Mull to Iona. These trips allow some time ashore, and there is no difficulty in finding out about such services when you arrive. Tourist information centres and many hotels have brochures.

If voyaging to the Outer Hebrides feels like sailing to the edge of the world, taking a ferry to the ancient isles of Orkney and Shetland (the Northern Isles) is equally exhilarating. Two major ferry companies ply these routes, and in summer it's essential to book ahead.

Orkney

Northlink Ferries Ltd run roll-on/roll-off car ferry services from Aberdeen (eight hours) or Scrabster (one hour 45 minutes) on the mainland to Stromness in Orkney, and also services from Lerwick in Shetland (www.northlinkferries.co.uk).

A passenger ferry runs from May to September from John o'Groats to Burwick on South Ronaldsay (tel: 01955-611 353; www.jogferry.co.uk). The crossing takes around 40 minutes. Connecting buses can be boarded on Orkney, and there are cars for hire.

Once on Orkney, a dozen or so smaller islands can be visited by local ferries. The Kirkwall tourist office has more details.

Shetland

Northlink Ferries has six sailings weekly taking 12 hours 30 minutes between Aberdeen and Lerwick, Shetland's main port, on modern roll-on/roll-off vessels with cabins, shops, restaurants and cafeterias.

BELOW: ferries are the ideal way of exploring the islands.

Once again, local ferries ply between the small islands.

Northlink Ferries Ltd: routes, timetables and fares may be obtained from Ferry Terminal, Stromness, Orkney, KW16 3BH; tel: 0845-600 0449; www.northlinkferries.co.uk.

Pleasure Cruises

On Loch Katrine, which has supplied Glasgow with water since 1859, the **SS Sir Walter Scott**, Scotland's only screw steamer in regular passenger service, makes three daily return-trip voyages between the Trossachs and Stronachlachar piers from April until the end of October. The morning trip permits a 15-minute landing at Stronachlachar, while the two one-hour afternoon trips are non-landing. Enquiries to Trossachs Pier Complex, Loch Katrine, Callander FK17 8HZ; tel: 01877-332 000; www.lochkatrine.co.uk.

Clyde Cruises operates several different river cruises out of Glasgow including day and evening cruises along the Clyde in and around the city and a 2½-hour sightseeing cruise into the countryside. They also run the new city RiverLink river bus, a novel way of seeing some of Glasgow's attractions, which departs from several points in the city centre. For further information contact Clyde Marine Cruises, Victoria Harbour, Greenock, tel: 01475-721 281; www.clydecruises.com.

Similar cruises from Gourock, with longer time ashore, can be enjoyed from the end of April to the end of September on Caledonian MacBrayne craft (see box on page 316).

Waverley, the world's last sea-going paddle steamer, sails on the Clyde (day trips) from Glasgow Science Centre, 50 Pacific Quay, Glasgow, from June until August. Tel: 0845-130 4647; www.waverleyexcursions.co.uk.

From April to October the **Maid of the Forth** sails from South

ABOVE: take a leisurely cruise on the PS Waverley paddle-steamer.

Queensferry, just outside Edinburgh, to Inchcolm Island which has a ruined medieval abbey; seals are often spotted during the voyage. Trips last about three hours with 1½ hours spent ashore. Contact Maid of the Forth, Hawes Pier, South Queensferry; tel: 0131-331 5000; www.maidoftheforth.co.uk.

From May to mid-September the 130-passenger **MV Sheerwater** sails each morning from Arisaig for a full day to the small islands (Rum, Eigg, Muck) of the Inner Hebrides. Several hours are spent ashore. Contact Arisaig Harbour, Inverness-shire PH39 4NH; tel: 01687-450 224; www.arisaig.co.uk.

During the summer months the **TSMV Western Isles** makes half- and full-day cruises from Mallaig past dramatic scenery to surrounding lochs, or to the islands of Rum and Canna, or to Skye, with landings. Contact Bruce Watt Sea Cruises, Mallaig; tel: 01687-462 320; www.knoydart-ferry.co.uk.

From May to September daily sailings (weather permitting) are made from Anstruther to the Isle of May aboard the **May Princess**. The trip lasts four to five hours, with two to three hours ashore to explore the island, whose cliffs, at least until July, are covered with breeding kittiwakes,

razorbills, guillemots and shags. Scotland's oldest lighthouse and the ruins of a 12th-century chapel can also be visited. Contact Anstruther Pleasure Trips, Pittenweem Road, Anstruther, Fife KY10 3DS; tel: 01333-310 103; www.isleofmayferry.com.

From Easter until mid-October **Anne of Etive** departs from Taynuilt on 1½- and three-hour cruises into Loch Etive. The route covered is inaccessible except by boat. If you are lucky you'll spot seals on the rocks, the golden eagle of Ben Starav and deer on the crags. Morning and afternoon departures from Sunday to Friday. Contact Donald Kennedy, Taynuilt, tel: 01866-822 430; e-mail: lochetive@aol.com.

Several companies run two- to four-hour cruises from Ullapool to the Summer Isles. Some are nature cruises, some are sunset cruises and some permit landing on the islands. Try Summer Queen Cruises; tel: 01854-612 472; www.summerqueen.co.uk.

Summer Isles Cruises also depart from Achiltibuie aboard the **Hectoria** from May to September. These last 3½ hours and permit landing on the islands. Contact Ian Mcleod; tel: 01854-622 200; www.summer-isles.com/summer-isles-cruises.asp..

The Hebridean Princess

The **Hebridean Princess**, more a stately country-house hotel on water than the usual run-of-the-mill luxury liner and accommodating only 49 passengers in elegant cabins, makes a series of cruises from Oban from March until October. The region covered is the northwest coast of Scotland, Inner and Outer Hebrides, the Orkney and Shetland Islands and even St Kilda. The route varies from cruise to cruise, with voyages lasting four

to eight nights, and the printed schedule may be altered to avoid bad weather. Cars can roll-on and roll-off the ship, thus enabling travellers to explore independently at the various ports of call. Bookings can be made through Hebridean International Cruises, Kintail House, Carleton New Road, Skipton, North Yorkshire BD23 3AN; tel: 01756-704 704; www.hebridean.co.uk.

Public Transport

By Bus

Major towns have their own bus services. For timetable information on all public transport services in Scotland contact **Traveline**, tel: 0871-200 2233; www.travelinescotland.com. In addition, there are bus services serving rural communities and linking the various towns. The national bus network is run by **Scottish Citylink**, tel: 0870-550 5050; www.citylink.co.uk. The visitor who intends to travel a lot on the buses should investigate the various tickets which allow unlimited

ABOVE: take the high road or the low road.

use of buses for specific periods. Contact Scottish Citylink or the tourist board for more details.

An unusual delight and a superb way to meet the people and learn something of their customs is to board one of the sadly diminishing Royal Mail Postbuses, which provide an essential post-and-passenger service in isolated parts of the country. To people in rural communities the familiar red Postbus is both a welcome friend and a lifeline to the world outside. The Royal Mail is reducing the service dramatically so check in advance where they run but you can hail a Postbus at any point along its route if you see one. Contact **Royal Mail Postbuses**, tel: 08457-740 740; www.postbus.royalmail.com.

By Taxi

The major cities have sufficient taxi stands. Outside the cities, you will probably need to phone for a taxi.

Private Transport

Scotland has an excellent network of roads which, away from the central belt, are usually not congested. Driving on the left is the rule and passengers must wear seat belts. In urban areas, the speed limit is either 30 or 40mph (48 or 64kmh), the limit on country roads is 60mph (97kmh), and on motorways and dual carriageways 70mph (113kmh).

In some parts of the Highlands and on many of the islands, roads are single track with passing places. The behaviour of drivers on these roads tends to show that good old-fashioned courtesy is not dead. On these narrow roads, please use the "passing places" to let oncoming vehicles pass, or to let others behind you overtake.

Radio Scotland (FM 92.4–94.7/ MW 810) broadcasts details of road conditions throughout the day, with details of particular problems,

accidents or emergencies. Its travel information includes details of ferry, rail or air travel hold-ups or changes. Local radio stations also broadcast travel and road information.

Even today you can travel many miles in the Highlands and on the islands without seeing a petrol station, so if you see one, fill up. If you are planning to drive on a Sunday in the Outer Hebrides, fill up your tank on the Saturday. This is because, in some places, strict Sunday observance means that filling stations will be closed.

Car Rentals

Self-drive rental costs £30–70 a day, depending on the type of car and the duration of the rental. Watch out for hidden costs when booking, especially online. The rates are reduced in the October–April off-season. For more detailed information, apply directly to the car rental companies. All the major car hire companies (such as Alamo, Avis, Budget, Europcar, Hertz and National) are represented throughout Scotland and at the airports. **Arnold Clark** (tel: 0141-237 4374) is Scotland's major car rental company.

Edinburgh

W.L. Sleigh Ltd (chauffeur-driven)
Turnhouse Road
Tel: 0131-339 9607

Glasgow

Little's Chauffeur Drive
1282 Paisley Road West
Tel: 0141-883 2111

The West Coast

Fort William
Easydrive
Lochybridge
Tel: 01397-701 616
Slipway Autos
Annat Point
Corpach, Fort William
Tel: 01397-772 404

Oban
Flit
Glencruitten Road
Tel: 01631-566 553

Inner Hebrides

Skye
Ewen MacRae
West End Garage, Portree
Tel: 01478-612 554

Outer Hebrides

Lewis
Lewis Car Rentals
52 Bayhead Street Stornoway
Tel: 01851-703 760
Stornoway Car Hire (Airport)
Tel: 01851-702 658

Benbecula
Ask Car Hire
Linicleat
Tel: 01870-602 818

South Uist
Laing Motors
Lochboisdale
Tel: 01878-700 267

Orkney

Kirkwall
W.R. Tullock
Castle Garage, Castle Street
Tel: 01856-875 500

Shetland

Lerwick
Bolts Car Hire
26 North Road
Tel: 01595-693 636

Bikers Welcome

Every summer, scores of motorcyclists don their leathers to tour Scotland's winding roads on two wheels. Glencoe, the Isle of Skye and the remote Applecross Peninsula are among the more popular routes. Furthermore, as increasing numbers of Scotland's 40- and 50-year-olds seek to rediscover their youth astride a growling Harley Davidson, B&Bs and many pubs have positively responded by displaying "Bikers Welcome" signs on their premises. **Scotland by Bike** is a new venture offering five- to 10-day tours and customised accompanied/ unaccompanied tours of the Highlands and islands on two wheels. Top of the range bikes can also be hired. For more information, tel: 0715-851 876; www.scotlandbybike.com.

A CCOMMODATION

HOTELS, YOUTH HOSTELS, BED & BREAKFAST

Types of Accommodation

A wide range of accommodation is available in Scotland, from hotels of international standard to simple Bed & Breakfast (B&B) accommodation. Prices vary from under £25 per person a night for Bed & Breakfast to well over £200 at the most luxurious hotels.

VisitScotland (www.visitscotland.com) operates a system of grading accommodation concentrating on assessment of quality (although symbols still indicate services available). Star gradings range from one star (fair and acceptable) to five stars (exceptional/world-class). These are applied to all types of accommodation, including hotels, Bed & Breakfasts and self-catering.

If you are planning a caravan or camping holiday, look out for the Thistle logo. The "Thistle Award" is bestowed by the industry and VisitScotland to parks that meet standards of excellence in environment, facilities and caravans.

Staying in Bed & Breakfast accommodation is not only economical, it is also a flexible and potentially interesting way to see the country. Local tourist offices operate a convenient booking service (for which there is usually a small charge) and, except at the height of the tourist season in July and August, it is not necessary to reserve in advance. Bed & Breakfasts in VisitScotland's scheme will, at a minimum, be clean and comfortable. With luck you may find the proprietor friendly and a mine of local information on local routes and things to see and do. Most of the better Bed & Breakfast establishments serve dinner on request, which is usually

excellent and modestly priced.

Particularly good value are Campus Hotels, the name given to Bed & Breakfasts and self-catering facilities offered by the Scottish universities in Aberdeen, St Andrews, Dundee, Edinburgh, Glasgow and Stirling, which are available during vacations. In addition, they offer the use of university facilities such as tennis courts and swimming pools *(see below)*.

There is also a vast choice of self-catering accommodation in chalets, flats, cottages and castles. A few websites to try are:
www.aboutscotland.com
www.assc.co.uk
www.cottages-and-castles.co.uk
www.scottish-holiday-cottages.co.uk
www.unique-cottages.co.uk.
The regional tourist information offices also have listings of self-catering accommodation.

Information on all types of accommodation is available from VisitScotland and local tourist information centres *(see page 359)*, or log on to their website, www. visitscotland.com, where you can find comprehensive listings, sorted by area, and refine your search to your specific requirements.

Except for the more expensive city hotels, prices quoted include breakfast. Approximate guides to prices per person per night in high season in a double room are:

£ = below £30
££ = £30–50
£££ = £50–80
££££ = more than £80

Note that, especially for the hotel chains, room rates vary widely according to demand, and weekend

rates in city business hotels are often much lower than weekdays. It's always worth enquiring about special offers: many hotels offer good-value short breaks outside the main holiday periods.

On occasions, the distinction between Bed & Breakfast establishments, guesthouses and private hotels becomes blurred, especially when the former have en suite facilities and serve dinner. All rooms in the following establishments have an en suite bath/shower unless otherwise stated.

Campus Hotels

Excellent accommodation is available during summer and Easter vacations and, on several campuses, throughout the year, at Scottish universities. Both B&B accommodation (some rooms en suite; no single supplement) and self-catering units are offered on a nightly or weekly basis. Access to the university's sports facilities is usually permitted.

The standard of accommodation is high, but so is the demand, so it's advisable to reserve a few months in advance.

Prices are usually between £20–30 per person per night.
Contact numbers are:
• Aberdeen – 01224-262 134
• Dundee – 01382-344 039 (B&B); 01382-573 111 (self-catering)
• Edinburgh – 0131-651 2007
• Glasgow – 0141-330 4116/330 2318
• Heriot-Watt – 0131-451 3669
• St Andrews – 01334-462 000
• Stirling – 01786-467 141/2
• Strathclyde – 0141-553 4148
• Napier (Edinburgh) – 0871-789 5832

EDINBURGH

Hotels

(If phoning from outside the area, use code: 0131.)

££££

Balmoral Hotel
1 Princes Street
Tel: 556 2414
Fax: 557 3747
www.roccofortehotels.com
188 rooms. Edinburgh's premier hotel, built in 1862 and reopened in 1991. All rooms recently underwent a tasteful £7-million refurbishment. Many rooms have a view of the castle.

Caledonian Hilton Hotel
Princes Street
Tel: 222 8888
Fax: 222 8889
www.hilton.com/caledonian
249 rooms. The grande dame of Edinburgh hotels is constantly being upgraded. Many rooms with view of the castle.

Dalhousie Castle Hotel
Bonnyrigg
Tel: 01875-820 153
Fax: 01875-821 936
www.dalhousiecastle.co.uk
34 rooms. A truly imposing 13th-century castle standing in parkland and forest through which flows the South Esk River. James VI, Queen Victoria and Sir Walter Scott all stayed here. The restaurant is in an atmospheric dungeon, and there is a chapel in the hotel.

Edinburgh Residence
7 Rothesay Terrace
Tel: 226 3380
www.townhousecompany.com
A taste of luxury in Edinburgh's West End Sporting 29 high-end suites, this hotel brings together plush design and contemporary trimmings.

George Hotel
19–21 George Street
Tel: 251 251
Fax: 226 5644
www.principal-hayley.com
195 en suite rooms. Very

central, well-established, grand old hotel.

The Glasshouse Hotel
2 Greenside Place
Tel: 525 8200
Fax: 525 8205
www.theetoncollection.com
65 rooms. Situated near the east end of Princes Street, this is a state-of-the-art building with the rooms surrounding a 2-acre (0.8-hectare) roof garden. The exterior rooms have splendid views to the New Town or across the Firth of Forth. Breakfast available on request, but the hotel has no restaurant: though there are many just minutes away.

Howard Hotel
34 Great King Street
Tel: 557 3500
www.thehoward.com
18 rooms. Three interconnected 18th-century town houses in the New Town result in a magnificent classical hotel. Garden.

Hotel Missoni
1 George IV Bridge
Tel: 220 6666
Fax: 226 6660
www.hotelmissoni.com
Opened in 2009, and splendidly located on Edinburgh's Royal Mile. This luxurious boutique hotel displays a dramatic use of colour and bold patterns.

Norton House Hotel
Ingliston
Tel: 333 1275
Fax: 333 3752
www.handpicked.co.uk
83 rooms. Baronial country house hotel in wooded grounds. Close to airport. Excellent restaurant and informal bistro.

Prestonfield House Hotel
Prestonfield
Tel: 225 7800
www.prestonfield.com
This beautiful 17th-century mansion is a celebrity hideaway hotel. 21 bedrooms combine antiquity with modernity; 2 miles (1km) south of

the Scottish Parliament. Excellent restaurant.

Radisson SAS Hotel
80 High Street
Tel: 557 9797
Fax: 557 9789
www.sas.radisson.com
238 rooms. A modern hotel situated on the Royal Mile. Well-equipped leisure centre.

The Scotsman
20 North Bridge
Tel: 556 5565
Fax: 652 3625
www.thescotsmanhotelgroup.co.uk.
68 rooms. A boutique hotel produced from a remarkably successful make-over of *The Scotsman* newspaper offices. Comfortable rooms have all mod cons and health club with pool.

Sheraton Grand Hotel & Spa
1 Festival Square
Tel: 229 9131
Fax: 228 4510
www.sheraton.com/grandedinburgh
265 rooms. Set back from busy Lothian Road and close to city centre. Complete leisure club.

£££

Bank Hotel
1 South Bridge
Tel: 622 6800
Fax: 622 6822
www.festival-inns.co.uk
Nine rooms. Former bank on the Royal Mile, now converted into café-bar with bedrooms.

Best Western Bruntsfield Hotel
69 Bruntsfield Place
Tel: 229 1393
Fax: 229 5634
www.bw-bruntsfieldhotel.co.uk
67 rooms. Well-established hotel 1 mile (1.5km) from Princes Street.

Channings
15 South Learmonth Gardens
Tel: 315 2226
www.channings.co.uk
41 rooms. A series of splendid Edwardian adjoining houses, minutes from city centre.

Comfortable reception area and lounges. Bedrooms individually furnished.

Hudson Hotel
7–11 Hope Street
Tel: 247 7000
Fax: 247 7001
www.festival-inns.co.uk
Swanky up-market hotel: cocktail bar and pleasing rooms with a contemporary twist – the ideal base from which to explore the city.

Malmaison
1 Tower Place, Leith
Tel: 468 5000
Fax: 468 5002
www.malmaison.com
100 rooms with cable TV in a former seamen's mission. The Malmaison is an award-winning contemporary hotel with stylishly designed rooms, on the waterfront of Leith. Haunted turret room.

Point Hotel
34 Bread Street
Tel: 221 5555
Fax: 221 9929
www.accorhotels.com
Cutting-edge minimalist hotel with colour-themed floors close to castle. Jacuzzis in suites. Attractive bar and restaurants.

Ramada Edinburgh Mount Royal
Princes Street
Tel: 0844-815 9017
www.ramadajarvis.co.uk
Centrally located, offering stunning views of the castle. Classic, fresh interiors create

ABOVE: the rooftop hydropool at the Sheraton Grand Hotel & Spa, Edinburgh.

a more than adequate base for the duration of any trip.

Royal Terrace Hotel
18 Royal Terrace
Tel: 557 3222
Fax: 557 5334
www.royalterracehotel.co.uk
107 rooms. Georgian terrace building on a cobbled street, minutes from east end of Princes Street. Leisure club and large private garden.

££

Ailsa Craig Hotel
24 Royal Terrace
Tel: 556 6055
Fax: 556 1022
www.townhousehotels.co.uk
18 rooms. Elegant, recently refurbished hotel with stunning views over the Forth and Calton Hill.

Albyn Townhouse
16 Hartington Gardens
Tel: 229 6459
Fax: 228 5807
www.albyntownhouse.co.uk
A striking Georgian town house with a warm, homely feel. Good location with most of Edinburgh's attractions easily accessible.

Ballantrae Hotel
8 York Place
Tel: 478 4748
Fax: 478 4749
www.ballantraehotel.co.uk
Modest yet reputable hotel offering a bar and classically furnished rooms. Good value for the more humble budget.

Edinburgh City Premier Travel Inn
1 Morrison Link
Tel: 0871-942 9025

Fax: 228 9836
www.travelinn.co.uk
281 rooms. Interesting bid to provide economical, comfortable, no-frills accommodation in centre.

Holiday Inn Edinburgh Citywest
107 Queensferry Road
Tel: 0870-400 9025
Fax: 332 3408
www.holiday-inn.co.uk
Friendly hotel with 101 rooms. 1½ miles (2.5km) west of city centre.

Travel Lodge
33 St Mary's Street
Tel: 0871-984 6137
Fax: 557 3681
www.travelodge.co.uk
193 rooms. Standard no-frills hostelry adjacent to Holyrood end of Royal Mile.

Guesthouses

(If phoning from outside area, use code: 0131.)

££

Salisbury Guest House
43–5 Salisbury Road
Tel/Fax: 667 1264
www.salisburyguesthouse.co.uk
Georgian listed building, relaunched in 2007 with 18 upgraded en suite rooms, and a licensed bar and garden café. Situated near to Holyroodhouse.

£

Ashlyn Guest House
42 Inverleith Row
Tel/Fax: 552 2954
7 rooms (5 en suite). Listed Georgian house close to the Botanic Gardens and five minutes' drive from the city centre.

Joppa Turrets
1 Lower Joppa
Tel/fax: 669 5806
www.joppaturrets.co.uk
Seven rooms (five en suite). On the beach at Joppa but close to bus routes and 5 miles (8km) from city centre.

Your best bet for low-priced accommodation in Edinburgh is a **B&B**. The Edinburgh and Lothians Tourist Board will help find one for you.
Tel: 08452-255 121
www.edinburgh.org/accommodation;
www.visitscotland.com

GLASGOW

Hotels

(If phoning from outside area, use code: 0141.)

££££

Blythwood Square

PRICE CATEGORIES

Approximate prices per person per night in a double room in high season:
£ = less than £30
££ = £30–50
£££ = £50–80
££££ = more than £80

11 Blythwood Square
Tel: 248 8888
www.townhousecompany.com
100 rooms. A boutique hotel and Glasgow's first luxury spa is located in a converted building dating back to 1823. The restaurant is in the former opulent ballroom.

Carnbooth House
80 Busby Road, Carmunnock
Tel: 644 3838
www.carnboothhouse.com
Eight suites. If you wish to stay in a country atmosphere yet only a few

miles to the south of the city, this sumptuous hotel in a converted schoolhouse could be the answer.

One Devonshire Gardens
1 Devonshire Gardens
Tel: 339 2001
Fax: 337 1663
www.hotelduvin.com
49 rooms. Part of the Hotel du Vin group this exquisite, luxury boutique hotel is on a tree-lined Victorian terrace in the residential area of West End. Each room is different and the service impeccable.

The standard rooms come in the **£££** price bracket.

£££

ABode Glasgow
129 Bath Street
Tel: 221 6789
www.abodehotels.co.uk
Trendsetting hotel combines luxurious rooms with stunning traditional architecture throughout. The restaurant is equally stylish.

Carlton George
44 West George Street
Tel: 353 6373
www.carlton.nl/george
64 rooms. Well-located for cultural attractions and shopping. The boutique-style decor combines Scottish tradition with a modern twist and there's excellent Scottish cooking with an unbeatable view at The Windows rooftop restaurant.

Glasgow Hilton
1 William Street
Tel: 204 5555
Fax: 204 5004
www.hilton.com
317 rooms. Modern 20-floor tower in the city centre, just off the motorway. Health and leisure club; excellent restaurant.

Malmaison
278 West George Street
Tel: 572 1000
Fax: 572 1002
www.malmaison.com
Stylish 72-room hotel in former Greek Orthodox church in city centre. Chic and comfortable.

Mar Hall
Mar Hall Drive, Bishopton
Tel: 812 9999
www.marhall.com
53 rooms. Luxury golf and spa resort just 10 minutes from Glasgow Airport. A host of original features but with all modern facilities incorporated.

Menzies Glasgow
27 Washington Street
Tel: 222 2929
www.menzies-hotels.co.uk
128 feng shui rooms and 12 suite apartments. Ten minutes from Central Station.

££

Best Western Ewington Hotel
132 Queens Drive
Tel: 227 2772
Fax: 422 2030
www.mckeverhotels.co.uk
43 rooms. Well-appointed terrace hotel in leafy street beside Queen's Park.

City Inn
Finnieston Quay
Tel: 240 1002
Fax: 248 2754
www.cityinn.com/glasgow
164 rooms. Pleasant property on the north side of the river with great deck. Close to Conference Centre and to Science Centre.

Crowne Plaza
Congress Road
Tel: 0871-942 9091
Fax: 221 2022
www.crowneplaza.com
289 rooms. Sited on the River Clyde next to the Scottish Exhibition Centre.

Hilton Glasgow Grosvenor
Grosvenor Terrace
Tel: 339 8811
Fax: 334 0710
www.hilton.co.uk
96 rooms. Hotel with striking facade near the Botanic Gardens, university and trendy Byres Road.

Millennium Hotel
George Square
Tel: 332 6711
Fax: 332 4264
www.millenniumhotels.co.uk
117 rooms. Situated in the heart of George Square next to Queen Street Station.

Novotel Hotel
181 Pitt Street
Tel: 222 2775
Fax: 204 5438
www.novotel.com
139 rooms. One of the more modern hotels, and close to trendy bars and restaurants. The headquarters of the city police is a neighbour.

Park Inn
2 Port Dundas Place
Tel: 333 1500
Fax: 352 2456
www.glasgow.parkinn.co.uk
100 well-equipped rooms. Ideally situated next to bus terminal, concert hall and 17-screen cinema. Duplexes available. PlayStations in all rooms, health club (no pool).

Radisson SAS Hotel
301 Argyle Street
Tel: 204 3333
Fax: 204 3344
www.sas.radisson.com
247 rooms. One of the city's newest hotels. Adjacent to Central Station.

Saint Jude's
190 Bath Street
Tel: 352 8800
Fax: 352 8801
www.saintjudes.com
Six rooms. A superb small hotel furnished in modern designer mode, attached to a smashing restaurant in the Merchant City. Fitness suite, jacuzzi and sunbed.

Sherbrooke Castle
11 Sherbrooke Avenue
Tel: 427 4227
Fax: 427 5685
www.sherbrooke.co.uk
21 rooms. Scottish baronial castle in own grounds on south side, about 3 miles (5km) from city centre. Handy for the Burrell Collection and Pollok Country Park.

Thistle Glasgow
36 Cambridge Street
Tel: 0871-376 9043
Fax: 333 9254
www.thistlehotels.com/glasgow
300 rooms. Good hotel in the heart of the city.

£

Argyll Guest House
970 Sauchiehall Street
Tel: 357 5155
www.argyllguesthouseglasgow.co.uk
20 rooms. Private hotel in Georgian terrace by Kelvingrove Park and a few minutes' walk from the art galleries and university.

Babbity Bowster
16–18 Blackfriars Street
Tel: 552 5055
Email: babbitybowster@gofornet.co.uk
Six rooms. Better known for its food, atmosphere and great folk music sessions, but also a handy base in the Merchant City and close to shopping and nightlife.

BELOW: the Hilton Glasgow Grosvenor Hotel.

PRICE CATEGORIES

Approximate prices per person per night in a double room in high season:
£ = less than £30
££ = £30–50
£££ = £50–80
££££ = more than £80

Express by Holiday Inn
122 Stockwell Street
Tel: 548 5000
Fax: 548 5048
www.hiexpress.co.uk
128 rooms. On north side of river, a tad away from the heart of the city. Close to the Glasgow mosque and the Citizens Theatre.

Holiday Inn Glasgow
161 West Nile Street
Tel: 352 8300
Fax: 352 8311
www.higlasgow.com
113 rooms. Ideally situated next to bus terminal, concert hall and 17-screen cinema. Duplexes available.

Ibis Hotel
220 West Regent Street
Tel: 225 6000
Fax: 225 6010
www.ibishotel.com
141 rooms. Don't be put off by the psychedelic appearance of this efficient modern hotel in a quiet part of the city centre. Compact rooms with work station and computer points. Close to motorway.

Kirklee Hotel
11 Kensington Gate
Tel: 334 5555
www.kirkleehotel.co.uk
Nine rooms. An Edwardian town house in an almost original condition in the West End conservation area. The extensive collection

ABOVE: Babbity Bowster, an 18th century townhouse.

of paintings and drawings adds to the atmosphere of a bygone age. One of the hidden gems of Glasgow.

The Pipers Tryst
30–4 McPhater Street
Tel: 353 5551
www.thepipingcentre.co.uk
Eight rooms. This small hotel is part of the Glasgow Piping Centre and is very close to the Royal Concert Hall and the city centre – and no, the sound of

bagpipes won't keep you awake at night.

Guesthouses

(If phoning from outside area, use code: 0141.)

£–££

Alamo Guest House
46 Gray Street
Tel: 339 2395
www.alamoguesthouse.com
10 rooms (Four en suite).

Situated on pleasant, quiet road alongside Kelvingrove Park. Good value and comfortable.

Euro Hostels
318 Clyde Street
Tel: 222 2828
www.euro-hostels.co.uk
Basic clean (and en suite) accommodation ideal for those seeking central location on a budget. Safe and friendly.

The Flower House Bed & Breakfast
33 St Vincent Crescent
Tel: 204 2846
www.scotland2000.com/flowerhouse
Four rooms. The flowers crowding round the front of the building explain the name. A warm, friendly, lovely guest house.

Glasgow Youth Hostel
7–8 Park Terrace
Tel: 0845-293 7373
www.syha.org.uk
Charming dorms sleep four to six. All rooms en suite. One of Scotland's best hostels, extensively refurbished following a fire.

McLays Guest House
268 Renfrew Street
Tel: 332 4796
www.mclaysgh.co.uk
62 rooms (39 en suite). Lots of singles. Well-appointed, comfortable guest house only a few minutes from the city centre.

THE BORDERS

Hawick

Mansfield House Hotel
Weensland Road
Tel: 01450-360 400
Fax: 01450-372 007
www.mansfield-house.com
12 rooms. Victorian country house hotel set in 10 well established acres (4 hectares). **££–£££**

Innerleithen

Traquair Arms
Traquair Road
Tel: 01896-830 229
Fax: 01896-830 260
www.traquairarmshotel.co.uk
15 rooms. Charming country house hotel with

excellent food, both Scottish and Italian. **££**

Jedburgh

Jedforest Hotel
Jedburgh, Roxburghshire TD8 6PJ
Tel: 01835-840 222
Fax: 01835-84226
www.jedforesthotel.com
The first hotel in Scotland. Stands in 35 acres (15 hectares) of a private estate on the banks of Jedwater River. **££–£££**

Kelso

Cross Keys
The Square
Tel: 01573-223 303

Fax: 01573-225 792
www.ckhkelso.co.uk
28 rooms. Old coaching inn set in town centre square with French character. **££**

The Roxburghe Hotel & Golf Course
Heiton
Tel: 01573-450 331
Fax: 01573-450 611
www.roxburghe.net
22 bedrooms. 18th-century house, 3 miles (5km) south of Kelso and nestling on the banks of the River Teviot. Superb public rooms and beautiful grounds. Fishing, clay pigeon shooting, croquet, tennis, championship golf course.
£££–££££

Kircudbright

Best Western Selkirk Arms
High Street

Tel: 01557-330 402
Fax: 01557-331 639
www.bw-selkirkarmshotel.co.uk
16 rooms. Pleasant hotel
with garden which, as the
scene of *The Selkirk Grace*,
will attract lovers of Robert
Burns. **££–£££**

Melrose

Burts Hotel
Market Square
Tel: 01896-822 285
Fax: 01896-822 870
www.burtshotel.co.uk
20 rooms. Tastefully
modernised old town house
in main square, close to the
ruined abbey. **£££**

Peebles

Castle Venlaw Hotel
Edinburgh Road, Peebles
Tel: 01721-720 384

Fax: 01721-724 066
www.venlaw.co.uk
12 rooms. A wide variety of
rooms in this pleasantly
situated 200-year-old castle
on the edge of Peebles. **£££**
Cringletie House Hotel
Edinburgh Road
Tel: 01721-725 750
Fax: 01721-720 244
www.cringletie.com
12 rooms. Elegantly
furnished hotel in its own
grounds 2 miles (3km) from
Peebles. Renowned
restaurant. **£££–££££**
**Macdonald Cardrona Golf
and Country Club**
Tel: 0844-879 9024
Fax: 01896-831 166
www.macdonaldhotels.co.uk/cardrona
Modern design surrounded
by nature offering a range of
facilities for the active visitor,
including top-class golf
course and spa. **££–£££**

Peebles Hotel Hydro
Innerleithen Road
Tel: 01721-720 602
Fax: 01721-722 999
www.peebleshotelhydro.co.uk
129 rooms. Château-style
hotel set in 34 acres (14
hectares) overlooking the
River Tweed. Leisure centre,
tennis, walking and riding.
Families welcome. **££££**
Tontine Hotel
High Street
Tel: 01721-720 892
Fax: 01721-729 732
www.tontinehotel.com
36 rooms. 1808-established
coaching inn, with views from
rooms to the River Tweed. **££**

St Boswells

Dryburgh Abbey Hotel
Tel: 01835 822261
Fax: 01835-823 945
www.dryburgh.co.uk

38 rooms. This hotel is
beautifully situated next to
Dryburgh Abbey and the
River Tweed. **£££–££££**

Selkirk

Glen Hotel
Yarrow Terrace
Tel/Fax: 01750-20259
www.glenhotel.co.uk
8 rooms. Small, friendly
hotel close to Ettrick Water,
good food. Traditional hearty
Borders breakfasts. Fishing
and horse riding. **££**
**Philipburn Country House
Hotel**
Linglie Road
Tel: 01750-20747
Fax: 01750-724 188
www.bw-philipburnhousehotel.co.uk
14 beautifully decorated
rooms, some with
balconies. Jacuzzi a nd
steam showers. **££–£££**

THE SOUTHWEST

Arran

**Auchrannie Country House
Hotel and Spa**
Brodick
Tel: 01770-302 234
Fax: 01770-302 812
www.auchrannie.co.uk
28 rooms. Mansion in 10
acres (4 hectares) of grounds
near bay and castle.
36-bedroom leisure, health
and spa resort nearby.
£££–££££
Kilmichael House Hotel
Glen Cloy, by Brodick
Tel: 01770-302 219
Fax: 01770-302068
www.kilmichael.com
The place to stay on Arran. In
acres of mature garden, this
luxurious country house with
award-winning restaurant
offers four individually styled
bedrooms, three suites and a
"wee dram" on your arrival.
£££–££££

Ayr

**Ramada Jarvis Caledonian
Hotel**
Dalblair Road
Tel: 0844-815 9005
www.ramadajarvis.co.uk
118 rooms. Town-centre

hotel close to beach offering
many rooms with fine views
and a leisure club. **££**

Dumfries

**Cairndale Hotel and
Leisure Club**
English Street
Tel: 01387-254 111
Fax: 01387-240 288
www.cairndalehotel.co.uk
91 rooms. Regular live
entertainment (*ceilidhs* in
summer), full leisure club;
activities include golf, walking and fishing. **££–£££**

Gatehouse of Fleet

Cally Palace
Tel: 01557-814 341
Fax: 01557-814 522
www.callypalace.co.uk
56 rooms. Magnificent public
rooms and comfortable
bedrooms in this Georgian
mansion set in forest and
parkland. Exclusive use of
18-hole golf course. **££££**
Murray Arms Inn
Ann Street
Tel: 01557-814 207
www.murrayarmshotel.co.uk
13 rooms. Attractive 18th-
century posting inn where

Robert Burns wrote *Scots
Wha Hae*. **££**

Girvan

Westin Turnberry Resort
Turnberry
Tel: 01655-331 000
Fax: 01655-331 706
www.westin.com/turnberry
221 rooms. Luxury country
club and spa. Elegance and
gracious service, especially
in the restaurants which
provide superb views and
food. Activities include horse
riding, squash, tennis and
golf, including Colin
Montgomerie Links Golf
Academy. **£££–££££**

Moffat

Auchen Castle Hotel
Beattock
Tel: 01683-300 407
Fax: 01683-300 727
www.auchencastle.com
25 rooms of which 15 in
castle and 10 in modern
wing. Set in 28 acres (12
hectares) of grounds with
spectacular views.
£££–££££
Buchan Guest House
Beechgrove

Tel: 01683-220 378
www.buchanguesthouse.co.uk
Pretty guesthouse a short
walk north of the city centre.
£–££
Moffat House Hotel
High Street
Tel: 01683-220 039
www.moffathouse.co.uk
20 rooms. An 18th-century

PRICE CATEGORIES

Approximate prices per
person per night in a double
room in high season:
£ = less than £30
££ = £30–50
£££ = £50–80
££££ = more than £80

ABOVE: Corsewall Lighthouse Hotel.

Adam mansion set in its own grounds. **££**

Newton Stewart

Kirroughtree House Hotel
Tel: 01671-402 141
Fax: 01671-402 425
www.kirroughtreehouse.co.uk
17 rooms. Cheerful and colourful Georgian mansion in large established landscaped gardens (croquet and pitch and putt available). Strong Burns associations. Renowned for traditional Scottish food. **£££–££££**

Stranraer

Corsewall Lighthouse Hotel
Kircolm
Tel: 01776-853 220
Fax: 01776-854 231
www.lighthousehotel.co.uk
Nine rooms and three suites. This warm and friendly hotel is set in the old lighthouse keeper's quarters. Located on a wild and windy headland miles from anywhere, this is a beautiful spot right off the beaten

track. Excellent five-course dinners. Advance booking recommended. **£££–££££** (includes dinner)
North West Castle Hotel
Tel: 01776-704 413
Fax: 01776-702 646
www.northwestcastle.co.uk
71 rooms. Comfortable hotel on seafront. Facilities include curling rink, gym, and indoor pool. **£££**

Troon

Marine Hotel
Crosbie Road
Tel: 01292-314 444
Fax: 01292-316 922
www.paramount-hotels.co.uk
89 rooms. Traditional hotel with some rooms overlooking the famous golf course. Health and fitness club. **£££**
Piersland House Hotel
Craigend Road
Tel: 01292-314 747
www.piersland.co.uk
30 rooms. Built for Sir Alexander Walker of whisky fame. Renovated in traditional style. Good restaurant. **££**

FORTH AND CLYDE

Airth

Airth Castle Hotel
Tel: 01324-831 411
Fax: 01324-831 419
www.airthcastlehotel.com
23 rooms in castle, plus 99 in adjoining country club. Historic castle, now converted into a fine hotel set in 17 acres (7 hectares) of grounds. **£££–££££**

Falkirk

Best Western Park Hotel
Camelon Road
Tel: 01324-628 331
Fax: 01324-611 593
www.bestwestern.com
55 rooms. Modern hotel close to Dollar Park and Mariner Leisure Centre. **££**
Macdonald Inchyra Hotel
Grange Road, Polmont
Tel: 0844-879 9044
Fax: 01324-7171 6134
Central reservations:
Tel: 0870-400 9191 (UK)

www.macdonald-hotels.co.uk
98 rooms. Fine country house hotel with beauty and fitness centre, tennis courts. **££**

Fintry

Culcreuch Castle Hotel
Fintry, nr Stirling
Tel: 01360-860 555
www.culcreuch.com
14 rooms. This 14th-century castle with pleasant modern rooms claims to be the oldest inhabited castle in Scotland. It stands in 1,600 acres (670 hectares) of glorious parkland with its own loch. Free fishing is available to guests. Such a wonderful setting makes it a very popular location for wedding parties. **£££**

Grangemouth

Grange Manor Hotel
Glensburgh
Tel: 01324-474 836

www.grangemanor.co.uk
Set in landscaped gardens, this hotel has spared no expense when it comes to decor – a beautiful wooden staircase graces the entrance hall. Ideally located for exploring central Scotland. **£££**

Stirling

Garfield Guest House
12 Victoria Square
Tel: 01786-473 730
Six rooms. Large Victorian house in quiet square, close to town centre. B&B only. **£–££**
Number 10
10 Gladstone Place
Tel: 01786-472 681
www.cameron-10.co.uk
Very central three-bedroom guesthouse in friendly house built in Victorian era. Within walking distance of castle and Old Town. Quiet residential area. **££**

Park Lodge Country House Hotel
32 Park Terrace
Tel: 01786-474 862
Fax: 01786-449 748
www.parklodge.net
Nine rooms. Part-Victorian, part-Georgian hotel in heart of town. Some rooms with four-poster beds. **££**
Stirling Highland Hotel
Spittal Street

TRANSPORT

ACCOMMODATION

EATING OUT

ACTIVITIES

A – Z

Tel: 01786-272 727
Fax: 01786-272 829
www.paramount-hotels.co.uk
96 rooms. Restored, listed
former school with
observatory. Good food in
Scholar's Restaurant.

Health and leisure club.
££
**Stirling Management
Centre**
Stirling University campus
Tel: 01786-451 712
Fax: 01786-450 472

www.smc.stir.ac.uk
75 rooms (all en suite).
Purpose-built conference
centre/hotel on bucolic
university campus 3 miles
(5km) from Stirling. Use of
pool and gym. **££**

Terraces Hotel
4 Melville Terrace
Tel: 01786-472 268
www.terraceshotel.co.uk
Revamped Georgian house,
close to the town centre.
Good food. **££–£££**

THE WEST COAST

Arisaig

Garramore House
South Morar
Tel: 01687-450 268
Email: garramorehouse@aol.com
Old hunting lodge con-
verted into a comfortable
guesthouse. Children and
pets are welcome. Set in
beautiful woodland
gardens with great views of
islands. Sandy beaches
nearby. **£**

Crinan

Crinan Hotel
Tel: 01546-830 261
Fax: 01546-830 292
www.crinanhotel.com
22 rooms. Some rooms
have private balconies; all
have stunning sea views of
the Sound of Jura. Dine in
Lock 16, the rooftop
seafood restaurant and eat
the "catch of the day".
From here, admire the seascapes and canal below.
££££

Eriska

Isle of Eriska
Ledaig by Oban
Tel: 01631-720 371
Fax: 01631-720 531
www.eriska-hotel.co.uk
19 rooms. Welcoming hotel
on private island joined to
the mainland by a short
bridge. Bedrooms vary in
size and each has its own
character. Terrific spa. Lovely
grounds with tennis, croquet
and 6-hole golf course,
driving range, golf academy.
££££

Fort William

Crolinnhe
Grange Road
Tel: 01397-702 709
www.crolinnhe.co.uk
Excellent guesthouse behind
town centre, very friendly,
good food and jacuzzi. **£££**
Inverlochy Castle Hotel
Torlundy
Tel: 01397-702 177
Fax: 01397-702 953

www.inverlochycastlehotel.com
17 rooms. One of Europe's
best stone-walled (castle)
hotels. Imposing public
rooms. Set in glorious
grounds with views of Ben
Nevis. Wonderful cuisine and
wine list. Snooker, tennis and
game fishing. **££££**
Moorings Hotel
Banavie
Tel: 01397-772 797
Fax: 01397-772 441
www.moorings-fortwilliam.co.uk
28 rooms. Three miles (5km)
from town at Neptune's
Staircase at the start of the
Caledonian Canal with
superb views of Ben Nevis.
£££

Gigha

Gigha Hotel
Isle of Gigha
Tel: 01583-505 254
www.gigha.org.uk
11 en suite rooms. Pleasant,
cosy hotel on this
community-owned island
and 10 minutes' walk from

pierhead. Good food,
especially fresh fish. **££**

Glenelg

Glenelg Inn
Tel: 01599-522 273
Fax: 01599-522 283
www.glenelg-inn.com
Seven rooms. Lively pub with
restaurant is the focal point
of this waterfront inn.
Bedrooms, which are
individually and tastefully
decorated, have grand views
of Skye. **££**

Glenshiel

Cluanie Inn
Tel: 01320-340 238
Fax: 01320-340 293
www.cluanieinn.com
10 rooms. Traditional
Scottish inn, fully
modernised, far away from it
all between Loch Ness and
Skye. Inviting roaring fires in
public rooms. **££**

BELOW: Lochalsh Hotel with Skye Bridge in the background.

PRICE CATEGORIES

Approximate prices per
person per night in a double
room in high season:
£ = less than £30
££ = £30–50
£££ = £50–80
££££ = more than £80

Inveraray

George Hotel
Main Street East
Tel: 01499-302 111
www.thegeorgehotel.co.uk
Atmospheric, friendly hotel serving delicious traditional food and real ales on tap in centre of town. A resident ghost and double jacuzzi reside among 27 rooms. ££££

Loch Fyne Hotel and Spa
Shore Street
Tel: 01499-302 980
www.crerahotels.com
With panoramic views of the loch and excellent spa facilities, this charming house offers spacious, beautifully furnished rooms in tranquil surroundings. A real hidden gem. ££££

Kyle of Lochalsh

Lochalsh Hotel
Ferry Road
Tel: 01599-534 202
www.lochalshhotel.com
38 rooms. Magnificently situated, comfortable hotel on the water's edge with superb views of Skye and the Cuillins. £–££

Loch Awe

Ardanaiseig Hotel
Kilchrenan, by Taynuilt
Tel: 01866-833 333
Fax: 01866-833 222
www.ardanaiseig.com
16 rooms plus two-bedroom cottage. Elegant country house hotel far away from it all. Beautiful furnished rooms. Woodland garden. Hotel boats for fishing; tennis, snooker. £££–££££

Taychreggan Hotel
By Taynuilt
Tel: 01866-833 211
Fax: 01866-833 244
www.taychregganhotel.co.uk
18 rooms. Old hotel around a cobbled courtyard on a secluded part of Loch Awe. Game and coarse fishing, boating, snooker. £££–££££

Loch Lomond

Ardlui Hotel
Ardlui
Tel: 01301-704 243
www.ardlui.co.uk
10 rooms. Friendly country house hotel on loch shore; good atmosphere, fine food, excellent walking. £££

De Vere Cameron House Hotel
Tel/fax: 01389 755565
www.devere.co.uk.
96 rooms. A handsome mansion house standing in 100 acres (40 hectares) by the side of Loch Lomond. Excellent leisure facilities

include a 9-hole golf course and a bustling marina for sailing and windsurfing. £££

The Lodge on Loch Lomond
Luss
Tel: 01436 860201
Fax: 01436 860203
www.loch-lomond.co.uk.
29 rooms. Luxurious modern loch-side hotel with magnificent views. Each bedroom has a sauna en suite. ££££

Loch Melfort

Loch Melfort Hotel
Arduaine
Tel: 01852 200233
Fax: 01852 200214
www.lochmelfort.co.uk
23 rooms. A relaxed atmosphere prevails in this splendid hotel, which looks out on magnificent scenery, about 20 miles (32km) south of Oban. Sample the fricassee of local shellfish with herb pasta ribbons and home-made puddings from the restaurant. ££££

Oban

Columba Hotel
Esplanade
Tel: 01631-562 183
Fax: 01631-564 683
www.obanhotels.com
50 rooms. Well-established hotel on waterfront. £££

Knipoch Hotel
Six miles (10km) south of Oban on the A816
Tel: 01852-316 251
Fax: 01852-316 249
www.knipochhotel.co.uk
22 rooms. Peaceful, elegant family-run hotel with well-appointed bedrooms. ££££

Manor House Hotel
Gallanach Road
Tel: 01631-562 087
Fax: 01631-563 053
www.manorhouseoban.com
11 rooms. Built in 1780 on a promontory with fine view of Oban Bay. Good restaurant. £££

Talladale

The Old Mill
Talladale
Tel: 01445-760 271
www.theoldmillhighlandlodge.co.uk
Six en suite rooms form part of a lodge built on a former horse mill. Spectacular views towards Torridon. £££

Tarbert (Loch Fyne)

Stonefield Castle Hotel
Tel: 01880-820 836
Fax: 01880-820 929
www.stonefieldcastle.co.uk.
32 rooms. Baronial mansion set in 60 acres (24 hectares) of glorious gardens and woodlands. £££

SKYE

Portree

Cuillin Hills Hotel
Tel: 01478-612 003
Fax: 01478-613 092
www.cuillinhills-hotel-skye.co.uk
28 rooms. A 19th-century former hunting lodge in large grounds just outside Portree. Views over Portree Bay to the Cuillins. ££££

Rosedale Hotel
Beaumont Crescent
Tel: 01478-613 131
Fax: 01478-612 531
www.rosedalehotelskye.co.uk
19 rooms. Comfortable waterfront hotel converted from former fishermen's houses. Some bedrooms are very small. ££

The Royal Hotel
Portree
Tel: 01478-612 525
www.royal-hotel-skye.com
25 rooms. Attractively furnished, traditional hotel offering no-nonsense, good-value food and lodgings overlooking the harbour. ££

Skeabost House Hotel
Skeabost Bridge
Tel: 01470-532 202
Fax: 01470-532 454
www.skeabostcountryhouse.co.uk
19 rooms. Former hunting lodge in 12 acres (5 hectares) of secluded woodlands and garden on the shore of Loch Snizort. Famous Sunday buffet lunch is served in sunny conservatory. Salmon

fishing, 9-hole golf course. £££

Viewfield House
Tel: 01478-612 217
Fax: 01478-613 517
www.viewfieldhouse.com
12 rooms. Idiosyncratic country house hotel in extensive wooded grounds overlooking the bay. Open mid-April–mid-October. Each room different, all large. Something of a time warp, although it has modern bathrooms. An experience. £££ (includes dinner)

Staffin

Flodigarry Country House Hotel
Tel: 01470-552 203

Fax: 01470-552 301
www.flodigarry.co.uk
19 rooms. Historic mansion beneath the Quiraing Mountains offering glorious

views. *Ceilidhs* held on Saturday night. Separate house where Flora MacDonald once lived has been tastefully converted into rooms. **££**

Sleat

Ardvasar Hotel
Tel: 01471-844 223
Fax: 01471-844 495
www.ardvasarhotel.com
10 rooms. Traditional white-washed hotel overlooks Sound of Sleat and Mallaig. 1 mile (1.6km) from Mallaig–Armdale ferry. **£££**

Eilean Iarmain (Isle of Ornsay) Hotel
Tel: 01471-833 332
Fax: 01471-833 275
www.eilean-iarmain.co.uk
12 rooms plus four suites in converted stables. Friendly 19th-century inn by the sea featuring Gaelic hospitality. Spectacular views. Famous for its seafood. **£££**

Dunvegan

Atholl House Hotel
Tel: 01470-521 219
Fax: 01470-521 481

www.athollhotel.co.uk
Nine rooms. Former manse; views of Loch Dunvegan. **££**
Roskhill House
Tel: 01470-521 317
www.roskhillhouse.co.uk
Built in 1890, the lounge was once the post office. Evening meals by prior arrangement. Pets welcome. **££**

Sligachan

Sligachan Hotel
Tel: 01478-650 204
Fax: 01478-650 207
www.sligachan.co.uk

22 rooms. Famous climbers' hotel, fully modernised, with views of the Cuillins and Loch Sligachin. Full of atmosphere. Range of real ales from Cuillin Brewery. Golf and fishing nearby. **£££**

Broadford

Tir Alainn
by Broadford
Tel: 01471-822 366
www.visitskye.com
Terrific views and a warm welcome are provided at this cosy 3-room B&B. **££**

THE INNER HEBRIDES

Iona

Argyll Hotel
Tel: 01681-700 334
Fax: 01681-700 510
www.argyllhoteliona.co.uk
The oldest inn on the island has 16 en suite rooms. Restaurant serves traditional food using the finest local produce. Open Feb–Oct. **££**
St Columba Hotel
Tel: 01681 700304
Fax: 01681 700688
www.stcolumba-hotel.co.uk
27 rooms. Situated close to the famous abbey, this tranquil hotel enjoys fine views across the water to Mull. **£££**

Mull

Druimard Country House Hotel
Dervaig
Tel/Fax: 01688-400 345
www.druimard.co.uk
Seven rooms. Victorian country house widely known for its interesting cuisine. Pleasant conservatory and informal atmosphere. **£££**
Western Isles Hotel
Tobermory
Tel: 01688-302 012
Fax: 01688-302 297
www.westernisleshotel.co.uk
28 rooms. Gothic-style building magnificently situated above Tobermory Bay. **£££**

Raasay

Isle of Raasay Hotel
Tel/Fax: 01478-660 222
www.isleofraasayhotel.co.uk
12 rooms. Take the ferry from Skye to the island of Raasay and escape into beautiful natural surroundings. Superb walking and birdlife. **££**

Tiree

Scarinish Hotel
Scarinish
Tel: 01879-220 308
www.tireescarinishhotel.com
Refurbished hotel with six en suite rooms. Dinner is served in the Old Harbour

Restaurant while the Lean To Bar is a friendly meeting place. Dogs welcome. **£££**

THE OUTER HEBRIDES

Barra

Castlebay Hotel
Castlebay
Tel: 01871-810 223
www.castlebay-hotel.co.uk
12 rooms. Overlooks the bay with its castle. Easy access to ferry. **£££**
Dunard Hostel
Castlebay
Tel: 01871 810443
www.dunardhostel.co.uk
Small, friendly family-run hostel, minutes from ferry terminal, bank and shops. **£**

Harris

Scarista House

Scarista
Tel: 01859-550 238
www.scaristahouse.com
Five rooms. Former manse run by very friendly couple. Superb views of sea, and bedrooms are comfortable; excellent restaurant using local produce. **£££**

Lewis

The Cabarfeidh
Manor Park, Stornoway
Tel: 01851-702 604
www.cabarfeidh-hotel.co.uk
Comfortable, recently refurbished hotel located close to ferry terminal and town centre. **£££**

North Uist

Lochmaddy Hotel
Lochmaddy
Tel: 01876-500 331
www.lochmaddyhotel.co.uk
Traditional white-washed Highland building; 15 rooms with en suite facilities. Close to the ferry terminal and with lovely sea views. Good restaurant serving game, local seafood and a fine selection of malts. **££–£££**
Tigh Dearg Hotel
Lochmaddy
Tel: 01876-500 700
www.tighdearghotel.co.uk
Stylish hotel with 8 designer rooms. Guests have use of

gym, sauna and steam room. Superb restaurant, views of the harbour. **£££**

CENTRAL SCOTLAND AND FIFE

Anstruther

The Spindrift
Pittenweem Road
Tel/Fax: 01333-310 573
www.thespindrift.co.uk
Eight rooms (seven en suite). Non-smoking B&B in Victorian house 10 minutes by car from St Andrews. **£**

Auchterarder

Duchally Country Resort
Gleneagles
Tel: 01764-663 071
Fax: 01764-662 464
www.duchally.com
Secluded country hotel set in parkland. The wide range of accommodation available includes self-catering lodges nestled in the beautiful Perthshire countryside. Ideal for golf fanatics with the Gleneagles courses just around the corner. **£££**

Gleneagles Hotel
Tel: 0800-389 3737 (UK)
Tel: 1866-881 9525 (US)
Fax: 01764-662134
www.gleneagles.com
275 rooms. Unbridled luxury is the name of the game at the "Palace in the Glen". Public rooms are very grand; bedrooms are tastefully furnished and comfortable. Health spa and leisure centre with three swimming pools. Activities include tennis, croquet, squash, clay pigeon shooting, fishing, horse riding, falconry, off-road driving and, of course, golf. **££££**

Blair Atholl

Dalgreine
Bridge of Tilt
Tel/fax: 01796-481 276
www.dalgreine-guest-house.co.uk
Six rooms (two en suite). Fine large house close to Blair Castle, superb walking, secluded garden. **££**

Blairgowrie

Altamount House Hotel
Coupar Angus Road
Tel: 01250-873 512
Fax: 01250-876 200

www.altamounthouse.co.uk
Seven rooms. Lovely country house, close to town centre, set in 7 acres (3 hectares) of gardens and wooded grounds. Excellent food. **££**

Callander

Arden House
Bracklinn Road
Tel/fax: 01877-330 235
www.ardenhouse.org.uk
Six rooms. With superb views of the Trossachs, this was the setting for the vintage BBC TV series *Dr Finlay's Casebook*. **£–££**

Callander Meadows
Main Street
Tel: 01877-330 181
www.callandermeadows.co.uk
Seek out this three-bedroomed den of tranquillity and you'll be rewarded with delicious fare in the restaurant and a great night's sleep. **££**

Roman Camp Country House Hotel
Callander
Tel: 01877-330 003
Fax: 01877-331 533
www.roman-camp-hotel.co.uk
14 rooms. Very plush hotel in converted 17th-century hunting lodge set in beautiful gardens that sweep down to the River Teith, in which fishing is available. Renowned for its cuisine. **£££–££££**

Carnoustie

Station Hotel
Station Road
Tel: 01241-852 447
Fax: 01241-855 605
www.stationhotel.uk.com
12 rooms. A family-run hotel from which it is but a giant step to the championship golf course and a small step to the station platforms. **£–££**

Crieff

Crieff Hydro Hotel
Tel: 01764-655 555
Fax: 01764-653 087
www.crieffhydro.com
213 rooms. Magnificent Victorian building, in 900

acres (360 hectares) of grounds. Superb accommodation, food and leisure facilities. **££££**

Dunblane

Cromlix House
Kinbuck
Tel: 01786-822 125.
Fax: 01786-825 450
www.cromlixhouse.com
14 rooms. One of Scotland's great country house hotels. All rooms are large and splendid, and antiques abound. Magnificent conservatory. Noted for its superb food and extensive wine list. Trout and salmon fishing, clay pigeon shooting, tennis and croquet all available. **£££–££££**

Dunblane Hydro Hotel
Perth Road
Tel: 01786-822 551
Fax: 01786-825 403
www.dunblanehydrohotel.com
206 rooms. Hotel with Victorian facade in 44 acres (18 hectares) of grounds. Excellent sports and leisure facilities. **£££**

Dunkeld

Hilton Dunkeld House
Tel: 01350-727 771
Fax: 01350-728 924
www.dunkeld.hilton.com
97 rooms. Splendid hotel, former home of the duke of Atholl, on the banks of the River Tay in 280 acres (112 hectares) of woodland. Extensive leisure facilities, including clay pigeon shooting and tennis. **££££**

Falkland

Luigino's Hotel
High Street
Tel: 01337-857 224
Fax: 01337-857 163
Three en suite rooms. A 17th-century coaching inn in conservation village, close to magnificent Falkland Palace. **££**

Glenisla

Glenisla Hotel
Kirkton of Glenisla

Tel: 01575-582 223
Fax: 01575-582 203
www.glenisla-hotel.com
Six rooms. Friendly, comfortable hotel in magnificent setting. **££**

Glenshee

Spittal of Glenshee Hotel
Tel: 01250-885 215
Fax: 01250-885 223
www.spittalofglenshee.co.uk
48 rooms. Slightly eccentric but very friendly and lively hotel in wonderful setting. Regular live entertainment. **££**

Killin

Ardeonaig House Hotel
By Killin
Tel: 01567-820 400
Fax: 01567-820 282
www.ardeonaighotel.co.uk
An award-winning, small country house exuding warmth and a personal touch with a South African wine list. 10 acres (4 hectares) of grounds by south shore of the Tay. **£££–££££**

Kinloch Rannoch

Macdonald Loch Rannoch Hotel
Tel: 0844-879 9059

TRANSPORT

ACCOMMODATION

EATING OUT

ACTIVITIES

A–Z

Fax: 01882-632 203
www.loch-rannoch.com
47 rooms. Converted shooting lodge in magnificent surroundings; excellent food, lively entertainment, wide range of leisure activities. **£££**

Perth

Ballathie House Hotel
Kinclaven by Stanley
Tel: 01250-883 268
Fax: 01250-883 396
www.ballathiehousehotel.com
43 rooms. Relaxing and civilised former shooting lodge on River Tay. Graciously proportioned public rooms. Comfortable bedrooms. **£££–££££**

Best Western Queens Hotel
Leonard Street
Tel: 01738-442 222
Fax: 01738-638 496
www.bestwestern.co.uk
50 rooms. Comfortable hotel with good leisure complex. Situated close to the city centre. **££**

Huntingtower Hotel
Crieff Road
Tel: 01738-583 771
Fax: 01738-583 777
www.huntingtowerhotel.co.uk
34 rooms. Country house hotel 3 miles (5km) west of Perth, standing in its own beautiful grounds. **££**

Murrayshall House Hotel
Scone
Tel: 01738-551 171
Fax: 01738-552 595
www.murrayshall.com
41 rooms. Sumptuously appointed, elegant country house in 300 acres (120 hectares) of parkland, 4 miles (7km) north of Perth. Superb food and wine served in luxurious dining room. Has two challenging 18-hole golf courses. **£££**

Parklands
St Leonards Bank
Tel: 01738-622 451
Fax: 01738-622 046
www.theparklandshotel.com
14 rooms. Classical Georgian town house, refurbished, overlooking the South Inch Park. **£££**

Ramada Jarvis Perth
West Mill Street
Tel: 0844-815 9105

Fax: 01738-643 423
www.ramadajarvis.co.uk
76 rooms. This is a comfortable hotel converted from a 15th-century watermill, situated in the city centre. **££–£££**

Salutation Hotel
34 South Street
Tel: 01738-630 066
Fax: 01738-633 598
www.strathmorehotels.com
84 rooms. One of Scotland's oldest hotels, where Bonnie Prince Charlie is said to have stayed. **££–£££**

Pitlochry

Atholl Palace Hotel
Atholl Road
Tel: 01796-472 400
Fax: 01796-473 036
www.athollpalace.co.uk
90 rooms, including turret suites. This majestic building is set in 50 acres (20 hectares) of grounds. Has health and sports facilities. **£££**

Dunfallandy Country House
Tel: 01796-474 128
www.dunfallandy.co.uk
Three spacious rooms. Georgian mansion set above the town, with glorious views of Tummel Valley. **££**

Killiecrankie Hotel
Tel: 01796-473 220
Fax: 01796-472 451
www.killiecrankiehotel.co.uk
10 rooms. Good country house hotel in beautiful setting overlooking the Pass of Killiecrankie, 3 miles (5km) north of Pitlochry. **£££**

Knockendarroch House Hotel
Higher Oakfield
Tel: 01796-473 473
Fax: 01796-474 068
www.knockendarroch.co.uk
12 rooms. Victorian mansion overlooking the town and Tummel Valley; two rooms have 4-poster beds. **££**

St Andrews

Cleveden House
3 Murray Place
Tel/Fax: 01334-474 212
www.clevedenhouse.co.uk
Seven rooms (five en suite). Five minutes' walk from Old

ABOVE: enjoy the luxury of a hotel afternoon tea.

Course, beach and town centre. **££**

The Inn on North Street
127 North Street
Tel: 01334-473 387
Fax: 01334-474 664
www.theinnonnorthstreet.com
13 rooms. Late Victorian building close to the Old Course and beaches. **£££**

Rusacks Hotel
Pilmour Links
Tel: 0844-879 9136
Fax: 01334-477 896
www.macdonaldhotels.com
68 rooms. Grand, refurbished Victorian hotel remodelled on golfing theme and overlooking the legendary 18th hole of the Old Course. **££££**

The Russell Hotel
26 The Scores
Tel: 01334-473 447
Fax: 01334-478 279
www.russellhotelstandrews.co.uk
10 rooms. A grand Victorian terraced house overlooking St Andrew's Bay and just minutes from the famous Old Course. Individual bedrooms are decorated with coordinating soft

furnishings; lovely views. **£££**

St Andrews Old Course Hotel
Tel: 01334-474 371
Fax: 01334-477 668
www.oldcoursehotel.co.uk
134 rooms. Large luxury hotel overlooking the famous 17th "Road" Hole of Old Course. Well-equipped health club. **££££**

St Fillans

Achray House Hotel
Tel: 0845-557 0447
www.achray-house.co.uk
Nine rooms. Welcoming small hotel with superb views across Loch Earn (fishing possible). Mountain bikes for guests' use. **££**

Four Seasons Hotel
Tel: 01764-685 333
Fax: 01765-685 444
www.thefourseasonshotel.co.uk
12 rooms plus six chalets. Comfortable, unpretentious Scandinavian-type hotel at eastern end of Loch Earn; good food. **£££**

THE EAST COAST

Aberdeen

Aberdeen Marriott
Overton Circle, Dyce
Tel: 01224-770 011
Fax: 01224-722 347
www.marriott.com
155 rooms. Luxurious hotel with full leisure facilities, close to airport. **£££**

Adelphi Guest House
8 Whinhill Road
Tel: 01224-583 078
www.adelphiguesthouse.com
A dedicated family-run guesthouse in an elegant terrace. Good quality accommodation with all modern facilities at a reasonable price. Situated close to the centre of Aberdeen. **£–££**

Atholl Hotel
54 Kings Gate
Tel: 01224-323 505
Fax: 01224-321 555
www.atholl-aberdeen.co.uk
34 rooms. Elegant granite Victorian hotel in the West End. **£££**

Brentwood Hotel
101 Crown Street
Tel: 01224-595 440
www.brentwood-hotel.co.uk
63 rooms. Situated in a pretty granite town house this is one of the most

comfortable small hotels in the area. Offers good rates at the weekend. **££–£££**

Caledonian Thistle Hotel
10–14 Union Terrace
Tel: 0871-376 9003
Fax: 0845-305 8342
www.thistlehotels.com
77 rooms. Business-oriented hotel in city centre, close to railway station, just off Union Street. **£££**

Marcliffe at Pitfodels
North Deeside Road, Cults
Tel: 01224-861 000
Fax: 01224-868 860
www.marcliffe.com
42 rooms. Sprawling country house hotel set in large grounds in western suburbs. Very well appointed, excellent food. **££££**

Alford

Kildrummy Castle Hotel
Kildrummy
Tel: 01975-571 288
Fax: 01975-571 345
www.kildrummycastlehotel.co.uk
16 rooms. Baronial mansion with lots of wood panelling, tapestries and grand staircase overlooking ruined 13th-century castle. Glorious gardens. Excellent

BELOW: St Andrews Old Course Hotel.

food accompanied by splendid wine list. **£££**

Ballater

Glen Lui Hotel
Invercauld Road
Tel: 01339-755 402
www.glen-lui-hotel.co.uk
19 rooms. This is a friendly country house hotel with superb views towards Lochnagar. Fishing, golf, and skiing available nearby. Good wine list. **£–££**

Hilton Craigendarroch
Braemar Road
Tel: 01339-755 858
Fax: 01339-755 447
www.craigendarroch.hilton.com
45 rooms. Excellent modern hotel with full leisure facilities, golf, fishing and shooting. **£££–££££**

Netherley Guest House
2 Netherley Place
Tel: 01339-755 792
www.netherleyguesthouseballater.com
Seven en suite rooms. Family-run guesthouse in centre of village, high standards of service. **££**

Banchory

Banchory Lodge
Dee Street
Tel: 01330-822 625
Fax: 01330-825 019
www.banchorylodge.co.uk
22 rooms. Large, well-furnished rooms, log fires and Victorian furnishings. On the banks of River Dee with private fishing; bicycles available for guests; two golf courses nearby. **££££**

Carrbridge

Dalrachney Lodge Hotel
7 miles (11km) north of Aviemore
Tel: 01479-841 252
www.dalrachney.co.uk
This beautiful Victorian hunting lodge will delight with delicious dinners, roaring fires, and views to die for. **££££**

Braemar

Invercauld Arms Hotel
Tel: 01339-741 605
www.shearingsholidays.com
68 rooms. Historic building

now offering high standards of accommodation and food. Minimum stay two nights. **££**

Moorfield House
Tel: 01339-741 244
Six rooms (two en suite). Very welcoming and friendly family-run hotel at edge of famous Braemar Highland Games Park. **£**

Dundee

Apex City Quay Hotel and Spa
1 West Victoria Dock Road
Tel: 01382-202 404
Fax: 01382-201 401
www.apexhotels.co.uk
152 rooms. Urban style at its best. Conveniently positioned in the centre of the City Quay development – the ideal option for both business and leisure. Good restaurant and bar. **£££**

Dundee Centre Premier Inn
Riverside Drive
Tel: 0871-527 8320
www.premierinn.com
40 rooms. Informal family hotel overlooking River Tay; indoor play area; close to Discovery Centre. **££**

Hilton Dundee
Earl Grey Place
Tel: 01382-229 271
Fax: 01382-200 072
www.hilton.com/dundee

PRICE CATEGORIES

Approximate prices per person per night in a double room in high season:
£ = less than £30
££ = £30–50
£££ = £50–80
££££ = more than £80

129 rooms. Modern hotel with good leisure facilities on the River Tay, with views across to Fife. **£££**

Shaftesbury Hotel
1 Hyndford Street
Tel: 01382-669 216
12 rooms. Victorian mansion in peaceful residential area yet close to city and university. **££**

Elgin

Mansion House Hotel
The Haugh
Tel: 01343-548 811
Fax: 01343-547 916
www.mansionhousehotel.co.uk
23 rooms. Tastefully restored baronial mansion with tower in woodland setting. Many rooms have 4-poster beds. Indoor pool and beauty salon. **£££**

Grantown-on-Spey

Culdearn House
Woodlands Terrace
Tel: 01479-872 106
Fax: 01479-873 641
www.culdearn.com
Nine rooms. Elegant Victorian house. Great selection of malt whiskies and good wine list. **££££** (includes dinner)

Tigh na Sgiath Country House Hotel
Dulnain Bridge
Tel: 01479-851 345
Fax: 01479-821 173
www.tigh-na-sgiath.co.uk
Eight rooms. Lovely old refurbished house in secluded grounds. Good food and wine. **£££–££££** (includes dinner)

Inverurie

Macdonald Pittodrie House
By Inverurie
Tel: 0844-879 9066
Fax: 01467-681 648
www.macdonaldhotels.co.uk
27 rooms. 17th-century

family house exudes character and luxury. Seek out the billiard room and snug bar. **£££–££££**

Montrose

Woodston Fishing Station
St Cyrus
Tel: 0759-556 4338
Fax: 0785-464 3348
www.woodstonfishingstation.co.uk
A family run B&B (and self-catering guesthouse) on the St Cyrus Nature Reserve. Perfect for walking and fishing. **£££**

Nairn

Golf View Hotel
Seabank Road
Tel: 01667-452 301
Fax: 01667-455 267
www.crerarhotels.com
42 rooms. Victorian hotel overlooking the Black Isle. Leisure centre, tennis and nearby golf course.
£££

Peterhead

Waterside Inn
Fraserburgh Road
Tel: 01779-471 121
www.swallow-hotels.com
105 rooms. On the banks of River Ugie and not far from sea. Full leisure facilities. **££**

Portsoy

Boyne Hotel
2 North High Street
Tel/Fax: 01261-842 242
www.boynehotel.co.uk
12 rooms. Charming building in beautiful fishing village. Golf, fishing, whisky trail close by. **£–££**

The Station Hotel
Seafield Street, Portsoy
Tel: 01261-842 327
www.stationhotelportsoy.co.uk
Golfers, walkers and wildlife enthusiasts will enjoy this handy base that includes 14 en suite rooms and a restaurant with great food.
£££

THE NORTHERN HIGHLANDS

Alchiltibuie

Summer Isles Hotel
Tel: 01854-622 282
Fax: 01854-622 251
www.summerisleshotel.co.uk
Delightful hotel with suites and log cabins in tiny village at the end of a 15-mile (24km) track with glorious views over the Summer Isles. Open Easter–Oct.
£££–££££

Aviemore

Aviemore Highland Resort
Tel: 0844-879 9152
www.aviemorehighlandresort.com
Four hotels catering for every budget. Luxury self-catering lodges, a range of leisure amenities including golf and spa and several restaurants are all part of this striking development in the heart of Aviemore.
££–£££

Hilton Coylumbridge
Tel: 01479-810 661
Fax: 01479-811 309
www.hilton.com

175 rooms. In the heart of the Grampians and an ideal centre for outdoor leisure. Good for families: large wooded grounds and play area for kids. Leisure centre with pool and spa.
£££–££££

Beauly

Lovat Arms Hotel
High Street
Tel: 01463-782 313
Fax: 01463-782 862
www.lovatarms.com
22 rooms. All rooms feature a clan tartan and many have canopied or half tester beds. Produce from farm served in dining room. **£££**

Priory Hotel
The Square
Tel: 01463-782 309
Fax: 01463-782 531
www.priory-hotel.com
36 rooms. Comfortable privately owned hotel in an attractive village square next to priory ruins. Scrummy afternoon tea. **££**

Cromarty

Royal Hotel
Marine Terrace
Tel: 01381-600 217
Fax: 01381-600 813
www.royalcromartyhotel.co.uk
20 rooms. Comfortable, welcoming family hotel with great view of the Cromarty Firth where dolphins swim among parked oil rigs. **££**

Dingwall

Tulloch Castle Hotel
Tulloch Castle Drive
Tel: 01349-861 325
Fax: 01349-863 993
www.tullochcastle.co.uk
19 rooms. Elegant country house hotel dating back to 12th century in superb surroundings, ideal for a relaxing break. **£££**

Dornoch

2 Quail Restaurant and Rooms
Castle Street, Dornoch

Tel: 01862-811 811
www.2quail.com
This three-bedroom Victorian house prides itself on a home-from-home ambience and excellent cuisine. Your hosts will be more than happy to advise on the best fairways in the area. **£££**

Drumnadrochit (on Loch Ness)

Drumnadrochit Hotel
Tel: 01456-450 218

TRANSPORT

Fax: 01456 450793
www.drumnadrochithotel.co.uk
29 rooms. Modern hotel close to Loch Ness and the visitor centres for "monster watchers". £–££

Fort Augustus

Carn a' Chuilinn
Tel: 01320 366387
www.carnachuilinn.co.uk
A welcoming B&B on the edge of a picturesque village and close to the centre of Inverness. Good-value, family-run accommodation offering no frills, just pristine lodgings and good food. £

Lovat Arms Hotel
Tel: 01456 459250
www.thelovat.com
25 rooms. Long-established friendly hotel near centre of village, close to loch and Caledonian Canal. Large selection of malt whiskies. £££

Gairloch

The Old Inn
Tel: 0800 542 5444
Fax: 01445 712445
www.theoldinn.net
14 rooms. Charming hotel in mountain and sea setting. Excellent food and real ale ("Taste of Scotland" accredited). Good for wildlife-watching. ££–£££

Invermoriston

Glenmoriston Arms Hotel
Tel: 01320-351 206
Fax: 01320-351 308
www.glenmoriston-arms-hotel.co.uk
Eight rooms. This 200-year-old coaching inn nestles in a lovely glen close to Loch Ness. £££

Inverness

Glenmoriston Town House Hotel
Ness Bank, Inverness
Tel: 01463-223 777
www.glenmoristontownhouse.com
An award-winning, 30-room boutique hotel that oozes style and class; and that's even before you dine in the award-winning restaurant. £££–££££

Bunchrew House Hotel
Bunchrew
Tel: 01463-234 917
Fax: 01463-710 620
www.bunchrew-inverness.co.uk
14 rooms. Every inch a 17th-century Scottish baronial home, yet comfortable and relaxed. Stands in 20 acres (8 hectares) of shores on the Beauly Firth, 3 miles (5km) west of Inverness. Afternoon tea on the lawn is a delight. £££

Columba Hotel
Ness Walk
Tel: 01463-231 391
Fax: 01463-715 526
www.oxfordhotelsandinns.com
76 rooms. Refurbished hotel on banks of River Ness. Close to town centre. £££

Culloden House Hotel
Culloden
Tel: 01463-790 461
Fax: 01463-792 181
www.cullodenhouse.co.uk
28 rooms. An architectural gem 3 miles (5km) east of Inverness, associated with Bonnie Prince Charlie and the Battle of Culloden. Magnificent public rooms, 4-poster curtain-framed beds. Dine in the Adam Room on local produce cooked in the French manner. 40 acres (16 hectares) of lovely grounds. Tennis, sauna, solarium, snooker. ££££

Dunain Park Hotel
Tel: 01463-230 512
Fax: 01463-224 532
www.dunainparkhotel.co.uk
11 rooms. Georgian country house, 4 miles (6km) from Inverness on A82, set in 6 acres (2.5 hectares) of gardens and grounds. Wide variety of bedrooms, some with 4-poster beds. Auld Alliance (marriage of French and Scottish produce and skills) is served accompanied by a fair selection of wines. Indoor swimming pool, sauna, croquet. £££–££££

Ramada Jarvis Inverness
33 Church Street
Tel: 0844-815 9006
Fax: 01463-711 206
www.ramadajarvis.co.uk
106 rooms. Elegant city hotel alongside the River Ness with all facilities. £££

Rocpool Reserve Hotel
14 Culduthel Road
Tel: 01463-240 089
Fax: 01463-248 431
www.rocpool.com
11 rooms. Top-notch boutique hotel, beautifully appointed. Close to city centre and Inverness castle. ££££

Whinpark Guest House
17 Ardross Street
Tel/Fax: 01463-232 549
www.whinparkhotel.com
10 rooms. Victorian house situated in quiet area close to River Ness. £–££

Kincraig

Ossian Hotel
Tel: 01540-651 242
Fax: 01540-651 633
www.kincraig.com/ossian
Nine rooms. Pleasant, small Highland hotel just off the main road providing friendly service. Vegetarian meals and lovely dinners. ££

Kingussie

Scot House Hotel
Newtonmore Road
Tel: 01540-661 351
Fax: 01540-661 111
www.scothouse.com
Nine rooms. Friendly, welcoming hotel in centre of village. ££

Lochinver

Albannach Hotel
Baddidarroch
Tel: 01571-844 407
www.thealbannach.co.uk
Five rooms. Delightful 19th-century house set in a walled garden. All comforts for those who enjoy the outdoors. Excellent home cooking, and vegetarians welcome. ££££ (includes dinner)

Inver Lodge Hotel
Iolaire Road
Tel: 01571-844 496
Fax: 01571-844 395
www.inverlodge.com
20 rooms. A modern hotel with superb loch views. ££££

Newtonmore

Balavil Sport Hotel
Tel: 01540-673 220
Fax: 01540-673 773

www.mckeverhotels.co.uk
50 rooms. Refurbished building on main street with excellent leisure facilities. ££

Scourie

Eddrachilles Hotel
Badcall Bay
Tel: 01971-502 080
Fax: 01971-502 477
www.eddrachilles.com
11 rooms. Beautifully maintained hotel on 320 acres (130 hectares) of waterfront property with stunning sea views. Close to Handa Island bird sanctuary. Open Mar–Oct. £££

Strathpeffer

Ben Wyvis Hotel
Strathpeffer
Tel: 01997-423 387
www.crerarhotels.com
With its commanding views over the town and lying in the shadow of Ben Wyvis, this is a comfortable hotel with its own 32-seat cinema. ££££

Ullapool

Ceilidh Place
14 West Argyle Street
Tel: 01854-612 103
Fax: 01854-612 886
www.theceilidhplace.com
24 rooms (10 en suite). With bookshop, café, restaurant and concert hall, this is not only a good hotel but is also the cultural centre of Ullapool. Bunk House with nine cheaper rooms is spartan but immaculate and great value for families. £–£££

Harbour Lights Hotel
Garve Road
Tel: 01854-612 222
www.harbour-lights.co.uk
19 en suite rooms. Comfortable hotel close to the picturesque shores of Loch Broom. A short walk from the village. ££

ACCOMMODATION   EATING OUT   ACTIVITIES   A – Z

PRICE CATEGORIES

Approximate prices per person per night in a double room in high season:
£ = less than £30
££ = £30–50
£££ = £50–80
££££ = more than £80

ORKNEY

Albert Hotel
Kirkwall
Tel: 01856-876 000
Fax: 01856-875 397
www.alberthotel.co.uk
19 rooms. Newly refurbished hotel in the centre of town. Orkney ales and whiskies.
£££

Barony Hotel
Birsay
Tel: 01856-721 327
Fax: 01856-721 302
www.baronyhotel.com
Panoramic views to

Boardhouse Loch and Brough of Birsay. Ideal for birdwatching and trout fishing. **££**

Foveran Hotel
St Ola, Kirkwall
Tel: 01856-872 389
Fax: 01856-876 430
www.foveranhotel.com
Eight rooms. Family-run hotel set in 35 acres (14 hectares) overlooking Scapa Flow.
£££

Lynnfield Hotel
Holm Road, Kirkwall

Tel: 01856-872 505
Fax: 01856-870 038
www.lynnfieldhotel.com
10 rooms. Formerly the home of the distillery manager: you can taste the "guid stuff" – and it's free. Good local cooking.
£££

Thira Guest House
Stromness
Tel: 01856-851 181
www.thiraorkney.co.uk
Purpose-built and roomy guesthouse with views over Hoy Sound. **£–££**

SHETLAND

Buness House
Baltasound, Unst
Tel: 01957-711 315
Fax: 01957-711 815
www.users.zetnet.co.uk
Four rooms. 17th-century building on island of Unst, most northerly isle in Britain. Close to Hermaness nature reserve and fine cliff scenery. **££–£££**

Busta House Hotel
Busta, North Mainland
Tel: 01806-522 506
Fax: 01806-522 588
www.bustahouse.com

22 rooms. Country house hotel 23 miles (37km) north of Lerwick, dating from 1588 and with private harbour and slipway. **££–£££**

Grand Hotel
Commercial Street, Lerwick
Tel: 01595-692 826
www.kgqhotels.co.uk
24 rooms. Oldest purpose-built hotel in Shetland, fully refurbished. Convenient location close to harbour and town centre. **££**

Shetland Hotel
Holmsgarth Road, Lerwick

Tel: 01595-695 515
www.shetlandhotels.com
65 rooms. Modern hotel with leisure complex. Views of the harbour and Isle of Bressay. **££**

Sumburgh Hotel
South Mainland
Tel: 01950-460 201
www.sumburghhotel.co.uk
32 rooms. Former laird's house, close to airport and Jarlshof ancient monument. Two bars serving local Auld Rock ale. Superb beaches nearby. **££**

HOSTELS AND CAMPING

Youth Hostels

There are about 60 YHF hostels in Scotland, many of them in the Highlands. The hostels provide low-cost accommodation, usually with dormitory-type bedrooms, although these days there are some twin and double rooms and even en suite facilities. The hostels are open to members of the International Youth Hostel Federation (IYHF), or you can join the SYHA at any hostel. They admit children from five years and up; there is no upper age limit. You can stay in a hostel for one night without becoming a member. To join the Youth Hostels Association is free

for five–17-year-olds and £8 for adults. Accommodation costs between £9 and £19 a night depending on the time of year and the facilities at the hostel.

For more information, contact the **Scottish Youth Hostels Association (SYHA)**, 7 Glebe Crescent, Stirling, FK8 2JA. Tel: 01786-891 400 Central info and reservations line: 0845-293 7373, www.syha.org.uk

Independent Hostels

Scotland has a growing network of excellent independent hostels which provide similar

accommodation to the SYHA hostels but with the advantage that you don't have to join any organisation to use them. Prices are very reasonable and the facilities are often surprisingly good; large dormitories are gradually being replaced by 2- and 4-bed rooms. Moreover, many of these hostels are in remote locations.
For more information, contact **Independent Backpackers Hostels Scotland**, The Secretary, SIM, PO Box 7024, Fort William PH33 6YX.

Camping

There are many campsites

around Scotland and these are normally open April–October. Expect to pay up to £10 to pitch a tent. Many hostels allow camping. For detailed information on Scottish campsites contact; **ScottishCamping.com Ltd**, Blairs College, South Deeside Road, Aberdeen AB12 5LF; tel: 01224-860 347; www.scottishcamping.com. They will also answer any camping queries.

PRICE CATEGORIES

Approximate prices per person per night in a double room in high season:
£ = less than £30
££ = £30–50
£££ = £50–80
££££ = more than £80

E ATING OUT

RECOMMENDED RESTAURANTS, CAFÉS & BARS

Scottish Cuisine

More than 50 years have elapsed since that distinguished travel writer H.V. Morton wrote: "Scotland is the best place in the world to take an appetite." The country is renowned for its produce from river and sea, from farm and moor. Fish is something of a speciality, with salmon being particularly good; kippers and Arbroath smokies (haddock smoked over wood) are delicious, too. Shellfish are excellent and exported all over the world, while Aberdeen Angus beef and Border lamb are both renowned. Various dishes are distinctly Scottish, such as haggis – which is probably more enjoyable if you don't know what should be in it (the heart, lungs and liver of a sheep, suet, oatmeal and onion).

Over the past decade culinary skills have come to match the quality of the produce, and today it is possible to enjoy superb meals in Scotland served in the most elegant of restaurants as well as in simple small spaces with scarcely more than half a dozen tables. The hours at which restaurants, especially smaller ones away from the main cities, serve meals tend to be less flexible than in many other countries. High tea, served from 5 to 7pm, usually consists of fish and chips or an egg dish followed by lashings of scones and pancakes, all accompanied by gallons of tea.

Dr Samuel Johnson once remarked, "If an epicure could remove by a wish, in quest of sensual gratifications, wherever he had supped he would say breakfast in Scotland." No doubt he would say the same today. There is surely no better

way to start the day than with a bowl of porridge followed by Loch Fyne kippers and Scottish oatcakes.

On a more mundane level, there is no shortage of fast-food outlets of one sort or another throughout Scotland. For a cheap and enjoyable takeaway meal, you could do a lot worse than try the humble "chippie" (fish and chip shop).

Lunch is almost invariably considerably less expensive than dinner, and nearly all restaurants have set menus, which are about half the price of an à la carte dinner.

Taste of Scotland

The *Taste of Scotland* scheme invites eating places to apply for membership. Its original and continuing objective is to promote restaurants and producers that are believed to offer the very best

of Scottish cuisine. All members are inspected before being admitted to the scheme; more than 400 restaurants, bistros and cafés are listed on its website where quality, service and in many cases considerable innovation can be guaranteed. Visit www.taste-of-scotland.com.

However, it's not only the above that offers an insight into the best of Scotland's culinary treats. Visit-Scotland runs a nationwide quality-assurance scheme called "Eat Scotland", providing visitors with a handy reference for quality eateries. Visitors to Glasgow and Edinburgh can discover the latest gossip on cafés and restaurants in *The List's Eating and Drinking Guide*, while the wonderful Outer Hebrides now have their very own "Speciality Food Trail" (www.foodhebrides.com).

BELOW: flying the flag for Scottish cuisine.

EDINBURGH

(If phoning from outside area, use code: 0131.)

Scottish

Restaurant at the Bonham
35 Drumsheugh Gardens
Tel: 274 7444
Daily, breakfast, lunch, dinner
A blend of classic and contemporary cuisine served in the dining room of an elegant up-market, boutique hotel. Organic Scottish produce with modern flavours. Leave room for stunning desserts. Light bites served in the lounge. **£££**

Restaurant Martin Wishart
54 The Shore, Leith
Tel: 553 3557
Lunch, dinner. Closed Sun, Mon
One of the best restaurants in the city (one of three with

a Michelin star), opened in 1999. Imaginative and dynamic cooking. Menu changes daily. **£££**

A Room In The West End
26 William Street
Tel: 226 1036
Daily lunch, dinner
The simplicity of the decor belies a talent for producing unusual culinary dishes with a distinctly modern Scottish theme. Licensed but operates a bring your own bottle policy, too. **££**

Sweet Melindas
11 Roseneath Street
Tel: 229 7953
Lunch, dinner. Closed Sun and Mon lunch
Excellent food and wine at reasonable prices in a joyous atmosphere in a south neighbourhood restaurant. Daily changing

seasonal menu. Booking advisable. **££**

Contemporary/ International

The Balmoral Hotel Number One Restaurant
1 Princes Street
Tel: 557 6727
Daily lunch, dinner
This Michelin-starred restaurant oozes style and panache without being pompous. Culinary treats such as baby spinach soup with salt-cod ravioli; sirloin with smoked mash; and gingerbread soufflé. Eat at lunchtime to safeguard your budget or splash out on an evening tasting menu. **£££**

Oloroso
33 Castle Street
Tel: 226 7614
Daily lunch, dinner
Stunning setting in a penthouse space with glass walls and a roof terrace. Excellent food that is cooked to precision. **£££**

The Witchery by the Castle
352 Castlehill, Royal Mile
Tel: 225 5613
Daily lunch, dinner
Imaginative Scottish cuisine. Two restaurants, each with unusual atmosphere. Upstairs is dark and atmospheric – while downstairs is bright with a small outdoor terrace for fine weather. Excellent wine list. **£££**

Fish and Seafood

Café Royal Oyster Bar
17a West Register Street
Tel: 556 1884
Daily lunch, dinner
An Edinburgh institution where the ambience is everything. Stained glass and polished wood; always bustling, and seafood is the house speciality. **£££**

Creelers
3 Hunter Square
Tel: 220 4447

Daily lunch, dinner
Like its sister establishment on the Isle of Arran, Creelers specialises in imaginative cooking of fresh seafood, plus game and vegetarian dishes. **££–£££**

Fishers
1 The Shore, Leith
Tel: 554 5666
58 Thistle Street
Tel: 225 5109
Daily lunch, dinner
Sister seafood restaurants, the former looking out over the water of Leith, the latter in a converted city warehouse. It's not all fish here, there's plenty of choice for meat eaters, too. **££–£££**

The Shore Bar & Restaurant
3–4 The Shore, Leith
Tel: 553 5080
Daily lunch, dinner
Fresh Scottish fish and shellfish at an 18th-century inn with traditional dining and a changing blackboard menu in the bar. **££**

Skippers Bistro
1a Dock Place, Leith
Tel: 554 1018
Daily lunch, dinner
Intimate, cosy restaurant with wood-panelled booths. Friendly service and some of the best seafood in town. **££–£££**

Chinese

Kweilin
19 Dundas Street
Tel: 557 1875
Lunch, dinner. Closed Mon
Large space serving authentic Cantonese dishes, especially strong on seafood. It's been consistently popular since 1984. **££**

Rendezvous
10a Queensferry Street
Tel: 225 2023
Daily lunch, dinner
Edinburgh's oldest Chinese restaurant (over 50 years) continues to thrill with its reasonably priced à la carte and buffet menu. **££**

BELOW: fine dining at Restaurant Martin Wishart.

ABOVE: there are plenty of cafés in Edinburgh at which to stop for a bite.

French

La Garrigue
31 Jeffrey Street
Tel: 557 3032
Lunch, dinner. Closed Sun
Friendly and relaxed. People come to this stylish French bistro-style restaurant to sample the excellent cooking skills of Jean Michel Gauffre. **££**

Le Sept
5 Hunter Square
Tel: 225 5428
Daily lunch, dinner
This long-established restaurant specialises in fish and crêpes. Simple, pub-style tables (a few outdoors). **££**

Indian

The Himalaya
171 Bruntsfield Place
Tel: 229 8216
Lunch, dinner. Closed Sun lunch
The interior is a little cramped, but the simple yet tasty tandoori dishes definitely won't disappoint. Be warned... the naan breads are huge. Takeaway menu, too. **£–££**

Kalpna
2 St Patricks Square
Tel: 667 9890
Lunch, dinner. Closed Sun lunch and all day Sun Oct–Apr
Make sure you book ahead at this restaurant serving Gujarati and southern Indian vegetarian food. Excellent, good value lunchtime buffet. **£**

Lancers Brasserie
5 Hamilton Place
Tel: 332 3444
Daily lunch, dinner
Popular venue, which is renowned for its curries, serving Bengali and northern Indian cuisine. Modest wine list. **££**

Suruchi Too
121 Constitution Street, Leith
Tel: 554 3268
Daily lunch, dinner
An authentic taste of India in Scotland's capital. All regions of the subcontinent are represented here from the hottest Punjabi curry to grilled Scottish salmon Indian-style. **£–££**

Italian

Centotre
103 George Street
Tel: 225 1550
Mon–Sat 7am–midnight, Sun 10am–10pm
Northern Italian flavours abound in this classy former bank turned bistro-bar slap bang in the city centre. For balsamic on bread, a bowl of olives and a glass of white wine, here's your answer. **££**

Valvona & Crolla Caffè Bar
19 Elm Row
Tel: 556 6066
Mon–Sat 8.30am–5.30pm (6pm on Fri and Sat), Sun 10.30am–3.30pm
Located at the rear of a fabled deli. Breakfast and lunch only, and queues not infrequent. It is open for dinner during the Festival in August. **££**

Valvona & Crolla Vin Caffè
Multrees Walk
Tel: 557 0088
Mon–Sat 9.30am–late, Sun noon–5pm
Most wonderful Italian restaurant, on the first floor of the newer of the two delis in the Multrees Walk precinct. **££**

Vittoria on the Walk
113 Brunswick Street
Tel: 556 6171
Daily lunch, dinner
A terrific atmosphere and great food assured in this family-run Edinburgh institution with another branch, Vittoria on the Bridge, at 19 George VI Bridge. Book ahead for a weekend table. **££**

Mexican

Viva Mexico
41 Cockburn Street
Tel: 226 5145
Mon–Sat lunch, daily dinner
Cosy restaurant with an atmosphere that transports you back to old Mexico. Food can be on spicy side. Good selection for veggies. Great margaritas. **££**

Thai

Thai Lemongrass
40–1 Bruntsfield Place
Tel: 229 2225
Daily lunch, dinner
The 20-minute walk (5 minutes taxi) south up Lothian Road will whet your appetite for this authentic Thai cuisine bursting with flavour; attentive staff. **££**

Thai Orchid
5a Johnston Terrace
Tel: 225 6633
Daily lunch, dinner
Opened in 1996 this was one of the first Thai restaurants in Edinburgh and is now located near the castle. Authentic food with herbs and spices flown directly from Thailand. **££**

Vegetarian

David Bann's Vegetarian Restaurant
56 St Mary's Street
Tel: 556 5888
Daily lunch, dinner
An extensive and varied well-prepared global menu from a very experienced vegetarian chef. **££**

Henderson's Restaurant
94 Hanover Street
Tel: 225 2131
Mon–Sat 8am–10.45pm
A popular basement vegetarian restaurant, Henderson's also now has a bistro, a deli and a bakery. **£–££**

Bistros

The Lot
4 Grassmarket
Tel: 225 9924
Mon–Sat 11am–late, Sun noon–6pm
An arts venue as well as a bistro, this is located in a converted church near the castle. Good value, wholesome food and a pleasant meeting place. **£**

Olive Branch
91 Broughton Street
Tel: 557 8589
Daily 10am–late
(Also Holy Corner, Bruntsfield)
Wicker chairs, an airy ambience and a wide-ranging menu of salads, classic burgers and even soup in a mug won't disappoint. Great for Sunday brunch. **£**

Cafés

Café at the Scottish Parliament
Holyrood Road
Tel: 348 6072

TRANSPORT

ACCOMMODATION

EATING OUT

ACTIVITIES

A – Z

Mon–Fri 10am–5.30pm, Sat–Sun
10am–3.30pm
Why not stop for a bite to
eat or a coffee before or
after your tour of this
extraordinary building. **£**

Elephant House
21 George IV Bridge
Tel: 220 5355
Daily 8am–11pm
Popular coffee house
serving a huge range of
exotic teas and coffees,
plus great cakes and
pastries. **£**

Filmhouse
88 Lothian Road
Tel: 229 5932
Sun–Thur 10am–11.30pm, Fri–Sat
10am–12.30am
This is no ordinary cinema,
showing a rash of cutting-
edge European films. It's
also a convivial place for all
ages to meet. Menu ranges
from baked potatoes and
filled rolls to salads and hot
meals. Wide range of drinks
including 11 draught beers
and five real ales. **£**

Glass & Thompson
2 Dundas Street
Tel: 557 0909
Mon–Sat 8am–6pm, Sun
10.30am–4.30pm
Café-cum-bistro serving
Mediterranean-style goodies.
Excellent cakes, pastries and
buttery shortbread. **£**

Pubs and Bars

Good areas to try include
the Royal Mile,
Grassmarket, Rose Street,
Haymarket, George Street
and West Register Street.
The Living Room and the
Opal Lounge on George
Street will appeal to the hip
and trendy.

NEAR EDINBURGH

Some top restaurants on
the outskirts of Edinburgh:

Champany Inn
Linlithgow
17 miles (25km) from Edinburgh
Tel: 01506-834 532
Mon–Sat lunch, dinner
Aberdeen Angus is the

speciality, and from the grill
come entrecôte, pope's eye,
porterhouse, sirloin and rib
eye. The seafood is just as
excellent. **£££**

Open Arms Hotel
Dirleton
Tel: 01620-850 241
Daily lunch, dinner
Pleasant restaurant
overlooking village green
and 16th-century castle
ruin. **£££**

Rhubarb Restaurant
Prestonfield House Hotel
Priestfield Road
Tel: 225 7800
Daily breakfast, lunch, dinner
Deep reds and plush,
elegant surroundings greet
the discerning diner within
this period building. Scottish
and international cuisine.
£££

GLASGOW

(If phoning from outside
area, use code: 0141.)

Scottish

(These restaurants do not
serve only Scottish food.)

Babbity Bowster
16 Blackfriars Street
Tel: 552 5055
Daily lunch, dinner
Friendly upstairs restaurant
serving Scottish food.
Renowned for its Burns
Night supper. **££**

Michael Caines at ABode
129 Bath Street
Tel: 572 6011
Daily lunch, dinner
This restaurant continues
to win awards and praise
among foodies seeking fine
Scottish/French cuisine
and Mediterranean
flavours. This is a slightly
formal though convivial
dining experience within
the renowned ABode Hotel.
Booking essential. **£££**

No. Sixteen
16 Byres Road
Tel: 339 2254
Daily lunch, dinner
An unassuming, even off-
putting, shopfront belies
an excellent cuisine
prepared with the best
Scottish ingredients

combined with flavours
from here, there,
everywhere. Imaginative
wine list. **££–£££**

International

The Bistro
1 Devonshire Gardens
Great Western Road
Tel: 339 2001
Daily breakfast, lunch, dinner
Set in the classy West End
hotel; guests feast on
Scottish-influenced cuisine
with a twist. **£££**

City Merchant
97 Candleriggs
Tel: 553 1577
Daily lunch, dinner
West coast seafood is a
speciality. **£££**

Stravaigin
28–30 Gibson Street
Tel: 334 2665
Fri–Sun lunch, daily dinner; café/
bar 11am–midnight
Stravaigin is a Scots word
for "wandering about",
which this restaurant's
"Global Twist" menu does
– and with great success.
Attractive, inexpensive
wine list. Café/bar on first
floor serves just as
excellent but less
expensive food. Open late.
£££

Stravaigin 2
8 Ruthven Lane
Tel: 334 7165
Daily lunch, dinner
Offshoot of Stravaigin (see
above) but more a brasserie
than a restaurant. Innovative
fusion dishes. Pre-theatre
menu is good value. **££**

Two Fat Ladies
88 Dumbarton Road
Tel: 339 1944
Daily lunch, dinner
Small and gets very busy, so
book in advance if you want
to sample the excellent
contemporary food, usually
fish and game. **££–£££**

The Ubiquitous Chip
12 Ashton Lane
Tel: 334 5007
Daily lunch, dinner
The Chip is much more than
a Glasgow institution.
Beloved by media types, it
also attracts more than its
fair share of celebrities, for
both the food and the
ambience. **££**

Fish and Seafood

Harry Ramsden's
251 Paisley Road
Tel: 429 3700
Daily noon–9pm

BELOW: Rogano, renowned for its seafood.

More than 10 years on the south bank of the Clyde and still the best fish and chips in town. **£**

Mussel Inn
157 Hope Street
Tel: 0843-289 2283
Daily lunch, dinner
Mussels, scallops and oysters are the stars of this restaurant opened by a collective of west coast shellfish producers. **££**

Rogano
11 Exchange Place
Tel: 248 4055
Daily lunch, afternoon tea, dinner
A glamorous Art Deco institution where oysters and fish soup are specialities. Very expensive, although the downstairs casual Café Rogano is more affordable. **£££**

Chinese

Amber Regent
50 West Regent Street
Tel: 331 1655
Mon–Sat lunch, daily dinner
Up-market, with a wide selection of Cantonese and Szechuan dishes. Booking essential. Pre-theatre menu. **££**

Peking Inn
191 Hope Street
Tel: 332 7120
Mon–Sat lunch, daily dinner
Delightful Cantonese/Pekinese restaurant serving tasty seafood. Booking essential, particularly at the weekend, when long queues are likely. **£–££**

French

Brian Maule at Chardon d'Or
176 West Regent Street
Tel: 248 3801
Mon–Fri lunch, Mon–Sat dinner
Brian Maule used to be head chef at the renowned Le Gavroche restaurant in London. Here he produces a refined marriage of the Auld Alliance (Scottish and French) cuisine served in a dining room decorated with Post-Impressionist art. **£££**

La Vallée Blanche
360 Byres Road
Tel: 334 3333
Tue–Sun lunch, dinner

Here you will find classical French cuisine with a Scottish twist, utilising the best of local produce. Also an extensive collection of French wines. **££–£££**

Greek

Konaki
920 Sauchiehall Street
Tel: 342 4010
Mon–Sat lunch, daily dinner
No-nonsense, pleasant Greek restaurant whose owners are from Crete and so serve excellent Greek food. Good choice for vegetarians. **£–££**

Indian

Ashoka
108 Elderslie Street
Tel: 221 1761
Daily lunch, dinner
This is the original Ashoka, located near the Mitchell Library and the best of several Indian restaurants in the vicinity. **££**

Mother India
28 Westminster Terrace
Tel: 221 1663
Fri–Sun lunch, daily dinner
Beautiful Indian home cooking in relaxed atmosphere. Especially pleasing for vegetarians. Licensed but also BYOB. **££**

Shish Mahal
66–8 Park Road
Tel: 339 7899
Mon–Sat lunch, daily dinner
Established in 1964 as one of the original curry houses and still run by the same family. **££**

The Wee Curry Shop
7 Buccleuch Street
Tel: 353 0777
Mon–Sat lunch, daily dinner
also 29 Ashton Lane
Tel: 357 5280
Mon–Sat lunch, daily dinner
This child of Mother India serves delightful no-nonsense food chosen from a concise menu at half a dozen tables within view of the chef. **£–££**

Italian

L'Ariosto
92–4 Mitchell Street
Tel: 221 0971

ABOVE: the elegant Willow Tea Rooms.

Daily lunch, dinner
This place looks tiny from the front, but inside it opens out onto a traditional Italian courtyard, although this one is indoors. Tuscan cuisine at its very best. **£££**

The Battlefield Rest
56 Battlefield Road
Tel: 636 6955
Mon–Sat 10am–10pm
This was a former tram stop, complete with waiting room and ticket office. Now it is a popular eating spot; the lunchtime menu and pre-theatre menu are good value. **£–££**

Di Maggio's
21 Royal Exchange Square
Tel: 248 2111
61 Ruthven Lane
Tel: 357 0874
1038 Pollokshaws Road
Tel: 632 7924
West Nile Street
Tel: 333 4999
Daily noon–12am, (Sun noon–11.30pm)
Straightforward, no-nonsense Italian cooking at an affordable price. A favourite with students. **£**

Fratelli Sarti
121 Bath Street
Tel: 204 0440
133 Wellington Street
Tel: 572 7000
42 Renfield Street
Tel: 572 7000
Daily lunch, dinner, Mon–Fri breakfast
All three restaurants are warm, friendly Italian establishments with a traditional menu – and wild boar pizza – and a long

wine list. Each restaurant has its own specialities. **£–££**

Jamie's Italian
1 George Square
Tel: 404 2690
Daily noon–11pm (10.30pm on Sun)
The latest of Jamie Oliver's Italian-style restaurants opened here in July 2010 in the old GPO building. The passion ordinary Italians have for their food is reflected here with straight-forward menus offering the best of simple, rustic seasonal fare. **££**

La Lanterna
35 Hope Street
Tel: 221 9160
Mon–Sat lunch, dinner
Basement restaurant opposite Central Station much frequented by Glasgow's Italian community. **££**

La Parmigiana
447 Great Western Road
Tel: 334 0686
Mon–Sat lunch, dinner
Many Glaswegians consider this to be the best Italian restaurant in the city (est. 1978) with its predominantly Milano cuisine and splendid wine list. **££–£££**

Ristorante La Fiorentina
2 Paisley Road West
Paisley Road Toll
Tel: 420 1585
Daily lunch, dinner
Upmarket Italian restaurant south of the river but pretty near the city. Classic Tuscan cooking meets modern Mediterranean with a classy wine list and excellent seafood. **££–£££**

Thai

Thai Fountain
2 Woodside Crescent
Tel: 332 15099
Lunch, dinner. Closed Sun
Excellent Thai cuisine in
elegant setting. **££**

Miscellaneous

The Arches Café Bar
253 Argyle Street
Tel: 565 1035
Daily noon–12am
The Arches is an arts venue
under the main railway
bridge at Central Station.
This café-bar is in the cellar
underneath and it has been
set up like a minimalist jazz
bar. Small, good-value
menu using locally sourced
products. **£–££**

Art Lovers' Café
Bellahouston Park, 10 Dumbreck
Road
Tel: 353 4770
Daily 10am–5pm
On the ground floor of
House for an Art Lover (see
page 174). Light
refreshments and à la carte
available, and children
catered for. Booking is
advised for lunch. **£–££**

Café Gandolfi
64 Albion Street
Tel: 552 6813
Daily 9am–11.30pm

The grandfather of modern
Glasgow café life. Fresh
Scottish ingredients with a
slight Mediterranean twist
are the staple of this
Merchant City eatery. **££**

Kember and Jones
134 Byres Road
Tel: 337 3851
Mon–Sat 9am–10pm, Sun 9am–
6pm
Once in a while a
delicatessen/café opens
that truly excites. Here,
plates arrive groaning
under the weight of a club
sandwich or huge platters
that are a speciality. Italian,
Spanish and French
influences are all to be
found in a convivial
atmosphere. **£–££**

The Living Room
150 St Vincent Street
Tel: 0870-220 3028
Daily lunch, dinner
Relaxed, informal dining is
offered in an airy
atmosphere. Great
selection of food including
old favourites, such as
steak and ale pie or the
more slow roasted shoulder
of lamb. **££**

Pancho Villas,
26 Bell Street
Tel: 552 7737
Mon–Sat 9am–5pm, Sun 11am–
4.15pm
Owned and run by a

Mexican, this is about as
good as Mexican eating
gets in the UK. With the
quality of its food and its
Merchant City location, it
attracts a wide mix of
people and can get busy.
£–££

Willow Tea Rooms
217 Sauchiehall Street
Tel: 332 0521
Mon–Sat lunch, daily dinner
Most tourist attractions
have a tearoom. In this
case it's the tearoom that
is the attraction. Charles
Rennie Mackintosh
designed the interior of this
for tearoom baroness Kate
Cranston, and it's still
possible to take lunch here
or enjoy afternoon tea. **£**

Vegetarian

Grassroots Café
97 St Georges Road
Tel: 333 0534
Daily 10am–10pm
Cosy Charing Cross
establishment. As well as
vegetarian food, they also
cater for vegans and people
on gluten- and wheat-free
diets. **£**

The 13th Note
50–60 King Street
Tel: 553 1638
Daily noon–12am
Strictly vegetarian and

vegan, based mainly on
Greek dishes, but with
other influences as wide
ranging as Italy and the Far
East. **£**

Pubs and Bars

The city centre offers a
bewildering choice – try the
Merchant City area, George
Square, Argyle Street, Hope
Street and Sauchiehall
Street for starters. The
suburbs (particularly Byres
Road and Shawlands) and
surrounding towns are also
very well supplied with
excellent pubs, many
providing very good food as
well.

NEAR GLASGOW

Gleddoch House Hotel
Langbank, Renfrewshire (near
Glasgow airport)
Tel: 01475-540 711
Daily lunch, dinner
An outstanding, elegant
restaurant on the outskirts
of Glasgow featuring
Scottish dishes in a small
hotel which has a first-class
18-hole golf course and a
host of other facilities.
Booking essential.
£££.

THE BORDERS

Cringletie House Hotel
Edinburgh Road, Peebles
Tel: 01721-725 750
Sun lunch, daily dinner
The restaurant of this
gracious country house
hotel has had a good
reputation for many years.
For some of the best
cooking in the Scottish
borders try the seven-
course tasting menu.
Booking advisable. **£££**

**Kailzie Gardens
Restaurant**
Kailzie, Peebles
Tel: 01721-722 807
Daily 10am–5pm
An unpretentious restaurant
housed in the old stable
square and carefully
converted to retain as many
original features as
possible. Under new
management in 2010 this is
traditional home cooking at

its best. Relaxed and
homely atmosphere and
especially popular for
afternoon tea. **£**

Simply Scottish
6–8 High Street, Jedburgh
Tel: 01835-864 696
Daily coffee, lunch, dinner
Bistro-style café using good
local produce to create
imaginative, tasty meals.
Traditional Scottish food.
£–££

Wheatsheaf Hotel
Main Street, Swinton
Tel: 01890-860 257
Wed–Sun lunch, daily dinner
A small Berwickshire
village yields this genuine,
award-winning country inn
that has a surprisingly
extensive and imaginative
menu specialising in
Scottish game and
seafood.
££–£££

THE SOUTHWEST

Creebridge House Hotel
Minigaff, Newton Stewart
Tel: 01671-402 121
Daily lunch, dinner

Imaginative cuisine served in
the brasserie, and the
chance to sample real ales.
The main restaurant

overlooks the landscaped
gardens. **££–£££**

Enterkine House
Annbank by Ayr

Tel: 01292-521 608
Sun–Fri lunch, daily dinner
Traditional Scottish food and
exquisite wines served in

elegant dining room in a recently restored country house hotel in 310 acres (130 hectares) of fields, rivers and woodland. **£££**
Fouters
2a Academy Street, Ayr
Tel: 01292-261 391
Tue–Sat lunch, dinner

An attractive cellar restaurant which for aeons has been serving creative Scottish dishes, cooked from local produce. **££**
Kilmichael Country House Hotel
Brodick, Isle of Arran
Tel: 01770-302 219

Wed–Mon dinner only
The four-course evening meal complete with canapés in this beautiful retreat will make your island stay memorable. **£££**
MacCallums of Troon Oyster Bar
The Harbour, Troon

Tel: 01292-319 339
Tue–Sun lunch, Tue–Sat dinner
A somewhat eclectic seafood menu which is served in an unpretentious high-roof stone shed right next to the fish market on the harbour. Great atmosphere. Try the grilled lobster and chips. **££**

FORTH AND CLYDE

The Drovers Inn
Inverarnan by Ardlui
Tel: 01301-704 234
Daily lunch, dinner
A 300-year-old pub, at the northern end of Loch Lomond, exuding real character. Forget "theme bar". The kilts, real ale, stuffed animals and cock-a-leekie soup are the real thing – even 17th-century outlaw Rob Roy drank here. **£–££**

Macdonald Houstoun House
Uphall, Edinburgh West
Tel: 0844-879 9043
Daily dinner only
The Tower Restaurant serves excellent Scottish food from local produce in the handsome dining room of a 16th-century house. A prodigious wine list from around the world and a splendid selection of malts. **££–£££**

The River House
The Castle Business Park, Craigforth, Stirling
Tel: 01786-465 577
Daily lunch, dinner
In a stunning loch-side setting at the foot of Stirling Castle, the first thing you notice is the design of the modern building, which is based on a "crannog", a traditional Scottish building. Good cooking using local produce. **££**

Ziggy Forelles
52 Port Street, Stirling
Tel: 01786-463 222
Daily from 10am–9pm (10pm Thur–Sat)
A sleek, modern restaurant and bar in the centre of Stirling, it offers a range of stalwarts on the menu from ribs to home-made burgers to pastas, pizzas and steaks, using local produce. Free Wi-fi available **£–££**

THE WEST COAST

Airds Hotel
Port Appin
Tel: 01631-730 236
Daily lunch, dinner
An inviting old inn on the edge of Loch Linnhe. Serves beautifully presented, delicious, first-class cuisine. Excellent wine list. **£££+**
Coast
104 George Street, Oban
Tel: 01631-569 900
Mon–Sat lunch, dinner
Loch Melfort mussels and West Coast crab tart are

just a few of the delicious dishes on offer. **££–£££**
The Kilberry Inn
Kilberry Road, Kilberry
Tel: 01880-770 223
Tue–Sun lunch, dinner
Scottish Restaurant of the Year 2009, the Kilberry Inn (with rooms) is reached by a single track road between Tarbert and Lochgilphead. The menu, with mackerel, crab, beef and lamb, is a wonderful tribute to local producers. Superb. **££–£££**

Loch Fyne Oyster Bar
Clachan Farm, Cairndow
Tel: 01499-600 236
Daily breakfast, lunch, dinner
Increasingly popular – with the finest of oysters served in this café-cum-restaurant, smokehouse and produce shop at the head of Loch Fyne. Superb oysters but also langoustines and food from the smokehouse – eel, mussels, etc. Leave room for excellent Scottish cheeses. Good, inexpensive wine list. Booking advisable. **££**

The Waterfront
The Pier, Oban
Tel: 01631-563 110
Daily lunch, dinner
This is an excellent seafood restaurant close to the ferry terminal (**££**) but for a simple, inexpensive taste of the sea you can't beat fisherman **John Ogden**'s tiny green shack also at the ferry terminal, serving takeaway crab, mussels and fish that he catches himself and all manner of pickled delights. **£**

SKYE

Kinloch Lodge
Sleat
Tel: 01471-833 333
Daily lunch, dinner
Lady Claire Macdonald, one of Scotland's best-known cookery writers, presides over the dining room, which offers a full five-course menu each night, with variety and imagination to the fore. Very expensive but a real treat. **£££**

Lochbay Seafood Restaurant
Stein, Waternish
Tel: 01470-592 235
Tue–Fri lunch, dinner
Halibut, shark, skate and ling may well be the specials on the menu in the atmospheric informal restaurant, which consists of two cottages built in 1740. If this is too esoteric, then there are always crab, lobster, scallops and

oysters. Reservations advisable.
££
Three Chimneys Restaurant
Colbost, by Dunvegan
Tel: 01470-511 258
Mon–Sat lunch (Apr–Oct only), daily dinner all year
Seafood Platter and Lobster Feast are two of the many mouth-watering creations served during a candlelit dinner in this

atmospheric restaurant in what was formerly a croft. But do leave room for scrumptious desserts. **£££+**

PRICE CATEGORIES

Average cost of a three-course evening meal per person, excluding wine:
£ = below £18
££ = £18–30
£££ = above £30

THE INNER HEBRIDES

ABOVE: lobster pots ready for the next catch.

Café Fish
The Pier, Tobermory, Isle of Mull
Tel: 01688-301 253
Daily lunch, dinner
Seafood such as squat

lobster is the speciality.
Though Tobermory isn't
lacking in eateries, this cosy
restaurant has the edge
over many. Booking for

dinner essential **££**
The Chip Van
Fisherman's Pier, Tobermory, Isle of
Mull
Tel: 01688-302 390
Mon–Sat 12.30pm–9pm (closes
7pm winter)
Enjoy an alfresco meal on
the seafront from the Les
Routiers award-winning
team. **£**
The Glassary
Sandaig, Isle of Tiree
Tel: 01879-220 684
Thur–Sun lunch, daily dinner
Unquestionably the best
place to eat on the island.
Simplicity is the key, with
a regularly changing menu
drawing on Tiree's renowned
reputation for beef, lamb
and seafood. It's important
to book ahead. **££**

Mediterranea
Salen, Isle of Mull
Tel: 01680-300 200
Thur–Sun lunch, daily dinner
In the midst of the
Hebrides, visitors will
discover this authentic
Italian restaurant. Excellent
Italian food cooked with
the finest of local Mull and
Scottish ingredients.
££
**The Water's Edge
Restaurant**
Tobermory Hotel, Main Street,
Tobermory, Isle of Mull
Tel: 01688-302 091
Daily dinner only
You will find the likes of
local specialities such as
Croig lobster, Lagganulva
lamb and venison on the
menu. **£££**

THE OUTER HEBRIDES

Scarista House
Scarista, Isle of Harris
Tel: 01859-550 238
Daily dinner. Closed Jan–Feb
This three-bedroomed,
18th-century former manse,
packed with character
and affording views over
Scarista Sands, is an
impressive, delightful
retreat in itself. Add the
opportunity to dine in style

on carefully selected locally
reared meats and wonderful
desserts and you'll be
loathe to leave this hidden
Hebridean gem. Advance
booking essential. **£££**
Langass Lodge
Locheport, Isle of North Uist
Tel: 01876-580 285
Daily dinner only
Nature abounds outside this
fascinating former sporting

lodge complete with its own
Neolithic stone circle. The
cuisine is as inspirational as
the scenery, with generous
servings of fresh-from-
the-sea crab, Hebridean
smokehouse selection, fish
and local meat for main
courses, and tasty desserts.
Booking essential. **££–£££**
Skoon Art Café
Geocrab, Isle of Harris

Tel: 01859-530 268
Tue–Sat 10am–4.30pm (Fri–Sat
only in winter)
For a warm welcome,
delicious home-baking,
hearty soups and views of
the Hebrides (and excellent
local paintings), this is a
recommended stop on
your journey through the
land of Harris tweed.
£

CENTRAL SCOTLAND AND FIFE

**Andrew Fairlie at
Gleneagles**
Gleneagles Hotel, Auchterarder
Tel: 01764-694 267
Mon–Sat dinner only
Two-Michelin-starred
restaurant, definitely one of
Scotland's best, set in an
exclusive resort hotel.
Superb French food
confidently served in opulent

surroundings; the puddings
are works of art. **£££+**
The Cellar
24 East Green, Anstruther
Tel: 01333-310 378
Wed–Sat lunch, Tue–Sat dinner
(open Mon Jun–Aug)
Just off the harbour, a walled
courtyard leads to an
atmospheric restaurant
serving splendid seafood.
Excellent wine list – French
and New World bins –
complements the food.
Booking essential. **£££**
Dean's at Let's Eat
77 Kinnoull Street, Perth
Tel: 01738-643 377
Tue–Sun lunch, dinner
Award-winning bistro-style

restaurant in city centre, with
a pleasant, relaxed
atmosphere. **££–£££**
Kind Kyttock's Kitchen
Cross Wynd, Falkland
Tel: 01337-857 477
Tue–Sun 10.30am–5pm
Just opposite the palace, this
small tearoom serves home-
cured ham, free-range eggs,
freshly baked bread and
scones. **£**
Monachyle Mhor
Balquhidder
Tel: 01877-384 622
Daily lunch, dinner
A gourmet's delight and five-
star hidden gem. Lunch and
dinner served in the hotel's
conservatory. **£££+**

Peat Inn
Peat Inn by Cupar, Fife
Tel: 01334-840 206
An 18th-century village inn
with an international
reputation, only 6 miles
(10km) from St Andrews. A
limited menu lists the very
best of Scottish produce
cooked imaginatively and
served stylishly in beautiful
dining rooms. Superb wine
list includes half-bottles.
Booking essential. **£££+**
Redrooms at Perth Theatre
High Street, Perth
Tel: 01738-472 709
A lively place for lunch and
pre-theatre dinner. Good
coffee bar. **£**

THE EAST COAST

Agacan
113 Perth Road, Dundee
Tel: 01382-644 227
Daily lunch, dinner
Lively, popular Turkish
restaurant. Enjoy the
mezze, kebabs and stuffed
pittas. Takeaways an
option. **£**

The Beautiful Mountain
11–13 Belmont Street, Aberdeen
Tel: 01224-645 353
Mon–Sat 8am–4.30pm
Tuck into a wholesome
breakfast, enjoy coffee and
cakes or a first-rate light
lunch with delicious soups,
salads and sandwiches.
One of the best cafés in
town. **£**

But'n'Ben
Auchmithie, near Arbroath
Tel: 01241-877 223
Wed–Mon lunch, Wed–Sat, Mon
dinner
Lunch, high tea and dinner
are served in a traditional
cottage with quarry tile
floors and open fires in this
out-of-the-way coastal
village. The produce is local,
cooking is traditional, and
you can sample the famous
Arbroath smokies. **££**

Café Society
9 Queen's Road, Aberdeen
Tel: 01224-208 494
Daily lunch, Mon–Sat dinner
After more than 15 years
dishing out contemporary/
fusion cuisine to the locals,
this busy restaurant
continues to appeal, with
tasty salads, staple special
burgers and a spirited staff.
£–££

Cornerstone Coffee House
118 Nethergate, Dundee
Tel: 01382-202 121
Mon–Sat 9am–4pm
Plain cooking with no
pretensions. Clean,
pleasant café where a good,
inexpensive meal can be
enjoyed. **£**

Foyer Restaurant & Gallery
Trinity Church, 82a Crown Street,
Aberdeen
Tel: 01224-582 277
Tue–Sat 11am–11.30pm
Enjoy good contemporary
British cuisine in an
architecturally altered
church which also houses
an art gallery and is part of
an organised charity for
young homeless and
disadvantaged people.
Child-friendly. **£–££**

Green Inn
9 Victoria Road, Ballater
Tel: 01339-755 701
Daily dinner only
In a village well served with
excellent, yet expensive,
restaurants, this inn on the
village green serves
imaginative tasty dishes
prepared with local produce.
£££

Old Boatyard
Fishmarket Quay, Arbroath
Tel: 01241-879 995
Daily from 10am
Located in Arbroath's newly
developed harbour, this
attractive modern building
retains a traditional feel
within. Great choices for
dishes from the sea, but
plenty of other options and
some tasty desserts,

including home-made ice
cream. **£–££**

Rama Thai
32 Dock Street, Dundee
Tel: 01382-223 366
Daily lunch, dinner
The packed tables of people
feasting on steamed king
prawns and excellent green
curry tell you this is where to
spice up your Dundee
dining. Imaginative menu.
£–££

Rocpool Reserve
Culduthel Road, Inverness
Tel: 01463-240 089
Daily lunch, dinner
Located in the centre of
Inverness, this elegant
boutique hotel has a fine
restaurant, Chez Roux. Part
of the Roux brothers'
empire, this is superb
Scottish produce presented
with a French twist.
Excellent wine list. **£££**

The Seafood Restaurant
Bruce Embankment, St Andrews
Tel: 01334-479 475
Daily lunch, dinner

BELOW: dishing it up at Fife farmer's market.

A classy destination beside
the sea that offers evening
diners plates of succulent
lobster, prawns, halibut and
scallops while they gaze out
to sea. **££–£££**

Silver Darling
Pocra Quay
North Pier, Aberdeen
Tel: 01224-576 229
Mon–Fri lunch, Mon–Sat dinner
The name derives from the
local term for herring.
Wonderful ambience, just
across from the fleet
landing its catch. Soon it
will be on your table, often
sumptuously cooked in
Provençal style. **£££**

Twin City Café
4 City Square, Dundee
Tel: 01382-223 662
Mon–Sat 7.30am–5.30pm, Sun
10.30am–4.30pm
Enjoy a latte or cappuccino
here after a tiring stint of
shopping. Wide-ranging
daytime menu with a Middle
Eastern influence. Friendly
service. **£**

THE NORTHERN HIGHLANDS

Achin's Bookshop
Inverkirkaig, Lochinver
Tel: 01571 844262
Apr–Oct daily10am–5pm
Simple, excellent home-
cooking in Scotland's
immaculate and well-
stocked, most remote
northerly bookshop. Hearty
soups and toasties. Quality
craft goods also on sale. **£**

Badachro Inn
by Gairloch

Tel: 01445 741255
Daily lunch, dinner
Popular pub on a sheltered
bay with a garden by the
sea. Wonderful prawns and
a variety of other seafood
dishes. Check times for
winter opening. **££**

Café 1
75 Castle Street, Inverness
Tel: 01463 226200
Mon–Sat lunch, dinner
Popular bistro serving ultra-

fresh contemporary Scottish
dishes. Good wines. **££**

The Cross
Tweed Mill Brae, Kingussie
Tel: 01540 661166
Tue–Sat dinner only
Superb Scottish cuisine
served in an old tweed mill
converted into a delightful
eating space. Superb wine
list – clarets, half-bottles,
dessert wines. Great
cheeseboard. Also good

accommodation in nine
bedrooms. **£££**

Culloden House Hotel
Culloden, near Inverness
Tel: 01463 790461
Daily lunch, dinner
Dine in the exquisite Adam
Room in this architectural
gem 3 miles (5km) south of
Inverness, choosing from a
"Tastes of Scotland" menu,
which reflects a modern
Scottish cuisine using the

highest quality ingredients. **£££**

Glen Mhor Hotel
9–12 Ness Bank, Inverness
Tel: 01463-234 308
Daily breakfast, lunch, dinner
Nico's Seafood and Grill House has a pleasant riverside setting and serves bistro-style food using local produce. **££**

Kishorn Seafood Bar
Kishorn, Strathcarron
Tel: 01520-733 240
Mar–Nov Mon–Sat 10am–5pm, Sun noon–5pm (until 9pm July–Sept)
An immaculate road side wooden building that serves

the freshest of shellfish prepared while you wait. Great seafood platter. Eat in or takeaway. **£–££**

Kylesku Hotel
Kylesku
Tel: 01971-502 231
May–Sept Tue–Sun dinner only
Beautifully situated small restaurant with own smokery serves delicious moderately priced meals. **££–£££**

Loch Ness Country House Hotel
Fort William Road near Inverness
Tel: 01463-230 512
Daily lunch, dinner
Formerly the Dunain Park

Hotel. Scottish cuisine with a twist is served in this Georgian country house set in lovely gardens. Also afternoon tea and light meals; the set lunch menu is good value. Just outside Inverness on road to Loch Ness. **££–£££**

Shorehouse Seafood Restaurant
Tarbet, Scourie
Tel: 01971-502 251
Apr–Sept Mon–Sat, July–Aug daily but call in advance
As the name suggests, seafood including hot smoked mackerel dominates the menu, using

produce caught from the restaurant's own boat in Loch Laxford. **££**

Tea Store
Argyll Street, Ullapool
Tel: 01854-612 995
Mon–Sat 8.30am–4pm (Sun summer only 9am–3pm)
This is the place for your breakfast with the locals. **£**

Tigh-an-Eilean
Shieldaig
Tel: 01520-755 251
Daily dinner only
Excellent, traditional country cooking in a little restaurant in a small hotel on the shores of beautiful Loch Carron. **££–£££**

ORKNEY

Creel Restaurant
St Margaret's Hope
South Ronaldsay
Tel: 01856-831 311
May–mid-Oct Wed–Sun dinner only
Historic seafront house offering innovative modern cooking with strong Orcadian influence and fresh ingredients including prime Orkney beef, and seaweed-fed lamb from North Ronaldsay. Booking

advised. **£££**

Foveran Hotel
St Ola, Kirkwall
Tel: 01856-872 389
Daily dinner only
Scandinavian-style building offering outstanding seafood and wide variety of other dishes. Advance booking essential. **£££**

Hamnavoe Restaurant
35 Graham Place, Stromness
Tel: 01856-850 606

Tue–Sun dinner only
Small family-run restaurant using fresh ingredients. Seafood is the speciality and there are vegetarian options, too. **££**

Kirkwall Hotel
Harbour Street, Kirkwall
Tel: 01856-872 232
Daily lunch, dinner
A prime example of Scottish cuisine at its best. Home-made beef pie topped with

flaky pastry, and Orkney fudge cheesecake laced with whisky are just a few dishes on offer. **££**

The Watersound Restaurant
The Sands Hotel, Burray
Daily lunch, dinner
Tel: 01856-731 298
Full à la carte menu using local produce. The hotel was originally built as a fish store in 1860. **££**

SHETLAND

Braewick Café
Eshaness, North Mainland
Tel: 01806-503 345
Seasonal opening times vary (10am–5pm high season)
From this clifftop location enjoy simple, local fare in a child-friendly environment. **£**

Busta House Hotel
Busta
Tel: 01806-522 506
Daily lunch, dinner
Restaurant specialises in Shetland lamb and fish dishes. Good choice of

vegetarian dishes and fine selection of malts. Bar meals also available. **££–£££**

Hay's Dock Café Restaurant
Hay's Dock, Lerwick
Tel: 01595-741 569
Daily lunch, Tue–Sat dinner
Located in the Shetland Museum and with great views over the harbour, this café/restaurant offers light meals, coffee and afternoon tea as well as a first-class evening meals featuring local produce. **£–££**

Peerie Shop Café
Esplanade, Lerwick
Tel: 01595-692 816
Mon–Sat 9am–6pm
Freshly made soups, toasties, smoothies, scones and muffins, and a whole range of lattes are served up in a stylish atmosphere. **£**

Queen's Hotel
24 Commercial Street, Lerwick
Tel: 01595-692 826
Daily lunch, dinner
The seafood is modestly priced and tasty, and if you're lucky, you might spot a whale out at sea from the window. **££**

Wind Dog Café
Gutcher, Yell
Tel: 01957-744 321
Daily 9am–5pm (Sat–Sun from 10am)
Opposite the post office, this café offers breakfasts, coffees, light lunches and teas. Exceptional cakes. **££**

BELOW: haddock in the smokehouse.

A CTIVITIES

FESTIVALS, THE ARTS, NIGHTLIFE, SHOPPING AND SPECTATOR SPORTS

THE ARTS

Museums, Galleries and Places of Interest

From its Neolithic standing stones to the clan system and a string of philosophers, inventors and architects at the forefront of the 17th- and 18th-century Enlightenment, Scotland's innumerable museums and galleries offer the visitor a fascinating insight to its history and culture. A few major ones are listed below. See relevant chapters for details of many others.

Edinburgh
The National Gallery and Royal Scottish Academy
The Mound
Tel: 0131-624 6200
www.nationalgalleries.org
The impressive **National Gallery** is one of five National Galleries of Scotland and Edinburgh's second most-visited attraction. Extensively refurbished in recent years, within its impressive stone walls at the foot of the Mound visitors will find Scotland's greatest collection of fine art, spanning the early Renaissance to the 19th century. Among the masterpieces are works by Rembrandt, Raphael and Monet, and *The Skating Minister* painted by the Scottish artist Raeburn.

Reopened in 2003, the **Royal Scottish Academy** building is also to be found here with various temporary exhibitions showcased over two floors. The new **Weston Link** beneath the two galleries exhibits works by Monet and includes a café and a 200-seat lecture theatre.

The Scottish National Portrait Gallery
1 Queen Street
The first such purpose-built gallery in the world, its portraits offer a visual history of those who have shaped the nation, including royals, poets, philosophers and heroes. (Closed until autumn 2011 for refurbishment.)
The Scottish National Gallery of Modern Art and the Dean Gallery
75 Belford Road
These huge buildings sit in extensive grounds about 15 minutes' walk west of Princes Street. The Modern Art Gallery exhibits both contemporary works and those from the 19th century, while Dada and Surrealist art sits alongside works by Paolozzi in the Dean.

All of the above are free and open daily 10am–5pm, with exceptions.
The Fruitmarket Gallery
45 Market Street
Tel: 0131-225 2383
www.fruitmarket.co.uk
Open Mon–Sat 11am–6pm, Sun noon–5pm; charge.
A not-for-profit gallery, offering visitors inspirational contemporary art.
National Museums of Scotland
Chambers Street
Tel: 0131-225 7534
www.nms.ac.uk
Open daily 10am–5pm; free.
From steam engines and mummies of ancient Egypt to the history of Scotland's sporting greats and the influence of the Picts, Romans and Vikings, the **National Museum** and adjoining **Royal Museum** house thousands of fascinating exhibits, including natural history specimens. (Partly closed while the Royal Museum is being revamped – due to open during 2011.)

National War Museum
Edinburgh Castle
Tel: 0131-247 4413
www.nms.ac.uk
Apr–Oct daily 9.45am–5.45pm, until 4.45pm Nov–Mar; charge.
National Museum of Flight
East Fortune Airfield, East Lothian
Tel: 0131-247 4238
Apr–Oct daily 10am–5pm, Mar, Sat–Sun only; charge.

The Borders
Paxton House
by Berwick-upon-Tweed
Tel: 01289-386 291
www.paxtonhouse.co.uk
Apr–Oct daily 11am–5pm; charge.
Housed within one of the UK's finest examples of an 18th-century Palladian country house, Paxton House contains paintings from 1760–1840, including works by Scottish artists Raeburn and Wilkie.

Glasgow
Entry to all Glasgow museums is free.
Kelvingrove Art Gallery and Museum
Argyle Street
Tel: 0141-276 9599
www.glasgowmuseums.com
Mon–Sat 9am–5pm, Sun 11am–5pm.
Spread across 13 museums, the city of Glasgow owns one of the richest collections in Europe. Reopened in 2006 following a three-year, £28-million refurbishment, Kelvingrove is arguably the city's masterpiece, with its sprawling space containing more than 8,000 exhibits, including a World War II Spitfire plane hanging from the ceiling and paintings by Monet and Van Gogh.

Museum of Transport
Tel: 0141-287 2720
www.glasgowmuseums.com
This wonderful world of old Glasgow trams, the world's oldest pedal cycle, steam locomotives and famous Scottish-built cars such as the Argyll, and Johnson and Albion, has moved to new purpose-built premises alongside the River Clyde (spring 2011) and is being renamed the Riverside Museum. (Check website for developments.)

The Burrell Collection
Pollokshaws Road
Tel: 0141-287 2550
www.glasgowmuseums.com
Mon–Thur and Sat 10am–5pm, Fri and Sun 11am–5pm
More than 9,000 works of art from around the world.

National Museum of Rural Life
East Kilbride
Tel: 0131-247 4369
www.nms.ac.uk
Daily 10am–5pm; charge.

Ayrshire

Burns National Heritage Park
Murdoch's Lone, Alloway
Tel: 01292-443 700
www.burnsheritagepark.com
Daily 10am–5.30pm; charge.
Discover the area that inspired Scotland's most famous poet.

Aberdeen

Duff House
Banff
Tel: 01261-818 181
www.duffhouse.org.uk
Apr–Oct daily 11am–5pm, Nov–Mar Thur–Sun 11am–4pm; charge.
Designed by William Adam in 1735, this Baroque mansion house contains the Dunimarle Library (open by appointment only), a rare collection of more than 4,000 volumes and works by Boucher and El Greco.

Inverness

Inverness Museum and Art Gallery
Castle Wynd
Tel: 01463-237 114
www.invernessmuseum.com
Mon–Sat 9am–5pm; free.
Reopened in 2006 following a multi-million pound refurbishment, here is the place to discover the history of the Highlands, including the impact of the infamous Clearances.

Shetland Islands

Shetland Museum and Archive
Hays Dock, Lerwick
Tel: 01595-695 057
www.shetland-museum.org.uk
Mon–Sat 10am–5pm, Sun noon–5pm; charge.
Following a multimillion pound refit, the new Shetland Museum and Archive opened in 2007.

Outer Hebrides

Taigh Chearsabhagh Museum and Arts Centre
Lochmaddy, North Uist
Tel: 01876-500 293
www.taigh-chearsabhagh.org
Mon–Sat 10am–5pm
Museum and gallery with changing displays of local life and history.

Inner Hebrides

The Old Byre Heritage Centre
Dervaig, Isle of Mull
Tel: 01688-400 229
www.old-byre.co.uk
Apr–Oct Wed–Sun 10.30am–6.30pm.
This small museum offers an excellent insight into the history and wildlife of Mull and Iona.

Music

Although hardly a swinging country – other than when dancing the Highland Fling – Scotland has its fair share of after-dark activities.

The Royal Scottish National Orchestra and the Scottish Chamber Orchestra are excellent and give regular concerts in both Glasgow and Edinburgh, as well as travelling to other parts of the country. The Scottish Opera and Scottish Ballet operate similar schedules.

Folk music abounds, with clubs in every town. Information is available locally and through newspaper advertisements.

Ceilidhs

In the Highlands and islands, especially in isolated villages, the inhabitants hold occasional *ceilidhs*, which might be defined as informal social gatherings with folk music and formation dancing. There is always an experienced caller to ensure that all dancers keep in step during the energetic reels. A useful resource for the latest *ceilidhs* and folk music locations can be found at www.footstompin.com; tel: 0131-441 3135. Details of events can often be obtained from local tourist boards. Hootenanny pub in Inverness is one of the most lively locations to experience a *ceilidh*.

Some regular and more commercial *ceilidhs*, which are tailored for tourists (see also www.hi-arts.co.uk), are:

Edinburgh

King James Thistle Hotel
Leith Street
Tel: 0871-376 9016
www.thistlehotels.com
Dinner and show, Apr–Oct. Nightly at 7pm.

Prestonfield House
Priestfield Road
Tel: 0131-225 7800
www.prestonfield.com
"A Taste of Scotland" show, including dinner.
Mid-Apr–Oct, Sun–Fri at 7pm.

Dunkeld

The Taybank
Tay Terrace
Tel: 01350-727 340
www.thetaybank.com
Described as "Scotland's Musical Meeting Place". Sessions Tue–Sun plus special events.

Inverness

Hootenanny
64 Church St
Tel 01463-233 651
www.hootenanny.co.uk
The place for hearing traditional music. *Ceilidhs* most nights, June–mid-Sept, Mon–Thur.

BELOW: the CCA on Sauchiehall Street, Glasgow.

Edinburgh Festival Tips

• **Programmes** can be obtained from the festival offices, the tourist information office or city bookshops.
• **For online information** about all of Edinburgh's festivals visit www.edinburghfestivals.co.uk.
• **Advance bookings** are taken for International Festival performances from April and for Military Tattoo performances from December the previous year. Demand for seats at the latter, particularly, is very high, and early booking is recommended. For Fringe events, it is often only necessary to book in advance for big-name or short-duration shows. Bookings are taken from around mid-June.
• **The Hub** on Castlehill is open year-round. You can book here for all the main festivals.
• *The Guide* magazine is published every day during the summer festivals, with full up-to-date listings; look also in the Scottish newspapers and *The List* magazine for reviews.
• **To avoid queues** at the venue and telephone booking fees, visit one of the Fringe sales points at the Festival Fringe office or The Hub.
• **Spontaneous festival goers** should head for one of the top Fringe venues, such as the Pleasance (60 The Pleasance), Assembly Rooms (54 George Street) or Gilded Balloon at Teviot Row House in Bristo Square.

Lerags/Oban
The Barn
Cologins, Lerags (3 miles/5km) south of Oban
Tel: 01631-564 501
Folk band most Sunday afternoons.

Ullapool
The Ceilidh Place
14 West Argyll Street
Tel: 01854-612 103
www.theceilidhplace.com
Regular traditional music events, check website or call.

Theatre

Theatre flourishes, with audiences responding to innovation. Glasgow's Citizens Theatre and Tramway Theatre and Edinburgh's Traverse Theatre are internationally renowned for mounting new plays and experimental works. Aberdeen, Dundee, Perth and Inverness are all home to first-class repertory theatres, while during the summer months the Pitlochry Festival Theatre puts on professional performances.

Commercial theatre, too, is still alive and kicking in the major cities. Its main venues are the Lyceum and Festival theatres in Edinburgh and the King's in Glasgow.

Aberdeen
Aberdeen Arts Centre
33 King Street
Tel: 01224-635 208
www.aberdeenartscentre.org.uk

Dundee
Dundee Rep Theatre
Tay Square
Tel: 01382-223 530
www.dundeereptheatre.co.uk

Edinburgh
Edinburgh Playhouse
18–22 Greenside Place
Tel: 0131-557 2692
www.edinburghplayhouse.org.uk
Festival Theatre
13–29 Nicholson Street
Tel: 0131-529 6000
www.fctt.org.uk
King's Theatre
2 Leven Street
Tel: 0131-529 6000
www.fctt.org.uk
Royal Lyceum
30B Grindlay Street
Tel: 0131-248 4848
www.lyceum.org.uk
Theatre Workshop
34 Hamilton Place
Tel: 0131-225 7943
www.theatreworkshop.com

BELOW: the Tramway arts centre.

Traverse Theatre
Cambridge Street
Tel: 0131-228 1404
www.traverse.co.uk

Glasgow
Centre for Contemporary Arts
350 Sauchiehall Street
Tel: 0141-352 4900
www.cca-glasgow.com
Citizens Theatre
119 Gorbals Street
Tel: 0141-429 0022
www.citz.co.uk
The King's Glasgow
297 Bath Street
Tel: 0844-871 7648
Theatre Royal
282 Hope Street
Tel: 0844-871 7647
Tramway Theatre
25 Albert Drive
Tel: 0141-276 0950
www.tramway.org
Tron Theatre
63 Trongate
Tel: 0141-552 4267
www.tron.co.uk

Inverness
Eden Court Theatre
Bishops Road
Tel: 01463-234 234
www.eden-court.co.uk
This flagship theatre project reopened after major refurbishment in 2008.

Mull
Mull Theatre
Druimfin
Tel: 01688-302 673
Mull Theatre is one of Scotland's foremost touring theatre companies. Following the closure of its "Little Theatre" in Dervaig, a new production centre is being built outside Tobermory.

Perth
Perth Theatre
185 High Street
Tel: 01738-621 031
www.mulltheatre.com

Pitlochry
Pitlochry Festival Theatre
Tel: 01796-484 626

Stirling
MacRobert Arts Centre
University of Stirling
Tel: 01786-466 666
www.macrobert.org

Arts Festivals

Edinburgh
During the annual Edinburgh

International Festival and others such as the Fringe, Jazz, Film and Book festivals – there is a vast choice of quality cultural events in the city every night, ranging from opera and experimental theatre to soon-to-be-famous comedy talents *(see also page 155)*.

Edinburgh International Festival, tel: 0131-473 2000; www.eif.co.uk; Aug–Sept

Edinburgh Fringe Festival, tel: 0131-226 0026; www.edfringe.com; Aug

Military Tattoo, tel: 0131-225 1188; www.edintattoo.co.uk; Aug

Edinburgh International Film Festival, tel: 0131-228 4051; www.edfilmfest.org.uk; June

Edinburgh International Jazz and Blues Festival, tel: 0131-467 5200; www.jazzmusic.co.uk; July–Aug

Edinburgh International Book Festival, tel: 0131-228 5666; www.edbookfest.co.uk; Aug

Imaginate Children's Theatre Festival, tel: 0131-225 8050; www.imaginate.org.uk; May

Glasgow

Celtic Connections, 2–3 weeks in January. International Celtic music festival. Tel: 0141-353 8000; www.celticconnections.com

Glasgow International Jazz Festival, June. Tel: 0141-552 3552; www.jazzfest.co.uk

World Pipe Band Championships, August. Tel: 0141-221 5414; www.rspba.org.

Ayr and Ayrshire

Burns an' a' that! Festival for two weeks at end of May and beginning of June in celebration of Robert Burns. Held mainly in Ayr but also throughout Ayrshire. Poetry, theatre and music. Tel: 01292-290 300; www.ayrshire-arran.com

Dumfries

Dumfries & Galloway Festival of Arts, 10 days end of May to beginning of June. Tel: 01387-260 447; www.dgartsfestival.org.uk

Perth

Perth Arts Festival, 10 days end of May to beginning of June. Tel: 01738-621 031; www.perthfestival.co.uk

Other Festivals

Edinburgh

International Science Festival, two weeks in April
Tel: 0131-553 0322
www.sciencefestival.co.uk

Edinburgh Hogmanay, 29 Dec– 1 Jan. www.edinburghshogmanay.org. A

ABOVE: festival fun in Edinburgh.

festival to see out the old and to bring in the New Year. Frenetic celebrations culminate in the largest New Year's Eve (Hogmanay) street party in Europe (great fireworks).

Calendar of Events

In addition to the festivals above, the following cultural and sports events are staged annually in Scotland. For a small country, Scotland's villages, towns and cities host a staggering number events. Since 2003, over 162 international events have collectively generated over £300 million for the national economy. From the Shetland Island Games to the Open Golf Championships in St Andrews and Edinburgh's international cultural festivals, events are both hugely popular and big business for the country.

However, while contemporary blockbusters such as Edinburgh and Glasgow's Hogmanay (New Year's Eve) parties, the musical extravaganza "T in the Park" (Kinross) and Edinburgh's cultural festivals annually attract tens of thousands of revellers, Scots also continue to hold dear national and local celebrations of historical dates and figures. The following offers a snapshot of the diversity and richness of the nation's annual events calendar.

January

Burns Night
Haggis, neeps and tatties and

an "address tae the haggis" is accompanied by the skirl of bagpipes as families and dedicated Burns societies settle down across the land, and indeed across the world, to toast the birth of Rabbie Burns, the nation's most beloved poet, on 25 January 1759; www.rabbie-burns.com/www.worldburnsclub.com

Up-Helly-Aa
On the last Tuesday of January, scores of Shetland Islanders dressed in Viking costume lead an atmospheric torchlit procession through the streets of Lerwick followed by the burning of a Viking longship.

February

Fort William Mountain Film Festival
From footage of sea-kayaking adventures in the Outer Hebrides to climbing in Dumbarton, this action-packed festival attracts scores of outdoor enthusiasts and film buffs alike. Tel: 01397-705 005; www.mountainfilmfestival.co.uk

March

Spring into Easter at events organised by Scotland's five winter ski resorts; www.ski-scotland.com

April

The Glasgow Art Fair. Scotland's National Art Fair. See also www.glasgowartfair.com

Malt lovers should head for the Highlands for the **Spirit of Speyside Whisky Festival**; www.spiritofspeyside.com. Also at the end of September. Alternatively, head to the Northern Isles for the **Shetland Folk Festival**; www.shetlandfolkfestival.com

May

Head for Loch Fyne as 200 yachts battle for supremacy in the **Brewin Dolphin Scottish Series**, and for nightly festivities in the picturesque fishing port of Tarbert; www.scottishseries.com

June

St Magnus Festival, Orkney. A spectacular, week-long celebration of the arts. Tel: 01856-871 445; www.stmagnusfestival.com

July

The Wickerman Festival, Dumfries and Galloway. This is one of Scotland's hottest music festivals. Tel: 01854-613 746; www.thewickermanfestival.co.uk

Hebridean Celtic Festival, Outer Hebrides. Tel: 01851-621 234; www.hebceltfest.com

T in the Park, Kinross, Fife. More than

100 bands and thousands of pop music fans converge outside Kinross for two days of non-stop partying; www.tinthepark.com

August

Piping Live!, Glasgow. You'll hear many a skirl of the pipes at this extravaganza; www.pipinglive.co.uk Equestrian-lovers will enjoy the spectacular Perthshire setting of the **Blair Castle International Horse Trials**; www.blairhorsetrials.co.uk

September

Fort William Mountain Bike World Cup. Almost 20,000 spectators converge on Lochaber to watch the thrills and spills of the world's best in action; www.fortwilliamworldcup.com Alternatively, join members of the Royal Family for bagpipes, caber-tossing and Highland dancing at the renowned **Braemar Highland Gathering**; www.braemargathering.org

October

First held in 1892, the **Am Mòd Nàiseanta Rìoghail** (Royal National Mod) is Scotland's main festival of the Gaelic language, arts and culture. This competition-based festival is held annually in October and always at a different Scottish location. Tel: 01463-709 705; www.the-mod.co.uk Alternatively, try to spot Nessie as you run all 26.2 miles (42km) of the annual **Loch Ness Marathon**; www.lochnessmarathon.com However, if it's wet 'n' wild action you are after, then head for the Inner Hebridean Isle of Tiree to watch some of the world's best windsurfers defy gravity at the **Tiree Wave Classic**; www.tireewaveclassic.com Of course, there's also the chance to understand why the population of Mull trebles for four days during the acclaimed **Tour of Mull Rally**; www.2300club.org

November

St Andrew's Day. On 30 November, Scots celebrate their patron saint.

December

Join thousands of festive revellers to welcome in the **New Year** in Glasgow's George Square or Edinburgh's Princes Street. Note: it's strongly advised to purchase tickets in advance. www.glasgowshogmanay.org.uk and www.edinburghshogmanay.org

Listings Magazines

Edinburgh

The List is a listings magazine

covering Edinburgh and Glasgow. It is published fortnightly (www.list.co.uk). For a guide to gigs in the city try the *Gig Guide* (www.gigguide.co.uk).

Glasgow

Itchy, the Glasgow entertainment guide, is available at most bookshops in the city (www.itchyglasgow.co.uk).

NIGHTLIFE

Clubs, Pubs and Bars

Pubs and clubs are very popular with the locals everywhere in Scotland and are especially crowded around the end of the working day and at weekends. The scene is lively and while the drinking man's bar still exists, most pubs now have a relaxed and friendly atmosphere. Thanks to changes in Scottish licensing laws, even children are welcome in many pubs.

Edinburgh

The places to go are Cowgate and Grassmarket in the Old Town, and Broughton Street and George Street in the New Town. Most city-centre bars stay open until 1am, some even until 3am.
Bacaro, 7–11 Hope Street Lane. Tel: 0131-247 7004; www.bacaro-edinburgh.com
It it's an overdose of indulgence you require – from the champagne vault and caged DJ booth to the sumptuous velvets, leathers and silk interiors – Bacaro can provide.
Cabaret Voltaire, 36 Blair Street. Tel: 0131-220 6176; www.thecabaretvoltaire.com
In the subterranean caverns that underpin the streets of the Cowgate district, this thriving venue hosts some of the best-known club events in the capital.
The Caves, 12 Niddry Street South. Tel: 0131-557 8989; www.thecavesedinburgh.com
An atmospheric venue with huge arches that support Edinburgh's South Bridge splitting it into vaulted rooms. A spacious balcony overlooks the stage.
City, 1a Market Street. Tel: 0131-226 9560; www.citypeople.info
Edinburgh's very own super-club with four bars and plenty of areas to party, dance or chill.
Espionage, 4 India Buildings, Victoria Street. Tel: 0131-477 7007; www.espionage007.co.uk
A thriving labyrinth of clubbing activity spread over five floors with a good

range of music and drinks.
Jolly Judge, 7 James Court, off Lawnmarket. Tel: 0131-225 2669;
Recently reopened after refurbishment, this delightful little pub is still full of 17th-century charm, with low-beamed ceilings and a wide choice of malt whiskies. Can be difficult to find as it sits at the foot of a vennel (alley) in the historic Old Town.
Lava & Ignite, 3 West Tollcross. Tel: 0131-228 3252; www.lavaignite.com/edinburgh
Two rooms offering the ultimate clubbing experience, Lava includes amazing sound and laser technology, attracting top DJs for music lovers across the UK.
Liquid Room, 9c Victoria Street. Tel: 0131-225 2564; www.liquidroom.com
An exciting live music venue, this deep, subterranean basement promotes breaking acts and continues to support the bands that have made the Liquid Room what it is today.
Lulu, 125b George Street. Tel: 0131-225 5005; www.luluedinburgh.co.uk
With more than a hint of decadence – Swarovski Crystals embedded in the walls – Lulu is a nightclub to remember.
Opal Lounge, 51 George Street. Tel: 0131-226 2275; www.opallounge.co.uk
Distinguished bar appealing to a more discerning audience who are looking to unwind in style.
Shanghai @ Le Monde, 16a George Street. Tel: 0131-270 3913; www.lemondehotel.co.uk
Pulsating energy in the heart of Edinburgh's George Street, Shanghai combines oriental style with cutting-edge technology.
Siglo Bar & Club, 184 The Cowgate. Tel: 0131-220 1228; www.siglo-edinburgh.com
A spacious bar with a pleasant atmosphere and popular with students. Come early for a pre-club drink, grab a cocktail or settle in for a fantastic late night.

Glasgow

A vibrant and exciting city, Glasgow is said to have the largest population of gays and lesbians in the UK outside of London, and the gay nightlife scene

Hot Air Ballooning

Hot air balloon flights over Edinburgh, Lothians, Borders and Fife. For more information contact:
Alba Ballooning, 5 Primrose Gardens, Carrington, Midlothian; tel: 01875-830 709; www.albaballooning.co.uk.

is particularly active. The main clubs are around the central shopping area of Buchanan and Argyle Streets, with some in Sauchiehall Street.

The Arches, 253 Argyle Street. Tel: 0141-565 1000; www.thearches.co.uk
Scotland's original super-club, located in the cavernous Victorian vaults under Central Station. Check for music style and events.

Arta, 62 Albion Street. Tel: 0845-166 6028; www.socialanimal.co.uk
Older clubbers feel more at home in these opulent surroundings. This Mediterranean-themed bar and club is located in the trendy Merchant City. There's live music every weekend. Salsa is popular here.

Blue Dog, 151 West George Street. Tel: 0141-229 0707; www.bluedogglasgow.co.uk
One of the best cocktail bars in Glasgow, attracting a wide age group. Jazz-bar style where some dress up and others come in more casual attire.

Bon Accord, 153 North Street. Tel: 0141-248 4427; www.bonaccordweb.co.uk
If you want to experience a traditional real ale pub this is a good bet. As many as 10 ales offered at one time in comfy surroundings. Malt whisky is a speciality, too.

The Butterfly and the Pig, 151–3 Bath Street. Tel: 0141-221 7711; www.thebutterflyandthepig.com
Quirky pub with lots of music events throughout the week. It's quaint and small and can get crowded.

The Garage, 490 Sauchiehall Street. Tel: 0141-332 1120; www.garageglasgow.co.uk
Cheap and cheerful, a popular clubbing venue for students.

The Loft, 24 Ashton Lane. Tel: 0845-166 6028; www.socialanimal.co.uk
Stylish venue for grown-up drinking, popular with the 20s and 30s professional crowd. Things liven up

when the DJ starts playing and weekends are busy.

The Polo Lounge, 84 Wilson Street. Tel: 0141-553 1221; www.bluedogglasgow.com
Grandiose decor at this multi-roomed gay and lesbian bar. The emphasis is on camp party fun.

Rogano, 11 Exchange Place. Tel: 0141-248 4055; www.roganoglasgow.com
Although primarily considered an eating place, this is now a cool venue to go to for cocktails or champagne perhaps accompanied by some seafood from the oyster bar.

Tiger, Tiger, 20 Glassford Street. Tel: 0141-553 4888; www.tigertiger-glasgow.co.uk
Get glammed up to check out this lounge bar, restaurant and nightclub.

The Tunnel, 84 Mitchell. Tel: 0141-649 9199; www.tunnelglasgow.co.uk
Perennial favourite that can see more than 1,000 clubbers on a Saturday night. House, electro, hip hop, soul and more.

Tusk, 18 Moss Side Road. Tel: 0845-166 6017; www.socialanimal.co.uk
Located in the up-and-coming Shawlands district, this restaurant, bar and club complex has several different rooms, each with its own style. Check out the Buddha Main Room for house music or the Boudoir for a chill out.

Uisge Beatha, 232–6 Woodlands Road. Tel: 0141-564 1596; www.uisgebeatha.co.uk
The translation of the pub name, "water of life", hints that this is where to enjoy a few drams of fine malt (100 on offer) and meet kilt-wearing staff.

Comedy

Edinburgh

The Stand, 5 York Place. Tel: 0131-558 7272; www.thestand.co.uk

The Stand Comedy Club began life in 1995 and continues to uphold Edinburgh's comedy scene from this basement bar, where well-known Scottish comedians and promising new talent perform nightly.

Glasgow

Jongleurs, The Glasshouse, 20 Glassford Street. Tel: 08700-111 960 www.jongleurs.com
Many well-known comedians take the stage at the Glasgow branch of this chain of comedy clubs.

The Stand, 333 Woodlands Road. Tel: 0844-335 8879; www.thestand.co.uk
Following the success of its Edinburgh counterpart, this purpose-built comedy club opened it doors in 2000 and likewise delivers a high standard of comedy.

Casinos

Both Edinburgh and Glasgow provide opportunities for you to gamble away your money. At most casinos you will need to become a member before you play but membership is free (ID required). Men are expected to wear casual but smart dress.

Edinburgh

Circus Casino
Fountains Park
Tel: 0131-228 4446
www.gentingcasinos.co.uk
Gala Maybury Casino
5 South Maybury
Tel: 0131-338 4444
www.galacasino.co.uk
Mint Casino
Ocean Terminal, Leith
Tel: 0131-553 7505
www.gentingcasinos.co.uk

Glasgow

Gala Merchant City
16–18 Glassford Street
Tel: 0141-553 5410
Gala Princess Casino
528 Sauchiehall Street
Tel: 0141-332 8171
Gala Riverboat Casino
61 Broomielaw
Tel: 0141-226 6000
www.galacasino.co.uk for all three casinos.

Birdwatching

More than 450 species of birds have been recorded in Scotland, and some regions attract the rarest of species. Enormous seabird colonies can be seen on coastal cliffs and the islands. Outstanding for birdwatching are Shetland, Orkney, Handa Island, Isle of May, St Abb's Head, and Islay.

Birds of prey, from the buzzard to the merlin, are often seen in the Highlands, where golden eagles and the osprey can also be spotted. Ornithological information can be obtained from:
RSPB Scottish Office

Dunedin House, 25 Ravelston Terrace, Edinburgh EH4 3TP
Tel: 0131-311 6500.
www.rspb.org.uk/scotland
Scottish Ornithologists' Club
Waterston House, Aberlady, East Lothian EH32 0PY
Tel: 01875-871330
www.the-soc.org.uk
Scottish Wildlife Trust
Cramond House, Cramond Glebe Road, Edinburgh EH4 6NS.
Tel: 0131-312 7765
www.swt.org.uk
The SWT also manages many bird reserves.

SHOPPING

City Shopping

Glasgow is the UK's second shopping city (after London) in terms of retail space. With a plethora of attractive, modern shopping centres *(see page 176)* and a wide choice of designer boutiques, the city is ideal for the compulsive shopper.

In **Edinburgh**, the length of the Royal Mile is dotted with shops selling everything associated with Scotland, including Highland dress and tartan, Scottish heraldry, Celtic design jewellery, bagpipes, Scottish woollens, whisky and haggis. For shopping with a more international flavour, Princes Street is the main thoroughfare, concentrating on fashion chains, bookshops and several department stores, including Edinburgh's grand old dame founded in 1838, Jenners.

However, the equally up-market Harvey Nichols store, located on the fashionable Mulberry Walk off St Andrew Square is now giving Jenners a run for its money.

Rural Luxury

While Glasgow and Edinburgh dominate in terms of retail space, Inverness, Dundee and Aberdeen all have major retail developments, too.

If large mall shopping isn't your idea of holiday fun, there are three distinct high-class shopping experiences to be found north of Perth. House of Bruar, located just off the A9 on the northern fringes of Blair Atholl, is where fine tweeds and country clothes mingle with delectable delights in the sprawling delicatessen and bustling café.

Forty miles (64km) further north, in the new Macdonald Hotels Highland Resort, a line of designer boutiques that wouldn't look out of place in fashionable Knightsbridge is also to be found, while Falls of Shin, beyond Lairg, offers yet more luxury browsing on product ranges from Harrods.

House of Bruar: daily, all year. Tel: 0845-136 0111; www.houseofbruar.com
Falls of Shin (only Harrods outlet in Scotland): daily, all year. Tel: 01549-402 231; www.fallsofshin.co.uk
Macdonald Aviemore Highland Resort: Tel: 01479-815 474. "Spey Valley Shopping", international luxury brands in the Highlands. Daily. However, if you would rather browse for Scottish quality products online and save the hassle of lugging presents home, arguably the pick of the bunch is "Papa Stour" (www.papastour.com), where you can find everything from cowhide sporrans to real antlers from the Highlands.

VAT Refunds

Visitors to Scotland from non-EU countries can obtain a refund of value-added tax, which is added to most purchases. Many large stores will deduct the VAT from purchases at time of sale if the goods are being shipped abroad directly from the store. In other cases, obtain a receipt, which can be stamped by Customs officers who will inspect the goods at ports or airports of exit; the receipt can then be sent to the store, which will mail a VAT refund cheque.

What to Buy

There is a wide range of "typical" Scottish products, from tartan and heather-embellished souvenirs to cashmere and Highland crafts.

Textiles and Knitwear

Although the industry is in decline, woollens production is still very much in evidence in the Borders region, where you can tour a number of mills and make reduced price purchases at the factory shops, including **Lochcarron of Scotland**, Huddersfield Street, Galashiels. Similarly, there is a Woollen Mill Trail in Clackmannanshire, near Stirling, where a quarter of Scottish woollens were once produced.

Look out for cashmere and Harris tweeds as well as lamb's wool. Shetland knitwear, including Fair Isle jumpers, is also justly renowned. Sadly, the art of weaving Harris tweed is a dying tradition.

Glassware

There are a number of high-quality glass and crystal producers that

BELOW: highland bears for sale.

have come out of Scotland, including Caithness Glass, Selkirk Glass, Edinburgh Crystal and Stuart Crystal. There's also **Caithness Glass Visitor Centre** in Crieff (tel: 01764-654 014), where you can buy beautiful paperweights.

Ceramics and Crafts

Many regional potteries produce distinctive, high-quality lines, such as **Highland Stoneware**. Look out for local outlets, especially in the Highlands and islands.

Celtic-Style Jewellery

Contemporary silver or gold jewellery with Celtic-influenced designs is very popular and widely available, with varying quality. **Ortak** from Orkney is particularly popular; www.ortak.co.uk.

Scotch Whisky

Malt whisky is a major Scottish export. Many of the whiskies you see will be Moray whiskies, produced in the Speyside region, where over half the country's distilleries are located. There you can go on a "malt whisky trail" of more than seven distilleries and their on-site shops, including the famous Glenfiddich distillery in Dufftown. Whiskies from the Northern Highlands and Islay whiskies from the west coast island are also renowned. Islay has eight distilleries.

Speciality Foods

Delicatessens abound to tempt you with haggis (if you don't read the list of ingredients), smoked salmon and other smoked produce, cheeses, marmalade, porridge and oatcakes, butter shortbread and a number of other Scottish-made delectables – see the feature on *pages 121–3*. If you are self-catering, then fresh fish, often very fresh, can be an excellent buy. In the northwest, look out for fresh, hot-smoked salmon.

Outdoor Equipment

With a burgeoning outdoor adventure sports market, it's little wonder that the country has several excellent specialist adventure sports stockists. **TISO** (www.tiso. com) and **Nevisport** (www.nevisport. co.uk) both stock a wide range of outdoor equipment. However, for those heading into Scotland's snowy back-country, **Mountain Spirit** in Aviemore (tel: 01479-811 788; www.mountainspirit.co.uk) is the place to buy and hire ski-touring, Nordic, telemark and mountaineering equipment.

Participant Sports

Thanks to the Land Reform (Scotland) Act 2003, visitors to Scotland can enjoy some of the most enlightened access laws in Europe. Add the fact that the nation possesses natural terrain of thousands of miles of rugged coastline, remote beaches, deep glens, rushing rivers and the highest mountains (Munros) in the UK, and it's easy to understand why Scotland is rapidly becoming one of the best destinations in Europe to enjoy a myriad of outdoor sports. Whatever the weather, fishing, mountain biking, walking, horse riding, winter sports, sailing and surfing are just some of the popular activities to be enjoyed in its great outdoors.

Wildlife enthusiasts, too, flock to these shores (see *Birdwatching*, page 350) to enjoy wild sea and landscapes teeming with rare species. Indeed, within the boundaries of the Cairngorms National Park (www. cairngorms.co.uk) alone, over 25 percent of the UK's most threatened bird, animal and plant species can be found. Hikers and water sports enthusiasts also enjoy the forests, lochs and mountains of the Loch Lomond and Trossachs National Park.

VisitScotland's website (www. visitscotland.com) provides a host of information about available activities across the country, key destinations and reputable tour operators.

Alternatively, you can call its hotline (tel: 0845-225 5121; freephone +44

BELOW: cycling the scenic bike trails.

(0)1506-832 222 from the rest of the world) or request a specific brochure about golf, sailing, fishing, walking or cycling from its head office. Write to: VisitScotland, Ocean Point, 94 Ocean Drive, Edinburgh EH6 6JH.

Golf

Scotland is the home of golf, and, some would claim, it is the national sport.

There are hundreds of courses, most of them open to the public. Even the most famous courses, such as St Andrews, Carnoustie and Turnberry, are public "links" courses, and anyone prepared to pay the appropriate fee and who can produce a handicap certificate (usually about 20 for men, 30 for women) is entitled to play on them.

It is advisable to book ahead at the "name" courses. At **St Andrews** half of all start times on the Old Course (closed on Sunday) are allocated by ballot. To be included, contact the starter before 2pm on the day before you wish to play. A handicap certificate (24 for men, 36 for women) or a letter of introduction is required. If the Old Course is fully booked, there are six other courses to choose from (tel: 01334-466 666; www.standrews. co.uk; www.visitscotland.com/golf).

Walking

Scotland is a paradise for walkers, and walking is a rapidly growing tourism sector. There are 284 mountains over 3,000ft (900 metres) – these are called Munros – and across the country you can find a wide range of climbs and walks suitable for the expert or the novice. The mountains, although not that high, should not be treated lightly. A peak which, when bathed in brilliant sunshine, looks an easy stroll can, a few minutes later, be covered by swirling mist, and can become a death trap. The importance of proper equipment (compass and maps) and clothing cannot be over-emphasised.

VisitScotland has an excellent online walking guide (http://walking. visitscotland.com) with routes, safety tips and lots more useful information.

The Mountaineering Council of Scotland

The Old Granary, West Mill Street, Perth PH1 5QP
Tel: 01738-493 942
www.mcofs.org.uk

Ramblers Association Scotland

Kingfisher House, Auld Mart Business Park, Milnathort, Kinross KY13 9DA
Tel: 01577-861 222
www.ramblers.org.uk/scotland

Fishing

Some of Britain's best fishing is found in Scotland. Rivers and lochs of all shapes and sizes can be fished for salmon and trout. Salmon fishing need not be as expensive as most people believe, and trout fishing is available in far greater supply than is ever utilised. Local permits must be obtained; details are available from tourist offices.

The salmon fishing season varies from river to river, starting from January in some places and as late as March in others and running until October. The trout season is from mid-March to early October. Fishing for migratory fish (salmon and sea trout) is forbidden on Sunday.

Sea fishing is found around the entire coast, particularly Orkney and the Shetland Islands. Shark, halibut, cod, hake and turbot are just a few of the species that can be caught.

Surfing

The water may be colder than Brazil and Australia but with powerful Atlantic waves battering Scotland's coastline, and the north and eastern coastlines, dotted with reef breaks, also enjoying consistent sizeable swells, it's unsurprising that Scotland is one of the hottest emerging surf destinations in Europe.

The Isle of Lewis, Tiree and Machrahanish on the west coast are remote, popular destinations while the east coast beaches of Fraserburgh and Pease/Coldingham Bay (East Lothian) attract legions of hardy surfers. Yet it's the renowned Thurso East in the north of Scotland that is really making waves. In April, some of the world's best surfers may be seen shredding its waves during the O'Neill Highland Surf Open (www. oneill.com; www.c2csurfschool.com).

Sea-kayaking

With miles of coastline, dozens of remote and uninhabited islands, countless sea lochs and a rich diversity of marine life including otters, whales and dolphins to observe, Scotland is paradise for paddlers who seek adventure and tranquillity.

Whether you are a beginner or an expert, increasing numbers of operators are offering day, weekend and even week-long trips off the coast. Indeed, at weekends between April and October it's not unusual to see cars with kayaks on the roof driving out of the cities.

Some argue that the Uists of the Outer Hebrides, complete with turquoise waters and white sands

ABOVE: spoiling for a showdown on the shinty pitch.

offer some of Europe's best sea-kayaking. The Shetland Islands could also make such a claim.

Canoe Scotland (tel: 0131-317 7314; www.canoescotland.org) is a useful first point of contact for suitable locations to learn/hire.

There are also excellent sea-kayaking operators who offer tours and lessons. Try **Sea Kayak Shetland** (tel: 01592-841 160), **Wilderness Scotland** (tel: 0131 625 6635), **Skyak Adventures** (tel: 01471-820 002; www.skyakadventures.com) and **Uist Outdoor Centre**, North Uist (tel: 01876-500 480; www.seakayakouterhebrides.co.uk).

Skiing

Despite erratic snowfall in recent years, Scotland's five ski centres (Cairngorm, The Lecht, Glenshee, Glencoe and Nevis Range) continue to survive, albeit with at least three now also diversifying into activities such as hiking, mountain biking and even go-karting to balance the books. However, when the snow does fall (the main season is between January and April), groomed pistes and miles of challenging off-piste terrain become the playground for skiers, boarders and ski-mountaineers (www.ski-scotland.com).

Mountain Biking

If one sport has emphatically captured the imagination of the Scottish public and activity-minded visitors to Scotland alike, it is mountain biking. While in the early 1990s, keen mountain bikers were forced to seek out their own trails through glens and forests, today there are more than a dozen purpose-built mountain bike centres offering mile upon mile of graded track (green

for easy, black for experts) through forests, open countryside, and even down mountain sides. Such has been the explosion of interest in the sport that since 2002 alone the Forestry Commission Scotland (FCS), the largest landowner of public land in Scotland (www.forestry.gov.uk/scotland), has invested over £4 million in trail building projects.

Glentress (tel: 01721-721 736; www.thehubintheforest.co.uk) near Peebles reportedly attracted over 250,000 riders to its trails and continues to be one of Scotland's top tourist attractions. Its sprawling, marked trails (and wonderful café) are part of the **7Stanes** trail network (www.7stanes.gov.uk) that stretches across the Borders and Dumfries and Galloway.

While **Wolftrax** at Laggan in the Central Highlands (tel: 01528-544 786; www.basecampmtb.com) and the Cairngorms (tel: 01479-810 111; www.bothybikes.co.uk) are both highly popular centres, it's the **Witch's Trail** cross-country route and spectacular 1.6-mile (2.6km) downhill course in the shadow of Ben Nevis which annually attracts thousands of amateur riders (www.ridefortwilliam.co.uk). In September 2007, Fort William hosted the Mountain Bike World Championships.

Diving

Scuba divers won't be disappointed when they visit Scotland. Fish and plants abound in the clear waters that bathe the Scottish coast.

Outstanding sub-aqua areas with good facilities and experienced locals are the waters around Oban, the Summer Isles near Ullapool, Scapa Flow in Orkney and St Abb's Head on the southern part of the east coast.

Scottish Sub-Aqua Club
Caledonia House, South Gyle, Edinburgh EH12 9DQ
Tel: 0131-625 4404
www.scotsac.com

Spectator Sports

The most popular spectator sports are football (soccer), golf and rugby.

Football

Rangers and Celtic are the two rival football teams that dominate the top of the Scottish Premier League.
Rangers Football Club
Ibrox Stadium, Glasgow
Tel: 0871-702 1972
www.rangers.co.uk
Celtic Football Club
Celtic Park, Glasgow
Tel: 0871-226 1888
www.celticfc.co.uk

Scotland's national football stadium is at **Hampden Park**, Glasgow. Tel: 0141-620 4000, or 0141-616 6139 for the museum.

International rugby matches are played at **Murrayfield Stadium** in Edinburgh. Tel: 0131-346 5000; www.sru.org.uk.

Shinty

Many Scots are fiercely proud of the heritage of this ancient Celtic sport of the *camanachd* or "curved stick". It demands stamina, speed and courage from the 11 players in two opposing teams who defend their goal on a football-like pitch. Fort William and Kingussie are among the most famous teams, which compete in the annual shinty league and vie for the honour of contesting the greatest shinty prize of all, the Camanachd Cup. Contact the **Camanachd Association** (tel: 01463-715 931; www.shinty.com) in Inverness for information about fixtures.

Curling

It's an indigenous sport almost as old as the hills themselves and, like shinty, firmly embedded in Scottish sporting culture. Played by teams on ice rinks across the land, between September and March thousands of men and women of all ages descend on rinks to "throw" and "sweep" their weighty granite-fashioned curling stones from the "hack". Two teams vie with each other to place their "stones" inside the "house" of concentric rings. Over the years, Scottish curlers have won European, World and Olympic medals in the sport. Tel: 0131 333 3003; www.royalcaledoniancurlingclub.org.

A – Z

A HANDY SUMMARY OF PRACTICAL INFORMATION, ARRANGED ALPHABETICALLY

A dmission Fees

Libraries and many museums and galleries in Scotland are free to enter, including the Kelvingrove Museum and Art Gallery in Glasgow and the National Museums in Edinburgh. The National Trust for Scotland (NTS) and Historic Scotland (HS) *(see Heritage Organisations, page 356)* do charge admission to many of their properties. Some, like Edinburgh Castle, can cost as much as £13, so it's definitely worth asking about child and family discounts. The NTS offers substantial admission discounts to its members, so joining may be a worthwhile investment if you're planning to visit many properties. The Historic Scotland Explorer Pass is also a cost-saving option.

B udgeting for Your Trip

Scotland is a relatively compact country. However, while even the outermost islands are easily reached, fuel costs continue to be high. Expect to pay more than £1.15p per litre of fuel and much more in the Highlands – ironic, considering the oil is produced by the rigs just over Aberdeen and Shetland's horizon. While bus travel is inexpensive (Glasgow–Edinburgh for under £7; super savers are available for less), the same return journey by train can cost over £15. There are accommodation and food options for every budget, from the almost five-figure cost of a 5-star dining experience and a suite at the Gleneagles Hotel to paying less than £10 to pitch your tent in one of dozens of campsites the length and breadth of the country.

However, as a rule of thumb, budget at least £30 per day for travel and food, and, depending on how you like to travel, £10–£100 per night for accommodation *(see Money Saving Tips, page 9)*.

C hildren's Activities

Scotland is a child-friendly nation, but attitudes definitely vary from place to place. For example, in cities and larger towns, some of the more established bistros and cafés generally welcome kids and are equipped with high chairs. However, many a parent has found their evening plans disrupted when their tiny offspring are deemed unwelcome at restaurants. In truth, access sometimes depends as much on the attitude of the owner of the establishment as the law, though Scottish pubs must obtain a special licence to permit under-16s into their bar. Invariably, parents will find the remoter parts of the Highlands and islands much more accommodating, though it's worthwhile considering self-catering as a cast-iron option for eating and accommodation.

That said, there are literally scores of child-friendly attractions across the country, from the child-oriented interpretive walks and interactive displays to be found at Forestry Commission centres (www. forestry.gov.uk/Scotland) to the renowned Landmark Forest Theme Park in Carrbridge (Speyside) that

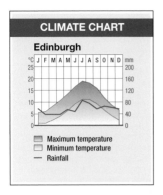

CLIMATE CHART

Edinburgh

- Maximum temperature
- Minimum temperature
- Rainfall

comes complete with tree top and red squirrel trail (tel: 0800-731 3446; www.landmark-centre.co.uk). Parents will find many tourist attractions, restaurants, hotels and bus/train routes offer substantially reduced rates for children.

Climate

No matter what you say about Scottish weather, you are bound to be wrong. There are those who rave about the cloudless two weeks they spent on Skye; others have made several visits and have yet to see the Cuillin Hills.

But it can be said that the west is generally wetter and warmer than the east. Summers are cool, with July temperatures averaging 13–15°C (55–59°F), though often peaking above 20°C (68°F) in the afternoon. Winters are cold, with January temperatures averaging 3–5°C (37–41°F), frost at night, and the higher mountains sometimes remaining snow-covered for months.

Rainfall is heavy, except on the east coast, and exceeds 100ins (25cm) in the Western Highlands. January, April, May and June are usually drier than July, August and September, but take an umbrella whenever you go.

Crime and Safety

Like any other country in the world, crime does exist in Scotland, though serious crime is predominantly confined to the major cities. In truth, pickpockets and credit card fraud are two of the greatest risks a visitor must guard against. Tourists should avoid carrying large sums of cash on their person and keep a close eye on their handbags.

Scotland's city centre streets are generally safe to walk around in the evening, though women travelling on their own should remain especially vigilant. Exercise common sense and avoid dimly lit streets. If eating or partying late into the night, it's advisable to call a taxi to get back to your hotel.

Should you be concerned for your safety, the emergency services (police, ambulance and fire) can be reached on tel: 999. Note that this is an emergency number only.

Note, too, that airport terminals carry out stringent security checks on passengers. Ensure you allow yourself plenty of time to get through security for your flight. This includes domestic short-hop flights to the Highlands and islands.

D isabled Travellers

Recent legislation means that all new buildings in Scotland must have appropriate facilities for disabled travellers, including wheelchair access. **First Scotrail** (tel: 0800-912 2901 assisted travel helpline; www.firstscotrail.co.uk) has ramps at station platforms for wheelchair-users to access trains, and such passengers also receive discounts on train travel. Visit its website and click on "Disabled Assistance" for further details.

While buses don't offer such facilities, **Caledonian MacBrayne** (www.calmac.co.uk) shore staff will assist wheelchair-users in negotiating the gangway on their ferries. There are also wheelchairs on many vessels.

While disabled toilet facilities are more commonplace in restaurants and cafés, it remains difficult for some disabled visitors to access some of the historic sites, though various (lower) parts of both Stirling and Edinburgh castles are accessible to wheelchair users (www.historic-scotland.gov.uk).

While there remains much work to be done, there are B&Bs, hotels and self-catering establishments across the country that provide facilities for disabled travellers.

Association of Scotland's Self Caterers (tel: 08705-168 571; www.assc.co.uk) has a list of such self-catering properties, or check out the VisitScotland website (www.visitscotland.com) for information.

Further advice on travel and services which are available for disabled visitors can be acquired from **Capability Scotland** (tel: 0131-337 9876; fax: 0131-346 7864; www.capability-scotland.org.uk).

E lectricity

220 volts is standard. Hotels usually have dual 220/110-volt sockets for razors. If you are visiting from abroad, you will probably need an adaptor to link other small electrical appliances to the three-pin sockets universal in Britain; it is usually easier to find these at home before leaving than in Scotland.

Embassies and Consulates

With the re-establishment of a Scottish Parliament in Edinburgh, many countries have opened consular offices in the capital *(if phoning from outside the area use code: 0131).*

Australia
5 Mitchell Street, EH6 7BD
Tel: 228 4771
Czech Republic
12a Riselaw Crescent, EH10 6HL
Tel: 447 9509
Denmark
48 Melville Street, EH3 7HF
Tel: 220 0300

BELOW: Kelvingrove Art Gallery and Museum in Glasgow.

KELVINGROVE
ART GALLERY AND MUSEUM

France
11 Randolph Crescent, EH3 7TT
Tel: 225 3377
Germany
16 Eglinton Crescent, EH12 5DG
Tel: 337 2323
India
17 Rutland Square, EH1 2BB
Tel: 229 2144
Ireland
16 Randolph Crescent, EH3 7TT
Tel: 226 7711
Italy
32 Melville Street, EH3 7HA
Tel: 226 3631
Japan
2 Melville Crescent, EH3 7HW
Tel: 225 4777
Jordan
11 Windsor Street, EH7 5LA
Tel: 466 9336
The Netherlands 7–9 North Saint
David Street, EH2 1AW
Tel: 524 9436
New Zealand
22 Hailes Grove, EH13 0NE
Tel: 222 8109
Norway
12 Rutland Square, EH1 2BB
Tel: 228 2444
Poland
2 Kinnear Road, EH3 5PE
Tel: 552 0301
Russia
58 Melville Street, EH3 7HF
Tel: 225 7098
Spain
63 North Castle Street, EH2 3LJ
Tel: 220 1843
Switzerland
255c Colinton Road, EH14 1DW
Tel: 441 4044
Taipei
1 Melville Street, EH3 7PE
Tel: 0131 220 6886
Ukraine
8 Windsor Street, EH7 5JR
Tel: 556 0023

Emergencies

For emergency services such as
police, ambulance, the fire service or
lifeboat service dial **999**.

Etiquette

There are no particular etiquette
issues in Scotland and general
manners, dress and attitudes do not
differ a great deal from the rest of the
United Kingdom.

Formal queuing is expected, as is
respect for others and Scottish
people, particularly in rural and
remote areas, are extremely friendly
and helpful.

Smoking is banned by law in all
public places; special designated
areas outside pubs are sometimes
provided. It is customary to buy a
round of drinks when out with a
group.

If invited into a Scottish household
it is appropriate to take a gift of, for
example, good wine or chocolates.
Avoid calling a Scottish person
English.

G ay and Lesbian Travellers

All of Scotland's cities have a gay and
lesbian scene, though arguably it's in
Glasgow and Edinburgh where the
most nightclubs and bars targeting
this sector of the community are to be
found. Edinburgh's Broughton Street
and Glasgow's Merchant City are the
two main "pink" areas of the
respective cities.

The best sources of information on
your travels are to be found in the
pages of the weekly entertainment
magazine; *The List* (www.list.co.uk) and
in the *Scotsgay* newspaper (www.
scotsgay.co.uk). For Edinburgh, check
out www.edinburghgayscene.com.

BELOW: the sun sets over a Scottish wind farm.

H ealth and Medical Care

It is advisable to have medical
insurance. Citizens of European Union
countries are entitled to medical
treatment under reciprocal
arrangements (EHIC card), and similar
agreements exist with some other
countries. No matter which country
you come from, you will receive
immediate emergency treatment free
at a hospital casualty department.

Although Scotland isn't normally
associated with mosquitoes, an
aggressive breed of biting midge
exists, especially in warm, humid
conditions in parts of the west coast,
and calls for a tough repellent from
June to September.

Heritage Organisations

**The National Trust for Scotland
(NTS)** is Scotland's premier
conservation body, caring for more
than 100 buildings or areas of
significant heritage interest. Its
properties range from single boulders,
such as the Bruce Stone in Galloway,
through magnificent houses and
castles including Culzean, Crathes
and Fyvie, to large areas of
outstanding countryside. These last
include Glencoe, Mar Lodge in the
Cairngorms, Kintail and Goat Fell on
Arran. Some properties are available
for holiday lets.

Membership allows free admission
to all its properties and those owned
by the English National Trust. Contact
the NTS at: 28 Charlotte Square,
Edinburgh EH2 4ET; tel: 0131-493
2100; www.nts.org.uk.
Historic Scotland (HS) is a
government body that looks after
more than 300 sites of historical or
archaeological interest. Its portfolio
ranges from the magnificent Borders
abbeys up to Stone Age sites in
Orkney and Shetland.

Membership gains free admission
to HS properties. Further information
from: Longmore House, Salisbury
Place, Edinburgh EH9 1SH; tel: 0131-
668 8800; www.historic-scotland.gov.uk.

I nternet

Scotland is well and truly on the
internet highway, with even some of
the remotest locations supported by
dial-up, broadband or even Wi-fi
services. However, don't yet expect
blanket coverage across the
Highlands. While many of the higher
graded hotels and guesthouses offer
internet facilities as standard (often
for a charge), many of the smaller

B&Bs have yet to follow suit. However, from Ullapool to Stranraer, public libraries across Scotland offer free (for at least 15 minutes) internet access on condition that you register on arrival.

There are of course, innumerable internet cafés around the country where you pay around £1 per 30 minutes or 60 minutes to surf the internet and access your email. Some also serve as Wi-fi hotspots; ideal for the visitor who arrives with a laptop. Unfortunately, just as one internet café business opens, it seems another shuts, making a mockery of attempts to list systematically key locations in cities and towns.

As a general rule, many are found in the student areas of a city. In Glasgow, Woodlands Road near Glasgow University is one such location, while Nicholson Street and Rose Street in Edinburgh both support internet cafés.

L ost Property

It's not always a case of "finders, keepers" – Network Rail (www. nationalrailco.uk) has stations with lost property and left luggage facilities. At **Glasgow Central** (railway station) the left luggage office is open daily on the main concourse between 6am– midnight (tel: 08457-114 141). The same number should be called to locate lost property (9am–5.30pm) in and around the station.

In Edinburgh, the lost property department at **Waverley Station** is on platform 1 (tel: 0131-550 2333; daily 7am–11.30pm). Note that lost property (including that which is left in taxis) found in and around the city centre may be handed in to the police HQ at Fettes Avenue (tel: 0131-311 3131).

Travellers in **Aberdeen** trying to track down their misplaced item(s) should contact the Lost and Found Department, Grampian Police, Queen Street (tel: 0845-600 5700). It's open 8.45am–4.30pm weekdays only.

While there's a left luggage (deposited items will be hand-searched) at **Inverness Railway Station** (open Mon–Sat, 8.45am–6pm, Sun noon–6.30pm), there is no lost property facility.

M edia

Newspapers

There are two quality dailies. *The Scotsman*, printed in Edinburgh, and *The Herald*, printed in Glasgow, both have good coverage of Scottish and

other UK and foreign news, as well as material on the arts and business. Dundee prints the quirky *Courier*. Much of the Highlands is covered by the *Press and Journal*, published in Aberdeen. It tries to live down its reputation for excessive parochialism, epitomised by the spurious headline on what proved to be a story about the sinking of the *Titanic*: "Aberdeen man lost at sea."

The most popular is the tabloid *Daily Record*, a stable mate of England's *Daily Mirror*. English dailies circulate widely in Scotland, and many have Scottish editions.

The four main cities each have evening papers. Scotland's most unusual Sunday newspaper is the *Sunday Post*, from the same stable as Dundee's *Courier*. It defies classification: perhaps the most helpful comment on it would be that it tries to be useful and inoffensive. *Scotland on Sunday* and the *Sunday Herald* are the two quality home-grown Sunday newspapers.

Throughout Scotland, there are many local weekly papers which you may find both entertaining and informative if you are interested in a particular region, or simply interested in newspapers. The *Caledonian Mercury*, founded in January 2010, is Scotland's first truly online newspaper and gives a good all-round view of Scottish news, sport, politics and entertainment.

Magazines

Scotland is poorly served by magazines. However, the *Scottish Field*, *Scots Magazine* and *Scotland Magazine* are good-quality monthly magazines which deal with Scottish topics. The *Edinburgh Review* is a literary review of consistent quality. *The List*, an Edinburgh-based listings magazine which appears every two weeks provides lively and comprehensive coverage of events in both Edinburgh and Glasgow.

Radio and Television

Radio and TV are excellent for the most part. Radio Scotland is the main BBC radio service, and national BBC radio stations also operate in Scotland, so it is possible to hear excellent Radio 4 (FM 92.4–94.6/LW 198), a mixture of news, current affairs and light entertainment, as well as classical music on Radio 3 (FM 90.2–92.4). Classic FM (FM 99.9–101.99) serves up the more familiar classics and some intriguing and challenging quiz games. Radio 2 (FM 88–90.2) concentrates on light

entertainment and sport. Sports fans will tune in to BBC Radio Scotland or Radio 5 Live (MW 693/909).

Radio 1 (FM 97.6–99.8), Absolute Radio (AM/MW 1215; formerly Virgin) and local radio stations run by both the BBC and commercial companies offer wall-to-wall pop and light music, interspersed with terse news summaries. Local stations tend to provide an unimaginative diet of pop music but can be useful sources of local traffic news and other important information.

Television services are provided by the BBC and commercial companies. BBC1 is a general TV service, mirrored (with a more down-market emphasis) by the commercial networks on STV, with channels varying according to region. BBC2 caters to a more specialist audience and minority groups. Satellite and cable channels are usually available in larger hotels.

Television reception is poor in some of the remoter areas and islands of Scotland.

Money Matters

Currency

The British pound is divided into 100 pence. The coins used are 1p, 2p, 5p, 10p, 20p, 50p, £1 and £2. Although the £1 coin is widely used, £1 notes (issued by the Royal Bank of Scotland) still circulate along with notes of £5, £10, £20, £50 and £100. It's best to keep notes to £20 and under as some shops, especially the smaller ones, can be suspicious of the larger denominations. (Technically, Scottish notes are legal tender in England and Wales, but some shops will not accept them; English banks will readily change them for you.)

Traveller's Cheques

Traveller's cheques can be cashed at banks, bureaux de change and many hotels, though the best rates are normally available at banks.

Credit Cards

MasterCard and Visa are the most widely accepted credit cards, followed by American Express and Diners Club. Small guesthouses and Bed & Breakfast places may not take credit cards, preferring payment in cash.

Banks

Scotland has its own banks: the Royal Bank of Scotland (RBS), the Bank of Scotland and the Clydesdale Bank. They still issue their own notes – although the RBS is the only one to issue the £1 note – which circulate alongside Bank of England notes.

Don't expect consistent opening hours. As a rough guide, most banks open Monday to Friday from between 9 and 9.45am to between 4 and 4.45pm (5.30pm on Thursday). In rural areas, banks may close between 12.30 and 1.30pm and may not be open later on Thursday. However, you will also find "travelling banks" – large trucks which go round the smaller villages at set times each week and can provide most banking services. These times are advertised locally.

Building societies, unlike banks, often open on Saturday morning.

Opening Hours

Generally shops open 9am–5/5.30pm Monday to Saturday. In many cities, towns and villages Sunday opening is becoming increasingly popular. Late night opening is often on a Thursday in the larger shopping conurbations. Larger supermarkets open for longer hours some even have 24-hour opening. Village stores and smaller towns often close one afternoon a week, generally a Wednesday or Thursday – though few towns are without a "wee shoppie" that stays open at all hours and can provide food, drink and assorted necessities. The shops on the islands of Lewis, Harris and North Uist are all closed on Sundays. For **banks** see above. For **post offices** see below.

Postal Services

Main post offices are open 9am–5.30pm Monday–Friday, and 9am–12.30pm on Saturday. Sub-post offices (which often form part of another shop) keep similar hours, though they usually close for one half-day during the week.

Public Holidays

Local, public and bank holidays can be frustrating for visitors, but generally there will be a supermarket open somewhere during the major public holidays, except for **25** and **26 December**, **1** and **2 January** and **Good Friday**. If you are having difficulty, try petrol stations, many of which have good small shops on the premises and are open until late, or even for 24 hours.

Other national holidays in Scotland are **May Day** (first Monday in May), **Spring Holiday** (Monday in late May)

ABOVE: keep in touch in the Highlands.

and **Summer Holiday** (first Monday in August).

Religion

Scotland supports a diverse mix of communities from across the world. While Christianity (both Catholicism and Presbyterianism) is followed by the majority of inhabitants, Islamic, Sikh, Buddhist and Jewish services are among the others available.

Sunday is the traditional "day of rest" in Scotland, though the diminishing numbers who attend church (or kirk as it's called in Scotland) would suggest this rest isn't being taken in church. However, most churches will welcome visitors who simply turn up at the door on a Sunday morning. Further information can be found at: www.churchofscotland. org.uk

The website www.upmystreet.com is also a useful reference point for locating churches, mosques and synagogues in the town or region of Scotland you will be visiting. The following religious contacts will be able to provide practical advice on their areas of worship.
Catholic Church
5 St Vincent Place
Glasgow G1 2DH
Tel: 0141-221 1168
Church of Scotland
121 George Street
Edinburgh EH2 4YN
Tel: 0131-225 5722
Baptist Union of Scotland
14 Aytoun Road
Glasgow G41 5RT
Tel: 0141-423 6169
Edinburgh Buddhist Centre
30 Melville Terrace
Edinburgh EH9 1LP

Tel: 0131-662 6699
Glasgow Buddhist Centre
329 Sauchiehall Street
Glasgow G2 3HW
Tel: 0141-333 0524
Scottish Episcopal Church
General Senate Office
21 Grosvenor Crescent
Edinburgh EH12 5EE
Tel: 0131-225 6357
Jewish Synagogue & Community Centre
4 Salisbury Road
Edinburgh EH16 5AB
Tel: 0131-667 3144
Sikh Temple
1 Sheriff Brae
Edinburgh EH6 6ZZ
Tel: 0131-553 7207
UK Islamic Mission
19 Carrington Street
Glasgow G4 9AJ
Tel: 0141-331 1119

Senior Travellers

If you are aged 60 or over, it's always worthwhile enquiring about discounts on buses, trains and at attractions. In Scotland, a Senior Railcard (www.senior-railcard.co.uk) costs £26 a year and can often save the holder almost 30 percent of the standard cost of a train journey. Swimming pools, leisure centres and the National Trust for Scotland (www.nts.org.uk) are among other locations where proving you're an OAP can prove beneficial to the wallet.

In addition to discounted fares, the most readily accessed seats on buses and trains are reserved for use by senior travellers. Unfortunately, that doesn't always mean that the younger person already sitting there will be willing to vacate their seat.

Saga (www.saga.co.uk) is among many tour operators that cater for the "grey market".

Telecommunications

When dialling from abroad, the international access code for the UK is 44, followed by the area code without the initial 0 (Edinburgh 131, Glasgow 141, Aberdeen 1224, etc.).

To reach other countries from Scotland, first dial the **international access code 00**, then the country code (eg Australia 61, France 33, Germany 49, Japan 81, the Netherlands 31, Spain 34, US and Canada 1).

Pre-paid **phonecards** are the most economical way of phoning abroad. You can either buy them before you leave home, online or from post offices and shops in various denomi-nations in Scotland. If using a US pre-paid phonecard, dial the company's access number: Sprint 0-800-890-877; MCI 0-800-279-5088.

Try to avoid using the telephone in your hotel as it is usually much more expensive.

The minimum charge for a call made at a public telephone is 20 pence. Most telephones accept only phonecards. Public call boxes are becoming rarer as mobile phone use increases.Direct dialling is possible to most parts of the world.

Mobile (cell) phone coverage is not as good in Scotland as the rest of the UK as only around 92 per cent of the country is covered, with rural areas particularly bad. You will need a GSM cellular phone for use in Scotland. It is possible to rent these but it is an expensive option, especially for a short stay. The cheapest option is to buy a local UK SIM card to use in the GSM phone; incoming calls will be free and local calls inexpensive. Check out all the options before travelling.

Time Zones

Scotland, like the rest of the UK, follows Greenwich Mean Time (GMT). In spring the clock is moved forward one hour for British Summer Time (BST), and in autumn moved back to GMT. Especially in the far north, this means that it is light until at least 10pm in midsummer.

When it is noon GMT, it is:
4am in Los Angeles
7am in New York and Toronto
noon in London and Dublin
2pm in Cape Town
10pm in Melbourne and Sydney

Tourist Information

In Scotland

General postal enquiries should be made to VisitScotland, OceanPoint One, 94 Ocean Drive, Leith, Edinburgh EH6 6JH. Tel: 0845-225 5121.

VisitScotland has an Edinburgh and Scotland Tourist Information Centre at 3 Princes Street in the centre of Edinburgh (tel: 0845-225 5121). Other tourist information is provided by 14 areas throughout Scotland. Their main information centres, with the areas covered, are:
Aberdeen City and Shire: 23 Union Street, Aberdeen AB11 5BP. Tel: 01224-288 828; email: aberdeen@ visitscotland.com; www.aberdeen-grampian. com. (Aberdeen City and Aberdeenshire.)

Angus and City of Dundee: Discovery Point, Discovery Quay, Dundee DD1 4XA. Tel: 01382-527527; email: dundee@visitscotland.com; www. angusanddundee.co.uk.
Argyll, the Isles, Loch Lomond, Stirling and Trossachs: 41 Dumbarton Road, Stirling FK8 2QQ. Tel: 08452-255 121; email: stirling@ visitscotland.com; www.scottish.heartlands. org. (Argyll and Bute, Mull, Islay, Clackmananshire, West Dumbarton and Clydebank, Falkirk and Stirling.)
Ayrshire and Arran: 22 Sandygate, Ayr KA7 IBW. Tel: 01292-290 300; email: ayr@visitscotland.com; www.ayrshire-arran.com.
Dumfries and Galloway: 64 White-sands, Dumfries DG1 2RS. Tel: 01387-245 555; email: dumfriestic@ visitscotland.com; www.visitdumfriesandgalloway.co.uk.
Edinburgh and the Lothians: 3 Princes Street (Waverley Market), Edinburgh EH2 2QP. Tel: 08452-255 121; email: info@visitscotland.com; www.edinburgh.org. (City of Edinburgh, East Lothian, Midlothian, West Lothian.)
Glasgow and the Clyde Valley: 11 George Square, Glasgow G2 1DY. Tel: 0141-204 4400; email: glasgow@ visitscotland.com; www.seeglasgow.com. (City of Glasgow, East Dunbartonshire, Inverclyde, South and North Lanarkshire, Renfrewshire.)
The Highlands and Moray: Castle Wynd, Inverness IV2 3BJ. Tel: 08452-255 121; email: inverness@visitscotland. com; www.visithighlands.com. (Moray, Aviemore Inverness, Fort William, Northern Highlands and the island of Skye.)
Kingdom of Fife: 70 Market Street, St Andrews KY16 9NU. Tel: 01334-472 021; email: standrews@ visitscotland; www.visitfife.com.
Orkney: West Castle Street, Kirkwall KW15 1GU. Tel: 01856-872 856; email: info@visitorkney.com; www.visitorkney.com.
Perthshire: Lower City Mills, West Mill Street, Perth PH3 1LQ. Tel: 01738-450 600; email: perth@

Useful Numbers

- Directory enquiries are provided by several companies. Numbers include **118500, 118888, 118118**
- International directory enquiries **118505** or **118866** or **118899**
- Operator assistance **100** for UK calls, **155** for international calls
- Emergencies – police, fire and ambulance **999**

visitscotland.com; www.perthshire.co.uk.
Scottish Borders: Murray's Green, Jedburgh, Roxburghshire, TD8 6BE. Tel: 01835-863 170; email: jedburgh@ visitscotland.com; www.visitscottishborders. co.uk.
Shetland: Market Cross, Lerwick, Shetland ZE1 0LU. Tel: 01595-693 434; email: info@visitshetland.com; www.visitshetland.com.
The Outer Hebrides: 26 Cromwell Street, Stornoway, Isle of Lewis HS1 2DD. Tel: 01851-703 088; email: stornoway@visitscotland.com; www.visithebrides.com. (Lewis, Harris, North Uist, Benbecula, South Uist, Barra and St Kilda.)

In addition, most towns have **Tourist Information Centres (TICs)**; not all are open in the winter months.

In London
VisitBritain
Britain & London Visitor Centre
1 Regent Street
London SW1 4XT
Tel: 0870-156 6366
E-mail: visitbritain@visitbritain.org
www.visitbritain.co.uk

Outside the United Kingdom
There are no longer any international tourist offices for Britain, so when you are planning your trip to Scotland, simply go to:
www.visitbritain.com
Alternatively, visit the websites of the region you wish to visit (see above).

Tours

From literary tours of Edinburgh's New and Old Town and wildlife tours on Mull to specialist adventure breaks by bike, foot and kayaking in the rugged Highlands, visitors are spoilt for choice with specialist tours.

The following are just a few of dozens to be found through local tourist information centres.
Mercat Tours
28 Blair Street, Edinburgh
Tel: 0131-225 5445
www.mercatours.com
Literary and ghost tours promise delight and fright.
Islay Birding
Port Charlotte, Isle of Islay
Tel: 01496-850 010
www.islaybirding.com
Award-winning operator who also runs bushcraft courses involving night navigation and sleeping in caves.
Wilderness Scotland
3a St Vincent Street, Edinburgh
Tel: 0131-625 6635
www.wildernessscotland.com

TRANSPORT

ACCOMMODATION

EATING OUT

ACTIVITIES

A – Z

Another award-winning operator who promises adventure and wildlife in abundance, as small groups explore the remotest corners of Scotland's Highlands and islands by sea-kayak, mountain bike, skis or on their own two feet.

Haggis Adventures
60 High Street, Edinburgh
Tel: 0131-557 9393
www.haggisadventures.com
Especially designed for travellers on a budget. Visitors are taken into the furthest reaches of the Highlands aboard their distinctive yellow "haggis" buses.

V isas and Passports

Your best starting point for a visa-related enquiry concerning entry to the UK is to contact the UK Foreign and Commonwealth Offices visa website (www.ukvisas.gov.uk).

Citizens of most EU countries don't require a visa (just a passport) to visit Scotland. For all other nationalities, it's best to check with the British consulate in your own country before travelling to access the latest advice on the documentation required to holiday/study/work in the UK.

W ater

It's the vital ingredient for Scotland's national drink, fills the nation's many lochs and reservoirs and runs freely from every household and hotel tap. While the taste varies across the country, the good news is that water drunk from the cold tap (unless stated otherwise) should be refreshing and perfectly safe to drink. However, if you would rather have the bottled variety, there's now also a bewildering array of mineral water brands on the market, including Scotland's Highland Spring.

If you want to tap into further information about Scotland's water resource visit www.scottishwater.co.uk.

Websites

The following website addresses could prove useful on your travels throughout Scotland:

Travel
www.visitscotland.com Scotland's national tourism agency which is also accessed through www.visitbritain.com.
www.visitbritain.com The UK's tourism agency which links through to www.visitscotland.com.
www.undiscoveredscotland.co.uk A very informative online guide to Scotland.

www.edinburgh.org The official tourist information site for Edinburgh.
www.eif.co.uk All you need to know about Edinburgh's famous Festival.
www.edintattoo.co.uk Find out about Edinburgh's Royal Military Tattoo.
www.seeglasgow.com The official destination marketing agency for Glasgow.

Eating and drinking
www.smws.co.uk Scotch Malt Whisky Society.
www.5pm.co.uk For last-minute deals on restaurant and bar food.
www.socialanimal.co.uk Online guide to restaurants, pubs and clubs in Scotland's cities and main towns.

Accommodation
www.syha.org.uk Scottish Youth Hostel Association.
www.assc.co.uk the Association of Scotland's self-caterers.

Entertainment
www.list.co.uk *The List* magazine highlights the latest and best entertainment venues and gigs across the Central Belt.
www.eventscotland.org A handy reference for key forthcoming festivals and sports events to be staged in Scotland.
www.scotchwhisky.net All you need to know about the distillation of Scotland's favourite tipple.

Outdoors
http://walking.visitscotland.com For everything from walking guides and operators to more than 800 suggested walking routes.
www.forestry.gov.uk/scotland Forestry Commission Scotland.

www.snh.org.uk Scottish Natural Heritage works with various conservation agencies to protect sensitive areas of fauna and flora throughout the country.
www.wildernessscotland.com For the traveller who seeks a tour operator who really does venture off the beaten track.
www.cruiselochness.com Take a variety of cruises along the length of Loch Ness.
www.metoffice.gov.uk Find out the latest weather reports around the country, including sea and mountain conditions.

Weights and Measures

Britain is only halfway to accepting the metric system: beer comes in pints and half-pints, and shop assistants will sell you "a quarter" of sweets or "half a pound" of cheese; yet pre-packaged goods cite weights in grams. Road signs give distances in miles, but fuel is sold in litres.

What to Wear

Given the climate, it follows that you should never be without a raincoat or a warm sweater. Neither should you be without light clothes in summer. For those attracted to the excellent opportunities for hill walking and rock climbing, it is essential to come properly prepared. In the mountains the weather can change very quickly.

Each year people suffer serious and needless harm through setting out without adequate clothing and equipment; the Highlands are no place to go on a serious hill walk in a T-shirt and light trainers.

BELOW: be prepared when out walking as weather conditions can change quickly.

FURTHER READING

History

The Scottish Enlightenment – The Scots Invention of the Modern World. A. Herman. Fourth Estate.
Mary Queen of Scots. Antonia Fraser. Weidenfeld & Nicolson.
Bonnie Prince Charlie. Fitzroy MacLean. Canongate.
A Concise History of Scotland. Fitzroy MacLean. Thames and Hudson.
Culloden and **The Highland Clearances**. John Prebble. Secker & Warburg.
A History of the Scottish People 1560–1830. T.C. Smout. Fontana.
A Century of the Scottish People 1830–1950. T.C. Smout. Fontana.
Scotland's Story. Tom Steel. Fontana.

Poetry

Many editions are available of Robert Burns's poems.
Last Poetic Gems. William McGonagall. Winter/Duckworth. Scotland's (and perhaps the world's) worst poet, who has become something of a cult.
Selected Poems. William Dunbar. Fyfield Books.

Miscellaneous

Aberdeen, An Illustrated Architectural Guide. W.A. Brogden. Scottish Academic Press.
A Companion to Scottish Culture. David Daiches (ed). Arnold.
Edinburgh: A Travellers' Companion. David Daiches. Arnold.
Exploring Scotland's Heritage. Her Majesty's Stationery Office.
Four Scottish Journeys. Andrew Eames. Hodder & Stoughton.
Glasgow. David Daiches. Andre Deutsch.
Glasgow Observed. John Donald. John Donald Publishers.
The Heart of Glasgow. Jack House. Richard Drew Publishing.
Hebridean Connection. Derek Cooper. Futura.
In Search of Scotland. H.V. Morton. Methuen.
A Journey to the Western Isles of Scotland and **The Journal of a Tour to the Hebrides**. Dr Samuel Johnson and James Boswell. Two accounts of the same trip made in the 18th century by the great lexicographer and his biographer. Oxford University Paperbacks.
The Munros: Scottish Mountaineering Club Hillwalkers' Guide. Donald Bennet and Rab Anderson. Scottish Mountaineering Club.
The Northeast Lowlands of Scotland. John R. Allan. Birlinn. From fishing and farming to the rich cultural life of the north-east of Scotland.
Scotland: An Anthology. Douglas Dunn. Fontana.
The Patter: A Guide to Current Glasgow Usage. Michael Munro. Glasgow District Libraries.
Portrait of Aberdeen and Deeside. Graham Cuthbert. Robert Hale.
Road to the Isles. Derek Cooper. Futura.

Send Us Your Thoughts

We do our best to ensure the information in our books is as accurate and up-to-date as possible. The books are updated on a regular basis using local contacts, who painstakingly add, amend and correct as required. However, some details (such as telephone numbers and opening times) are liable to change, and we are ultimately reliant on our readers to put us in the picture.

We welcome your feedback, especially your experience of using the book "on the road". Maybe we recommended a hotel that you liked (or another that you didn't), or you came across a great bar or new attraction we missed.

We will acknowledge all contributions, and we'll offer an Insight Guide to the best letters received.

Please write to us at:
Insight Guides
PO Box 7910
London SE1 1WE
Or email us at:
insight@apaguide.co.uk

Fiction

Kidnapped. Robert Louis Stevenson. Penguin. An historical novel set in the aftermath of the Jacobite rebellion.
Knots and Crosses. Ian Rankin. Orion. The first book in the Inspector Rebus series.
The Prime of Miss Jean Brodie. Muriel Spark. Penguin. An unconventional school teacher instructs her girl pupils on the ways of love and life.
A Scots Quair. Lewis Grassic Gibbon. Canongate. A trilogy following the life of Chris Guthrie, a woman from north-east Scotland at the turn of the 20th century.
The Thirty-Nine Steps. John Buchan. Penguin. The best-known of Buchan's thrillers, set in Scotland.
Trainspotting. Irvine Welsh. Vintage. A horrifying look at Edinburgh's drug scene.
Waverley. Sir Walter Scott. Penguin Classics.
Whisky Galore. Compton Mackenzie. Vintage Classics. A comic novel about a wreck of a cargo of whisky.
44 Scotland Street. Alexander McCall Smith. A series of lighthearted novels about the eccentric comings and goings in Edinburgh's New Town. Plus his **Isabel Dalhousie** series about an Edinburgh detective.

Other Insight Guides

More than 120 **Insight Guides** and **Insight City Guides** cover every continent, providing information on culture and all the top sights, as well as superb photography and detailed maps. In addition, **Insight Smart Guides** present comprehensive listings in a snappy, easy-to-find way, held together by an A–Z theme and with a street atlas showing major attractions, hotels and public transport; while **Insight Step By Step Guides** deliver self-guided walks and tours. **Insight Fleximaps** highlight all the main tourist sights and provide essential facts about the destination, while being printed on durable paper with a laminated finish – write on the map with a non-permanent marker pen and wipe it off later.

ART AND PHOTO CREDITS

INDEX